Maine Atlantic Salmon:

A National Treasure

by

Ed Baum

Published in the United States of America by:

Atlantic Salmon Unlimited
P. O. Box 6185
Hermon, Maine 04402 USA

ISBN 0-9660496-9-1

Library of Congress Catalog Card Number: 97-94393

First Edition

To

My father, Ray Baum Sr., who taught me how to fish and hunt
and who enkindled my love and appreciation for the Maine outdoors.
And, to Charles G. Atkins who, more than anyone else, inspired
my love and appreciation for Maine's wild Atlantic salmon.

Contents

Appendices

Foreword

Ed Baum has at last completed the difficult and arduous task, his labor of love, "Maine Atlantic Salmon: A National Treasure." And a treasure the Maine Atlantic salmon is and an important contribution this book will be to all who have had their lives touched by this magnificent creature. From the fisheries scientist to the lay person, this manuscript will have meaning. Mr. Baum's objectives—to inform and educate the reader about the biology of the Atlantic salmon, to chronicle 125 years of experience in Maine, and to emphasize the importance of the species to all of us—have been met.

The fisheries scientist most often reports on current activities; those events that are small parts of the whole. Seldom, and millions of words have been written about the Atlantic salmon, does the scientist pull all of the little stories together into one. And it is when this does happen, and only then, that the complexities surrounding this species and its restoration and management come to light, and even then the light may be somewhat scattered. However, the events of the past, the mistakes and the successes, can provide the building blocks for the future.

Ed, as most of us know him, has attempted to lay the foundation for the Atlantic salmon's future in Maine. He has provided definitions of the more important terms and concepts, "wild salmon, hatchery salmon, salmon stocks, and salmon populations," that will enable the reader to better understand some of the issues that have risen to the top in the last few years. And this will assist us all in understanding the the twists and turns that are likely to occur in the future.

The general overview of the salmon's freshwater and marine residencies with special reference to the salmon in Maine is the precursor to the more detailed descriptions of the Atlantic salmon of Maine that appear later. The writer has pulled together years of data pertaining to such subjects as run timing, population age structures in both freshwater and the marine environment, migration in the ocean, predators, and so forth. This wealth of information, important to future salmon management, is now contained in one location for all to use.

The great debate that endlessly revolves around predator control is addressed in a straightforward manner. Some of you will agree with Ed's conclusions and some of you won't, but we will all be able to appreciate the notion that attempting to control predators without first controlling the salmon's ultimate predator, Man, himself, will be of little value.

Ed's synthesis of the historical and present sport and commercial fisheries for Atlantic salmon of Maine origin is both informative and humorous. The description of the development of the historical commercial fisheries within Maine attests to the fact that Atlantic salmon were extremely abundant during that period. The description of the ocean commercial fisheries of the near past and present is thorough and the part that Maine played in documenting these fisheries as well as assisting in framing the present day management initiatives will be of interest to all readers. For the history buff the chronicle of the sport fishery for Atlantic salmon in Maine will provide many a chuckle, especially the section dealing with 'Presidential Salmon Tidbits.'

As we are taken step-by-step through the history of Atlantic salmon restoration in Maine, beginning in the 1860's and concluding with the formation of the Atlantic Salmon Authority and the issues surrounding this body, the politics, the good and the ugly, of salmon restoration and management is brought to the forefront. An understanding of the behind-the-scenes activities that occurred and are presently occurring is vital to all of us if we are to have a hand in the future of the Atlantic salmon in

Maine.

It will be interesting for the reader to note that the state political process effectively abandoned the salmon program in 1989 because of severe financial constraints, a time that unfortunately coincided with dramatic shifts in the marine environment that would lead to significantly declining salmon runs. And in 1993 the petition to list the Atlantic salmon as an endangered species fully ignited the political engine and sent everyone scurrying to protect their interests. During this period of intense turmoil the Atlantic Sea Run Salmon Commission was abolished and replaced by the Atlantic Salmon Authority, the body that is to take Atlantic salmon restoration and management into the next century.

However, there are significant concerns regarding the Atlantic Salmon Authority. The Authority has yet to define its role in the future of Maine's Atlantic salmon restoration program and, according to Ed, it is not likely that the Authority will be provided with the resources required to work effectively throughout Maine. Given the information provided, the reader may also come to the same conclusion that Ed has, "the jury is still out on whether the Atlantic Salmon Authority represents a genuine effort at beginning a new chapter in the State of Maine's efforts to restore and manage Atlantic salmon or if this is the final chapter of the book on Maine Atlantic salmon as we have known them."

The reader is given a snapshot of the future of Maine Atlantic salmon interwoven with the likely outcome of the petition to list the Atlantic salmon as an endangered species. Of interest to the reader will be Mr. Baum's recipe (list of issues that must be dealt with) for successfully taking the Atlantic salmon program into the future. Hopefully, the reader will take to heart the issue of public apathy, the author's perceived number one threat to future Atlantic salmon restoration and rational management in Maine.

The importance of Charles G. Atkins to the Atlantic salmon of Maine is chronicled, a fitting final chapter. This pioneer fisheries scientist was instrumental in providing a firm biological foundation for the beginnings of Atlantic salmon restoration in Maine, and throughout New England for that matter. A book could be devoted to this man alone for his accomplishments go far, far beyond the Atlantic salmon. As Mr. Baum writes, Charlie is the Thomas Edison of fish culture in America. I couldn't agree more.

Hopefully, the reader will feel as I do and applaud Ed Baum's efforts in putting this story and his philosophies to paper. It has been long overdue. Good reading and enjoy, but remember Mr. Baum's idiom, "Just when you think you know something about the Atlantic salmon, reality redefines itself and you begin to question what you thought you knew."

—Larry Stolte

Acknowledgments

Although I originally planned to accomplish this project "all by myself," I soon realized that I would need help if I were to finish the task and maintain my sanity. Consequently, there are four special people to whom I will be forever indebted to—without their help my dream of writing this book would still be just that. First, I thank my wife, Peggy, for her editorial assistance, guidance, encouragement, and constant support (as well as for putting up with my many mood swings and keeping her awake during many a sleepless night!). Second, I thank my friend and colleague Larry Stolte, Merrimack River Atlantic Salmon Program Coordinator for the U.S. Fish and Wildlife Service, for his indispensable technical reviews and comments, appraisals of various drafts of the manuscript, and some of the old photos that I used in Chapter 4. Both Peggy and Larry were always there to give me the impetus and encouragement that I needed to go forward with a much better product after they had finished "commenting" upon my original thoughts. Third, I thank Tom Chamberlain, of Graphiti Publishing in Belfast, for his help and guidance in putting all of the pieces of the puzzle together and turning them into a book. Tom's assistance with the format and publishing details were also extremely helpful. Fourth, and certainly not the least, I thank Pearl Bustard for her excellent typing skills in the preparation of earlier portions of the original manuscript. Always cheerful, eager, and willing to tackle anything from spreadsheets to complex manipulations of text, Pearl's help was invaluable to me.

Many other individuals also contributed small, yet significant, pieces of the puzzle that has now been put together to form *Maine Atlantic Salmon: A National Treasure*. Among them, I especially thank the following:

- The Atlantic Salmon Federation, St. Andrews, New Brunswick, for awarding the 1994–1995 Bensinger-Liddell Memorial Atlantic Salmon Fellowship* to me. Their vote of confidence and assistance with some of the costs associated with producing this book made it possible for me to expand the scope of my original project dramatically.
- Current Atlantic Salmon Authority (formerly Atlantic Sea Run Salmon Commission) staff, including: Randy Spencer, Gregg Horton, Norm Dube, Melissa Evers, Ken Beland and Ernie Atkinson who, in the course of their professional careers, collected or provided some of the most recent biological information pertaining to Maine Atlantic salmon. Literally hundreds of former Atlantic Sea Run Salmon Commission staff, seasonal assistants, summer interns, college students, and volunteers were also involved in the collection of biological data pertaining to Maine Atlantic salmon that is found within these pages.
- I also gratefully acknowledge the invaluable assistance of my colleagues from the United States Fish and Wildlife Service, especially those at Craig Brook and Green Lake National Fish Hatcheries and the Maine Fisheries Coordinator's Office staff (with special thanks to my longtime colleague and friend, Jerry Marancik).

*The Bensinger-Liddell Memorial Atlantic Salmon Fellowship is awarded in alternate years by the Atlantic Salmon Federation (in North America) and the Atlantic Salmon Trust (in Europe). The purpose of the award is for overseas travel, study, and research benefitting the conservation or management of wild Atlantic salmon. The fellowship is named in memory of international conservationists B. E. Bensinger and P. J. Liddell. No restrictions are placed on the use of the funds, duration of the proposed program, or the professional background of the applicant. Further information regarding this program may be obtained from the Atlantic Salmon Federation in St. Andrews, New Brunswick, Canada or the Atlantic Salmon Trust in Perthshire, Scotland, UK.

- I thank NOAA—National Marine Fisheries Service staff, both in Woods Hole and Gloucester, Massachusetts, who have made significant contributions to the Maine Atlantic salmon restoration program in recent years, especially to our knowledge of salmon in the marine environment.
- Additionally, I acknowledge the valuable input of biologists from the Maine Departments of Inland Fisheries and Wildlife and Marine Resources in the collection of Atlantic salmon habitat and biological data during the past 50 years.
- To Maine Atlantic salmon anglers Bill Modeen and Joe Robbins, I thank you for sharing the locations of some of the Atlantic salmon fishing pools illustrated on the East Machias, Machias, and Pleasant river maps. Now, how about showing us where the *really* good salmon fishing pools are?
- Alfred Fenton, Bowdoin College alumnus and Charles G. Atkins enthusiast, cheerfully provided some of the biographical information presented in Chapter 7. If Atkins were alive today Mr. Fenton and I (along with Larry Stolte) would probably start the first Charlie Atkins fan club!
- Finally, I thank Kendall Warner, with his 45 (and still counting!) years of experience as a fishery scientist with the Maine Department of Inland Fisheries and Wildlife, for his review and comments of Chapter 4.

Undoubtedly, I have forgotten to thank someone who willingly helped with this undertaking. If so, please be assured that it was not intentional—your help and thoughtfulness was deeply appreciated.

Preface

Salmon—is there any one word in the English language which is more universally recognizable when seen or spoken? Whether it is pronounced "sam-*on*" or "sam-*mon*" or "*sal*-mon,"the mind instantly conjures up vivid images from the influence the species has had on your life. *Atlantic Salmon*—is there any one species of fish which has touched the lives of so many? Perhaps you are an angler who has fished for salmon in Maine, Canada or Europe. Or maybe you own a hydroelectric or water control dam which is an obstacle to salmon. Nowadays, you may be a commercial salmon farmer, rearing Atlantic salmon for sale in the local supermarket or restaurant. If you are of Native American ancestry, the salmon may have a unique religious or cultural significance to you. If you are engaged in forestry, agriculture or aquaculture in Maine, the salmon has often influenced your business, if not your life. Whether you are a state legislator or Maine representative to Congress, the salmon is often the subject of debate and concern. You may also be a state, federal or privately employed biologist, engineer, law enforcement officer or university professor — again, the Atlantic salmon is often a part of your everyday life. You may be a doctor, conducting research into the benefits of Omega-3 fish oil* found in salmon in warding off heart disease, or a lawyer, involved in a controversial legal question brought about by the presence of Maine salmon. You may have been raised learning to eat fish on Friday, or perhaps you enjoy the annual tradition of eating Atlantic salmon on the 4th of July—with fresh peas, of course! Maybe you are even one of those rare individuals who "hate to eat fish." If so, even you have been touched by the salmon that your mother tried to make you eat as a child. Maine Atlantic salmon have also touched the lives of many people far beyond the state of Maine — from New Brunswick to Labrador in Canada and on to West and East Greenland, to the Faroe Islands, and to the British Isles and Scandinavia.

Whether an angler, businessman, businesswoman, homemaker, Native American, farmer, forester, engineer, game warden, biologist, doctor, lawyer, professor, legislator, fish eater, non-fish eater, governor, president of the United States, foreign commercial fisherman, international negotiator — you will discover in the following pages that innumerable people have been touched by Maine Atlantic salmon.

And so we come to the simple purposes of this treatise: (1) to inform and educate the reader about the biology of the species, (2) to chronicle 125 years of restoration and management efforts in Maine in a single-source document, and (3) to articulate the importance of Maine Atlantic salmon populations, not only to the citizens of Maine and the United States, but to the international community as well. I believe that this monograph will serve to demonstrate the value of Atlantic salmon to society and to provide a small contribution to the future conservation and management of the species in Maine. While some cynics may want to cite this manuscript as the obituary for Maine Atlantic salmon, I harbor no such thoughts. On the contrary, the Atlantic salmon of Maine has maintained itself for centuries in spite of humankind's abuse and neglect. No matter how hard we continue to try to destroy the species in the future, I have no doubt that Maine Atlantic salmon will endure, for it truly is a *National Treasure.*

*"*Omega-3 fatty acids have been credited with significantly reducing some risks of heart disease and high blood pressure, and alleviating migraine headaches, arthritis and some allergies. In every 100 grams of Atlantic salmon, there are 1.4 grams of Omega-3s."* The Palatable Properties of Omega 3 by W. S. Brewster, Atlantic Salmon Journal, Autumn 1987.

Glossary of Life History Terms Relating to Maine Atlantic Salmon

The exact meaning of the many names for the various life-stages of Atlantic salmon in North America is often confusing. Therefore, many State and Federal resource agencies in the United States have adopted a system similar to that which is based upon the terminology commonly used in Canada and elsewhere (Allan 1967; Allan and Ritter 1975; Ritter and Harger 1974). The various life history stages that follow are listed in chronological order from salmon egg to post-spawning adult — a period of up to seven years for some Maine Atlantic salmon on their first spawning migration.

LIFE-STAGE	*DEFINITION*
Green egg	The stage from spawning until faint eyes appear.
Eyed egg	The stage from the appearance of faint eyes until hatching.
Alevin	The period after hatching of the egg when the salmon is entirely dependant upon the yolk sac for nutrition. In the natural environment, alevins are buried within the substrate of the stream bottom.
Sac-fry	Synonymous word for alevin; more commonly used in fish culture, where the young salmon can be observed in a hatching tray or trough.
Fry	Commonly used to designate the stage from alevin to the end of June of the year of hatching. (Note: this date is not appropriate for all rivers because of the wide variation in the growth and development of salmon in North America).
Unfed fry	Atlantic salmon of hatchery origin that have fully absorbed the yolk sac and have not been fed artificial foods.
Fed fry	Atlantic salmon of hatchery origin that have fully absorbed the yolk and have begun feeding upon artificial foods.
Parr	The period which follows the fry stage; subdivisions have been adopted based upon the age and size of the young salmon.[2]
O+ Parr	The period from July 1 to December 31 of the year of hatching. O+ Parr are less than one year old.
1 Parr	The period from January 1 to June 30 one year after hatching.
1+ Parr	The period from July 1 to December 31 one year after hatching.
2 Parr	The period from January 1 to June 30 two years after hatching.
2+ Parr	The period from July 1 to December 31 two years after hatching.
3 Parr	The period from January 1 to June 30 three years after hatching.
3+ Parr	The period from July 1 to December 31 three years after hatching.
Precocious parr	An Atlantic salmon that becomes sexually mature in freshwater without ever going to sea. Nearly all precocious parr are males, although a few females have been documented on rare occasions.
Fingerling	An obsolete, non-specific term for parr that is often found in the literature prior to 1960.

Underyearling	An obsolete, non-specific term for parr (or fingerling), often found in the literature prior to 1960.
Pre-smolt	Parr that have commenced the smoltification process in preparation for migration to sea. Another commonly used term for this stage is silvery parr.
Smolt	A silvery-colored, juvenile Atlantic salmon during its active migration to sea in the spring. Smolts (unlike parr) are able to survive the natural transition from fresh to salt water.
1+ Smolt	The birth date of Atlantic salmon is arbitrarily set at April 1. Since smolts migrate to sea between April and June, a 1+ smolt migrates 1+ years after hatching.
2+ Smolt	The period from January 1 to June 30 of the year of migration. The migration year is two years after hatching.
3+ Smolt	The period from January 1 to June 30 of the year of migration. The migration year is three years after hatching.
Post-smolt	The life stage during the first year of life at sea, from July 1 to December 31 of the year the salmon left the river as a smolt.
Salmon	Any adult salmon after the post-smolt stage, regardless of age or state of sexual maturity.
1SW salmon	A one sea-winter (SW) salmon has passed one December 31st since becoming a smolt.
2SW salmon	A two sea-winter (SW) salmon has passed two December 31st's since becoming a smolt.
3SW salmon	A three sea-winter (SW) salmon has passed three December 31st's since becoming a smolt.
Maiden salmon	Any virgin salmon (1SW, 2SW, 3SW) found in freshwater on its first spawning migration.
Bright salmon	A fresh-run salmon which has entered its natal stream. Synonymous with maiden or virgin salmon.
Grilse	A 1SW salmon that has matured (or is about to mature) after one winter at sea. This term is applied to salmon in their natal river, not while at sea.
MSW salmon	Multi sea-winter (MSW) salmon have matured (or are about to mature) after two or more winters at sea. (Note: also see repeat spawner).
Kelt	A spawned out (spent) adult salmon (male or female) that is found in the freshwater portions of rivers, normally between November of the year of spawning until the salmon returns to sea the following year.
Black salmon	A synonymous term for kelt. Occasionally referred to as a slink, racer, or snake.
Post-kelt	A spent salmon that has left the freshwater environment, until December 31 one year after spawning.
Mended-kelt	Infrequently used term for a post-kelt that has regained the weight lost during the first spawning cycle and has resumed feeding and growth at sea.
Repeat spawner (RS)	An adult salmon when found in freshwater on its second (or greater) spawning migration. Alternatively termed a previous spawner.
Short-absence RS	Consecutive year repeat spawners that have spent less than one year at sea before spawning again. Short-absence repeat spawners are often referred to as SARS.
Long-absence RS	Alternate year repeat spawners that have spent one year (or more) at sea before spawning again. Long-absence repeat spawners are often referred to as LARS.

Photo by Paul J. Fournier

1

Atlantic Salmon Fundamentals

1 The Importance of Wild Salmon

Definition of a Wild Atlantic Salmon

One of the more commonly posed questions in Maine, particularly in recent years, is "How does one define a *wild* Atlantic salmon?" The question necessitates an answer from two points of view—one purely biological and one based upon practicality or philosophy. From a purely biological perspective, wild Atlantic salmon, and all of their ancestors, have spent their entire life cycle in the wild, with no known impacts from human intervention. Using this definition, wild salmon would probably only be found in the remote, pristine environments of North America and similar areas of Europe.[1] Unfortunately, there is no way to identify these individual fish, because they don't appear to be different from many other wild salmon, either physically or genetically. From a practical or philosophical perspective, a wild Atlantic salmon must be defined utilizing the "degree of wildness" approach. Most fishery scientists establish that line at two generations, based upon the following criteria: parental origin and how much of the fish's life cycle was also spent in the wild. To put it succinctly, a wild salmon is a salmon that has spent its entire life cycle in the wild, and its parents were also spawned and continuously reared in the wild. Beyond that, it doesn't matter—not because it is unimportant, but because there is no practical way to tell the difference between individuals. With the first definition in mind there probably are no wild salmon in Maine, or many other areas of the world. With the second there are, and—more importantly—there can be a lot more in the future if humankind has the will and desire to do so.

The Value of Wild Salmon to the State of Maine

Throughout history, wild Atlantic salmon populations have been threatened by the activities of humankind. In freshwater, habitat alteration and degradation, dams, predation, poaching, sport fisheries, and even well-intentioned fisheries management programs take their toll annually, while at sea, predation, adverse environmental conditions, and commercial fisheries are continually contributing to the survival of the fittest individuals. The wild Atlantic salmon of Maine are no exception.

The decline of wild Atlantic salmon stocks in Maine's rivers is symptomatic of a century of failed fishery management policies throughout the United States. Even now, current policies continue to incorporate schemes that utilize technology designed to "improve" upon nature. These schemes are conceived to circumvent habitat degradation and to provide "mitigation" that is politically and socially palatable to society. The decline (and, in some instances, the extinction) of wild salmon stocks in the face of currently available technologies has caused some people to question whether or not the protection and preservation of wild salmon are worth the effort.

After all, there are numerous state, federal, and private hatcheries in New England, and aquaculture facilities in the Bay of Fundy that are literally bursting with millions of Atlantic salmon—why not simply stock these salmon in Maine rivers and produce a large number of adult salmon for anglers to pursue? In the meantime, any of those fish which survive and reproduce in Maine rivers can be regarded as a bonus, and if there aren't enough spawners this time around simply stock more hatchery-reared fish next year. After all, a salmon is a salmon—right? *Wrong!* The question becomes "Why wild Atlantic salmon?"

Wild Atlantic salmon, whether considered in the biological or the practical context, have the best chance of long-term survival in the natural environment. The loss of wild stocks *is irreversible*—once lost, they are gone for eternity. Wild salmon are a valuable genetic resource, which should be protected for future generations. Who knows what the future holds—perhaps 50 years from now hatchery stocks will have become so inbred and susceptible to diseases and predators that wild salmon stocks may be the only ones able to survive.

1. Even this would be difficult to ascertain, since all salmon stocks have undoubtedly been subjected to some form of human interference, whether it be from sport and/or commercial fisheries, native sustenance fisheries, or environmental alterations such as global warming.

Wild salmon stocks are valuable because they spawn naturally (without human intervention) and spend the next 4–6 years being reared in and subjected to a natural environment and the process of natural selection. Over time this leads to genetic diversity and results in important physiological (example: disease resistance), morphological (examples: fish size and condition), and behavioral (examples: run timing and maturity) differences. Conversely, the protected environment of cultured salmon stocks circumvents the natural mortality factors which produce healthy, wild salmon stocks adapted to survival in nature. Additionally, catastrophic events, such as a disease outbreak, are less likely in the wild environment than in cultured environments.

The conservation and rehabilitation of wild Atlantic salmon stocks in Maine rivers should be given the highest priority over all other salmon restoration and management programs.

Atlantic salmon require high quality riverine habitats and, as such, their presence has often been referred to as an indicator of the health of our own human environment. The restoration of Atlantic salmon and other anadromous fish has provided much of the stimulus for pollution abatement and for the construction of fish passage facilities in Maine rivers. Wild Atlantic salmon are also inexorably linked to our overall quality of life, often serving as a "barometer of health" for Maine ecosystems.

The study of wild Atlantic salmon populations can help humankind to learn more about the biological systems which operate within our rivers. Salmon population trends and related biological information may provide valuable insight into and enhance our knowledge about the use and management of cultured stocks, whether in restoration programs or in the aquaculture industry.

Tangible economic benefits to the State of Maine from angling and related "eco-tourism" can be substantial when runs are large enough to allow for a harvest. And numerous studies, including some in Maine, have shown that anglers prefer wild salmon to stocked salmon. It is also within the realm of possibility that commercial benefits could again be produced from healthy, wild Maine Atlantic salmon runs.

In addition to direct, measurable, economic benefits it has been shown that many members of society derive tremendous satisfaction from the knowledge that uncommon or unusual animals (for example, eagles and whales) share our environment, and most people are willing to pay something to maintain them. Therefore, the esthetic value of wild Atlantic salmon runs in Maine, along with their overall value to society, should be underscored.

In Maine, the cultural values and traditions that were once strongly associated with wild salmon runs can also provide a valuable link to our past. The first recorded rod catch of a wild Atlantic salmon in Maine dates back to 1832 in the Dennys River, and numerous records of angling traditions date back to the 1880's in other Maine rivers. Our ancestors enjoyed the resource while it was abundant; they (and we) also nearly destroyed it for future generations. It is up to the current generation to prevent this heritage from being lost forever. Who among us would be content to stand on the banks of Maine's Atlantic salmon rivers and watch the species swim into extinction?

The State of Maine is in the enviable position of being the home of the last remaining wild Atlantic salmon stocks in the United States of America. If those stocks are lost they can never be replaced. For this reason, and this reason alone, Maine's wild Atlantic salmon stocks are a resource of *national* importance.

Salmon Stock Concepts

A *stock* of fish may be defined as a species or unit of a species that is a race, a population, or a subpopulation (adapted from Booke 1981). Most often, a stock is an arbitrarily (or philosophically) designated unit which is defined for management purposes, and the term is often used in the context of defining exploitation or harvest levels. Thus, depending upon the context in which it was used, discussing the Dennys River salmon stock as a component of the Maine stock would be biologically correct. Similarly, the Maine salmon stock may be considered to be a component of the North American Atlantic salmon stock, while the North American salmon stock may be defined as a component of the West Greenland salmon stock. Salmon stocks, therefore, originate in rivers, inhabit different geographical areas, and, what is more important, usually possess different biological characteristics.

On the other hand, a salmon *population* is usually thought of as a group (or groups) of Atlantic salmon spawning in a particular stream, or portion of it, at a particular season which, to a substantial degree, do not interbreed with any group spawning in a different place or in the same place at a different season (adapted from Ricker's 1972 definition of a stock). The premise for defining salmon populations is usually based upon genetics. In the case of Atlantic salmon their homing behavior to different streams results in genetic differentiation because the local populations do not breed with each other. Thus, literally thousands of local breeding populations comprise what scientists term the North Atlantic salmon stock. Protecting wild salmon populations is extremely important because they are locally adapted to specific streams in which they are more suited to reproduce and survive. Examples of local adaptation include run timing and migratory behavior. The more complex the life cycle of a unique salmon population, the more difficult it would be to try to recreate a local salmon population that has been lost.

The native breeding range of Atlantic salmon in the Northern Hemisphere and worldwide migration routes are illustrated in Figure 1. As a species, the Atlantic salmon does not exhibit a lot of genetic variation, although North American stocks possess 58 pairs of chromosomes, while European stocks possess 56 pairs of chromosomes. However, a recent study has identified a certain gene (3.00-kb allele) which is unique to European Atlantic salmon and another (2.77-kb allele) which is almost always found in North American salmon (Taggart et al. 1995). It is the frequency of occurrence of those genes that varies geographically, and genetic differences increase with increasing geographic distance between stocks. To put it another way, adjacent salmon populations tend to be more genetically similar than populations that are farther apart. On a worldwide basis, three general races of Atlantic salmon have been identified; they inhabit the Baltic Sea, Western Europe, and Iceland, and Eastern North America (Verspoor 1986; Cross 1989). An earlier study (Moller 1970) divided North American Atlantic salmon into three major groups: Newfoundland-Labrador, New Brunswick-Nova Scotia, and Maine. Saunders (1979) has conservatively estimated that there may be as many as 1,000 distinct Atlantic salmon populations and stocks within North America.

The process of natural selection ensures the continuance of local populations and stocks by favoring reproduction among those individuals that have adapted to their local environment and by eliminating those that are unable to do so. Thus, a salmon stock may also be defined as a successfully, naturally reproducing population or group of populations. All rivers pose different physical and biological constraints upon salmon populations; therefore, natural selection varies among rivers resulting in different salmon stocks. Salmon stocks are reproductively isolated from each other and are locally adapted to each river that they inhabit. Therefore, to be self-sustaining maintaining genetic isolation and local adaptations is important. While salmon homing is very precise (±98% for Maine salmon), it is not perfect. If a local population (called a *deme*) is extirpated (another word biologists often use for *eliminated*) due to environmental or human causes, strays from nearby rivers may result in the reestablishment of the local population. This is most likely to be the case if strays originate from the same or nearby river systems with similar environments.

Many scientists often refer to groups of local populations as a *metapopulation*. This "population of populations" concept may be thought of as a group of local breeding populations connected by an exchange of individuals through straying (Hanski and Gilpin 1991). Alternatively, the connection may also be the result of certain stocking practices. Atlantic salmon differ in their physical appearance, their development, and their behavior. These differences are a result of their genetic makeup and their environment. Therefore, to sustain local salmon populations over time maintaining a good geographical distribution of locally adapted stocks within the overall population is extremely important.

Genetics Concepts

Since a stock is often an arbitrary unit, the process of identifying and quantifying salmon stocks can be a very complex process. Geneticists estimate that each Atlantic salmon carries between 50,000 and 100,000 genes (Youngson and Hay 1996), and each gene consists of two components termed *alleles* (one from each parent). Consequently, in recent years much scientific effort has been expended on the development of sophisticated stock identification techniques that are designed to measure genetic differences between salmon stocks. The reader should keep in mind that genetics studies are used for at least three different reasons: to demonstrate differences among individuals, to differentiate between stocks (and populations) or regions, and to

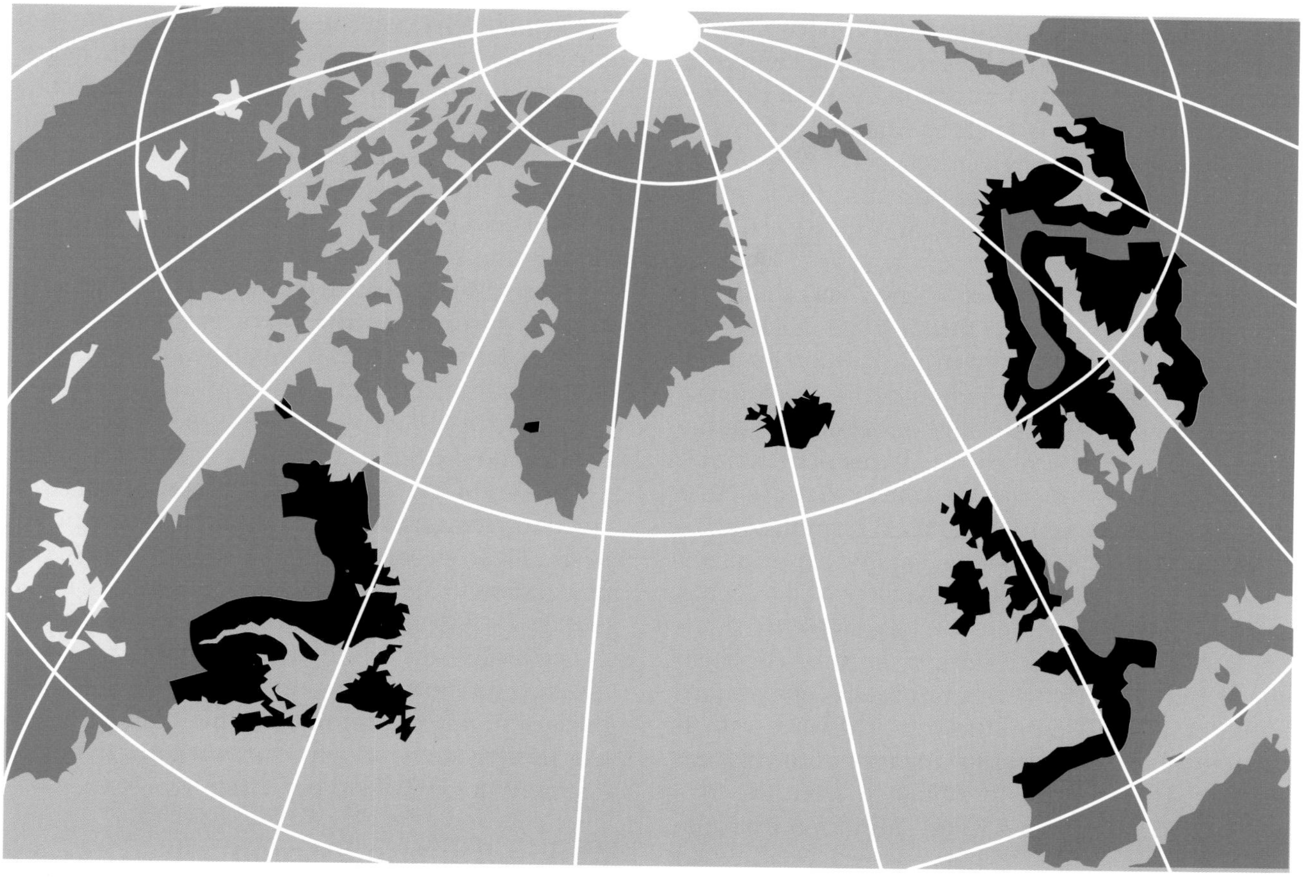

Figure 1. Native breeding range of Atlantic salmon in the Northern Hemisphere (above) and world-wide migration routes (below).

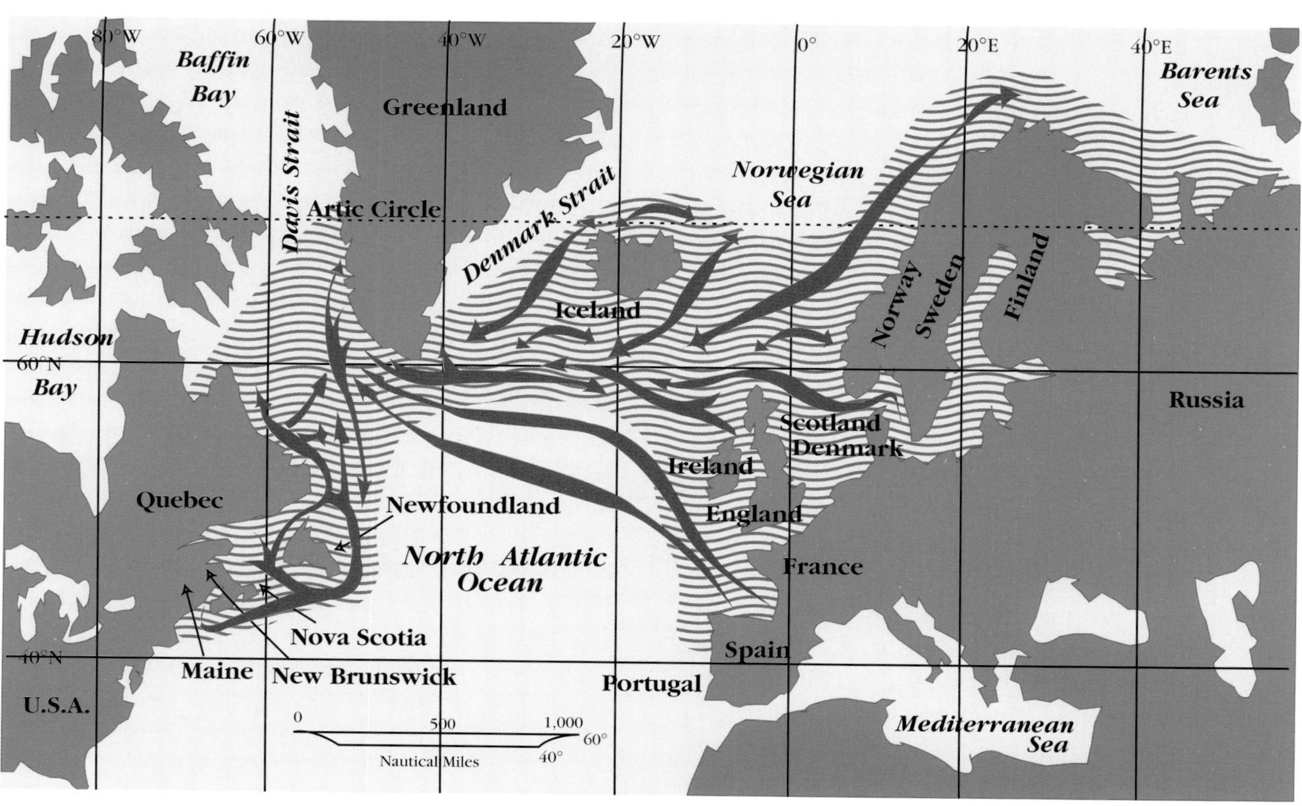

document how genetic differences vary over time. The terminology used in these studies is often confusing and difficult to understand (for all but geneticists), with terms such as heterogeneity, homozygosity, inbreeding depression, outbreeding depression, dehydrogenase polymorphism, putative recessive homozygotes, and Castle-Hardy-Weinburg equilibriums!

It has been argued that Maine rivers have lost their wild salmon stocks through the stocking of large numbers of hatchery-origin salmon over the last 125 years. After all, Penobscot River Atlantic salmon were stocked throughout much of Maine from 1872 to 1921, while Canadian stocks (primarily originating from the Miramichi River in New Brunswick) were sometimes used from the 1920's to the mid-1960's. However, many experiments conducted in Maine using both native Maine stocks and nonnative Canadian stocks repeatedly demonstrated the superior performance of the local stocks in Maine rivers. Therefore, the use of nonnative stocks in Maine stocking programs was ultimately abandoned in 1969 in favor of using local stocks that were initially obtained from the Machias and Narraguagus rivers, and then from the Penobscot River. By 1991, the State of Maine had further refined the stock concept to the point of adopting a river-specific policy for all Maine rivers that had viable Atlantic salmon populations at the time. While it is tempting to conclude that Maine Atlantic salmon stocks may have become hybridized from the release of nonnative stocks from Canada, caution must be exercised in the use of stocking records alone to make generalized conclusions about the origin of Maine salmon stocks. Many studies conducted in Maine (and elsewhere) have shown that stocking is often ineffective because: (1) few, if any, adults return, (2) some return but do not breed, and (3) some breed, but unsuccessfully due to differences in developmental timing and behavioral inhibition.

A number of studies of the genetic composition of Maine Atlantic salmon stocks have been completed in recent years (Bentzen and Wright 1992; King and Smith 1994; Kornfield 1994; May et al. 1994; Roberts 1976; Schill and Walker 1994) and additional studies are continuing. These studies have focused primarily upon the seven Maine rivers with wild salmon runs (Dennys, East Machias, Machias, Pleasant, Narraguagus, Ducktrap, Sheepscot) and the Penobscot River, which currently contains a mixture of wild and hatchery-origin salmon. Most of the studies listed above have independently revealed small, yet statistically significant differences among Maine's Atlantic salmon stocks. More recent studies conducted by geneticists at the U.S. Geological Survey Research Center in Leetown, West Virginia, indicate that the most "unique" Atlantic salmon in Maine occur in the lower Penobscot River (Cove Brook), the lower Kennebec River (Togus Stream), and the Ducktrap River. However, many of these studies also contain *caveats,* cautioning the reader that the reasons for these differences are not well understood. Additional research is always recommended, with representative samples from all Maine stocks collected over space and time, and using the latest techniques—which seem to become more sophisticated about every six months.

In summary, Maine Atlantic salmon stocks are currently defined and managed on a river-specific basis. Thus, each river that contains a breeding population of salmon is considered to possess its own stock. While there may not be conclusive evidence to support this theory for all of Maine's rivers that contain salmon populations, it is presently the best biological approach to managing the species until it can be shown that an alternative management policy would be better.

Maine Atlantic Salmon Populations

While there will probably always be a continuing debate about the number and origin of Maine Atlantic salmon stocks, there can be no doubt that there are two distinct Maine Atlantic salmon populations, and these are made up of a number of stocks collectively referred to as a *stock complex (Figure 2).* The largest Maine Atlantic salmon population may be defined as the *Maine* Atlantic salmon population, encompassing the Penobscot, Machias, and Narraguagus rivers' stocks. Secondary salmon stocks which also contribute to the Maine salmon population include the Dennys, East Machias, Pleasant, Ducktrap, and Sheepscot rivers, and several smaller stocks (such as tributaries to the lower Kennebec River, the lower Androscoggin River, Tunk Stream, St. Croix River, etc.). Penobscot salmon stocks were historically used in to bolster salmon runs in all other Maine rivers during periods of low abundance (1872–1921, 1940's, and since 1970), while Machias and Narraguagus salmon stocks(and, to a lesser extent, a few other rivers such as the Dennys) were used to bolster Penobscot salmon runs, and others, during periods of low abundance (mostly in the 1950's and 1960's).

The second distinct Maine Atlantic salmon population is not actually a Maine population at all, but one that originates in Canada. The *Saint*

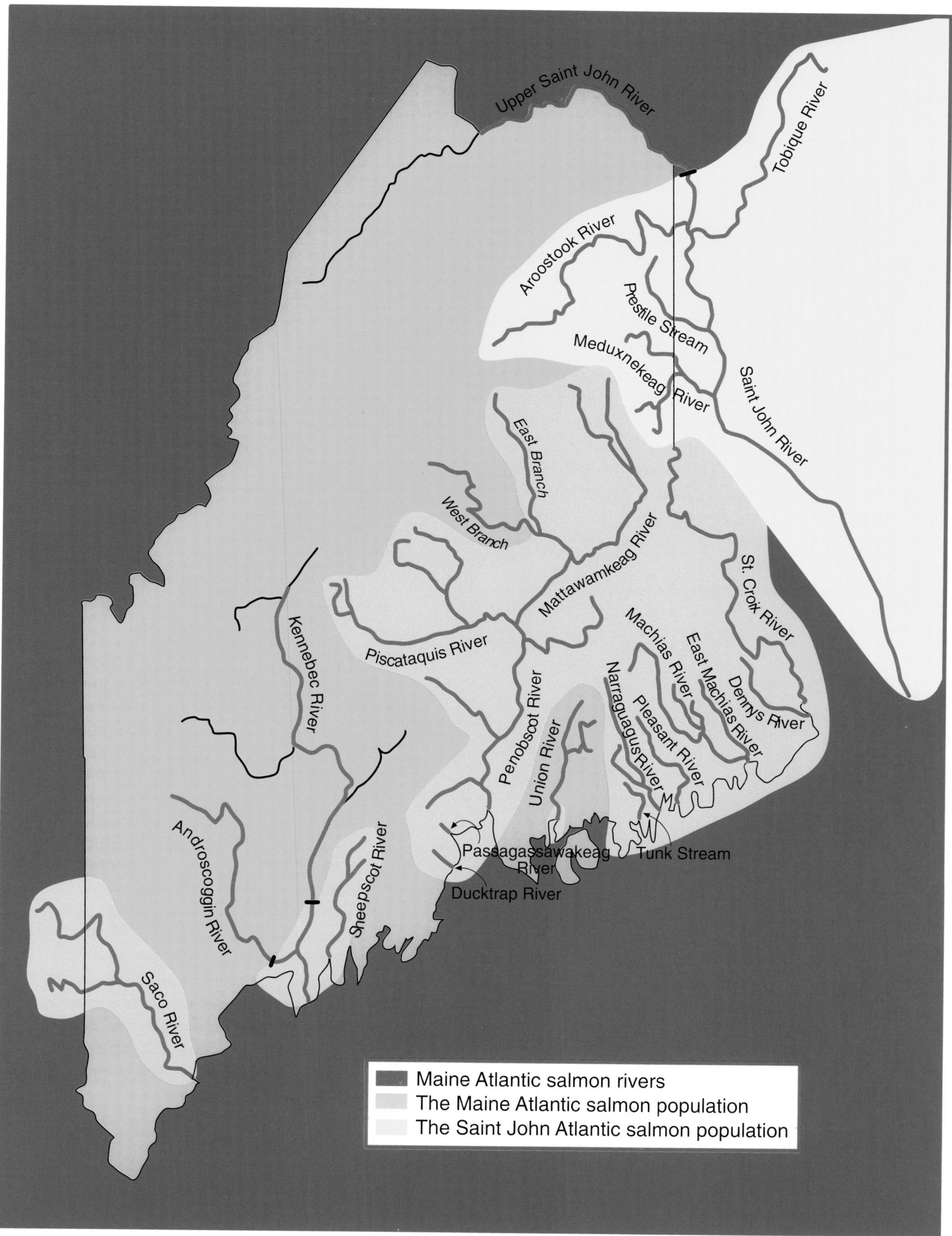

Figure 2. Maine Atlantic salmon rivers and salmon populations.

John population consists of the Saint John River as the primary stock, with secondary stocks originating in the many tributaries to the system. Maine salmon stocks which contribute to the Saint John population include the Aroostook and Meduxnekeag rivers and Prestile Stream, all of which are found in Aroostook County in northern Maine.

The Maine salmon population is characterized by the production of mostly two-year smolts (with the balance as three-year smolts) which result in predominantly two sea-winter adult returns. The Saint John salmon population, on the other hand, is characterized by the production of predominantly three-year smolts (with the balance as two-year smolts) which produce primarily one sea-winter adult returns. There has been only one documented stray salmon from Canada (a tagged smolt released in the Miramichi River in 1972 and recovered in the Penobscot River in 1974) and only 11 known stray salmon from Maine identified in Canadian rivers (ten in the Saint John River system and one in the Sops Arm River, Newfoundland).[2]

While geneticists may not always agree upon how many individual salmon stocks (or populations) there are in Maine rivers, there can be no doubt that the overall Maine population is dissimilar from the Saint John and other North American salmon populations. These notable differences between Maine and Canadian salmon are demonstrable in such areas as age at smoltification, age at maturity, adult run timing, fecundity, exploitation rates in distant water fisheries, and migration routes at sea. While it is not always possible to distinctly separate genetically inherited from environmentally induced traits, there is evidence in the scientific literature that some of those traits have genetic components. As well, some recent genetics studies of Maine Atlantic salmon have shown genetic differences between Maine and Canadian salmon, although geneticists are quick to point out that they do not know exactly how to interpret those differences. Additional research is always recommended, and the debate continues.[3]

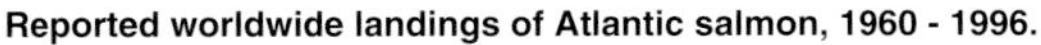

Reported worldwide landings of Atlantic salmon, 1960 - 1996.

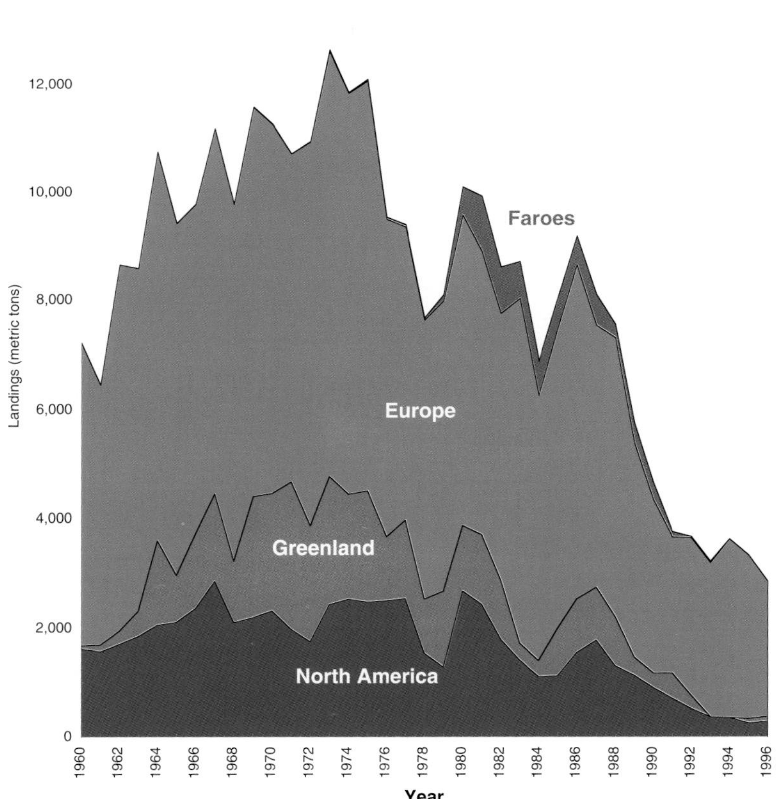

The precipitous decline in worldwide landings of Atlantic salmon since the early 1970's may be attributed to declining abundance and the Draconian management measures that have been instituted in an effort to preserve remaining stocks. The situation is most acute for North American salmon where some of the lowest marine survival rates for 2SW salmon have been observed in recent years.
Despite the nearly complete closures of commercial and sport fisheries, overall stock abundance remains low. Scientists are unable to explain the cause(s); however, it is suspected that this may be a cyclical phenomenon.

2. All of the Maine "strays" were of hatchery-origin and all had ample time to return to Maine to spawn that year.

3. The subject of genetics usually doesn't provide the clear-cut answers that most people seek, since these types of studies usually raise more questions than they answer.

2

Biology of Maine Atlantic Salmon

2 Biology of Maine Atlantic Salmon

Overview of Stream Life

The Atlantic salmon is an anadromous fish, which means that it spends most of its adult life in the ocean but returns to freshwater to reproduce. Between the juvenile growth and adult breeding stages in freshwater Maine salmon undertake impressive migrations covering thousands of miles at sea. Most adult salmon enter Maine rivers during the spring and early summer (May–July); however, fresh run or *bright salmon* are common from April to early November.

Upon first entry into freshwater, Atlantic salmon are called bright salmon because of their extremely silvery coloration and light blue-brownish backs. They will often have a few sea lice *(Lepeoptherius salmonis)* attached to their bodies, but these are usually harmless, dropping off within a day or two after the fish have entered freshwater. As the fish mature sexually in the river,[4] they become darker colored and mottled. By fall, they are almost bronze colored and often have large reddish spots on the head and body. Male salmon acquire the characteristic elongated lower mandible and hook, or *kype*, on the tip of the lower jaw.

Spawning normally takes place in Maine from mid-October through mid-November and is triggered by photoperiod and water temperature; spawning is usually completed within 7 to 10 days. Since early migrants may spend up to five months in the river, it is important that deep, cool, well-shaded resting pools are available in order

4. Actually, the sexual maturation process, as measured by hormone levels, has been shown to begin while the salmon is still at sea.

Bright salmon just in from the sea are very silvery in color. Determining the sex of early-run salmon is as much an art as it is a science.

A female salmon early in the season. Note the general shape of the head and overall coloration.

A male salmon in the fall. Note the kype on the tip of the lower jaw.

A female salmon in the fall. Note the differences in coloration at spawning compared to the female above.

Top: Two males court a female salmon on a redd. Left: A female salmon cutting or digging a redd. Below: Spawning salmon often roil the surface of the stream and frequently can be heard before they are seen.

to offer protection for the salmon until they spawn in the fall.

Suitable spawning areas consist of coarse gravel or rubble (up to fist-size rocks) in moving water that provides oxygen to incubating eggs. Salmon spawning areas are called *redds*. While female salmon may prepare up to four redds, one or two redds per female is the norm. Atlantic salmon redds consists of several *egg pits*. The female digs each egg pit by turning on her side and vigorously flapping her tail. The digging is accomplished primarily by the water currents produced by the fish's undulating movements, rather than by a lot of body contact with the gravel. This activity is known as redd digging or cutting. Frequent rest periods are taken between digging activities while the male (which usually mates with more than one female) spends his time courting the female or driving off other males.

When the egg pit is completed, the female settles into the depression, the male swims into position beside her, and some of the eggs and sperm (milt) are deposited. Water currents in the egg pit mix the sperm and eggs to ensure efficient fertilization and hold the eggs in the depression. When spawning is completed in the first egg pit, the female moves upstream to dig another, and another, and so on, until all her eggs have been deposited. As each successive egg pit is made, the displaced gravel is carried downstream to cover eggs in the pit below. The eggs, which are orange or amber in color, spherical in shape, and about 5 to 7 millimeters in diameter (roughly the size of a pea), are usually buried to a depth of 12 to 20 centimeters (5 to 8 inches) but may be found as deep as 45 centimeters (18 inches). As many as 8 egg pits have been found in individual Maine salmon redds.

An intensive survey conducted by fishery biologists in the 1970's of Atlantic salmon spawning activities in Maine's Downeast rivers revealed that spawning is usually initiated at water temperature between 7° and 10.5°C (45° and 51°F) and occurs between October 13 and October 17 each year. The onset of spawning activity varies from river to river and is thought to be due to slight differences in water temperatures. For example, spawning occurs earlier in portions of the Machias and Narraguagus rivers than it does in the East Machias and Pleasant rivers. The average depth of water observed at salmon spawning sites in Maine is 36 centimeters (14 inches) and ranges from 22 to 74 centimeters (8.5 to 29.0 inches). Surface water velocity over spawning areas average 49 centimeters/second (1.6 feet/second) and ranges from 27 to 83 centimeters/second (0.9 to 2.7 feet/second). While the average Maine salmon redd is 2.4 meters (7 feet, 10 inches) long and 1.4 meters (4 feet, 7 inches) wide, redds up to 5.6 meters long (18 feet, 3 inches) and 6.1 meters (20 feet) wide have been measured. The average area of Maine Atlantic salmon redds is about 3.8 square meters (4.5 square yards); however, individual redds as large as 15 square meters (18 square yards) have been found.

Frequently, young male salmon 10 to 15 centimeters (4 to 6 inches) long are sexually mature and participate in the spawning act. Experiments have shown that these fish, termed *precocious* parr, are just as capable of fertilizing eggs as adult salmon, and the presence of a larger male is not required for spawning to occur (Jones and King 1972).

The number of eggs deposited by any female will, of course, depend upon her size. A fecundity (egg production) study involving salmon from the Machias and Narraguagus rivers in the 1960's revealed that the egg number per individual female ranged from 3,528 to 18,847. Since each female produced an average of about 800 eggs per pound of body weight (range: 523 to 1,385 per pound), a 10-pound female salmon will produce about 8,000 eggs. Interestingly, the smallest maiden spawners are the most productive in terms of eggs per fish with one sea-winter (1SW) salmon (or grilse) producing 1,600 eggs per pound of body weight, as compared with two sea-winter (2SW) salmon producing 887 eggs per pound and 690 eggs per pound for three sea-winter (3SW) salmon (Figure 3).

If you find the current names for the various life history stages of Atlantic salmon confusing (alevin, fry, parr, smolt, grilse, salmon, kelt), consider the following terminology used in the 1600's (Kendall 1935). A salmon in its first year was known as a salmon-smolt, in the second year it was known as a mort, in the third a spraid, in the fourth a soar, in the fifth a sorrel, in the sixth a forket-tail, and finally in its seventh year it was finally termed a salmon!

Unlike all of the species of Pacific salmon which are semelparous (meaning that they die after first spawning), the Atlantic salmon may live to spawn several times. About 20% of the post-spawners, or *kelts*, may return to the sea in the fall, but the majority overwinter in the river and return to the ocean the following April or May. Having lost an average of 28.5% (and as much as 48%) of their body weight between river entry and spawning in the fall, due to the effects of starvation (adult salmon do not feed in fresh water) and the rigors of migration and spawning, these thin, dark fish are often called *black salmon*, or *racers*, if caught by anglers in the spring. Most salmon that live to repeat the spawning cycle will spend 12 to 15 months in the ocean before returning to the river to spawn again, although a few will reenter the river later in the fall after only three to five months in the ocean.

Salmon that return to spawn again after less than one year are termed short-absence, or consecutive year, repeat spawners, while those that return after more than one year are termed long-absence, or alternate year, repeat spawners. Most (±90%) Maine repeat spawners are the long-absence type; short-absence repeat spawners are most often associated with salmon of hatchery origin, and those, more often than not, originally spawned as grilse. Occasionally, a Maine Atlantic salmon will survive long enough to spawn four times and live to the ripe old age of ten.

The eggs deposited in the fall usually hatch during March or April. The *alevins*, or sac-fry as they are also called, are about one-half inch in length and have a large yolk sac protruding from their bellies. When the yolk sac is almost completely absorbed, the young fry swim out of the gravel and begin feeding in the river. This takes about six weeks and normally occurs about mid-May in most Maine rivers. Studies of Maine salmon have shown that most fry emerge at night (96.6% during hours of darkness), undoubtedly as a protective measure against predation. Various studies in Maine and elsewhere have shown that an average of only about 8% of the eggs originally deposited in the fall survive to the emergent fry stage. This is undoubtedly one reason why

Atlantic salmon parr (bottom) exhibit red and black spots on their sides as well as 8 to 11 vertical bands, termed parr marks. Smolts (top) no longer exhibit parr marks, becoming very silvery except for the outer margins of their fins.

Figure 3. Average number of eggs produced by Maine Atlantic salmon.

Repeat Spawners—11,350 eggs
(858 per pound of ripe body weight)

Three Sea-Winter Salmon—10,200 eggs
(690 per pound of ripe body weight)

Two Sea-Winter Salmon—7,560 eggs
(887 per pound of ripe body weight)

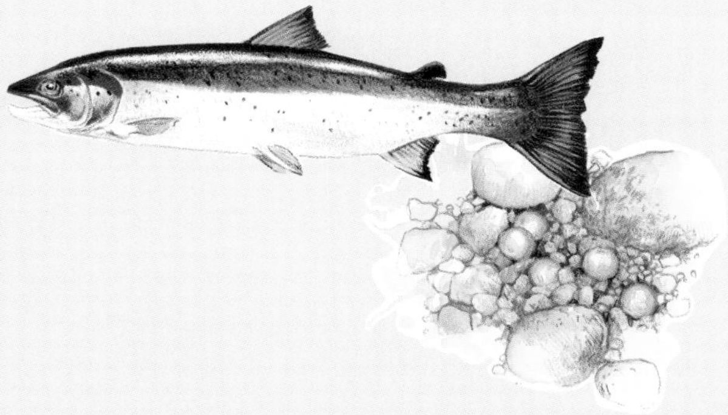

One Sea-Winter Salmon—3,040 eggs
(1,680 per pound of ripe body weight)

The Egg of the Salmon

The fecundation of the egg is a wonderful phenomenon. The egg in relation to the milt presents one of the most astonishing spectacles, if rightly viewed, which microscopist and "philosopher" can witness. To those of your readers who have not given any attention to this subject, it may be thus briefly described.

The egg of the salmon of the size of a pea consists of a semi-transparent spherical mass, whose tough external covering is penetrated by a very minute funnel-shaped opening, termed the micropyle. The milt of the male contains a vast assemblage of exceedingly minute organisms, styled spermatozoids. Perhaps a hundred thousand of these spermatozoids may be equal in bulk to one egg. Taking a minute quantity of milt on the point of a fine needle, and putting it into a drop of water in contact with an egg, the careful observer may witness the following consequences with a good microscope: The number of spermatozoids wandering vigorously round the passive egg, traveling over its surface with considerable activity. Suddenly one reaches the minute funnel-shaped micropyle; it enters, and the mouth of the micropyle contracts. Suddenly, pulsation begins in the egg, a new life has dawned and the micropyle speedily closes. Other spermatozoids continue wandering over its surface, but in fifteen or twenty minutes grow weary, languish, drop off and die. But vivid pulsations continue in the egg, and the new creature is forming. Let us carry the thoughts which may crowd upon us to a further issue. We have had under view two imperfect lives, that of the active spermatozoid and that of the passive egg. But the moment the spermatozoid enters the micropyle a new and a perfect physical life begins, which, as we shall presently see, already possesses absolute knowledge of a special kind, requiring only a short time for its manifestation.

Two of these eggs thus "fertilized" are conveyed far away, say to Australia, and these placed in a river in which salmon had never been. The eggs are hatched, the young fish in due time migrate to a sea of which their ancestors had no experience, and return to a river of which they knew nothing, and where there are no teachings to be gained from the experience of others of their kind. How did they obtain this absolute knowledge of an unknown sea and whence did they gather the instinct that it was essential that they should return to the river in which they were born, at stated periods? Ages of experience in others of their kind were not there to aid them, and migration is said to be the result of experience. It is clear that out of two imperfect lives a new life possessing absolute knowledge—knowledge not gained by experience or teaching—has been produced. Is this to be explained by the formula of words, that the instinct which impels the resulting creature to migrate to a sea and return to a river of which its ancestors knew nothing is "an inherited habit"? Or is not the gulf between the imperfect lives of the egg and the spermatozoid on the one hand, and the resulting perfect life of the impregnated egg on the other, with its absolute knowledge, infinite to us, passing the power of language to describe, and failing which, we apply to it a formula of words?

It seems to me that the conception which is so often designated as an "inherited habit," is a manifestation of design, infinite in its variety, endless in its future attainments, and crudely spoken of in the two often misleading language of philosophy by the barren term "evolution," which, properly used and interpreted, indicates only a part of design. The possession of absolute knowledge by the embryonic salmon, and all similar cases, is fatal to the materialistic view of evolution. How the results of experience can be conveyed from the parent to the spermatozoid or to the egg—for habit is derived from the female as well as from the male—we may never fully understand, but that it is an effort infinitely beyond the mere "potency of matter" we may adoringly believe.

EXCERPT FROM THE 1880 *REPORT OF THE COMMISSIONERS OF FISHERIES AND GAME FOR THE STATE OF MAINE*, EXPLAINING WHY THE SALMON RETURNS TO THE RIVER OR PLACE WHERE FIRST PLANTED.

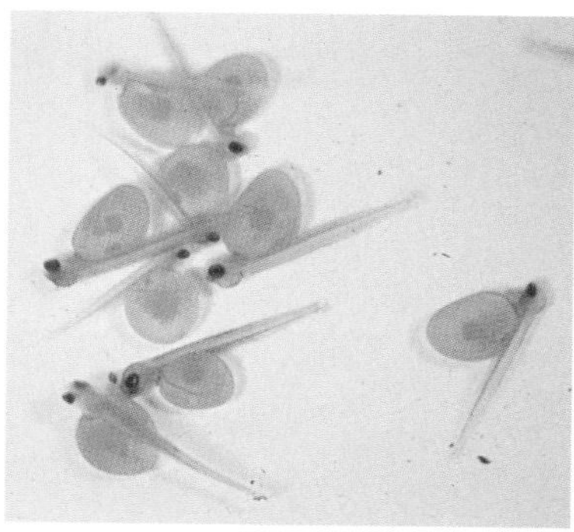

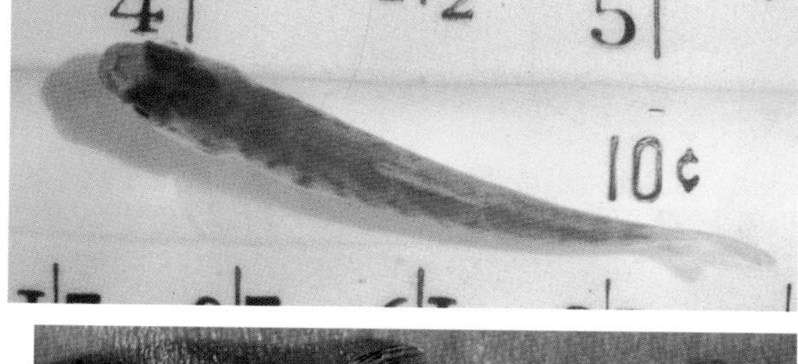

From egg deposition in the fall to smolt migration in the spring, most Maine Atlantic salmon spend 2– or 3 –years in freshwater. Three or more year classes may occupy the stream simultaneously. The life history stages shown are (clockwise from upper left): eggs, eyed eggs, alevin or sac-fry, fry , parr, smolt.

fish cultural programs originated—the false belief that they could improve upon nature.

Salmon fry first feed on plankton (microscopic plants and animals), but, as they grow in size, their diet consists primarily of insect larvae and insects such as blackflies, stoneflies, caddisflies, and so forth. As they increase in size they also occasionally eat small fish, such as alewives, dace, or minnows. As growth continues, the small salmon are called *parr* because of the eight to eleven pigmented, vertical bands (termed parr marks) on their sides. These bands are thought to help camouflage the salmon from predators during their period of stream life. Salmon parr closely resemble small brook trout. However, unlike trout, they have black *and* red spots on their sides, and a well-forked tail.

About 80% (range: 70 to 90%) of the parr in Maine streams remain in freshwater for two years, while the other 20% stay an additional year. Obviously, a salmon stream must provide extensive nursery areas where the young salmon can find sufficient food and protection from predators during this stage of its life history, since up to three year-classes of young salmon may occupy nursery areas simultaneously.

Following two or three years of stream life, the approach of spring heralds the time to leave freshwater and the salmon parr undergo several changes. Outwardly, the fish become thinner and their tails become elongated and more deeply forked; the parr marks disappear as the fish turn very silvery. Inwardly, drastic changes occur to enable them to adapt to life in the sea. For example, the kidneys of a salmon must now be able to excrete salt rather than retain it. The salmon, now termed a *smolt*, migrates downstream to the ocean during the period mid-April to mid-June. While most smolts leave Maine rivers at age two or three, one-year-old and four- and five-year-old smolts have been documented; however, these are very rare in Maine rivers.

While salmon parr are very territorial, demersal (bottom-dwelling) animals in streams, as smolts they become pelagic (free-swimming) animals that

Maine Atlantic salmon spend from one to three winters at sea before returning to their river of origin to spawn. One sea-winter salmon, or grilse (A), weigh from 2 to 4 pounds upon their return, while two sea-winter salmon (B) range from 7 to 12 pounds. Three sea-winter salmon (C) normally weigh from 13 to 19 pounds, while repeat spawners (D) weigh as little as 5 pounds or more than 30 pounds, depending upon their size the last time that they spawned.

are usually found near the surface (top 1 to 2 fathoms) of the sea. The smolts' newly acquired silvery coloration creates an effective camouflage that appears dark when viewed from above and light when viewed from below the surface of the sea.

Maine Atlantic salmon smolts range from 13 to 23 centimeters (5 to 9 inches) in length, depending upon their age and the productivity of the streams in which they live. The average length of several thousand wild smolts measured in the Narraguagus River in the 1960's was 16 to 18 centimeters (6.5 to 7.2 inches) for two-year smolts and 17 to 20 centimeters (6.9 to 7.8 inches) for three-year smolts. Interestingly, three-year-old smolts averaged only 1.1 centimeters (less than 1/2 inch) longer than two-year-old smolts.

As with all forms of life, Atlantic salmon are exposed to various natural enemies. Fish that may prey upon young salmon in freshwater include chain pickerel, smallmouth bass, American eels, and even an occasional large brook trout. Such birds as American and red-breasted mergansers, belted kingfishers, double-crested cormorants, gulls, and ospreys are known to consume Maine Atlantic salmon parr and smolts. The role of predators will be discussed in a later section.

It has been shown that the survival of Atlantic salmon in freshwater is less variable than it is at sea (Reddin 1988). Thus, it is within the ocean that the greatest variations in survival occur—precisely the area most difficult to study and the area where fishery scientists have the least amount of knowledge about the life of the Atlantic salmon.

Overview of Ocean Life

Once in the estuary, Atlantic salmon begin to feed voraciously on insects and crustaceans and, as they migrate further into the marine environment, on other species of fish. Initially, primary foods consist of euphasids (shrimp-like animals), amphipods (flea-like animals), and decapods (10-legged crustaceans), followed in a few weeks by the addition of herring, sand lance, capelin, and shrimp (Dutil and Coutu 1987). As the salmon mature in the ocean, the life cycle is completed by a spawning migration back to freshwater. Most salmon return to the river where they were spawned and reared; however, a few occasionally wander into other rivers. Studies involving the release of 1.5 million tagged hatchery-reared smolts into Maine rivers have shown that, on average, only 1 to 2% stray into other rivers. It is unknown if many (or any) of these fish successfully reproduce in those rivers or whether or not they eventually return to their rivers of origin.

While in the ocean, Maine Atlantic salmon are subjected to attack from seals, porpoises, many species of birds, and many other species of fish. The mortality rate during life at sea is extremely high; for every 100 smolts that leave the river, only a small percentage survive to return to Maine as adult fish. Additionally, Maine salmon were also heavily exploited in commercial fisheries until recently (see Chapter 3).

Maine Atlantic salmon spend varying lengths of time in the ocean. Fish that spend one winter at sea are called one sea-winter (1SW) salmon, or *grilse*, while older salmon are simply called *salmon*, or multi sea-winter (MSW) salmon. Scale samples examined from more than 2,000 wild Narraguagus River salmon in the 1960's and 1970's revealed that in any year, 1SW salmon comprised 1–2% of the spawning run, 2SW salmon 80–90%, and 3SW salmon 3–5%. The balance of the salmon run (5–10%) was composed of salmon that had previously spawned one or more times. Similar data from other rivers have shown that this age structure is typical for Maine salmon runs. The percentage of three sea-winter salmon and repeat spawners has declined to fewer than 1% in recent years, apparently because of commercial fisheries that operated from the early 1960's to the early 1990's. These largest of Maine salmon were extremely vulnerable to commercial fisheries, with exploitation rates estimated to be as high as 90% in some years (i.e., 9 of every 10 fish were harvested before they had a chance to return to Maine!). With the closure of the Newfoundland and Greenland fisheries in 1992 and 1993, respectively, the proportion of 3SW salmon and repeat spawners in Maine salmon runs should increase in future years. However, it may take several generations for the numbers of these fish to increase substantially.

The average Maine adult salmon is 72–76 centimeters (28–30 inches) long and weighs from 3.5–5.5 kilograms (8–12 pounds), although they can weigh as much as 14 kilograms (30 pounds). The largest Atlantic salmon caught on rod and reel in Maine in recent years weighed more than 28 pounds, although fish larger than 20 pounds are uncommon.

Where do Maine salmon go during their years at sea? First, based upon commercial and research vessel catches of salmon in the North Atlantic, it has been shown that they prefer 4–8°C (40–46°F)

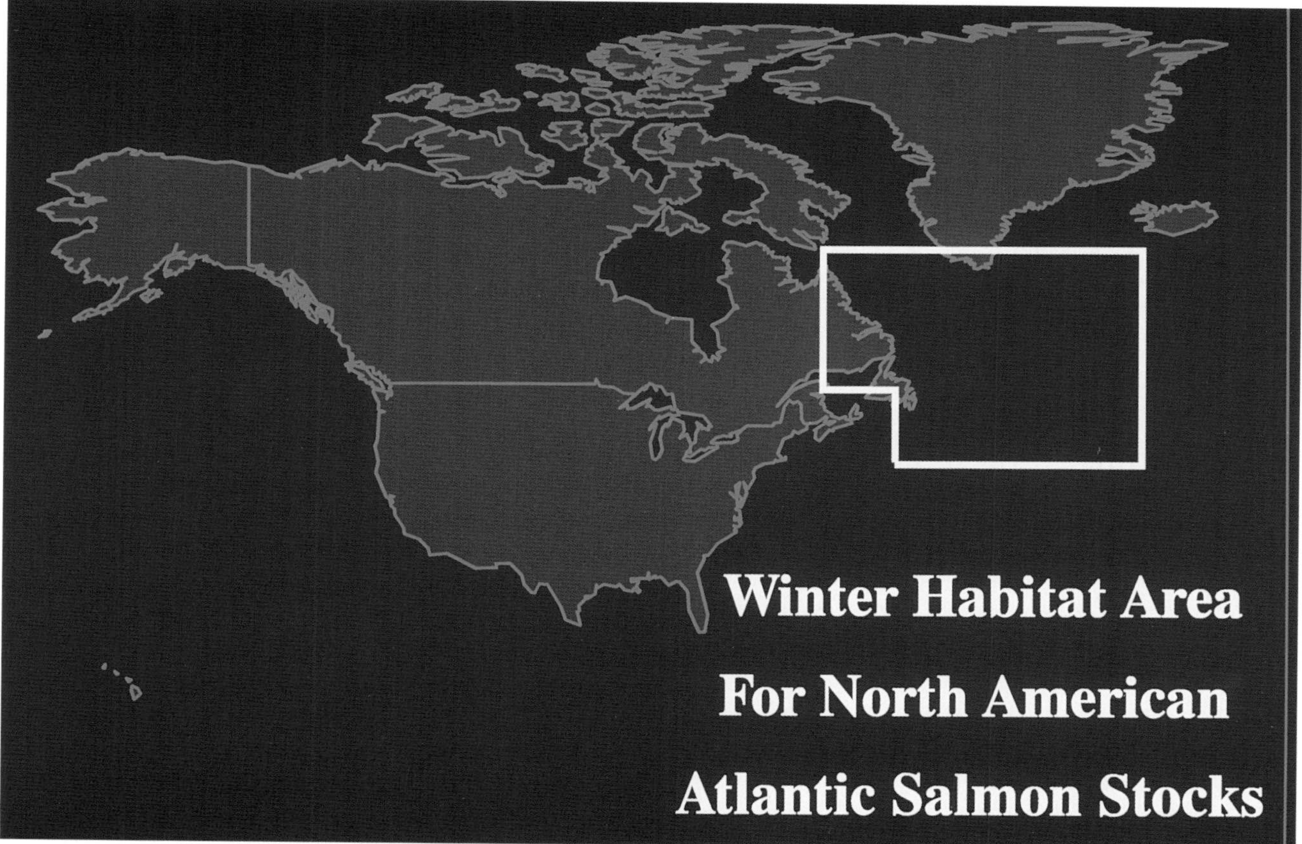

The winter habitat area for North American Atlantic salmon stocks is based upon the salmon's preferred water temperatures at sea.

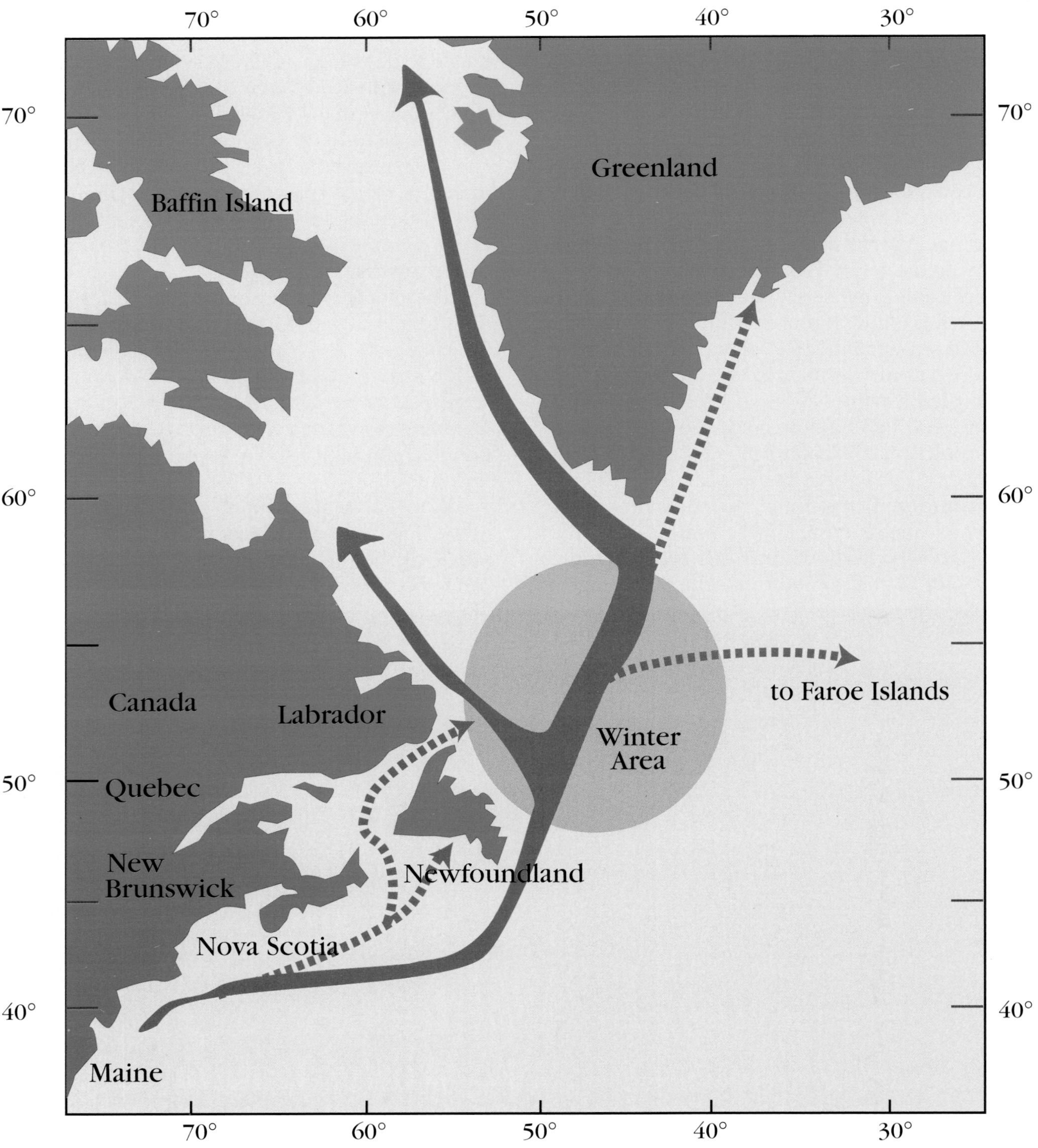

Figure 4. Known migration routes of Maine Atlantic salmon.

water temperatures, although they can be found in waters ranging from 3 to 13°C (38 to 56°F) (Reddin and Shearer 1987). The lower lethal temperature for salmon in the ocean has been reported to be -0.7°C (31°F) (Saunders et al. 1975), while the upper lethal temperature in freshwater is about 30°C (86°F). Second, tagging experiments involving adults and hatchery smolts have taken some of the mystery out of the ocean life of Maine salmon. Tag returns have been reported from commercial fisheries in Nova Scotia, Newfoundland, Labrador, and West and East Greenland—more than 2,850 miles from home! While some Maine salmon go to Greenland, others only go as far as Newfoundland and Labrador, and a few tagged Maine adventurers have been taken in the Faroe Islands (located between Iceland and Scotland) in recent years. The Greenland area is a common feeding ground for many European and North American salmon stocks.

Most Maine salmon migrate to sea in May and by mid-June they are found off the coast of Nova Scotia. In July they may be found off the south and east coasts of Newfoundland, and some are found as far north as Labrador by August. Maine salmon apparently spend their winters in the Labrador Sea, since salmon tagged as smolts, as well as those tagged as adults, have been recovered in the same areas during the fall. The known migration routes of Maine Atlantic salmon are illustrated in Figure 4.

During their second summer at sea, some Maine salmon return to the coasts of Newfoundland and Labrador, while others migrate to East or West Greenland, and still others have already returned to Maine rivers to spawn as grilse. This, no doubt, is Nature's way of not putting all of its "salmon eggs" in one basket!

By calculating the length of time at sea between the release and recapture of tagged salmon originating in Maine, migrations of more than 40 kilometers (25 miles) per day have been documented (assuming straight line migration). Faster daily rates of migration undoubtedly occur, since salmon do not swim in straight lines. Greenland tag returns from adult fish originally tagged in the Machias, Narraguagus, and Penobscot Rivers on their first spawning migration have shown that some Maine salmon can make the journey to Greenland waters more than once in their lifetimes!

Biological Aspects of Maine Atlantic Salmon

The overviews of the stream and ocean life stages of Atlantic salmon presented a thumbnail sketch of the complicated life cycle of Maine Atlantic salmon, that is illustrated in Figure 5. The following sections present more detailed information about Maine salmon collected by state and federal biologists during the last 50 years of study. How big do Maine salmon grow? When do they migrate? What are the impacts of predators such as seals and cormorants? Where and how fast do they migrate at sea? The answers to these and other frequently asked questions about Maine Atlantic salmon are unraveled throughout the following pages.

Adult Run Timing

Initially, it would seem that describing when adult Atlantic salmon return to Maine rivers would be a relatively straightforward task—monitor the timing of catches in sport fisheries and in fishway traps and simply add up the numbers. However, salmon are not so easily monitored, since they are often present before fishing seasons open and after seasons close. Similarly, operating fish-counting facilities under all environmental conditions is not always possible, and, in most instances, those counting facilities are not 100% efficient at catching all of the salmon that are present. For example, periods of high (or low) water may render fishways and traps inoperable; conversely, such conditions may also render those counting facilities more (or less) efficient at capturing salmon in the area at that time. Rod and trap catches in May are also not usually representative of the actual numbers of salmon present at that time of year. While the combined rod and trap catch of salmon in the Penobscot River in May amounts to about 5% of the average annual total run, in reality it is more likely that about 20% of the salmon run occurs

> *Maine's Passamaquoddy Indians had distinct names for Atlantic salmon and landlocked salmon, calling the sea salmon* Plláhm *and the freshwater salmon* Tagewahnahn *(Atkins 1874). Members of Maine's Penobscot Indian Nation use the word* Skwameku *to describe the Atlantic salmon.*

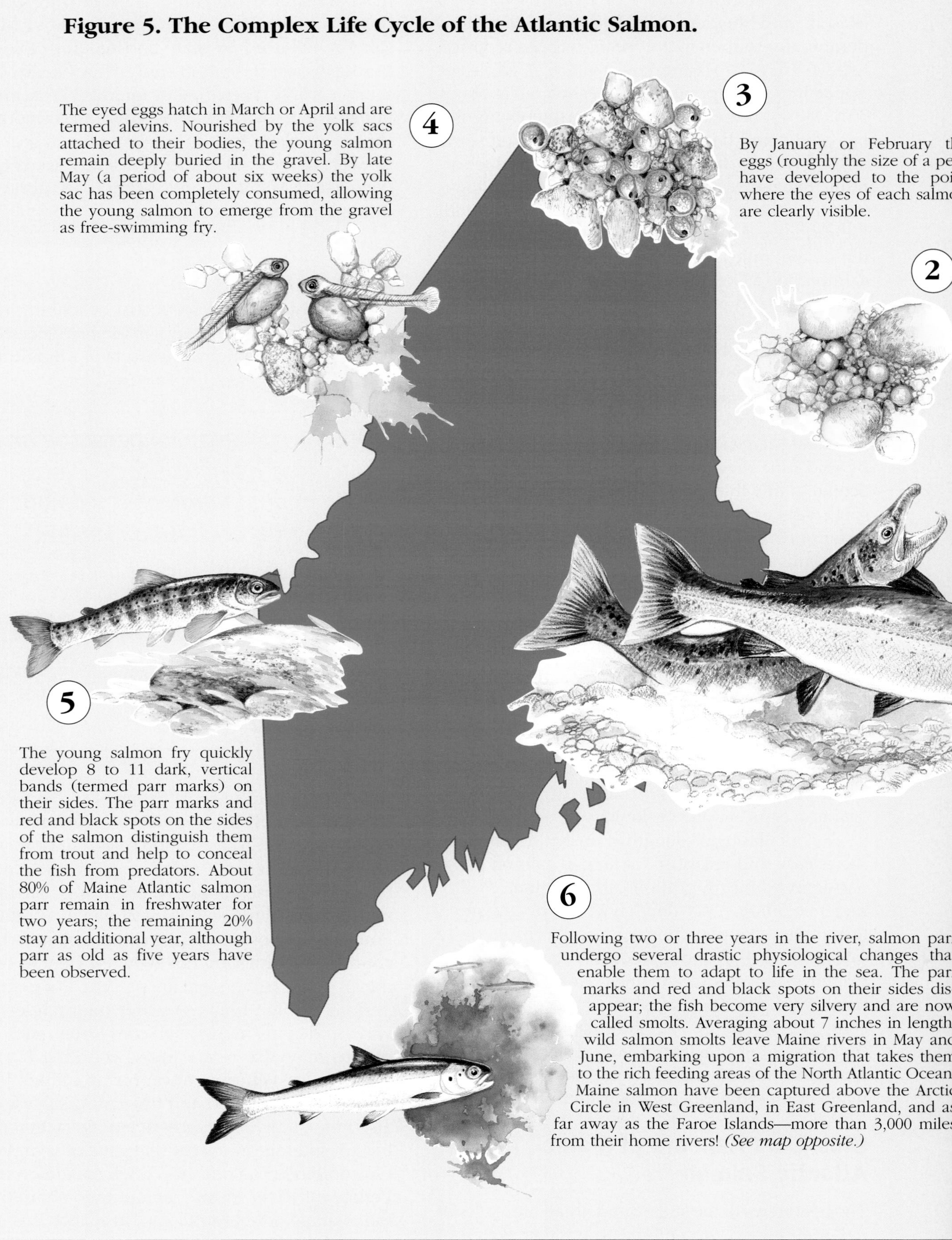
Figure 5. The Complex Life Cycle of the Atlantic Salmon.
3
By January or February th eggs (roughly the size of a pe have developed to the poi where the eyes of each salmo are clearly visible.
4
The eyed eggs hatch in March or April and are termed alevins. Nourished by the yolk sacs attached to their bodies, the young salmon remain deeply buried in the gravel. By late May (a period of about six weeks) the yolk sac has been completely consumed, allowing the young salmon to emerge from the gravel as free-swimming fry.
2
5
The young salmon fry quickly develop 8 to 11 dark, vertical bands (termed parr marks) on their sides. The parr marks and red and black spots on the sides of the salmon distinguish them from trout and help to conceal the fish from predators. About 80% of Maine Atlantic salmon parr remain in freshwater for two years; the remaining 20% stay an additional year, although parr as old as five years have been observed.
6
Following two or three years in the river, salmon parr undergo several drastic physiological changes that enable them to adapt to life in the sea. The parr marks and red and black spots on their sides disappear; the fish become very silvery and are now called smolts. Averaging about 7 inches in length, wild salmon smolts leave Maine rivers in May and June, embarking upon a migration that takes them to the rich feeding areas of the North Atlantic Ocean. Maine salmon have been captured above the Arctic Circle in West Greenland, in East Greenland, and as far away as the Faroe Islands—more than 3,000 miles from their home rivers! *(See map opposite.)*

average female Maine Atlantic salmon will osit about 7,200 eggs in the one or two ls that she prepares. Suitable spawning s consist of very coarse gravel or rubble (up bout 4 inches in diameter) and are located reas of moving water. A mixture of coarse wning material is necessary in order to re that the eggs, which incubate at an aver- depth of 5-8 inches below the gravel, are plied with an adequate supply of oxygen.

m mid October through early November nale salmon deposit their eggs into sever- al egg pits that are collectively termed a redd. Spawning, which is motivat- ed by decreasing daylight (photoperiod) and water tem- peratures of 45-50°F, nor- mally takes place in water averaging 14 inches deep. It is common for precocious male parr to ist the adult males in the fertilization cess. Spent salmon are termed kelts and ny will survive to spawn again in later rs despite the fact that they lose nearly 6 of their original body weight. Most of ine's repeat spawners are biennial or alter- e year spawners, although some spawn in secutive years.

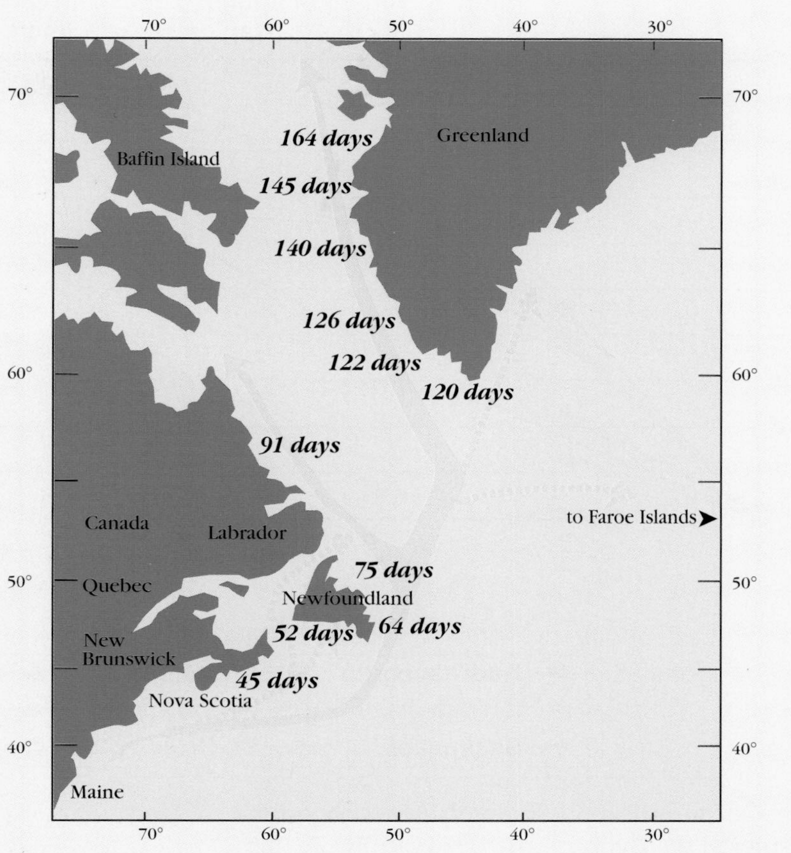

Maine Atlantic salmon spend varying lengths of time at sea. Those that spend one year are termed one sea-winter salmon (anglers call these fish grilse), while older salmon are termed multi sea-winter salmon (or simply, salmon). Smolts migrate at an average rate of 9.5 miles per day (adults, because they are larger and can swim faster, average 16.5 miles per day), and reach the south coast of Newfoundland in 50-60 days, mid-Labrador in 90-110 days, southern Greenland in 120 days, and northern Greenland (above the Arctic Circle) in 160 days.

Atlantic salmon return to spawn by retracing their original migration routes. Less than 10% return as one sea-winter salmon (95% of which are males) at an average weight of just under 4 pounds. The majority (about 90%) return as two sea-winter salmon averaging approximately 9 pounds. In recent years three sea-winter salmon and repeat spawners have made up about 1% of adult returns to Maine rivers. The average weight of three sea-winter salmon is about 16 pounds, while repeat spawners can reach weights approaching 30 pounds.

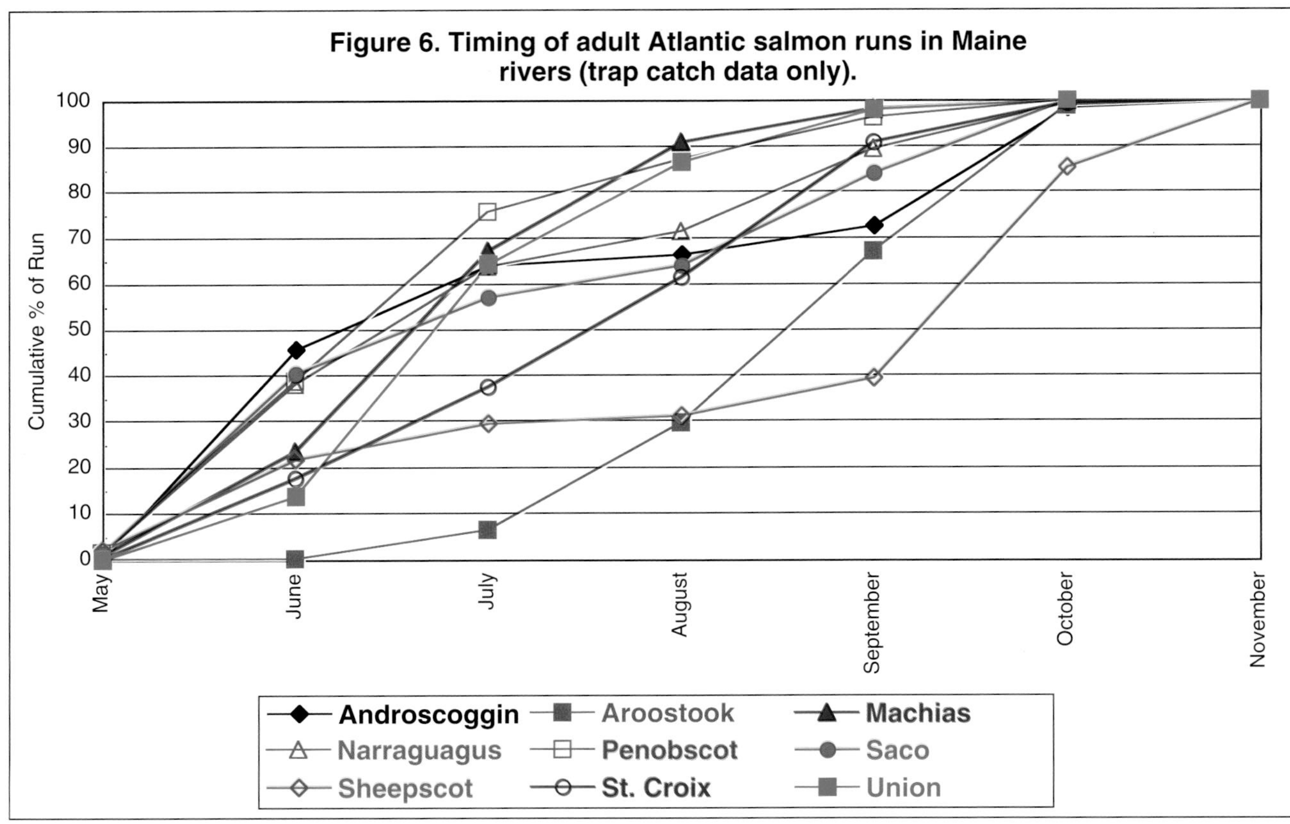

during that month (and some of *those* fish originally entered the river in April). To complicate this task even further, Maine Atlantic salmon do not always migrate in an upstream direction. Returning to tidewater after migrating several miles upriver earlier in the year is common for an Atlantic salmon. They may migrate back into the same (or even a different) river later in the year.

Maine rivers contain salmon populations that are classified as early run or late run, based upon the timing of adult entry into freshwater. In early runs most of the salmon enter freshwater during the period May through mid-July, while in late runs most of the salmon enter after that time. As evidenced by fishway trap catches and historical rod catches, the Penobscot River has the earliest salmon run each year, with other early runs occurring in the Dennys, East Machias, Narraguagus, Kennebec, Androscoggin, and Saco Rivers. Late salmon runs occur in the St. Croix, Machias, and Ducktrap rivers and a few Maine rivers contain salmon runs that exhibit tendencies for both early and late returns (see Figure 6 and Table 1). The Pleasant River in eastern Maine and the Sheepscot River in central Maine are good examples of this.

Sizes of Adult Maine Atlantic Salmon

Since Maine salmon spend from one to three years in the ocean, the size of the returning adults varies with sea age. Various studies of the lengths of Maine salmon have shown no statistical difference between males and females; therefore, the information presented in Table 2 and Figure 7a is for both sexes combined.

Weight data for adult salmon of various age groups is not routinely collected because weighing a live Atlantic salmon is difficult under field conditions. Additionally, information from rod catches is difficult to use because anglers use various types of scales to weigh their fish, and slightly "exaggerated" weights are often provided. Detailed weight information is available, however, for some years from the Narraguagus, Machias and Penobscot rivers where individual salmon were carefully weighed by biologists under controlled field conditions. Information collected from Narraguagus River salmon in the 1960's and Penobscot River salmon in the 1980's was quite similar (Table 2). The relative sizes and weights for adult Maine salmon of all ages are illustrated in Figures 7a and 7b.

Although it has been suggested that Maine salmon are smaller now than they were in the "good old days," there is no evidence to support this. In fact, average length and weight data from Penobscot salmon collected by Charles Atkins in the 1870's shows that two and three sea-winter salmon were virtually the same size then as they are now. The *average* weight of those salmon used for spawning purposes at Craig Brook Hatchery

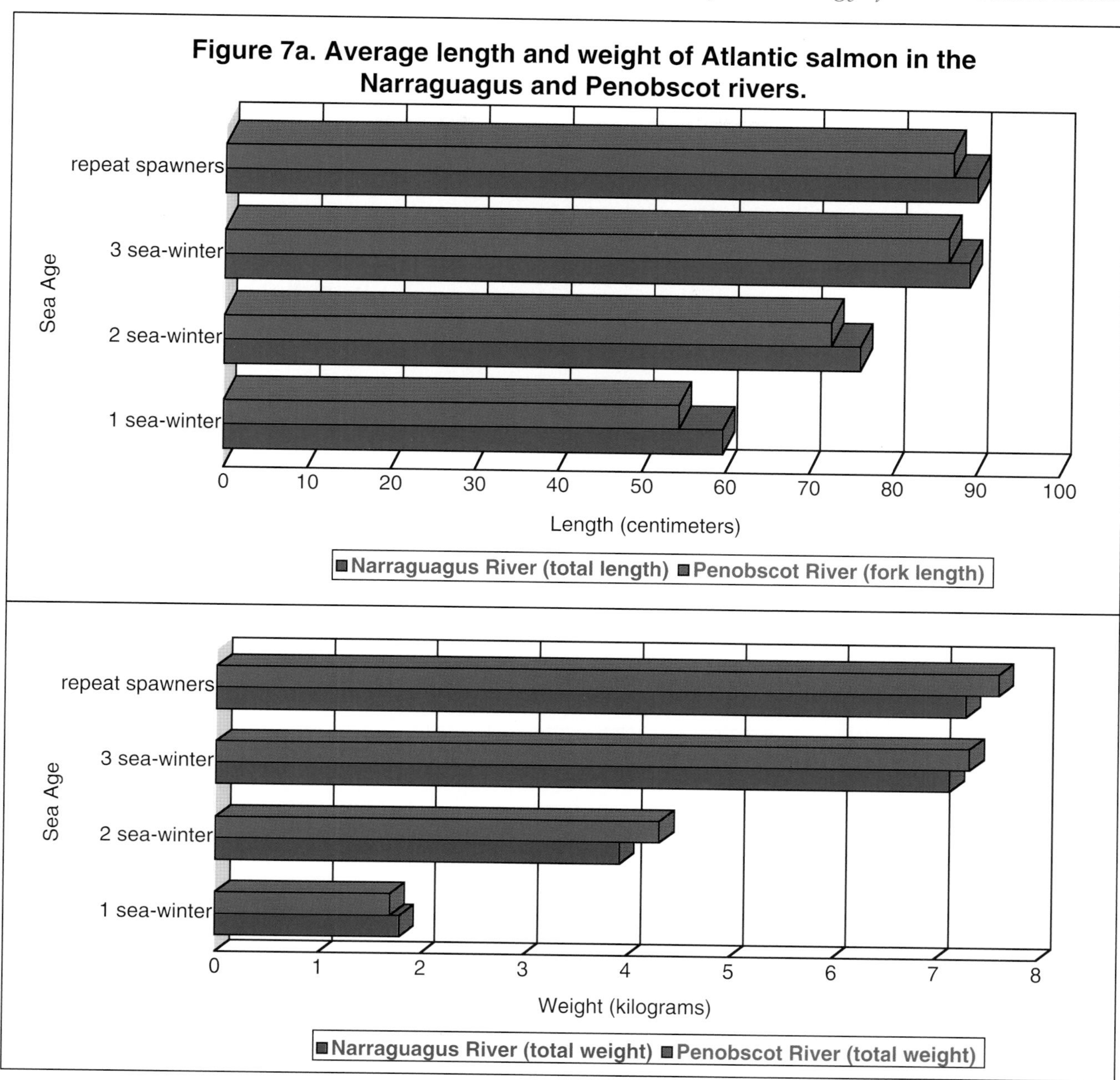

in the 1800's was greater because three sea-winter salmon and repeat spawners were more abundant in those times than they are now, and there was a bias toward the purchase of large salmon for broodstock purposes in the 1800's. As a matter of interest, the average length of Atlantic salmon of various ages measured in the Penobscot River during the past 25 years is illustrated in Figure 8. While there is a small amount of annual variation, the average length of fish at a given sea age has been remarkably similar over time.

Homing

The return of an adult salmon to its natal river is termed homing, and how a 17-centimeter (7-inch) smolt leaving the Machias River in the spring can swim to Greenland and return to the Machias River two years later as a 78-centimeter (30-inch) salmon is one of the great mysteries in life. Various theories have been postulated to explain this behavior in salmon, including those involving ocean currents, magnetic fields, pheromones (hormones secreted by the presence of other salmon), the odor or scent of the water, and the sun, moon, and stars. It has even been postulated that salmon movements are not directed, but occur at random or in a chaotic manner.

At one time it was thought that the imprinting of Atlantic salmon smolts occurred during a relatively short period (a few days to a few weeks) in the river of origin. However, modern theory suggests that salmon undergo a process of *sequential* imprinting (Harden-Jones 1968), whereby they are

Figure 7b. Atlantic Sea Run Salmon Commission biologists have accurately measured the length and weight of more than 1,700 adult Atlantic salmon from the Narraguagus, Machias and Penobscot rivers.

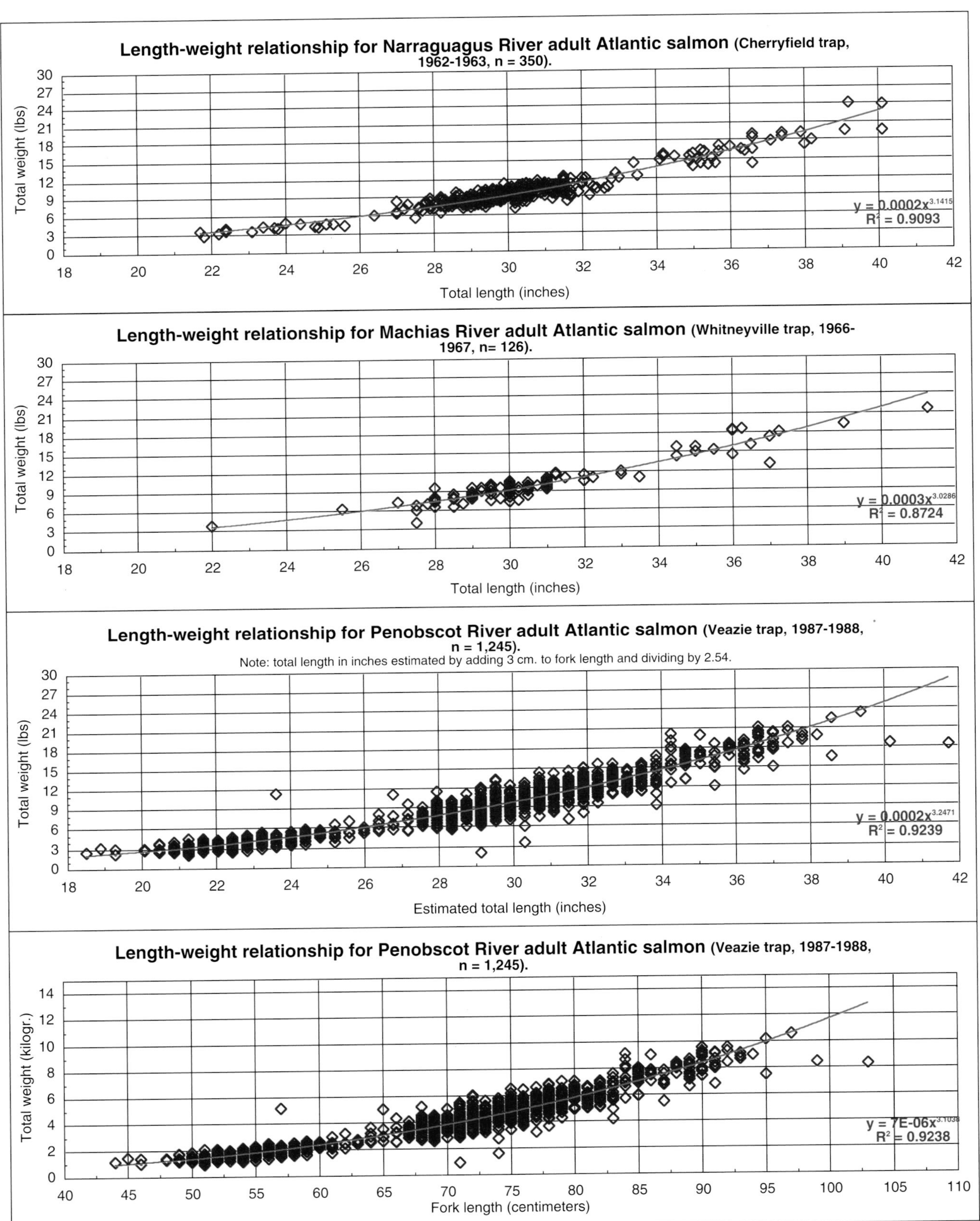

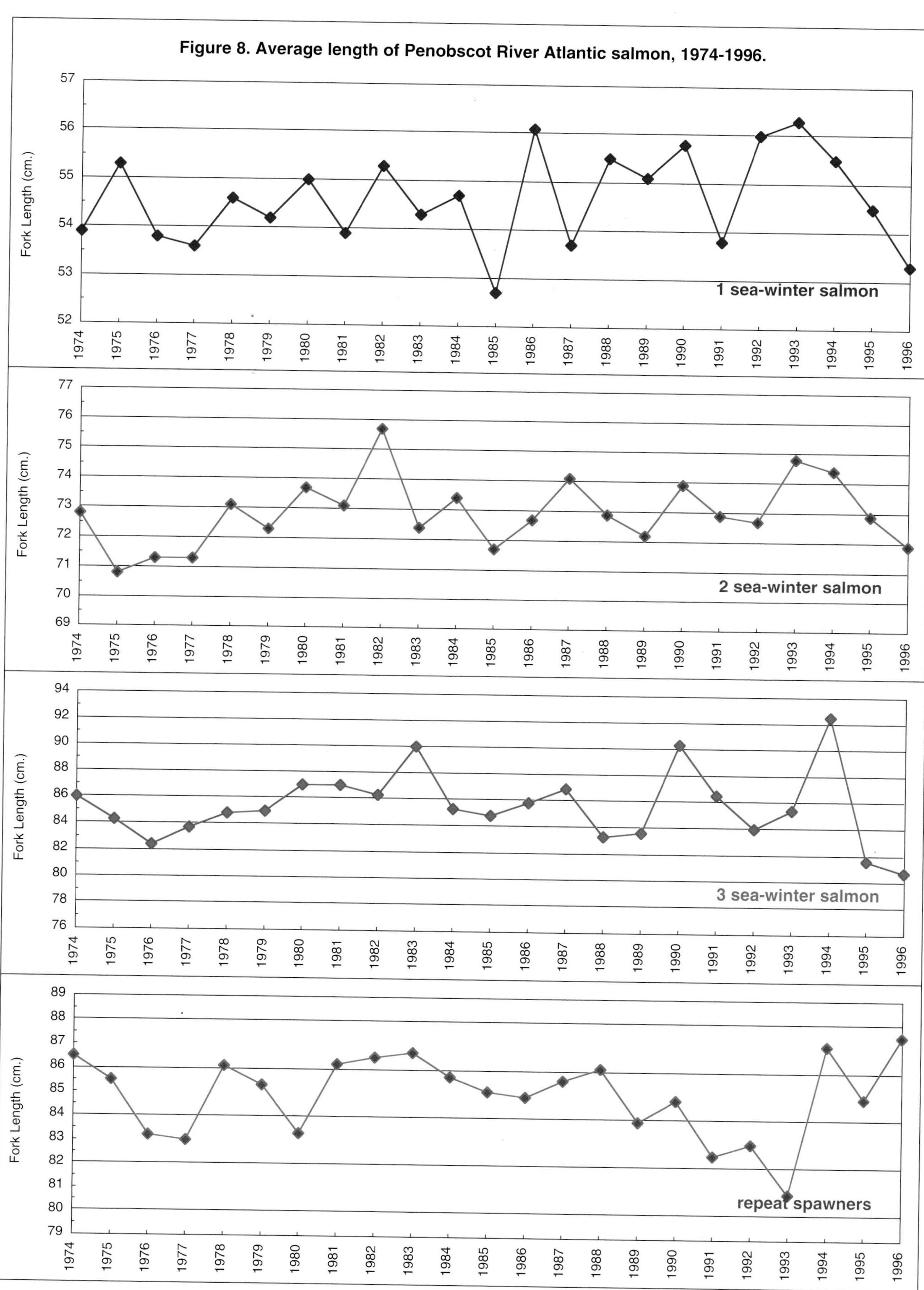
Figure 8. Average length of Penobscot River Atlantic salmon, 1974-1996.
Fork Length (cm.)
1 sea-winter salmon
2 sea-winter salmon
3 sea-winter salmon
repeat spawners
1974 1975 1976 1977 1978 1979 1980 1981 1982 1983 1984 1985 1986 1987 1988 1989 1990 1991 1992 1993 1994 1995 1996

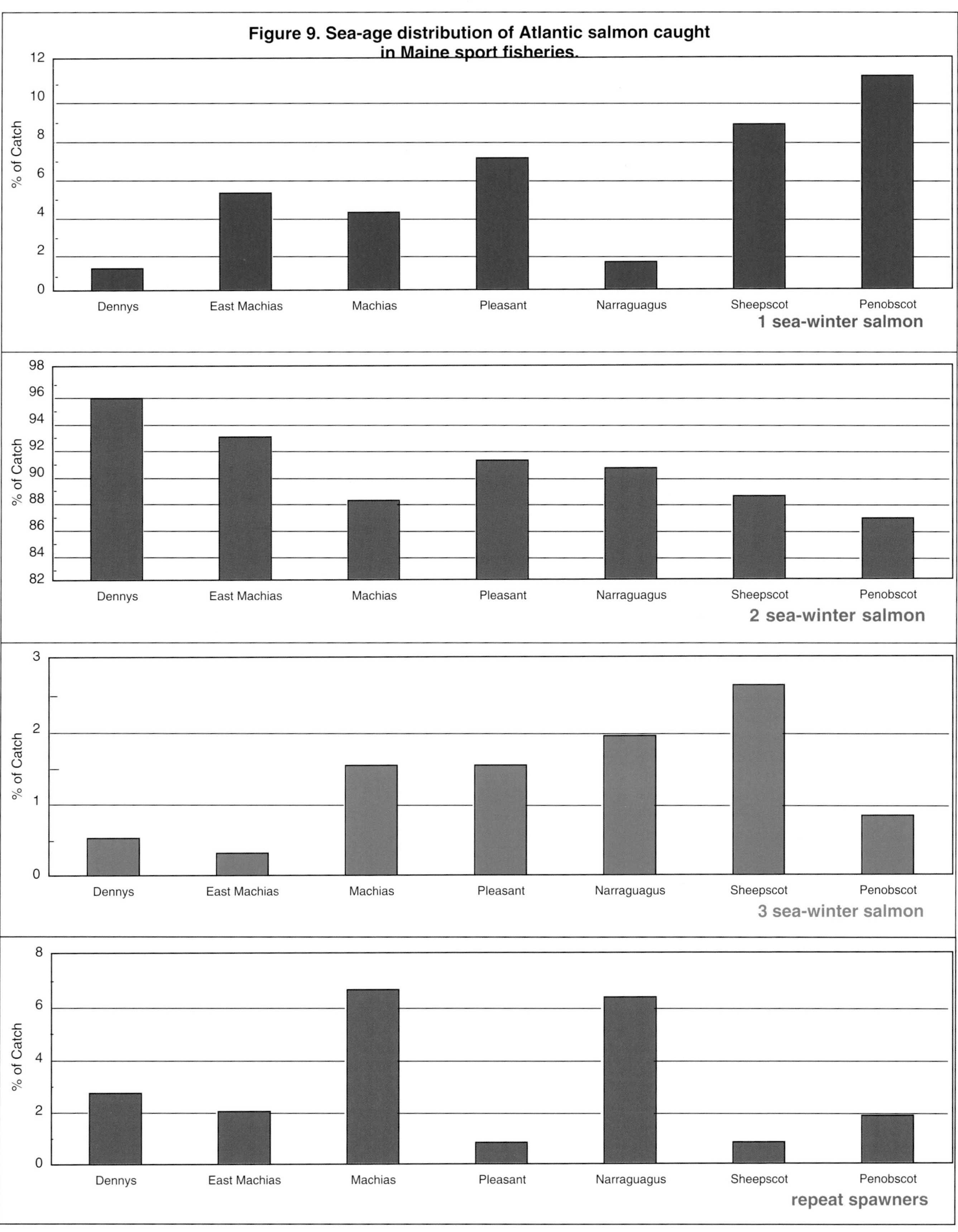
Figure 9. Sea-age distribution of Atlantic salmon caught in Maine sport fisheries.
% of Catch
12
10
8
6
4
2
0
Dennys
East Machias
Machias
Pleasant
Narraguagus
Sheepscot
Penobscot
1 sea-winter salmon
98
96
94
92
90
88
86
84
82
2 sea-winter salmon
3
1
3 sea-winter salmon
repeat spawners

Seals and Salmon…

Seals are known to kill a great many salmon in Penobscot Bay and the lower river. They enter and leave the weirs and traps without difficulty and cause great annoyance to the fishermen. When a seal enters a net, the fish are frightened and usually become meshed; the seal may then devour them at its leisure. The initial bite usually includes the salmon's head. Fishermen in some places report a noticeable increase in seals in the past few years, and a consequent increase in damage done to the salmon fishery. The state pays a bounty of $1 each for seal scalps, which serves to keep the seals somewhat in check, although the sagacity of the animals makes it difficult to approach them with a rifle and to secure them when shot. Within a few years some weir fishermen have been obliged at times to patrol the waters in the vicinity of their nets, in order to prevent depredations. In the Cape Rosier region, where some salmon trap fishing is done, seals were very troublesome in the early part of the season of 1896. Mr. George Ames, who set three traps in 1896 and took about 100 salmon, had knowledge of 13 other salmon that were destroyed by seals while in his nets. Similar instances of relatively large numbers of salmon killed by seals might be given. With salmon worth 20 to 50 cents a pound the loss of 10 or 12 salmon by seals, in a total catch of 75 to 100, is a matter of importance to the fisherman.

(Smith 1898)

continually learning their migration route from the time they leave the river as smolts until they return as adults from one to three years later. It has been shown that the olfactory sense (sense of smell) is extremely important to the adult salmon in successfully returning to their river of origin (Stabell 1984). This led to the belief that water odor (and/or pheromones) is one of the most important aspects of the homing process. It has been shown, however, that the olfactory sense is not required for smolt navigation through rivers and lakes when they are *leaving* their home river (Doving et al. 1984).

A maximum straying rate of three (meaning fewer than 3 of every 100 salmon returns to the wrong river) has been reported for North American and European Atlantic salmon (Stabell 1984). Results from the release of more than 1.5 million Carlin-tagged (an externally applied tag named after its inventor, Swedish scientist B. Carlin) hatchery-reared salmon smolts in Maine rivers during the period 1966–1992 suggests that Maine salmon fall within that range, since only 1–2% have been known to enter rivers other than where they were originally stocked. The highest incidences of straying were observed for those fish stocked at or near the head of tide (for example, at Ellsworth in the Union River), where the opportunity for imprinting in freshwater portions of the river was the shortest. While straying of Maine salmon does occur, it is also theoretically possible for many of

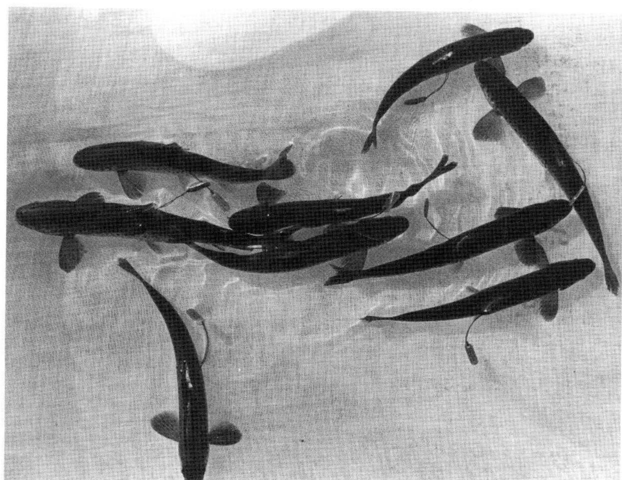

Carlin-tagged Atlantic salmon smolts prior to release in a Maine river. There is a one-inch section of polyethelene between the tag and the fish's body that allows the fish to grow without the tag becoming embedded in the flesh of the animal. These seven- to eight-inch salmon will return as 27 to 32-inch long adult salmon two years later.

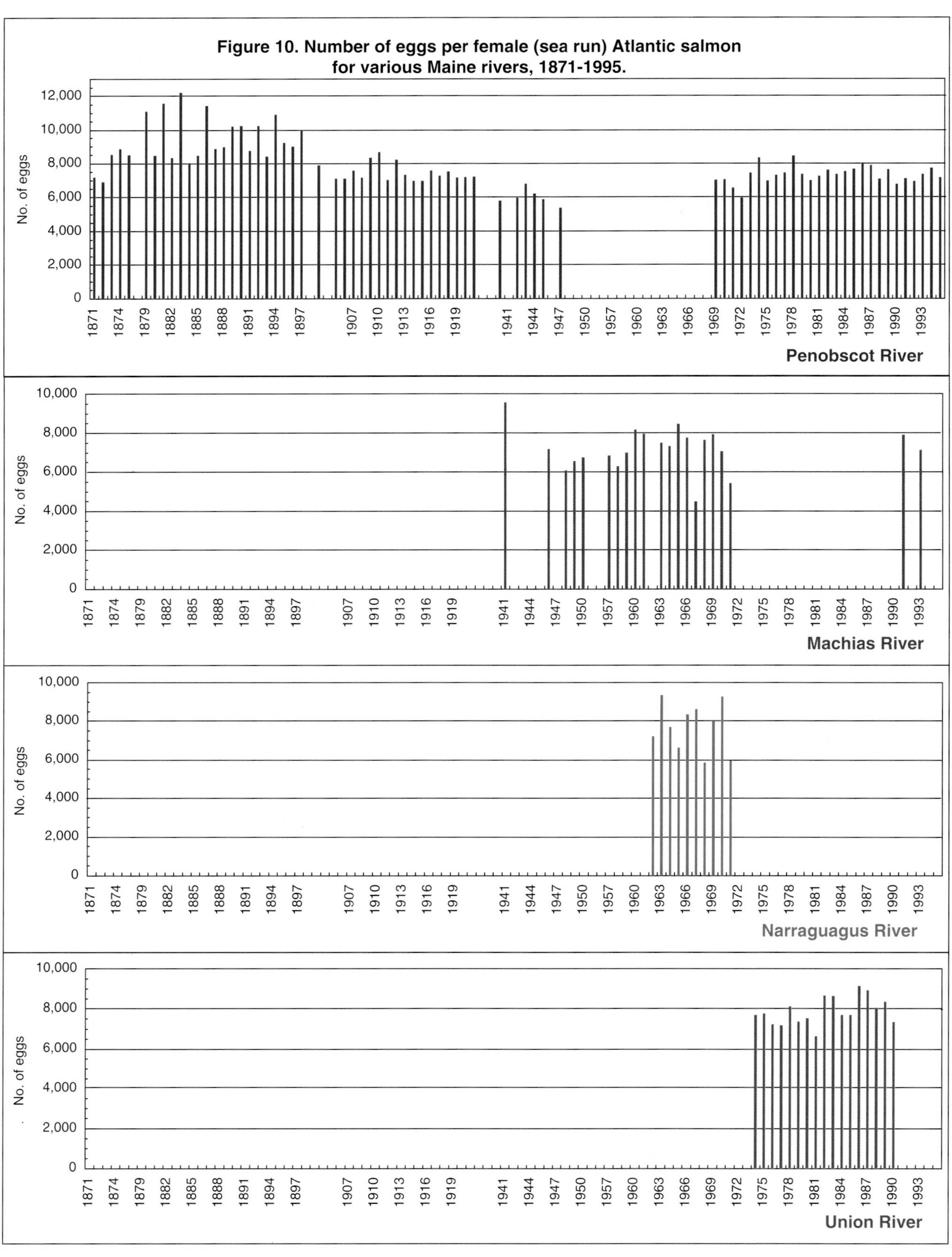
Figure 10. Number of eggs per female (sea run) Atlantic salmon for various Maine rivers, 1871-1995.
No. of eggs
12,000
10,000
8,000
6,000
4,000
2,000
0
1871 1874 1879 1882 1885 1888 1891 1894 1897 1907 1910 1913 1916 1919 1941 1944 1947 1950 1957 1960 1963 1966 1969 1972 1975 1978 1981 1984 1987 1990 1993
Penobscot River
Machias River
Narraguagus River
Union River

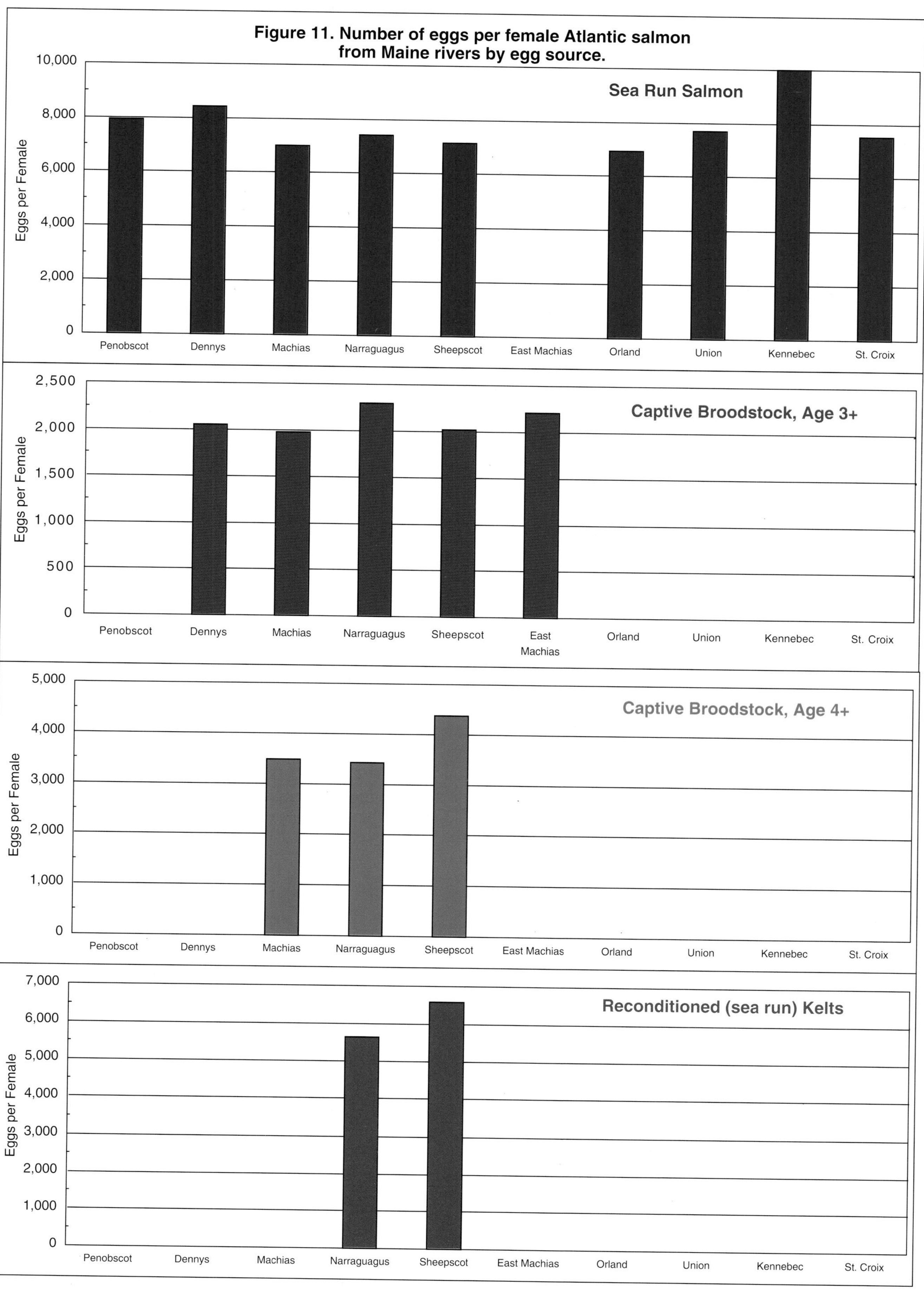
Figure 11. Number of eggs per female Atlantic salmon from Maine rivers by egg source.
Sea Run Salmon
Eggs per Female
10,000
8,000
6,000
4,000
2,000
0
Penobscot
Dennys
Machias
Narraguagus
Sheepscot
East Machias
Orland
Union
Kennebec
St. Croix
Captive Broodstock, Age 3+
Eggs per Female
2,500
2,000
1,500
1,000
500
0
Penobscot
Dennys
Machias
Narraguagus
Sheepscot
East Machias
Orland
Union
Kennebec
St. Croix
Captive Broodstock, Age 4+
Eggs per Female
5,000
4,000
3,000
2,000
1,000
0
Penobscot
Dennys
Machias
Narraguagus
Sheepscot
East Machias
Orland
Union
Kennebec
St. Croix
Reconditioned (sea run) Kelts
Eggs per Female
7,000
6,000
5,000
4,000
3,000
2,000
1,000
0
Penobscot
Dennys
Machias
Narraguagus
Sheepscot
East Machias
Orland
Union
Kennebec
St. Croix

those fish that do stray to ultimately return to their river of origin. The reproductive success of these strays (which originated from hatchery-reared salmon smolts) and whether or not this rate of straying is the same for wild-origin Maine salmon is unknown.

Age at Maturity and Sex Ratios

The age at maturity (i.e., the age when most adults return to spawn) for most Maine salmon is during the fifth summer of life—after two summers in the river and two summers at sea. Differences among Maine rivers are due to many factors, including genetics and environment. It should be kept in mind that the information shown in Table 3 and Figure 9 represent averages over time. Variations within any given year are apt to vary considerably from the "average."

Until the time for spawning is near, ascertaining the sex of mature Atlantic salmon readily is very difficult. Both sexes are similar in appearance in the ocean and upon entry into freshwater. Generally speaking, though, male salmon often have a large adipose fin whereas females have a small one. However, the problem with this statement is that many fish have a "medium" sized adipose fin! Another feature peculiar to males is that they have elongated, rounded heads, while females tend to have short, pointed heads. The problem with *this* theory is that many salmon seem to have heads shaped somewhere between long and round and short and pointed! In other words, determining the sex of individual salmon, especially early in the migration season, is as much an art as it is a science.

The sex ratios for Maine salmon of various sea ages are also quite different. Grilse (one sea-winter salmon) are predominantly (95–98%) males while older salmon are predominantly (55–75%) females. As with most aspects of fishery science, there are exceptions to the rule. For example, detailed records of Penobscot salmon collected for broodstock purposes at Craig Brook Hatchery revealed a 50/50 sex ratio, while similar data from Narraguagus River salmon in the 1960's revealed that, on average, about 60% were females. Most of the Penobscot salmon were of hatchery origin, whereas the Narraguagus salmon were of wild origin. Whether originating from releases of hatchery-reared salmon or from spawning in the wild, females usually comprise about 75% of the three sea-winter salmon and repeat spawners in Maine rivers. As with humans, the female of the species is predestined to outlive the male!

Fecundity and Weight Loss From Spawning

Detailed estimates of the numbers of eggs produced (fecundity) by 154 wild, female salmon from the Machias and Narraguagus Rivers ranged from 3,528 to 18,847, and egg numbers per pound of body weight from 523 to 1,385 (Baum and Meister 1971). Although older salmon produce a greater *total* number of eggs, the number *per unit* of body weight is highest for the youngest salmon (Figure 3).

The numbers of eggs produced per female for all Maine-origin Atlantic salmon broodstock used in hatchery programs since 1871 are reported in Appendix 1. The annual variation in eggs per female is illustrated in Figure 10, as is the number of eggs per female for the Penobscot and Union River broodstock spawned at Craig Brook National Fish Hatchery during "modern" times. Finally, the average number of eggs per female salmon for all Maine broodstock used in recent times is shown in Figure 11. In recent years new sources of eggs have been developed by reconditioning kelts originally spawned as adult sea run salmon and by rearing wild-origin salmon parr to maturity (at ages 3 and 4) in freshwater. As the reader can see from Table 4 (appendix) and Figure 11, there are differences in egg production among the various Maine salmon stocks.

Information pertaining to the weight loss of post-spawner Atlantic salmon, and, more importantly, its significance, is limited. In the years 1881 and 1882, Charles Atkins and his staff weighed 135 and 250 Penobscot River female salmon before and after artificial spawning at Craig Brook Hatchery. For those salmon weighed in 1881, the average weights before and after spawning were 15.67 and 11.85 pounds, respectively, representing a 24.4% loss of ripe body weight. Salmon weighed in 1882 salmon averaged 12.2 pounds before spawning and 9.4 pounds after spawning, representing a 23.0% loss of ripe body weight. In 1964 the average weight loss for 39 female salmon from the Narraguagus and Machias Rivers was 24%, ranging from 12 to 46% for individual fish. For these fish all of the weight information was collected at the time of spawning. In 1965 however, another 25 females were weighed at the time of capture (some 4–5 months prior to spawning) and again after spawning. For these salmon, the average weight loss was 28.5%, ranging from 18 to 47% (Baum and Meister 1971). In terms of overwinter survival and the ability to survive to return as a repeat spawner, the consequences of a 45% weight loss for an individual salmon are probably more severe than the consequences of a 15% loss in body weight. Interestingly, similar results were noted by Warner (1962) who gave the average loss in weight of 42 Maine landlocked salmon as 25% of ripe body weight.

Juvenile Production and Survival

The suitability of Maine salmon streams to produce juvenile salmon depends upon myriad factors that affect productivity—bottom substrate, gradient, cover, water depth, velocity and temperature, and the presence of competing species and predators, to name a few. It has been shown that age 0+ juvenile salmon prefer water depths of 10 to 15 centimeters (4–6 inches) and velocities of 50 to 60 centimeters/second (1.6–2.1 feet/second), while the age 1+ and older parr are more commonly found in riffles greater than 20 centimeters (8 inches) deep (Symons and Heland 1978). While Atlantic salmon parr occupy a wide range of water depths, most are found in water that is 24 to 36 centimeters (9–14 inches) deep (Rimmer et al. 1984). At all life stages, young salmon require cover in the form of rocks and boulders, aquatic vegetation, and/or overhanging stream banks. Cover provides the salmon with a source of food, since many aquatic insects are found on or around the bottom and nearby rocks and vegetation. Cover also provides the salmon with refuge from predators. The distribution of juvenile salmon during the winter is often markedly different from that observed in the summer. It has been shown that small salmon usually move into deeper riffles and pools and may often be found buried several centimeters beneath the bottom substrate.

Biologists use pulsed-DC electrofishing equipment to estimate the population densities of juvenile salmon. The fish are momentarily stunned and released after biological data has been collected. Here the author and several summer assistants sample the wild Atlantic salmon population in Cove Brook, a tributary to the lower Penobscot River.

Maine Atlantic Salmon Authority (formerly Maine Atlantic Sea Run Salmon Commission) biologists have conducted annual late-summer surveys of selected salmon nursery areas with the use of electrofishing equipment since the mid 1950's. In order to make inter- and intra-river comparisons, the production of juvenile salmon is expressed in terms of the density per "unit" of habitat where one unit equals 100 square meters. This system was first reported in 1957 by Dr. Paul Elson, world-renowned Canadian Atlantic salmon biologist, and is now used universally to describe Atlantic salmon production in both North America and Europe.

Estimates of juvenile salmon densities from various Maine rivers are shown in Table 5. Generally speaking, Maine's Atlantic salmon streams produce from 5 to 10 parr/unit of habitat, which is quite similar to other streams in this area of North America (i.e., New Hampshire, New Brunswick, etc.). While it is tempting to try to compare rivers (e.g., are the Dennys and Machias more productive than the Narraguagus and Sheepscot rivers?), in this instance the reader would truly be comparing the proverbial apples with oranges. The data in Table 5 were collected from various types of habitat, during different times, by different personnel, and utilizing different electrofishing techniques. Therefore, this information is useful in illustrating the variability in parr densities that is commonly observed in Atlantic salmon streams in this part of the world.

On the other hand, Atlantic salmon smolt production appears to be less variable than parr production in areas where two-year-old smolts predominate. For example, the average smolt production documented in a Maine stream was 3.0 smolts/unit (Meister 1962). This is very similar to that reported in a tributary to the Connecticut River (3.1 to 4.1 smolts/unit; Orciari et al. 1994), and the Big Salmon (3.1/unit; Jessop 1975), the Miramichi (4.7/unit; Elson 1975), and the Pollett (2.9/unit; Gee et al. 1978) rivers in New Brunswick.

The survival of juvenile salmon can be as variable as the production of parr in different types of habitats. In a review of the literature, Symons (1979) listed survival rates ranging from 9% to 20% from eggs to fry, 28% to 44% from fry to 1+ parr, and 35% to 55% from 1+ parr to smolts. Obviously, the survival rates for Maine salmon fall somewhere within these ranges, since the highest survival estimates would result in the production of 11 smolts per unit of habitat, while the lowest estimates would result in two smolts per unit of habitat. As a general "rule-of-thumb" one can expect Maine salmon rivers to produce about 19 fry per unit of habitat (±8% survival from egg to fry) resulting in about 6 parr per unit (±30% survival from fry to parr), and ultimately about 3 smolts per unit (±50% survival from parr to smolt). These estimates are based upon the commonly used standard egg deposition of 240 eggs per unit, yielding an average estimated survival from the egg to age 2+ smolt of 1.25% (i.e., 3 smolts per unit of habitat/240 eggs per unit of habitat).

In Maine, Atlantic salmon parr grow rapidly between late April and late August. They continue to grow at a much slower rate through October. Obviously, growth of juvenile salmon is dependent upon the quality of the habitat (i.e., variables such as water quality and food supply, which are independent of the density of fish) and the density of the fish (i.e., too many young fish in an area retards growth, development, and survival). However, the growth of Atlantic salmon parr in Maine streams is not as variable as one might expect. Generally speaking, Maine Atlantic salmon fry range from 5 to 8 centimeters (2–3 inches) in length and weigh 1–3 grams (a fraction of an ounce), while parr range from 10 to 25 centimeters (4–10 inches)

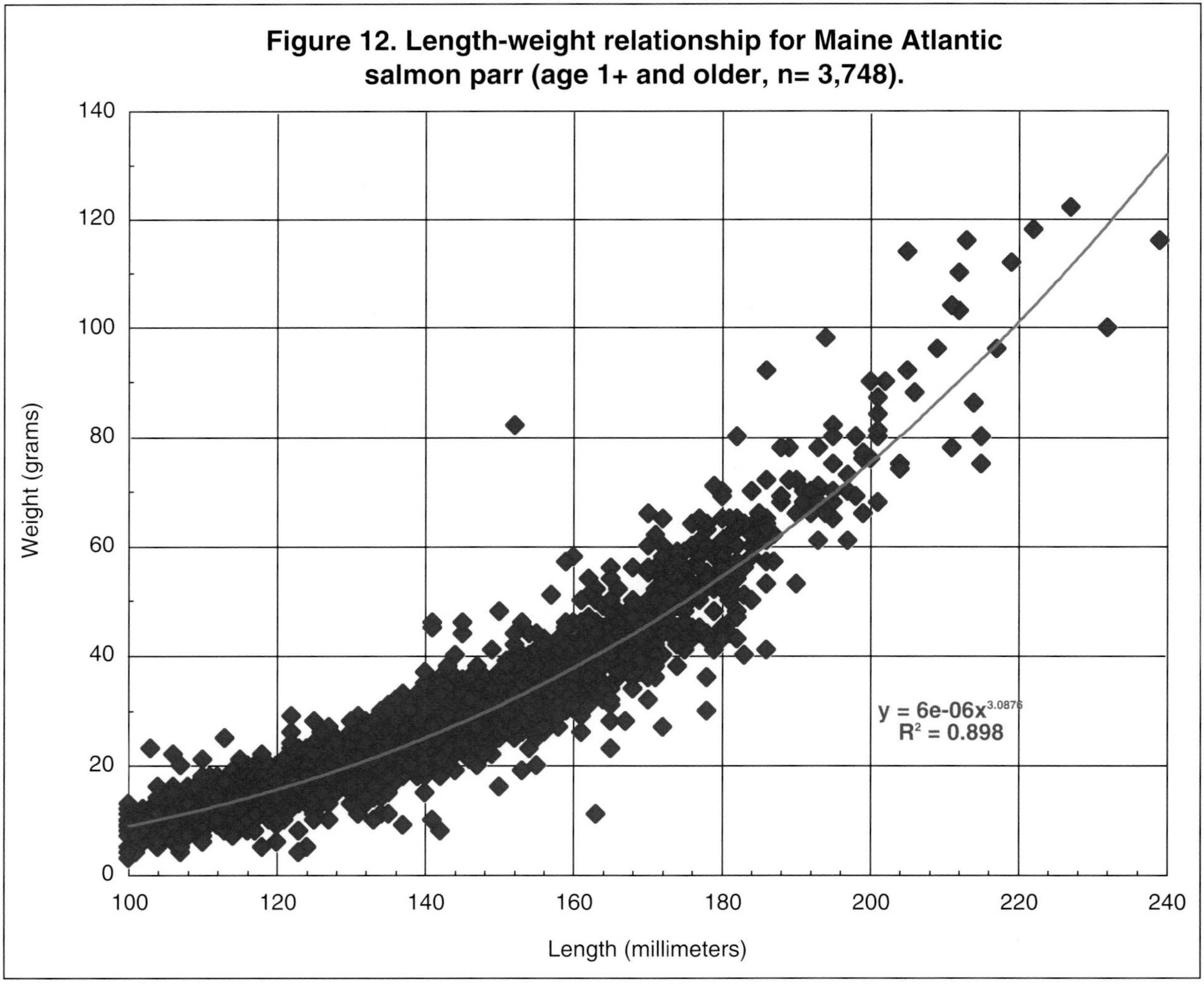

Figure 12. Length-weight relationship for Maine Atlantic salmon parr (age 1+ and older, n= 3,748).

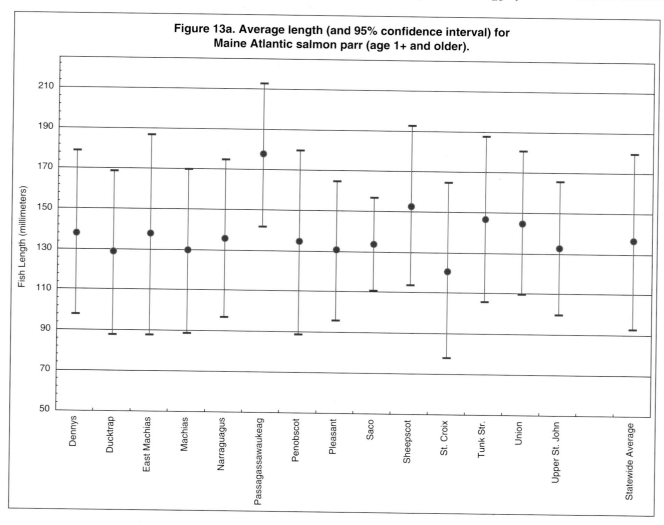

Figure 13a. Average length (and 95% confidence interval) for Maine Atlantic salmon parr (age 1+ and older).

Fish Length (millimeters)

210
190
170
150
130
110
90
70
50

Dennys
Ducktrap
East Machias
Machias
Narraguagus
Passagassawaukeag
Penobscot
Pleasant
Saco
Sheepscot
St. Croix
Tunk Str.
Union
Upper St. John
Statewide Average

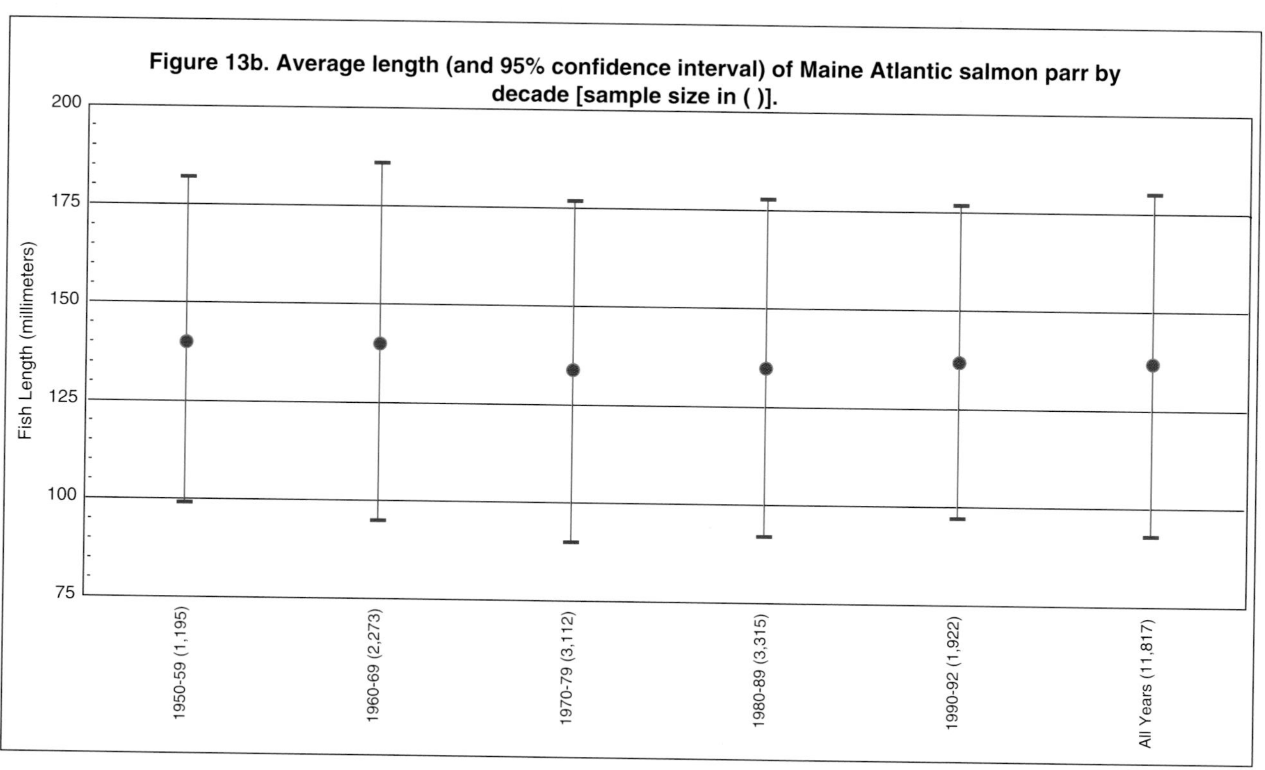

Figure 13b. Average length (and 95% confidence interval) of Maine Atlantic salmon parr by decade [sample size in ( )].

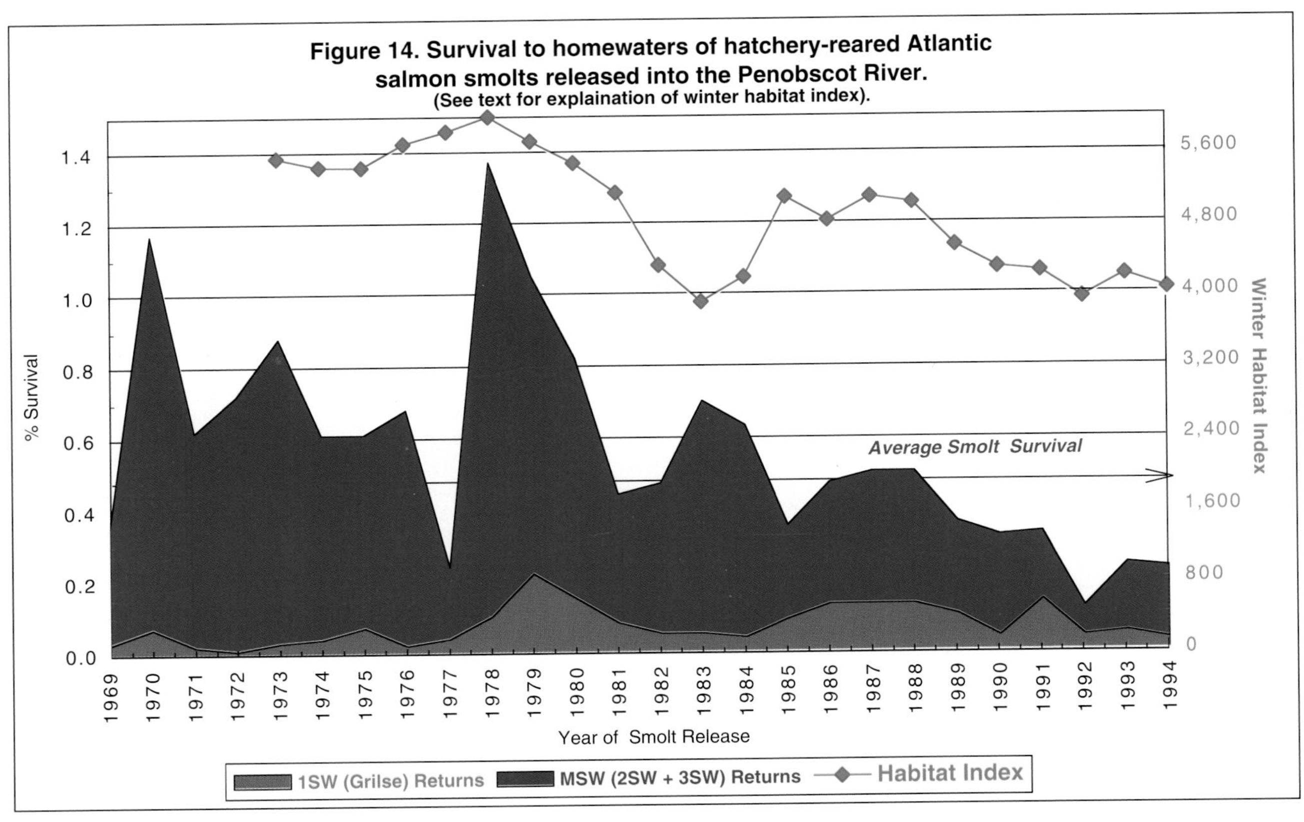

in length and weigh 10 to 100 grams (less than one to more than four ounces) during the late summer (end of August). The length-to-weight relationship for Maine juvenile Atlantic salmon is illustrated in Figure 12. Interestingly enough, the average length of age 1+ and older Atlantic salmon parr in Maine streams during the late summer is about 5.7 inches (14.5 centimeters, Figure 13a); this average length has remained relatively constant since the early 1950's (Figure 13b).

> *While the typical female Atlantic salmon in Maine deposits about 7,000 eggs into a redd, an average of only about 700 alevins (8%) will survive to emerge from the gravel the following spring. Of those, only about 3-5 will survive to the smolt stage.*

The survival from smolt to returning spawning adult salmon in Maine streams is challenging to measure, because of the difficulty associated with obtaining a *complete* count of the outgoing smolts and the returning adults. The most thorough information on this subject was collected in the 1950's in the Sheepscot River and Cove Brook (a tributary to the Penobscot River), when biologists estimated that wild smolt survival ranged from 3% (in Cove Brook; Meister 1962) to 15% (in the Sheepscot River; USFWS 1960). Studies conducted in the Narraguagus River, however, suggest that the survival of wild smolts to returning adults in that river ranged from 0.5% to 1.5% in recent years (Beland et al. 1995). The survival of hatchery-reared smolts (marked or tagged before release) in various Maine rivers since the 1960's has been extremely variable, ranging from 0 to 3% for individual lots of fish. Penobscot River hatchery smolt survival data (Figure 14) show a decline from 0.5 to 1.5% in the 1970's to 0.2 to 0.5% in the 1990's (Baum 1983, 1993; Baum et al. 1988). From sea surface temperature data collected in the Labrador sea during the winter (January–March) it appears that environmental conditions in the ocean since the mid-1980's have become less favorable for post-smolt survival than in the 1960's and 1970's. The low marine survival documented for many North American salmon stocks in recent years (as evidenced by the reduced abundance of 2SW salmon) parallels the adverse marine conditions observed, according to the ICES North Atlantic Salmon Working Group. There is

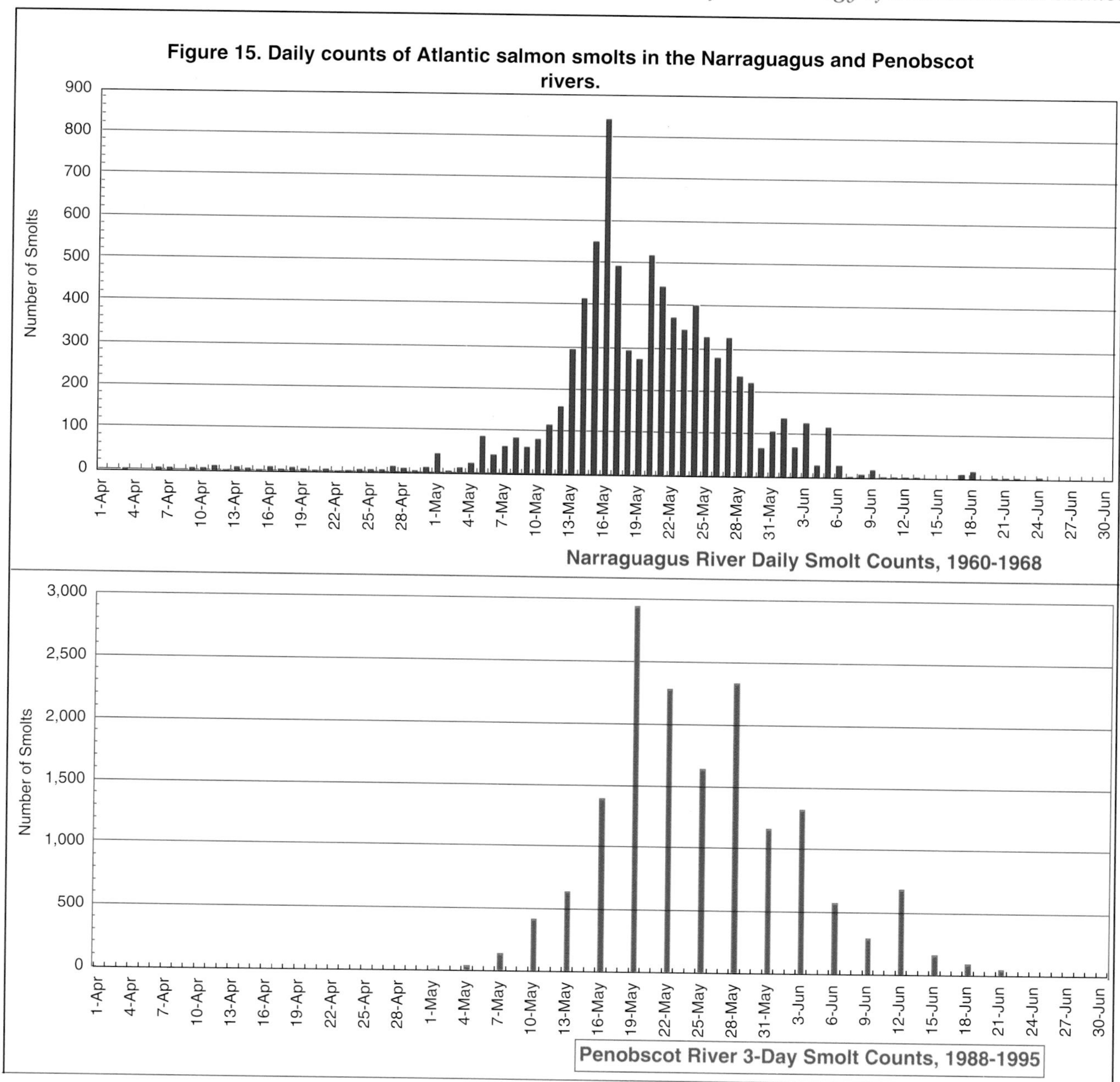

Figure 15. Daily counts of Atlantic salmon smolts in the Narraguagus and Penobscot rivers.

evidence from long-term commercial and sport catches that there have been similar periods of high and low salmon abundance in North America, therefore, it is possible that the marine survival of Atlantic salmon is cyclical.

Smolt Migrations

Atlantic salmon smolts migrate from Maine rivers each spring when they are physiologically able to survive in saltwater. The window of opportunity for smolts to leave freshwater lasts for a period of about six weeks and is influenced by water temperature, photoperiod (day length), light intensity, and river flow. The onset of migration often appears to be triggered when water temperatures reach about 10°C (50°F). Initially, migration is passive with smolts essentially being swept downstream (tail first) by the current. However, as the migration period progresses the fish often turn and swim downstream faster than the current. While migration can occur at any time of day, the most active period is from about 10:00 P.M. until about 2:00 A.M. Interestingly enough, this natural migratory behavior is thought to be a form of predator avoidance and is common for all life stages of juvenile salmon (fry, parr, and smolts).[5]

5. In contrast, adult salmon in Maine rivers are more active during the daylight hours. Adult salmon are, for the most part, crepuscular in their migratory behavior in that they are most active around dawn and dusk.

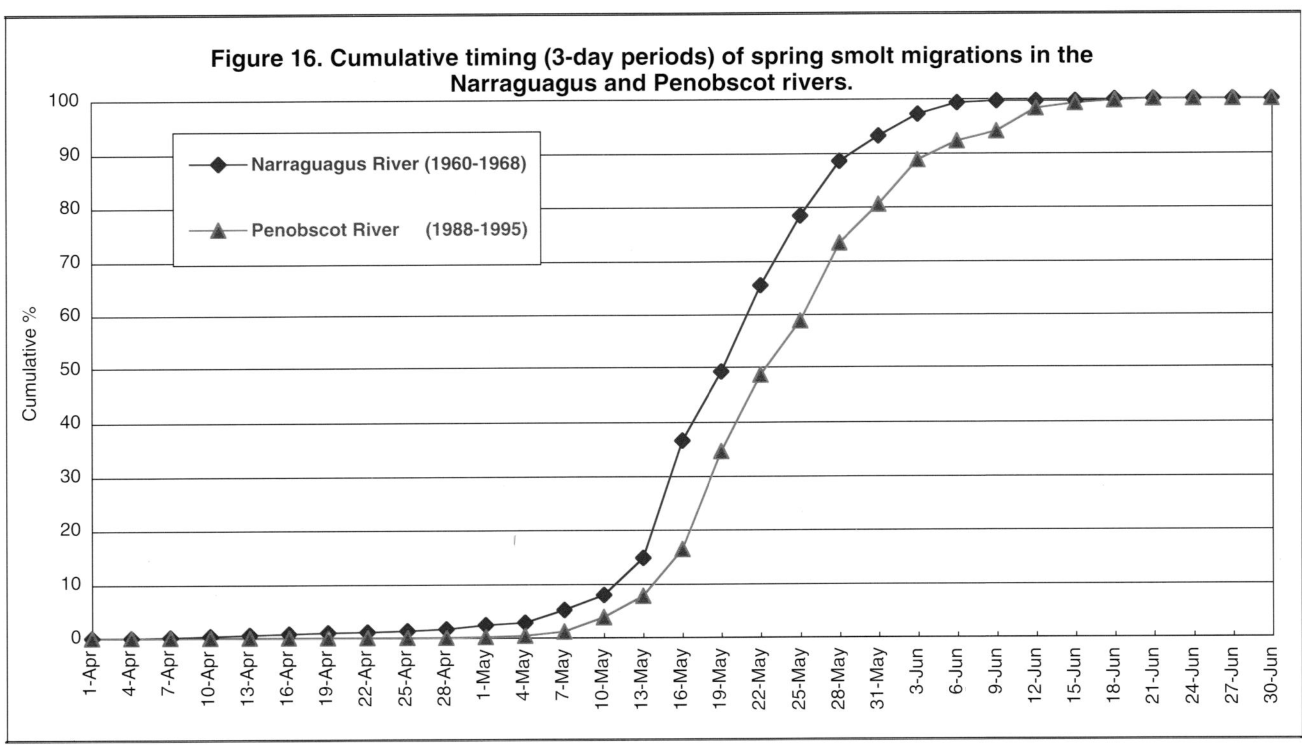

Figure 16. Cumulative timing (3-day periods) of spring smolt migrations in the Narraguagus and Penobscot rivers.

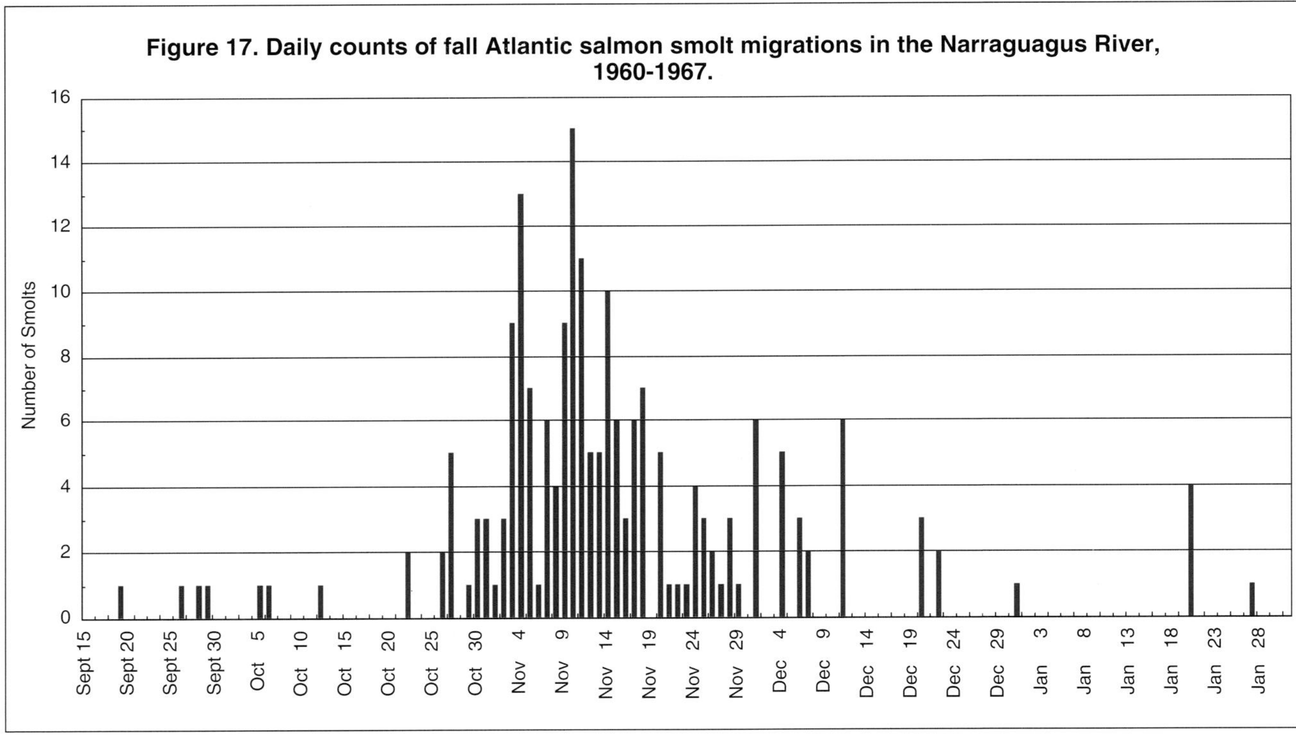

Figure 17. Daily counts of fall Atlantic salmon smolt migrations in the Narraguagus River, 1960-1967.

Smoltification is not influenced by the age of the salmon parr; instead, it is a function of the length of the fish. Parr which reach a minimum length of about 13 centimeters (5 inches) at the end of the growing season (around the middle of September) are likely to smoltify the following spring. Smolts exhibit schooling behavior and are pelagic or free-swimming, as opposed to parr that are solitary, territorial, demersal (bottom-dwelling) fish.

The first studies of smolt migration in Maine occurred in Hobart Stream (Little Falls Stream) in Edmunds Township during the late 1940's and early 1950's and involved the year-round operation of a weir used to count emigrating smolts and immigrating adults. During the late 1950's, a similar study was conducted on the Sheepscot River; and that study was followed by the Beddington weir studies on the Narraguagus River during the

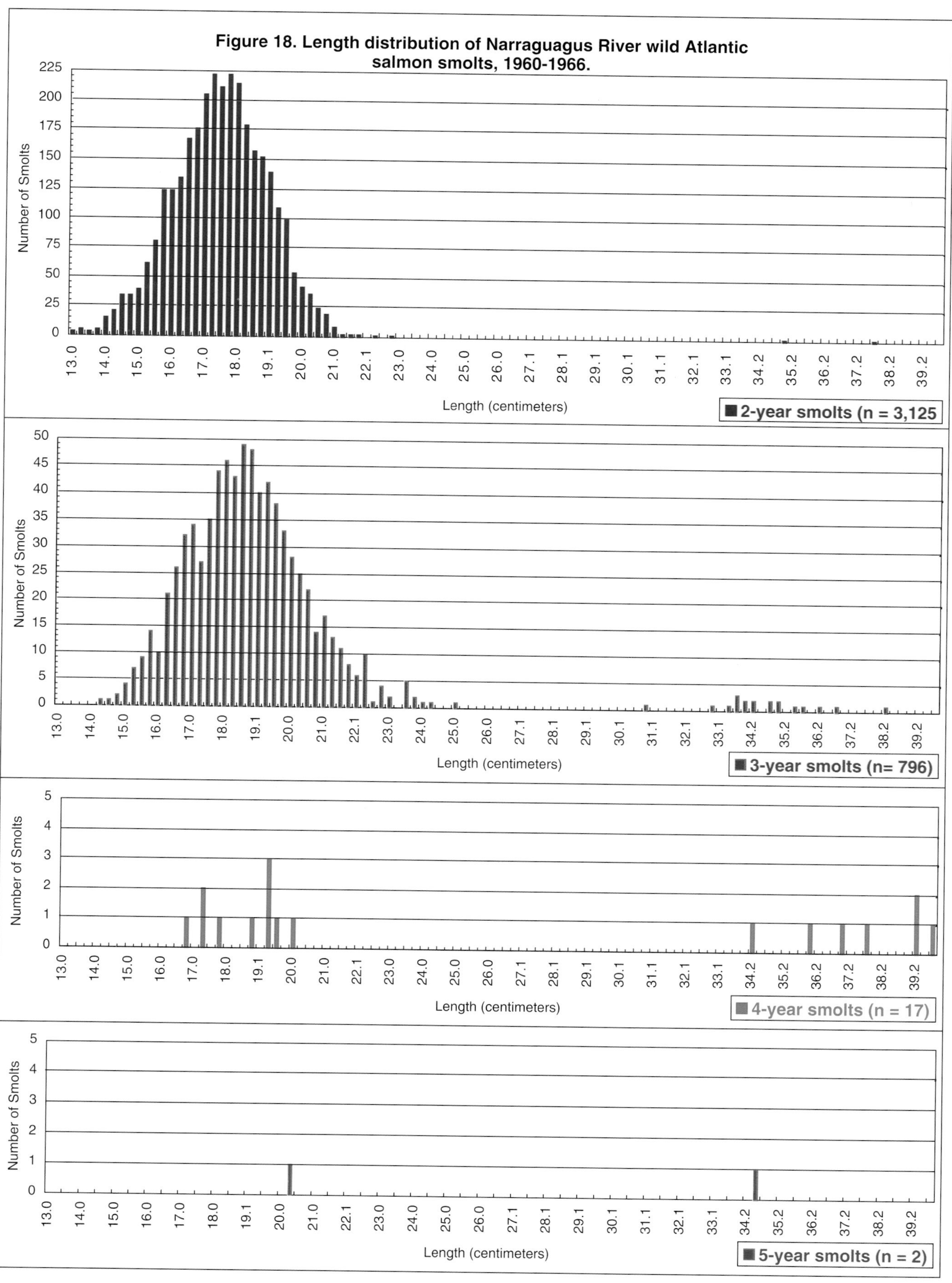
Figure 18. Length distribution of Narraguagus River wild Atlantic salmon smolts, 1960-1966.
Number of Smolts
Length (centimeters)
2-year smolts (n = 3,125
3-year smolts (n= 796)
4-year smolts (n = 17)
5-year smolts (n = 2)

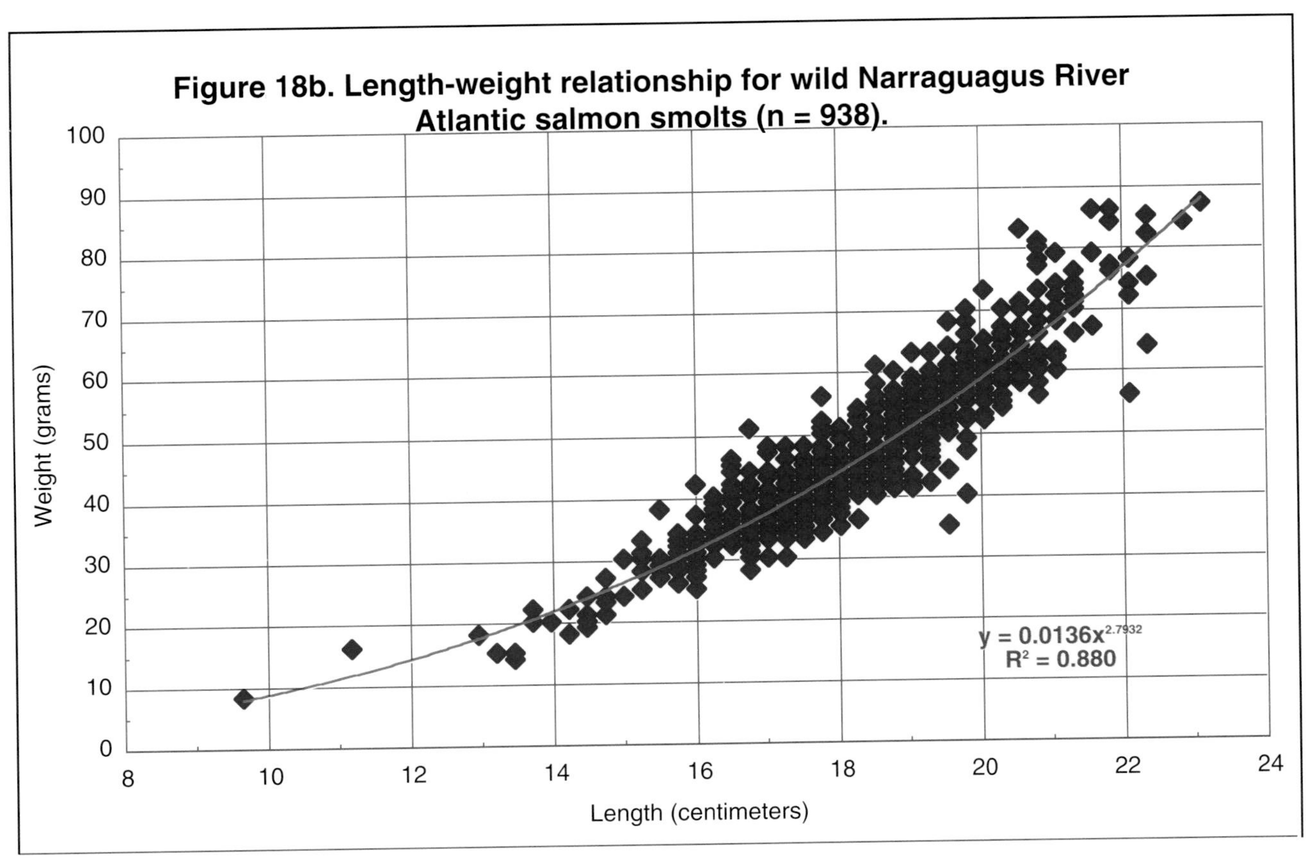

1960's. The most recent smolt migration data were collected on the Penobscot River at the Mattaceunk (Weldon) Dam by biologists from Great Northern Paper Company as part of studies designed to evaluate a new downstream fish passage facility.

The Narraguagus and Penobscot River smolt migration studies were conducted for many years during the 1960's and 1980's–1990's, respectively. Daily counts of smolts (total number = 8,316) at the Beddington weir on the Narraguagus River and at the Weldon Dam on the Penobscot River (total number = 16,114) are shown in Table 6 and Figure 15.

In all four rivers monitored, the smolt migration period began in late April or early May, peaked around the second or third weeks of May, and tapered off by mid-June. The Sheepscot River smolts appeared to migrate a little earlier than those in Hobart Stream in the 1950's. Similarly, the Narraguagus River smolt migration that was monitored in the 1960's occurred about a week earlier than the Penobscot River smolt migration that was observed in recent years (Figure 16).

Number and timing of smolts counted leaving Hobart Stream and the Sheepscot River during the 1950's

Time Period	Hobart Stream (1950–1951)		Sheepscot River (1957 and 1959)	
	No.	Accum %	No.	Accum %
April 11–20	–	–	10	0.7
April 21–30	–	–	244	16.9
May 1–10	64	39.8	681	62.2
May 11–20	61	77.7	336	84.6
May 21–31	14	86.4	223	99.4
June 1–10	12	93.8	9	100.0
June 11–20	9	99.4	–	–
June 21–30	1	100.0	–	–
Total	161		1,503	

In some areas where Atlantic salmon are found, up to one-third of the smolts have been shown to leave their natal streams in the fall (Youngson and Hay 1996) and Maine salmon are apparently no exception. Of the smolts counted at the Beddington weir on the Narraguagus River each spring, a small number of silvery parr (about 5%, ranging from 3 to 10% annually) from the same year class had moved downstream through the weir the previous fall (Figure 17). Most of the fall movements of these fish occurred during the month of November (73%), with smaller numbers leaving during December (14%)

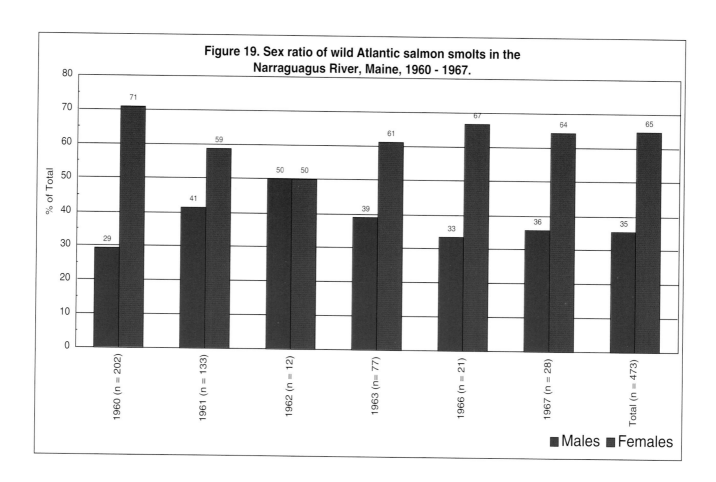

Figure 19. Sex ratio of wild Atlantic salmon smolts in the Narraguagus River, Maine, 1960 - 1967.

% of Total
80
70
60
50
40
30
20
10
0

1960 (n = 202): 29, 71
1961 (n = 133): 41, 59
1962 (n = 12): 50, 50
1963 (n= 77): 39, 61
1966 (n = 21): 33, 67
1967 (n = 28): 36, 64
Total (n = 473): 35, 65

■ Males ■ Females

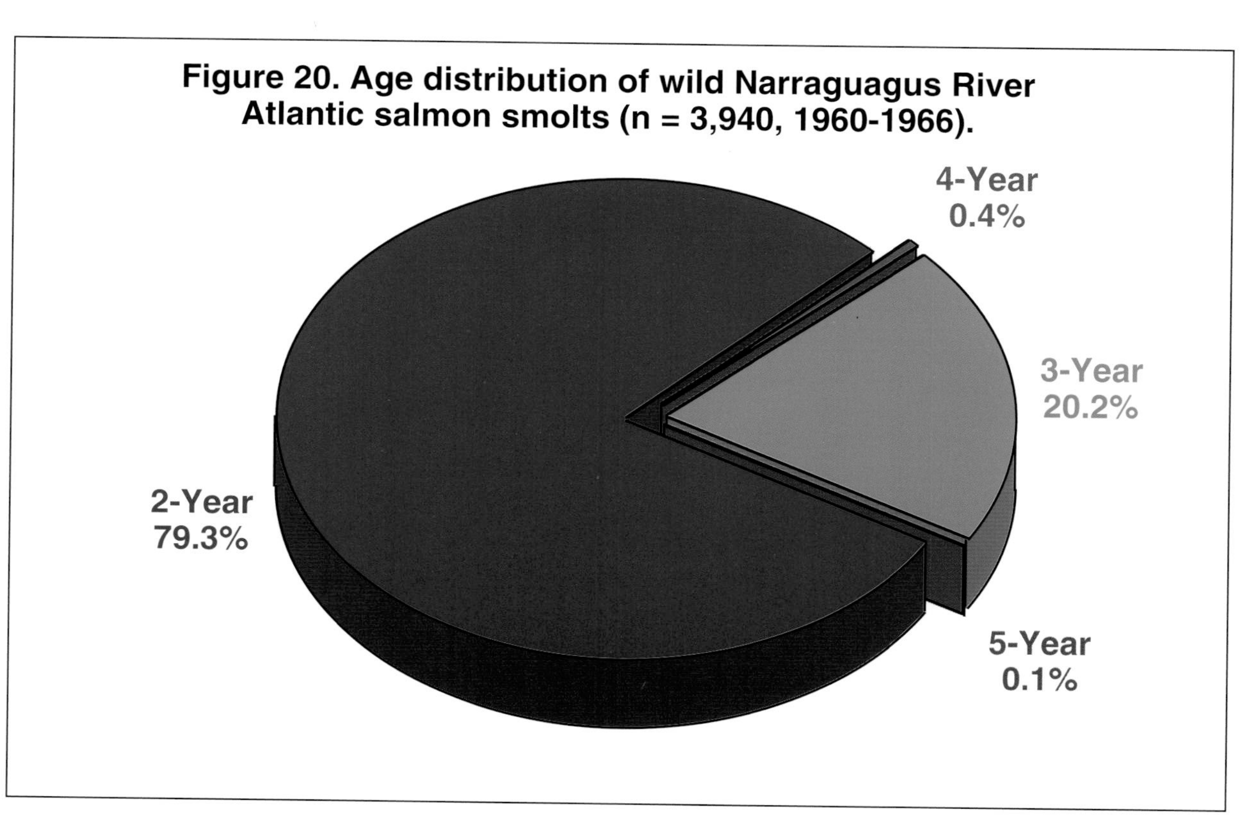

Figure 20. Age distribution of wild Narraguagus River Atlantic salmon smolts (n = 3,940, 1960-1966).

Scales T

Fishery scientists "read" scale samples from Atlanti
The most commonly observed types of Maine
F = FOCUS (CENTER) OF THE SCALE, FW = FRESHWATER GR

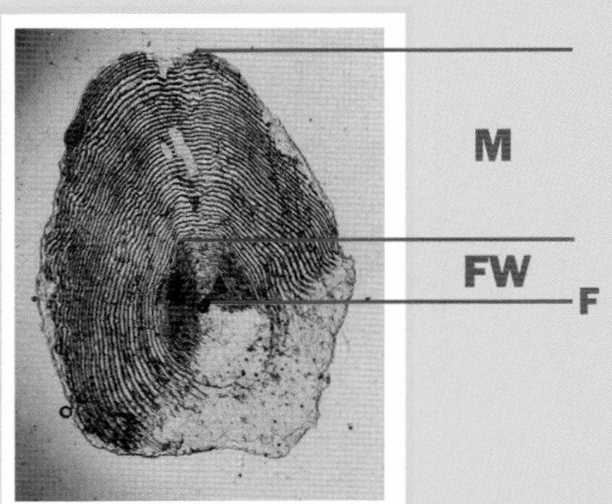

Age 1: 1 (Hatchery-origin)

A hatchery-origin, one sea-winter (1SW) salmon (or grilse). Note the very uniform growth pattern in the one year spent in the hatchery environment and the rapid growth during the one year at sea. The total age of this fish (from egg to spawner) is three years.

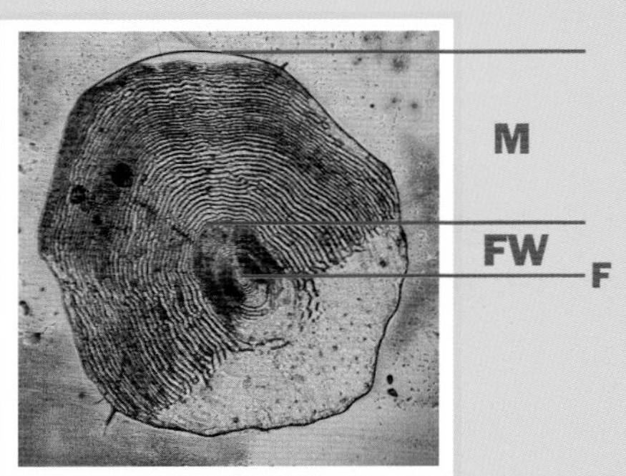

Age 2: 1 (Wild-origin)

A wild-origin, one sea-winter (1SW) salmon (or grilse). Note the irregular growth (rapid in summer, very slow in winter) during the two years spent in the river. The total age of this fish is four years.

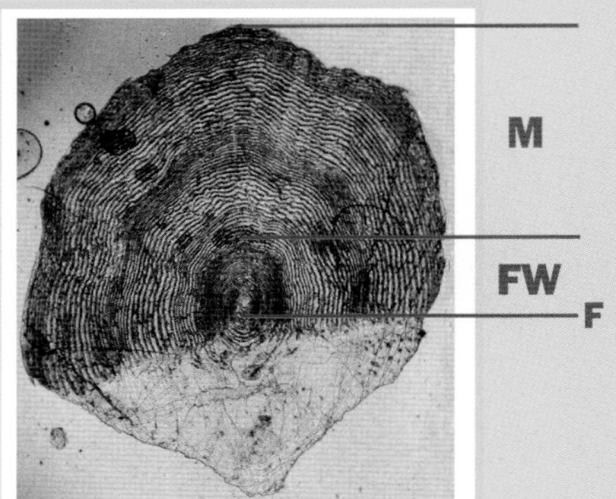

Age 2: 2 (Wild-origin)

A wild origin, two sea-winter (2SW) salmon that spent two years in the river. This type of scale is representative of about 80-90% of Maine Atlantic salmon. The total age of this fish is five years.

ll Tales!

non to determine the age and origin of individual fish.
tic salmon scale samples are illustrated below.
H ZONE, M = MARINE GROWTH ZONE, S = SPAWNING MARK

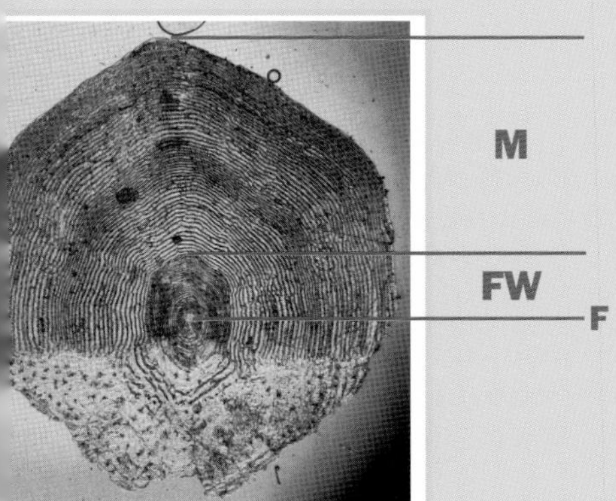

Age 3 : 2 (Wild-origin)

A wild origin, two sea-winter (2SW) salmon that spent three years in the river. Three-year smolts comprise about 10-20% of the smolts leaving Maine rivers. The total age of this fish is six years.

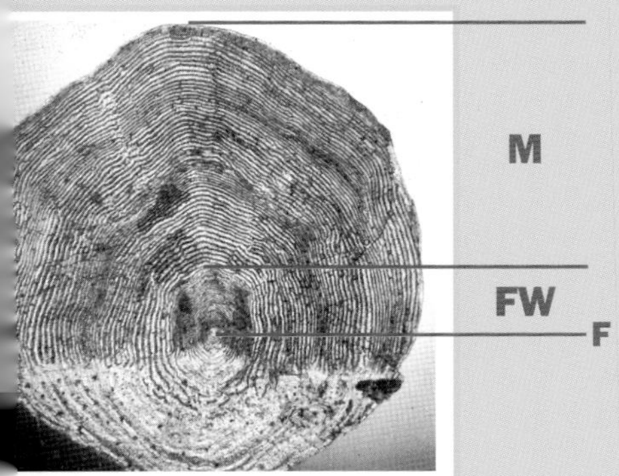

Age 2 : 3 (Wild-origin)

A wild origin, three sea-winter (3SW) salmon that spent two years in the river. Three sea-winter salmon comprise about 1-2% of the adults entering Maine rivers each year. The total age of this fish is six years.

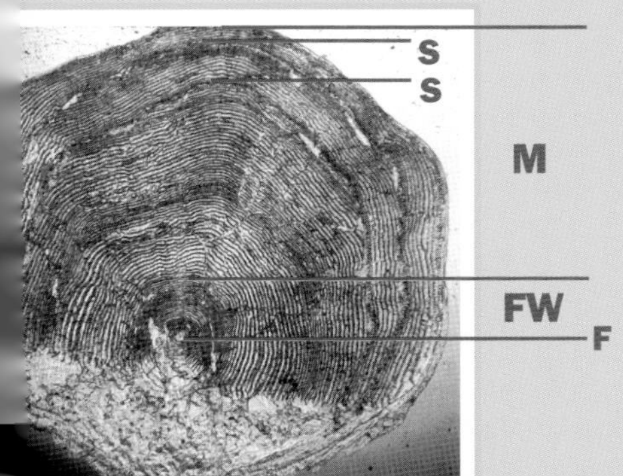

Age 2 : 2,S,1,S,1 (Wild-origin)

A wild-origin, repeat spawner that spent two years in the river and first spawned as a two sea-winter salmon. This fish returned to sea for another full year and returned to Maine to spawn a second time. It then returned to sea for another full year and was on its third spawning migration. The spawning marks are visible as blank areas that follow the perimeter of the scale. The total age of this most unusual Maine Atlantic salmon is nine years.

and October (9%). The remaining 4% was equally distributed during September and January.

The length distribution of wild-origin two-year and three-year smolts from the Narraguagus River is illustrated in Figure 18a, while the weight to length relationship for these wild smolts is shown in Figure 18b. Two-year smolts (n = 3,078) measured during the period 1962–1966 ranged from 13 to 24 centimeters in length (5.0 to 9.4 inches), while three-year smolts (n = 791) were only slightly longer, ranging from 14 to 25 centimeters (5.5 to 10.0 inches) The average length of two-year smolts was 17.5 centimeters (6.9 inches), while three-year smolts were only an average of 1.1 centimeters longer at 18.6 centimeters (7.3 inches). During the 1960's Atlantic Salmon Commission personnel sampled nearly 500 wild, Narraguagus River smolts at the Beddington weir (mostly from miscellaneous moralities) to determine what the sex ratio of the smolt run was each year. Overall, the sex ratio was 35% males and 65% females, although there were annual differences noted (see Figure 19).

Post-smolts leaving the coast of Maine in June reach Cape Breton Island (N.S.) within 45-50 days. The salmon arrive in southern Newfoundland by mid-August, and a few make the journey to the mid-coast of Labrador in 90 days. Because of their larger size, post-kelts are able to migrate faster than smolts. Swimming between 15-25 miles per day, these Maine salmon are able to reach the south coast of Greenland in 120 days, and northern Greenland waters above the Arctic Circle in 160 days.

While the majority of Narraguagus River smolts were either two or three years old, small numbers of four and five-year-old smolts were also documented (Figure 20).

Marine Migrations

Webster's dictionary defines the word *migrate* as "to move from one region to another with the change of seasons, as many birds and some fishes." For Maine Atlantic salmon, migration is a two-way street of precise, directed, well-oriented movements between habitats for feeding and reproduction. The feeding migration from Maine to various areas in the North Atlantic allows the salmon to take advantage of distant abundant food sources. Conversely, the return migration to Maine allows the adult fish to spawn in the protected environment of its natal stream. Migration patterns in salmon are predictable; they are not random movements. Although affected by water temperatures, currents, and oceanographic (or stream and estuarial) features, these parameters do not guide the salmon during its migrations. The guidance methods used by salmon migrating at sea are thought to be of the map and compass, or orientation, variety; while the stream phase of migration may be appetite driven, or controlled by various physiological factors.

Theories of ocean migration revolve around the salmon's ability to use a combination of electromagnetic fields, polarized light, and various celestial phenomena such as the sun, moon, or stars. Riverine migrations, however, appear to be largely based upon olfactory cues, or the sense of "smell," as experienced primarily through the fishes' lateral line. There are two "odor" theories, one based upon the distinctive odor of the home stream and the other that is based upon pheromones. The distinctive odors that are thought to be imparted by the soils and vegetation in the drainage, possibly combined with odors added by human activities such as waste treatment facilities, pulp and paper mills, and so forth, may allow the fish to "home in" on the "scent" of its natal stream. The pheromone theory is essentially related to the scent of the fish's next-of-kin. Pheromones are hormonal substances secreted by living organisms that stimulate behavioral or physiological responses in other individuals of the same species. Thus, it is possible that adult salmon returning to their home stream are homing in on the scent of other salmon that are living in upstream areas.

The importance of olfaction for salmonid migration has been well documented in the scientific literature (Stabell 1981). Fish that have had their sense of olfaction destroyed have a much lower rate of survival and a much higher rate of straying. While olfaction is important, genetics is probably the number one factor that controls navigation in Atlantic salmon. That is why a Saco River salmon can embark upon a feeding migration to

West Greenland along with salmon from Canada and Europe, yet return to the Saco to spawn.

Tagging studies conducted in Maine since 1962 have taken *some* of the mystery out of where Maine salmon go during their oceanic migrations. During the past 35 years more than 4,100[6] Atlantic salmon tagged (with externally applied Carlin tags) in Maine have been recovered in the North Atlantic Ocean. Those tags were returned from Greenland (43%), from Canada (48%), and a small number (1%) was returned from coastal areas of the United States (mostly from coastal areas of Maine). Although about 8% of the tag returns could not be assigned to a specific location, most were taken in either Canada or Greenland (Table 7). The timing and distribution of these tag returns are extensively reported in Chapter 3 under the heading "Distant Water Commercial Fisheries."

Although tagged salmon have been released into seven rivers in Maine, the majority were released into the Penobscot River; therefore, the latitude and longitude of Bangor are usually used to calculate distances traveled by individual Maine salmon. The average number of days at large, distances traveled, and estimated migration rates for tagged Maine Atlantic salmon of various ages is presented in Table 8.

Based upon the tag return data and average rates of migration presented above, the oceanic migrations of most Maine Atlantic salmon may be summarized in the following manner (Figure 4):

> Leaving the coast of Maine in mid- to late-June, post-smolts move northeasterly across the Gulf of Maine and along the south and eastern coasts of Nova Scotia, reaching the Cape Breton Island (N.S.) area within 45 to 50 days. Crossing the entrance to the Gulf of St. Lawrence, the salmon arrive at the southern end of Newfoundland in 60 to 65 days (mid-August). The post-smolts feed along the northeastern coast of Newfoundland and the southern half of Labrador for the balance of their first summer at sea. While a few Maine salmon have made the journey to the mid-coast of Labrador in as little as 90 days, most take from 105 to 110 days to make the trip. By mid-to-late October the post-smolts have roughly doubled in size (30–36 centimeters; 12–14 inches) and they congregate in the Labrador Sea for their first winter in the Atlantic Ocean. The following year, sometime between April and June, depending upon environmental conditions, the one sea-winter salmon (as they are now called) have three choices: some will migrate in an easterly direction (to Newfoundland and Labrador), others will migrate in a northerly direction (to East and West Greenland), and still others will migrate in a southerly direction back to Maine. Those individuals migrating north or east will spend another summer feeding in Canadian or Greenlandic waters and will return to Maine as two sea-winter salmon the following year. Those that migrate south will return to Maine rivers to spawn as one sea-winter salmon or grilse in the current year. By August of the second summer at sea these salmon have grown to a length of about 56 to 62 centimeters (22 to 24 inches). The proportion of nonmaturing (i.e., those migrating to Newfoundland-Labrador and Greenland) and maturing (i.e., those returning to Maine to spawn as grilse) one sea-winter salmon varies from year to year. Generally speaking, fewer than 10% of any year class will mature as one sea-winter salmon, although some scientists have postulated that there is evidence of a trend toward a higher rate of maturity as one sea-winter salmon in the last decade. This may partially explain the noticeable decrease in two sea-winter salmon and a noticeable increase in one sea-winter salmon (grilse) in North American rivers in recent years.

The migration rates for Maine post-kelts (i.e., those salmon tagged as adults) are similar to those documented for smolts, except that large salmon migrate faster than small salmon. Swimming up to 26 miles per day (assuming straight line migration), the average Maine salmon reaches the mid coast of Labrador or the southern coast of Greenland in 120 days and northern Greenland waters above the Arctic Circle in 5 months.

While the majority of Maine salmon migrate along the eastern shore of Newfoundland, there is evidence that a small number occasionally migrate along the western shore and through the Strait of Belle Isle found between the provinces of Quebec and Newfoundland. Additionally, the recent recapture of two Maine-origin tagged salmon in the Faroe Islands shows that a few nonconformists rejected the original three choices presented to them after their first winter in the Labrador Sea. Perhaps they decided to follow their European "cousins" back to Europe?

On their return to home waters, Maine salmon migrate along the coasts of Nova Scotia and New Brunswick, following the prevailing ocean currents in the Gulf of Maine. This leads the adult salmon to somewhere between the southern and mid-coastal areas of Maine, where they appear to migrate "Downeast" in search of their home river, whether it is the Kennebec, the St. Croix, or any of the other salmon rivers of Maine.

6. The total to date is 4,143 tags from Maine-origin salmon.

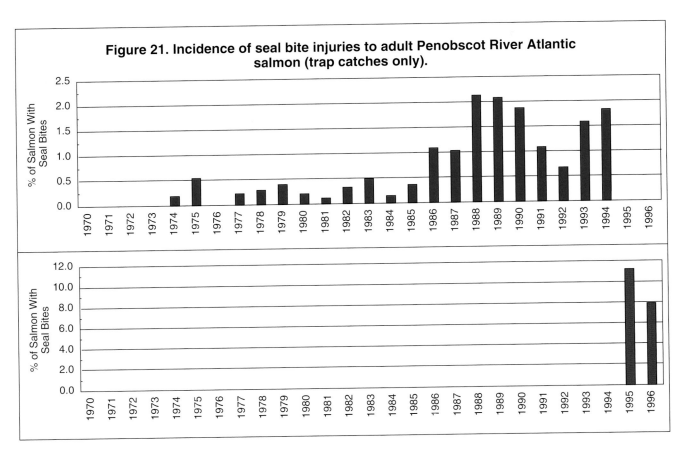

Figure 21. Incidence of seal bite injuries to adult Penobscot River Atlantic salmon (trap catches only).

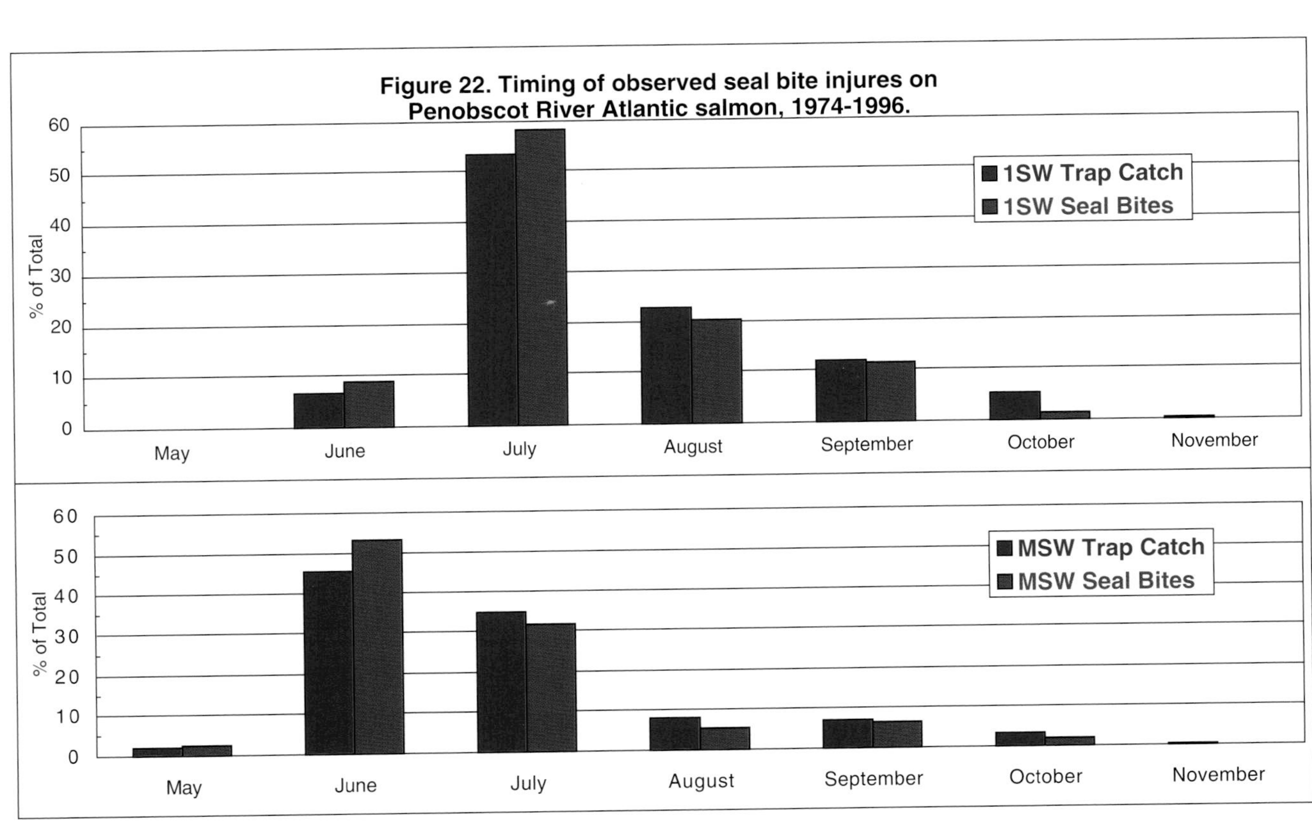

Figure 22. Timing of observed seal bite injures on Penobscot River Atlantic salmon, 1974-1996.

Predators Upon Maine Atlantic Salmon

SEALS

There are six species of seals in the North Atlantic, yet relatively little is known about their predation upon salmon. Since seals consume large quantities of fish, they are often blamed for recent reductions in Atlantic salmon populations. The high visibility of seals in rivers and estuaries also contributes to the perception that they must be a significant predator upon Maine salmon.

Since implementation of the federal Marine Mammal Protection Act (MMPA) of 1972, the number of harbor or common seals *(Phoca vitulina concolor)* in Maine has more than doubled to about 29,000 animals. The number of gray seals *(Halichoeurs grypus)* has also increased from about 30 in 1980 to somewhere between 600 and 1,200 in the early 1990's (NMFS 1996). There are an additional estimated 143,000 gray seals in eastern Canada, and their numbers have been increasing by an average of 13% per year during the past 20 years (Anthony 1994). Harbor seals can be up to 5 feet long and weigh 200 pounds, while gray seals can be up to 8 feet long and weigh 900 pounds. In Scotland, it has been estimated that one gray seal consumes 2.4 metric tons of fish each year.

Ringed *(Phoca hispida)*, harp *(Phoca groenlandica)*, and hooded *(Cystophora cristata)* seals are also becoming more common in the Gulf of Maine each year. These three species are called ice seals because they normally live and breed near pack ice in the North Atlantic. The reason for their increasing abundance this far south is unknown. The bearded seal (*Erignathus barbatus*) feeds primarily on crustaceans; therefore, it is unlikely that this species would prey on Atlantic salmon.

Seal predation upon adult Atlantic salmon has been well documented in the United Kingdom (Rae 1960, 1973; Soderberg 1975; Pierce et al. 1991), and there is evidence that it occurs in North America. Benoit (1989) tabulated the results of an examination of the stomach contents of 1,878 gray seals in Canada and found that salmon occurred in fewer than 1% of the stomachs which contained food. Similarly, the diet of 1,167 harp seals in Canada was examined by Lawson et al. (1995) and they reported that no Atlantic salmon were found. The most important food items were cod, herring, capelin, flatfishes, and mackerel. A recent study of the diet of harbor seals in the Bay of Fundy (stomach contents of 470 seals collected from 1988 to 1992) revealed that the most common foods of seals were cod, herring, pollack, and squid; the only anadromous fish found were remains from three blueback herring (Bowen and Harrison 1996). Most of the studies of seal feeding habits show that these animals are opportunistic predators, normally feeding upon what is seasonally and regionally available, often with a preference for small, schooling fishes. A recent study of the selected prey of harbor seals in New England revealed that the American sand lance (*Ammodytes americanus*) was the most dominant prey item of seals in waters adjacent to Cape Cod (Payne and Selzer 1989).

Associated with the documented increase in seal numbers along the Maine coast, there has also been an increase in the incidence of seal bite injuries to salmon in the Penobscot River, especially during the last decade (Figure 21). In many instances large, healed scars are noted on the posterior portions of salmon, most often near the ventral fins, vent, or caudal peduncle below the lateral line. Trap catch data from more than 44,000 Atlantic salmon examined at the Brewer and Veazie fishways in the Penobscot River during the period 1970–1996 include 827 records of seal bite injuries.[7] While, overall, only about 2% of the salmon examined during the past 25 years have exhibited seal bite injuries, the incidence has been increasing since the mid-1980's as evidenced by the following summary:

Years	Number of Salmon Examined	Number of Seal Bites Observed	% With Seal Bites
1970–1974	1,430	1	0.07
1975–1979	4,220	13	0.31
1980–1984	10,704	26	0.24
1985–1989	14,955	194	1.30
1990–1996	12,841	593	4.62
Total	44,150	827	1.87

It is interesting to note that most (88%) of the observed seal bites were recorded from MSW Penobscot River salmon, and that the majority of those fish were attacked during the month of June (53%). These data suggest that both 1SW and MSW salmon are equally vulnerable to seal predation, and that the attacks appear to occur throughout the run approximately in proportion to salmon abundance (Figure 22).

Seal bite injuries to salmon are also often reported by anglers fishing in the Downeast rivers

7. About 37% of the seal bite injuries observed on Penobscot River adult salmon in the last 25 years were recorded in 1995 and 1996. It is likely that personnel changes and a more concerted examination of fish for the presence of seal bite injuries may have contributed to the extraordinary increase in the noted incidence of seal induced injuries in recent years.

of Maine. For example, in 1986 anglers from the Two Rivers Salmon Club reported that 70% of the salmon they caught in the East Machias River that year had seal bites. The narrow, shallow estuaries of the small rivers of eastern Maine, in addition to their proximity to large aquaculture operations, probably contribute to the increased vulnerability of those salmon populations to seal predation. It is also possible that seals are attracted to these areas at certain times of the year by concentrations of other prey (e.g., alewives, blueback herring, smelt) resulting in more frequent incidental attacks upon salmon.

While seals occasionally attack Atlantic salmon, the overall magnitude and extent of predation upon Maine Atlantic salmon stocks remains unknown. In recent years 1–2% of the adult salmon examined at trapping facilities on the Penobscot River have survived an attack by a seal, but the number of salmon actually consumed (i.e., the number that did not survive the attack) cannot be ascertained. It is possible that the decline in cod and flatfish stocks in the Gulf of Maine and in populations of river herring in Maine rivers has contributed to the increase in predation by seals upon salmon. It is also possible that the increase in seal numbers during the past 20 years has had a significant impact on the major food supply of Maine Atlantic salmon at sea, sand lance, and capelin in particular.

Atlantic salmon anglers often call for lethal seal control programs in Maine rivers to "protect"[8] salmon; however, as with other predators (cormorants, for example), there is no biologically feasible or socially acceptable means of controlling seal numbers. Besides that, who could condone killing an animal with big brown (watery) eyes and a head that resembles a cocker spaniel?

8. So that anglers may harvest them instead?

DOUBLE-CRESTED CORMORANTS

The double-crested cormorant is one of the most despised birds in the State of Maine, particularly by many Atlantic salmon anglers. At nearly every public meeting held by the Atlantic Salmon Authority (or Atlantic Sea Run Salmon Commission) the subject of cormorant predation and the need to "control cormorants" is usually espoused vehemently. Salmon anglers frequently express the opinion that there are no demonstrable aesthetic, economic, or ecological benefits from the protection of cormorants. If only they were allowed to shoot cormorants—so the argument goes—Maine's Atlantic salmon populations would benefit greatly. Are cormorants as "evil" a predator as salmon anglers think? If so, what should or can be done about the problem?

The double-crested cormorant is an opportunistic predator that will eat any fish that is readily available. (Photo courtesy Joe Robbins)

The double-crested cormorant *(Phalcrocorax auritus)*, extirpated in New England by European settlers who ate cormorants and their eggs and used the bird's feathers for various items, is reported to have started renesting along the eastern Maine coast in the mid-1920's (Mendall 1936). The population expanded rapidly, and the breeding population had increased to about 10,000 nesting pairs by 1944 (Gross 1944). In the 1930's and 1940's, increasing concerns expressed by commercial fishermen about the negative economic impact of cormorant predation to marine fisheries resulted in a control program carried out by the Maine Department of Sea and Shore Fisheries between 1944 and 1953 (Dow 1953). During that period nearly 200,000 cormorant eggs were sprayed with oil. While the oil was apparently successful in destroying the eggs, the birds quickly renested and laid new clutches of eggs. Therefore, the practice failed to reduce the cormorant population, and the program ended in 1954.

In 1977 there were an estimated 15,333 breeding pairs of cormorants on 103 colonies in Maine; the number had increased to 28,760 pairs on 121 colonies by the mid-1980's and to 28,000 pairs on 135 colonies in the early 1990's (Krohn et al. 1994). These data show an 87% increase in the number of breeding pairs of cormorants in Maine between 1977 and 1985, with a slight decline or leveling off of the population since then.

Cormorant predation upon Maine Atlantic salmon smolts. The Atlantic Sea Run Salmon Commission was first alerted to the problem of cormorant predation upon Atlantic salmon in 1966, when more than 650 tags from hatchery smolts stocked in the Machias River were recovered from Old Man Island in Machias Bay. A detailed study of cormorant predation was initiated in 1967, and the results of that study were presented with the 1966 data in a report by Meister and Gramlich (1967). Ongoing studies were conducted into the early 1970's by Salmon Commission and US Fish and Wildlife Service personnel. These studies clearly demonstrated that the cormorant was a significant predator upon hatchery-reared smolts then, with more than 7,000 salmon tags eventually recovered on Old Man Island. One cormorant collected in the spring of 1968 in the estuary of the Machias River had 55 Carlin tags in its stomach. These tags came from a group of hatchery smolts stocked only four days earlier! Three unsuccessful attempts were made to eradicate the cormorant colony on Old Man Island in 1969 by applying the contact toxicant DRC-1347 to cormorant nests and eggs. A fourth application, placed in dead alewives used as bait near nests on the island, resulted in the unplanned deaths of many gulls that ate the bait intended for the cormorants. In 1970 and 1971 the Old Man Island colony was finally eliminated by shooting nesting adults at night. Within a few years, however, adult cormorants from nearby islands quickly repopulated the island.

In 1972 cormorants came under federal protection when the Migratory Bird Treaty Act of 1918 was amended to include 32 additional families of birds, including the cormorant family. Prior to March 10, 1972, cormorants were not protected by state or federal laws and could be killed without restriction, but after federal listing, cormorants could only be killed under a permit issued by the

Cormorant nests on Nitecap Island in Narraguagus Bay, 1970 (upper photo). Cormorants prefer to nest in trees. However, when the trees die (from the effects of cormorant guano), the birds readily nest on the ground as illustrated in the bottom photo taken on Flat Island in Penobscot Bay. The last photo illustrates a group of Carlin tags from hatchery-reared smolts eaten by a cormorant. The tags are regurgitated singly or in clumps of 25 or more tags!

U.S. Fish and Wildlife Service (USFWS). A federal permit was issued to the Maine Department of Marine Resources (DMR) between 1972 and 1981, and that agency issued 44 subpermits to Maine Department of Inland Fisheries and Wildlife and Atlantic Sea Run Salmon Commission (ASRSC) personnel, who reported shooting 2,800 cormorants. Between 1982 and 1988 subpermits were issued by either the Department of Marine Resources or Inland Fisheries and Wildlife, and, for the first time, permits were issued directly to the public. Since 1989, however, the Maine Department of Inland Fisheries and Wildlife has obtained an annual master permit from U.S. Fish and Wildlife and has sole authority for issuing subpermits. Until 1992 up to 50 subpermits were issued annually, with 160–590 cormorants reportedly shot annually (Krohn et al. 1994). Most of these birds were shot in the lower East Machias, Machias, Pleasant, Narraguagus, Union, and Penobscot rivers. In response to expanding federal requirements associated with the annual master permit, and increasingly complex administrative record keeping requirements, the Maine Department of Fisheries and Wildlife has referred all requests for permits to shoot cormorants directly to the U.S. Fish and Wildlife Service.

Besides the cormorant predation studies conducted in the Machias and Narraguagus Rivers during the period 1966–1972, additional studies were conducted by ASRSC and USFWS personnel in the Penobscot River between 1972 and 1982 and again from 1986 to 1988 (ASRSC, Penobscot River Annual Federal Aid Performance Reports). A recent Ph.D. thesis published at the University of Maine (Blackwell 1996) estimated that cormorants consumed fewer than 7% of the hatchery-reared smolts stocked in the Penobscot River in recent years (1992–1994) and that most of the predation occurred in the headponds of various mainstem hydrodams. While the headponds of main stem Penobscot River dams accounted for fewer than one half of 1% of the cormorant feeding areas, about 43% of the smolt predation occurred there. It should also be pointed out that smolts migrate primarily at night, whereas cormorants feed during the day. Thus, the combination of the behaviors of predators and prey with the presence of dams in the Penobscot River contributes to the level of predation. The studies previously referred to also estimated a very low level (1–2 %) of cormorant predation upon hatchery smolts released in the Penobscot River. All of the Maine cormorant predation studies have produced similar results that may be summarized as follows:

(1) Cormorants are opportunistic feeders—they will eat whatever is available to them, including Atlantic salmon. Besides hatchery smolts, more than 40 species of fish (including shellfish) have been found in Maine cormorant stomachs. Species identified to date include:

Freshwater and anadromous species

Alewife	Golden shiner
American eel (to 24")	Longnose sucker
American shad (to 22")	Pumpkinseed sunfish
Atlantic salmon	Rainbow smelt
Blueback herring	Smallmouth bass
Brook trout	Three-spine stickleback
Brown bullhead	White perch
Chain pickerel	White sucker
Common shiner	Yellow perch

Saltwater species

American sand lance	Northern lobster
Atlantic cod	Northern pipefish
Atlantic herring	Oceanpout
Atlantic mackerel	Periwinkle (3 species)
Atlantic menhaden	Rock crab
Atlantic silversides	Rock gunnel
Atlantic tomcod	Sand shrimp
Banded killifish	Shorthorn sculpin
Blue mussel	Snake blenny
Cunner	Summer flounder
Mummichog	Wrymouth
No. caridean shrimp	Yellowtail flounder

The wide variety of fish species eaten by cormorants points out the importance of buffer species of anadromous fish (smelt, alewife, etc.) during the annual Atlantic salmon smolt migration period in May and June. Predation upon Atlantic salmon smolts takes place almost exclusively within Maine rivers, for once salmon enter the marine environment they are rarely preyed upon by cormorants. In fact, Maine cormorants have recently been shown to feed mostly upon five marine species of fish—sculpins, sand shrimp, wrymouth, rock gunnel, and cunner (Blackwell et al. 1995).

(2) Predation by cormorants on individual groups of *hatchery-reared* smolts can be significant. This is because hatchery smolts are usually stocked in large groups, and they also exhibit little or no predator avoidance behavior (Hockett 1994). For example, known predation by cormorants upon various Machias River smolt groups in the mid-1960's was as high as 13.4% (Table 9). Cormorants prey upon all sizes of salmon smolts in direct proportion to their abundance. Although smolts larger than 20 centimeters (8 inches) may be less vulnerable to predation, the large two-year hatchery smolts that were released in the mid-1960's were just as vulnerable to predation as the smaller one-year smolts. Table 10 and Figure 23 illustrate why predation upon hatchery smolts released during the period 1966–969 was so high. Before 1970, all smolts were reared in uncovered raceways or pools

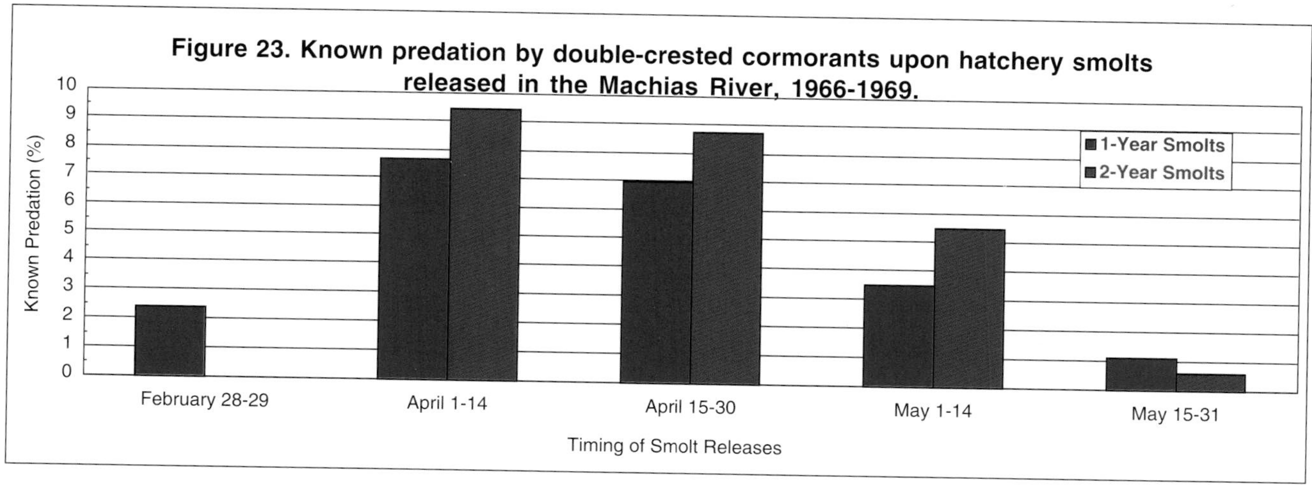

Figure 23. Known predation by double-crested cormorants upon hatchery smolts released in the Machias River, 1966-1969.

and were stocked in early April prior to smoltification. Smolts released in April were staying in the river for several weeks, making those lots much more susceptible to predation, while other lots released in May migrated to sea more directly and were less susceptible to predation by cormorants. Additionally, buffer species such as rainbow smelts and alewives are generally much more available in May. One group of smolts released in late February was preyed upon at a low rate (similar to late May) presumably because those smolts had 4-6 weeks to disperse in the Machias River before the cormorants returned from their southern wintering areas.

(3) Despite the thousands of cormorant stomachs examined over a 30-year period in Maine, there have been very few documented instances of cormorant predation upon wild Atlantic salmon smolts. This is not to infer that cormorants do not prey upon wild smolts—undoubtedly they do when the opportunity arises. Nevertheless, there is no evidence to suggest that cormorant predation upon wild smolts is a major factor in their survival.

(4) Behavioral differences help to keep the predator and its prey apart, since salmon smolts migrate primarily at night (when the birds are roosting) and cormorants feed primarily during the daylight hours (when the smolts are less active). Additionally, since salmon can migrate up to 25 miles per day, they are unlikely to spend much time in the areas where cormorants are feeding.

(5) Results of other cormorant predation studies have yielded conflicting results. For example, cormorant predation upon wild smolts in the River Bush (Northern Ireland) was two to three times *higher* than predation upon hatchery smolts (Kennedy 1987). Also, recent studies in New Brunswick and Nova Scotia suggest that mergansers eat more young salmon than cormorants do. Most scientists, including this one, agree that the majority of smolt mortality is not caused by bird predation.

Cormorant predation and what should be done about it in Maine. There is no evidence that double-crested cormorants inflict significant damage on Maine wild Atlantic salmon populations. Cormorants can and do eat Atlantic salmon smolts under certain circumstances. Nevertheless, cormorant predation is but one of the perils of life faced by Atlantic salmon throughout their five-year life cycle. Several management measures can be taken to reduce the impact of cormorant predation. These include releasing hatchery-reared smolts at a time when they are likely to migrate to sea rapidly (e.g., avoid April) and emphasizing fry stocking to produce more natural smolts that migrate to sea at the proper time and in small groups (as opposed to stocking large groups of hatchery smolts into small areas). Encouraging the production of buffer prey species for cormorants to feed upon (alewife, blueback herring, rainbow smelt, etc.) is another means of managing the impact of avian predation upon salmon smolts.

For those who remain convinced that cormorant "control" is necessary, the following must be considered seriously:

- Nesting colonies of cormorants would have to be permanently eradicated from large areas along the Maine coast, since previous efforts to eliminate cormorants on selected islands in Maine studies have shown that other cormorants quickly repopulate vacant areas.
- A long-term, annual control program would be necessary and this would be costly to carry out. Based upon previously conducted control programs in Maine, the probability of a successful control program is highly unlikely.
- Many other species of birds use the same is-

lands on which cormorants nest; cormorant control on those islands would probably have serious consequences for other local sea bird populations (e.g., eider ducks, gulls, terns, etc.).
- Negative public relations resulting from cormorant control programs could be enormous, pitting the salmon program against other bird-related activities that are popular with the public. Decreased overall support for Atlantic salmon restoration efforts would be a likely consequence.

BELTED KINGFISHER

Years ago, shooting belted kingfishers (*Megaceryle alcyon*) was fashionable because they are known fish eaters and because overzealous salmon anglers believed that these fish were eating too many young salmon. A study conducted by Elson (1962) on the Pollett River, a tributary to the Miramichi, suggested that killing avian predators in salmon streams could theoretically double smolt production. This study was often cited as the justification for killing kingfishers and mergansers. However, studies of kingfisher food preferences have shown that these little birds eat mostly minnows, insects, and amphibians. Although they will occasionally eat a small salmon if it is found in shallow water, there is no valid reason to be shooting these small, blue-jay sized birds in Maine. In addition, they are a protected species!

CHAIN PICKEREL

Introduced into the Penobscot River watershed in 1819 via Davis Pond in Eddington, the chain pickerel *(Esox niger)* rapidly increased its range naturally and through human intervention throughout all but the northern area of Maine. Regarding the pickerel, Maine Fisheries Commissioners Foster and Atkins said in their report of 1867: "they are the most ruthless destroyers amongst all the freshwater fishes, and in most waters their advent is misfortunate."

Pickerel predation has been shown to be significant for smolts that migrate through lakes and ponds. In a study conducted in the Narraguagus River drainage, 21% of the pickerel sampled in Beddington Lake contained smolts. Pickerel as small as 35 centimeters (14 inches) were found with up to four smolts in their stomachs, and individual fish consumed as many as seven smolts up to 20 centimeters (8 inches) in length (Barr 1962). The pickerel has also been implicated as a significant predator upon landlocked salmon in Maine lakes where 31% of pickerel stomachs examined contained salmon (Warner 1972).

The extent of pickerel predation upon salmon migrating through deadwater areas of Maine's larger rivers (especially those with headponds created by dams) may be significant. A recent study of pickerel predation upon hatchery-reared smolts stocked in the Penobscot River (van den Ende 1993) revealed that Atlantic salmon were the most important dietary items and that almost one-third of all pickerel captured had consumed smolts.[9]

SMALLMOUTH BASS

The smallmouth bass *(Micropterus dolomieui)*, originally introduced into Maine waters in the 1860's, is known to consume juvenile Atlantic salmon. Bass most often prey upon salmon fry and parr, since the two species inhabit similar habitats in rivers. It appears that the bass is not a significant predator upon Atlantic salmon smolts, since smolts leave Maine rivers in the early spring when water temperatures are cold and bass feeding activity is reduced. A University of Maine masters thesis study conducted in the Penobscot River in 1992 could not document bass predation upon any Atlantic salmon smolts (van den Ende 1993). In this study, 125 smallmouth bass were caught by angling, and the major prey items found were other fish (shiners, suckers, chubs, etc.), insects, and crayfish. The smallmouth bass, like most other predators of Atlantic salmon, are opportunistic feeders in that they normally eat what is most abundant and available to them at the time. Smallmouth bass are more likely to consume Atlantic salmon fry and parr, since both species are found in similar habitats within rivers.

AMERICAN EEL

American eels *(Anguilla rostrata)* are common in Maine rivers, and whether or not they are an important predator upon young salmon is unknown. While it is assumed that eels feed primarily on carrion, White (1933) reported finding the remains of 429 salmon fry in one 50.8-centimeter (20-inch) long eel! Obviously, if there were many eels in areas where large numbers of salmon fry were being stocked, the potential for eel predation upon salmon would be significantly increased. There is no evidence to suggest that eels are important predators upon older, live salmon; although, if an adult salmon dies in a fish trapping facility, eels will quickly feed on the carcass, usually entering through the vent of the fish.

---

9. This study should be viewed with caution in that it was based upon data from only 23 chain pickerel with food in their stomachs.

OTHER PREDATORS

There are many other documented mammalian (mink, otter, etc.), avian (mergansers, herons, gulls, ospreys, eagles, etc.), and piscivorus (striped bass, white and yellow perch, cod, sharks, etc.) predators upon Atlantic salmon. Of these, only the striped bass *(Morone saxatilis)* is considered possibly to be a significant predator upon Maine Atlantic salmon. This opinion is based upon the fact that striped bass numbers are increasing in Maine's coastal waters. In addition, Schulze (1994), using a mathematical technique termed *bioenergetics modeling*, concluded that the striped bass posed a potential threat to both shad and salmon populations in the Connecticut River.

> *Striped bass continue to win new devotees and provide fine sport for the angler in the estuaries of our rivers from Kittery to Calais. Fish of 8 to 10 pounds were common in the 1963 striper catch.*
>
> —From the Atlantic Sea Run Salmon Commission Newsletter, March 1964

Despite many fishery research studies conducted in Europe and North America, none has implicated any single predator species that is responsible for the major mortality of juvenile or adult Atlantic salmon. In fact, typically the removal of any single source of Atlantic salmon mortality often does not result in greater adult returns. Is it possible that cormorants, or other predators, prey primarily upon those individual salmon that are unlikely to survive the next two years at sea anyway?

THE ULTIMATE PREDATOR

The ultimate predator upon Maine Atlantic salmon is ubiquitous throughout the salmons' range in North American and Europe. This predator, responsible for the direct and indirect deaths of more Atlantic salmon than all other predators *combined*, is the human one. Consider just a few of the cumulative effects of the following activities of the ultimate predator:

- sport fisheries, commercial fisheries and poaching
- habitat alteration, destruction and degradation
- the addition of many poisons and toxins to the air, land, and water
- the establishment of upstream and downstream barriers to salmon migration
- the introduction of nonnative species of animals to the salmon's domain that compete for food and space and prey upon the salmon (e.g., brown trout, smallmouth bass, and chain pickerel)
- artificial manipulations of stream flows and water temperatures
- reductions in the genetic diversity of wild salmon populations through careless, improper, or accidental stocking practices
- the creation of artificial conditions that result in an imbalance between the ratios of predators and prey (e.g., cormorants like to feed in the headponds of hydrodams, seals are attracted to cages holding thousands of salmon in the ocean, etc.)

Considering the devastating effects of human predation upon Atlantic salmon, I find it amusing, and rather hypocritical, to entertain the notion of predator control, unless humans are willing and able to control the "ultimate" predator first!

Parasites and Diseases of Maine Atlantic Salmon

Fish diseases are normally separated into four categories: parasites, bacterial and viral diseases, nutritional diseases, and environmental diseases. While many parasites and diseases are known to infect Atlantic salmon, Maine salmon populations are fortunately infrequently affected by them. Most of the infestations occur under hatchery or other crowded rearing conditions where high densities of salmon are confined to small areas.

One of the most common freshwater external parasites found on adult salmon in hatcheries is Ich *(Ichthyopthirius)*, while the so-called freshwater "brackish water" louse *(Argulus spp.)* is most often observed on adult salmon in the wild. The common sea louse *(Lepeoptherius salmonis)*, found only on salmonids, is prevalent on Atlantic salmon at sea. This parasite normally dies and falls off the fish within 24 hours after entry into freshwater. A smaller, less harmful species of sea lice *(Caligus elongatus)* has been found on more than 80 species of fish and is less commonly found on wild Atlantic salmon. On juvenile salmon in Maine rivers, the common brook trout ecto (external) parasite *(Salmincola edwardsii)* has been occasionally observed. An internal parasite that was common 30 years ago in the liver of Atlantic salmon reared at the state hatchery in Enfield was a larval cestode, caused by the parasite *Diphyllobothrium sebago*. Overall, how-

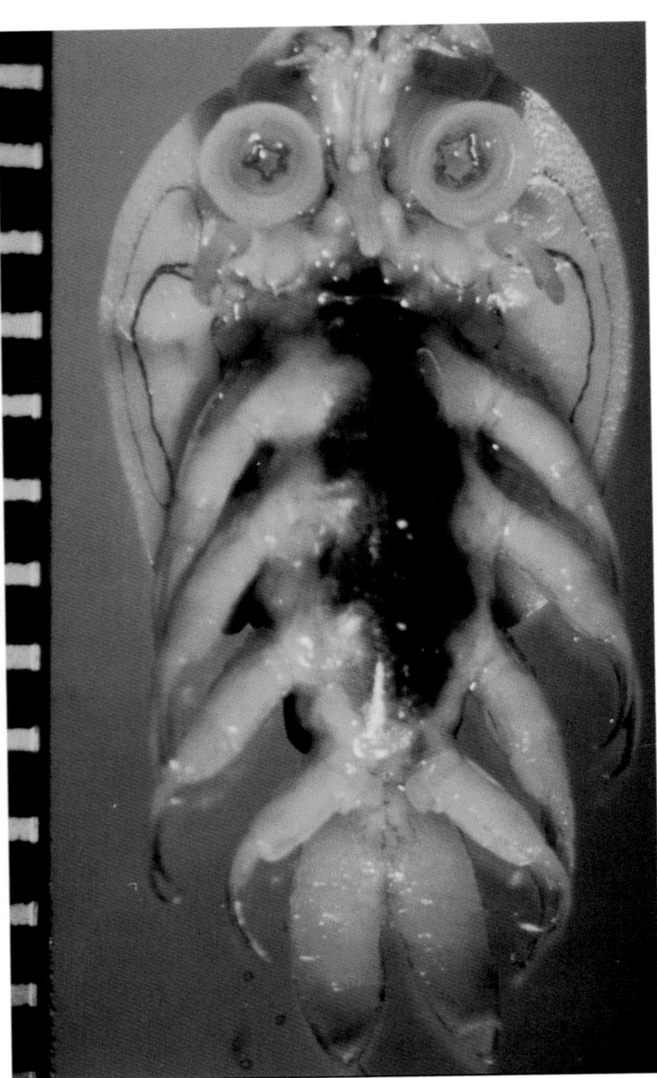

The brackish water louse *(Argulus canadensis)* is commonly found on adult Maine Atlantic salmon in brackish or fresh water. (Photo courtesy of Kip Powell)

ever, parasites are rarely the cause of significant mortality in wild salmon populations.

On the other hand, infectious diseases caused by bacteria and viruses have the propensity to cause significant mortalities in any species of fish. Consequently, if diseases are found in Atlantic salmon in hatcheries in clinical form (i.e., fish exhibiting visual signs of infection) all fish are sometimes destroyed (depending upon which disease is found) and the hatchery is thoroughly disinfected. Furunculosis *(Aeromonas salmonicida)* and enteric redmouth or ERM *(Yersinia ruckeri)*, the most commonly found bacterial diseases in Maine salmon, have been found at one time or another in both US Fish and Wildlife Service salmon hatcheries in Maine.[10] In saltwater, vibriosis or *vibrio* (most often caused by *Vibiro anguillarum)* is a common bacterial disease affecting most species of fish including farmed salmon; therefore, it is thought to also affect wild salmon populations. Vaccination of smolts before stocking into net pens has significantly increased their survival to maturity, although this could not be shown for Maine hatchery-reared smolts released into the wild (Baum et al. 1981). There have been recent reports of a new type of vibriosis, termed coldwater vibrio, which has been responsible for significant mortalities in the salmon farming industry in Maine and New Brunswick.

Several important bacterial diseases affect the gills and fins of juvenile salmon in hatcheries. These bacteria occur in most waters, and their outbreak is often associated with conditions that stress the fish (high temperatures and hatchery practices such as grading and moving). Fish that are overly stressed often exhibit severely eroded fins (termed

10. Furunculosis occurs in warmwater and coldwater species of finfish as well as shellfish populations. It is so widespread that all freshwaters in Maine with resident fish undoubtedly harbor the disease.

fin rot) that results from a combination of mechanical injury and secondary infection by these so-called *flexibacteria*. Another potentially very serious disease not found in Maine wild salmon but occasionally found elsewhere is bacterial kidney disease or BKD, which is caused by *Renibacterium salmoninarum*. A very serious viral disease that has not been found in Maine wild salmon but is very common in brook trout and rainbow trout is infectious pancreatic necrosis or IPN. Oddly, this disease causes little mortality in Atlantic salmon but can be extremely lethal for trout. A few extremely serious viral diseases are only found in European salmon (e.g., viral hemorrhagic septicemia or VHS) and West Coast salmon (e.g., infectious hematopoietic necrosis or IHN). Whirling disease (*Myxosoma cerebralis*), which is caused by an internal parasite, is not found in Maine. Although rare in New England, the existence of whirling disease is a major problem in the western part of the United States. This is one of the principal reasons for current Maine laws that prohibit the importation of Atlantic salmon from Europe and the west coast of North America.

> *Simply stated, disease is literally a lack of ease. It can be defined as a morbid process or condition in the body and its parts with characteristics which distinguish it from the normal state. Diseases can be infectious, that is, communicated from one host to another, or noninfectious. The course of a disease can range from short-term lethal effects to chronic, inapparent conditions which are detectable only at specific times.*
>
> *A Guide to Integrated Fish Health Management in the Great Lakes Basin*, F. P. Meyer et al. 1983.

Fungal diseases that grow on dead or decaying matter often attack dead fish eggs and then spread to nearby, healthy eggs. On juvenile salmon, fungal diseases are most often seen as secondary infections that occur on fish subjected to some form of injury.

Nutritional diseases affecting Atlantic salmon occur in hatcheries and are relatively rare today. However, dietary problems have occasionally occurred in the past due to protein or fat imbalances in the artificial food fed to salmon. Additionally, deficiencies in vitamins and minerals have sometimes resulted in mortalities of young salmon.

Environmentally induced diseases in salmon are caused by poor water quality conditions. For example, a supersaturation of nitrogen caused by heating water in hatcheries to speed development and growth can cause gas bubble disease in fry (also called popeye). If metabolic wastes such as ammonia accumulate to high levels, salmon in the sac-fry stage have been known to develop a condition known as blue-sac disease. Even too much air in the water supply or abrupt increases in temperature can be harmful, causing conditions termed, respectively, white spot disease and pinch off disease.

If you have visited either of the two federal hatcheries in Maine recently, you have probably noticed the extraordinary precautions taken to protect the salmon and their environment from diseases and parasites. In fact, most of the production areas of these hatcheries are not accessible to the public for that reason. The lessons of good animal husbandry have been developed and perfected over a long time; occasionally, a few lessons were learned the hard way.

Photo by Tom Carbone

3

Fisheries for Maine Atlantic Salmon

3 Fisheries for Maine Atlantic Salmon

Homewater Commercial Fisheries

Although commercial fishing for anadromous fish was reportedly practiced as early as 1628 at the mouth of the Androscoggin River, it was not until 1684 that the first laws to regulate fishing were enacted. At that time "the Town of Pemaquid and the region round and about were formed into a Ducal State under a Royal Grant to the Duke of New York, whereupon a tax was put upon fishermen for the purpose of revenue." All vessels not of the ducal state were required to pay into the public revenues four quintals[11] of merchantable fish if a decked vessel and two quintals of merchantable fish if an open boat.

In the late 1700's Penobscot River salmon were plentiful and used extensively for bartering as evidenced by these exchange rates:

2 pounds of salmon for 1 pound of codfish
5 pounds of salmon for 1 pound of pork
2 pounds of salmon for 1 pound of beef
3 pounds of salmon for 1 pound of flour
48 pounds of salmon for 1 bushel of corn
6 pounds of salmon for 1 pound of tea
15 pounds of salmon for 1 yard of sheeting

Commercial fishing for salmon took place with the use of primitive nets until they were gradually replaced by the introduction of weirs[12] in the 1780's. The use of weirs spread rapidly throughout Maine, with the first one reportedly installed in the Kennebec River in 1780 and in the Penobscot River in 1815. Stakes and brush were used until the 1890's, after which they were gradually replaced by various types of twine and netting. Examples of the most common types of weir used in the Penobscot salmon fishery are illustrated on the following pages (recreated from Smith 1898). These various types of weirs were constructed to conform to the topography of the bottom and shoreline, and the habits of the salmon as discovered by commercial fishermen through many years of fishing. The commercial harvest of salmon and other species was virtually unregulated since anadromous fish stocks were apparently abundant. For example, in June 1807 it was reported that 7,000 striped bass, ranging from 10 to 60 pounds in weight, were taken at the mouth of the Kenduskeag Stream in Bangor. Another local report from mid-May in 1812 reported that one haul of the seine by Mr. Luther Eaton of Eddington took 7,000 shad and 100 barrels of alewives.

Little or nothing was done to protect or enhance the fisheries in Maine until the Legislature passed a resolution on January 28, 1867, concerning the protection and restoration of sea fisheries. The first laws specifically pertaining to commercial salmon fishing were established for the Androscoggin, Kennebec, and Penobscot rivers. These laws established annual and weekly times closed to fishing and areas that were permanently closed (for example, within 200 yards of any dam or fishway). At this time every dam or artificial obstruction in any river frequented by salmon, shad, and alewives was also supposed to be "provided with a durable, efficient fishway."

In 1867, the Maine Fisheries Commissioners reported that 183 weirs and nets in the Penobscot River took 7,320 salmon, leading them to proclaim, "we can confidently say that the average yield of the Penobscot before its obstruction by dams could

11. In case you forgot, a quintal is equal to 100 pounds in the United States and 112 pounds in Great Britain!

12. A weir is essentially a fence made of stakes and brush, that is designed to lead the fish into a net or pound where they are captured.

Weirs Used In Penobscot Bay, 1890s

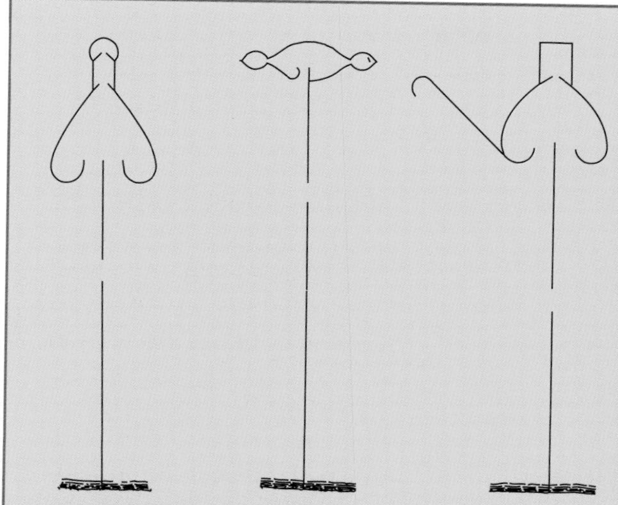

Left: Salmon weir, Penobscot. **Leader of stakes interwoven with brush, 175 yards long. "Great pond," brush, 42 feet long. "Middle pond" and "back pond," netting with board floor, each 10 feet long. Outer entrance, 16 feet wide; middle, 2 feet; inner, 1 foot. Value, $75.**
Center: Salmon weir, Bucksport. **Leader, brush, 4 to 8 rods long. Middle pond, 40 feet long, 8-foot entrance; inner side, brush; outer side, twine. Pockets, twine, 10 feet long, 10-inch entrances, wooden floor. Value, $25. Some weirs have only one (upstream) pocket.**
Right: "Hook weir," Orland. **A brush hook, about 50 feet long and extending down stream, is built on some of the weirs. It serves the purpose of leading the fish into the net. Value, $35.**

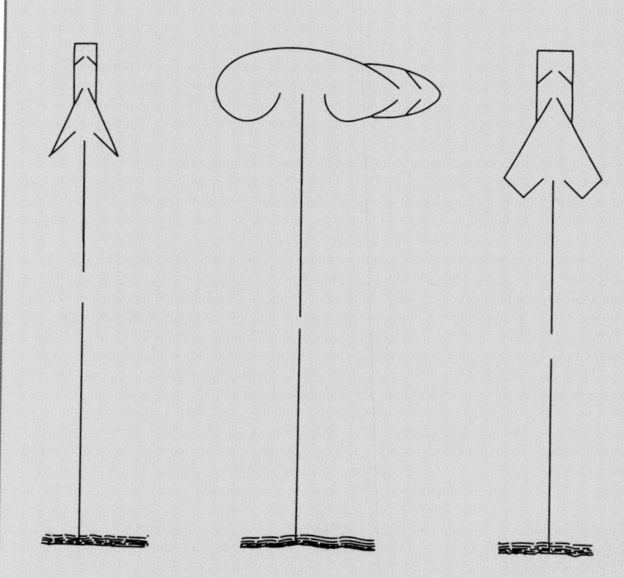

Left: Salmon weir, Castine. **Hedge, 200 feet long, made of stakes driven in mud interwoven with brush to low-water mark, covered with netting beyond. Great pound, 30 feet long, 30 feet wide at base, made of netting; entrance 8 feet wide. Inner pounds, 10 feet wide, with board floors; outer entrance, 2 feet wide, inner 1 foot. Value, $70.**
Center: Salmon weir, Stockton. **Leader or hedge, 400 yards long, all brush except 20 yards next to head, which piece is netting above low water mark and brush below. Main compartment or great pound, 60 feet long and 25 feet wide, with 10-foot entrance on each side of leader; smaller compartments, directed downstream, 21 feet long, with 2-foot entrance to first and 8-inch entrance to second. Value, $100.**
Right: Salmon weir, Stockton. **Leader, 200 feet long; brush from shore to low-water mark; remainder brush at bottom, netting at top. Head, 60 feet long; outer pound, 40 feet, middle pound, 12 feet, inner pound, 8 feet; brush below low-water line, netting above; plank floors in two smaller compartments. Value, $40.**

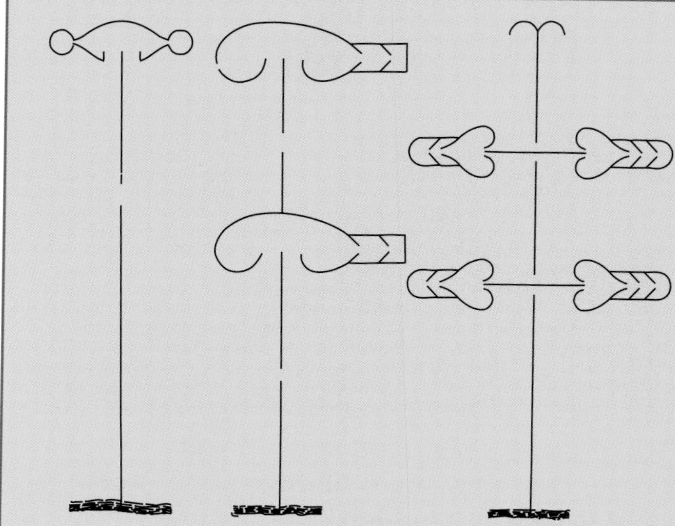

Left: Salmon weir, Winterport. **Leader, brush, 6 rods long. Heart, brush, or netting, 40 feet long, 20 feet wide, with 8-foot entrance on each side of leader; pockets, netting, 10 feet in diameter, 9-inch entrance, wooden floor. Value, $50.**
Center: "Up and down" Salmon weirs, Orland. **Constructed of brush except final compartments, which are of netting with wooden floors. Value of set, $65.**
Right: Salmon weir, built at Verona in 1889. **The most elaborate net used in the Penobscot region.**

not have been less than 100,000 salmon and 200,000 shad." By 1880 the catch had increased to 110,176 pounds of salmon (10,016 individual fish) which were taken in 230 weirs and traps and 36 gillnets. The gillnet fishery in the Hampden-Orrington-South Brewer section of the river was relatively unimportant; most of the weirs and traps were in the vicinity of Verona (Whitmore's) Island (Figure 24). In the mid-1890's the commercial fishing effort had declined by 20% as compared to 1880, while the catch had declined by nearly 50%, to 4,400–6,400 salmon per year.

Our State is best known by her salmon. Once the salmon of Maine were all quoted in the markets of the United States as from the Penobscot or the Kennebec—each river having its advocates for their local superiority of flavor, for the one or the other.

State of Maine Commissioners of Fisheries and Game, *1891–1892* Annual Report.

Unfortunately, many laws and regulations were frequently repealed or altered, often because of local pressure or action. The Maine Fisheries and Game Commissioners noted in 1892 that "the eight years exemption from obedience to the fishery laws of the State granted to the dam owners at Augusta virtually exterminated the Kennebec born salmon. When the present fishway was completed, a few surviving salmon passed up the river and were successfully hunted and killed at Waterville. We doubt that either frog or snake could escape the keen eyes or appetite of the French Village at Waterville Falls." Loopholes were sometimes created deliberately to circumvent existing laws. For example, fishing for salmon in the Penobscot River above the railroad bridge in Bangor was limited to three days per week between April 1 and July 15; however, fishing for alewives was legal at all times. The use of nets above tidewater in the Penobscot River was banned in 1883, although, in 1895, Maine residents were allowed to catch Atlantic salmon between the Bangor Dam and the mouth of the Seboeis River between 6:00 P.M. Wednesday and 6:00 P.M. Saturday each week.

Penalties for the violation of fisheries laws were severe for those times—$10 minimum, $50 maximum, *and* $10.00 for each salmon, $1.00 for each shad and $.20 for each alewife taken. However, from the examples noted above it seems that there were few prosecutions because of the existing laws.

After the turn of the century, commercial Atlantic salmon landings in Maine steadily declined in concert with the diminishing resource, although throughout history most of the catch continued to occur on the Penobscot River (Figure 25). There were a few "good" years during the early 1900's; however, the fishery was finally closed in 1948 after a reported catch of only 40 salmon in the Penobscot River (Cutting 1963).

Maine Sport Fisheries

The subject of angling for Atlantic salmon can be overwhelming—literally dozens of books have been written on the subject by world-renowned anglers who were vastly qualified to do so. Atlantic salmon fishing is unlike fishing for any other species in that the angler must fish for individual fish in specific locations. One difficulty the angler faces is the fact that salmon do not eat in freshwater; therefore, you are not trying to entice the fish into eating something upon which they normally feed. If the reader is looking for "inside" information on how to fish for Maine Atlantic salmon or "secret" tips on tackle and techniques to catch a 25-pounder, a tactful conversation with a local, knowledgeable angler on a

Jan Blake has fished for Maine Atlantic salmon for many years. Obviously, she knows how to do it successfully!

salmon river would probably be more productive than anything found herein. If, however, you have an interest in the history and traditions associated with salmon angling in Maine over the last 150 years, read on! As an added incentive, maps of the most popular (and productive) Atlantic salmon fishing pools in Maine rivers are scattered throughout the following pages. At least you will know where to go!

Historical Perspective

The first recorded "sport" catch of a Maine Atlantic salmon goes back to 1822 when a Captain Eldridge from Bucksport (while trolling for pollock with squid for bait) caught a salmon on hook and line near Seal Island (Meister 1964). Ten years later, an unidentified angler fishing the lower Dennys River was the first person in the United States to catch an Atlantic salmon by rod and reel. A small group of anglers fished for salmon below the dam in the Dennys River in the mid-1800's; then, in 1860, a fisherman of Scottish descent by the name of Kevin Brackett had the distinction of being the first person in Maine known to have caught an Atlantic salmon on an artificial fly (Bartlett and Robinson 1988).[13] Fly fishing for salmon in Maine spread to the Narraguagus River sometime during the 1860's, the St. Croix River in the 1870's, the Penobscot River in 1880, and the Aroostook River in 1890. "In 1885 more than six salmon were taken in the Bangor Salmon Pool by Fred Ayer who has demonstrated that fishing with a fly is as good on the Penobscot as in any salmon river in the world" according to an article in the *Bangor Whig*. At least 40 salmon were taken in the Bangor Salmon Pool during the 1885 season.[14]

While salmon angling was often thought of as a male-dominated sport until more modern times, there were several female pioneers. In 1885, Mrs. George W. Dillingham from New York was the first woman to catch a salmon in the Bangor Salmon Pool, while Miss "Jennie" Sullivan caught the first salmon of the season on April 3, 1901 (a 16 3/4 - pound fish!). Fifteen years later, on April 1, 1916, Jennette Sullivan again caught the first salmon of

Salmon in Maine Take the Fly

It has been said that while salmon in most other waters take the fly at some season, those in Maine streams have persistently refused it. It would be very gratifying to know why they have declined it, and still more so to learn their reasons for reconsidering the question and resolving to accept it. In proof that they now take the manufactured insect, we publish the following dispatch which was received at Portland from Bangor one day last week: J. F. Leavitt and H. L. Leonard, the rodman, have just returned from a trip and have brought with them the first salmon taken with a fly in Penobscot waters. This they took in Wassataquoik Stream, which empties into the east branch of the Penobscot half a mile above the Hunt Farm. They report that plenty more can be had in the same way.

Forest and Stream,
Volume XV, August 12, 1880.

13. Why an Atlantic salmon will strike at or take an artificial fly is the subject of much speculation. It is possible that this is a conditioned reflex (i.e., young salmon eat insects), or the fish may be angry or simply defending its territory. While all of these explanations may be true, in reality no one knows why Atlantic salmon take artificial flies.

14. Mr. Ayer reportedly caught 35 salmon in 1885 and another 27 in 1892!

Twelve-year old Ralph Andersen (left) and his thirteen-year-old brother Edmund (siblings of Miss Esther Anderson, mentioned in sidebar at right) proudly display a 22-pound salmon that they caught in the Bangor Salmon Pool. Ralph was the oarsman for Edmund who caught the fish—one of several that they took on this day in April of 1912. Note the way that these young fishermen dressed for a day of Atlantic salmon fishing! (Photo courtesy of Raymond Andersen)

the season, and this time the fish graced the table of President Woodrow Wilson! In 1902 Mrs. George Willey was acclaimed champion woman angler of the Penobscot when she was credited with taking three fish with an aggregate weight of 53 pounds (Kendall 1935).

On March 30, 1895, a 23-pound salmon was taken at the Bangor Salmon Pool while the river below was still covered with ice. Traditionally, angling for salmon in the Penobscot and other Maine rivers ceased after the middle of July. However, since many Maine anglers also fished Canadian rivers late in the season, a few continued this practice on the Penobscot by fishing well into the month

Wednesday of last week is reported as the banner day at the Bangor Salmon Pool. . . . The record for the season certainly belongs to little Miss Esther Andersen. This little miss is the ten-year-old daughter of Mr. and Mrs. Karl Andersen. Mr. Andersen comes pretty near being high line for the number of fish taken at the Pool this season and his little daughter seems to have inherited her father's ability with the rod. They had been out on the Pool less than half an hour when a salmon struck the fly and was hooked firmly. Little Miss Anderson was holding the rod while her father managed the boat and encouraged by her father the little girl held the big rod and the salmon straining at the end of the long line, reeling in the slack and meeting the rushes of the fish like a veteran. The fish was unusually lively and broke water repeatedly but the little girl gave him line or took in slack as she was told by her father and finally brought the fish into shallow water where Mr. Andersen gave him the gaff. The fish was a beauty weighing 10 pounds. It will be a long time probably before little Miss Andersen's feat is duplicated and she will retain the record of being the youngest person who ever landed a salmon at the Bangor Pool.

MAINE WOODS, PHILLIPS, MAINE, JUNE 14, 1897.

Maine Atlantic Salmon Fishing Clubs and Conservation Organizations

Name	Year Formed
Penobscot Salmon Club	1884 (incorporated 1923)
Dennys River Sportsman's Club	1936 (incorporated 1947)
Narraguagus Salmon Association	1947
Pleasant River Fish & Game Association	1950's
Maine Atlantic Salmon Federation (defunct)	1960
Sheepscot River Atlantic Salmon Association	1950's
Sheepscot River Salmon Club (new name for previous listing)	1960's
Veazie Salmon Club	1978
Atlantic Salmon for Northern Maine, Inc.	1978
Downeast Salmon Federation[16]	1981
Two-Rivers Salmon Club (Machias & East Machias Rivers)	1981
Northern Penobscot Salmon Club	1982
SALEN (SALmon ENhancement for the Upper Saint John River)	1982
Eddington Salmon Club	1982
Saco River Salmon Club	1983
Maine Council-Atlantic Salmon Federation[17]	1984
St. Croix International Atlantic Salmon Association	1984
Worumbo Falls Salmon Club (Androscoggin River, defunct)	1986
Union Salmon Association	1992
Friends of the Kennebec	1997

of August 1903. To their surprise angling continued to be worthwhile, as evidenced by eight salmon landed by one angler after July 15 that year.

Salmon fishing in the Penobscot River at the Bangor Salmon Pool was unlike fishing in any other river in Maine. For example, in 1905 Mr. Charles Eugene Taft, a New York sculptor, reportedly took a 19-pound salmon in the pool. Having no landing net, he shot the fish in the head with a light target rifle, thereby taking just one minute to play and land the fish! It was also during 1905 that Charles Bissell and Charles Halkins were reported to have taken 66 salmon weighing a total of 777 1/2 pounds, representing over half the reported catch for the entire year (113 salmon, weighing 1,322 pounds).

Due to the size of the Penobscot River and the tackle and techniques brought over from Europe during the 1880's, most of the salmon were caught from boats anchored in the river. In 1908 former state Fish and Game Commissioner H. O. Stanley described the experience in the following fashion: "the angler sits in his boat and lets out his line and guides his fly over any spot below him he desires. The current and eddies do the rest—giving the fly just the right motion. The first thing the angler knows he has a salmon—usually unexpectedly." Another angling technique called "harling" involved two anglers in the boat (called a "peapod" because of its shape and design) which was rowed so that their flies were dragged over salmon lies.[15] During this procedure, the anglers periodically made casts to present the fly at different angles and drifts (Hennessey 1987).

Known Sport Catches by River

Despite the nostalgia associated with accounts of Atlantic salmon fishing in the 1880's, the *1980's* were actually the halcyon days for Maine Atlantic salmon fishing. Although records prior to 1948 are often fragmentary, the greatest rod catches clearly occurred in Maine during the last 25 years. The 1990's have produced the second highest annual catches in Maine history (Table 11), even with the

15. While many salmon anglers have been known to lie about their fishing experiences, the term *salmon lie* actually refers to the places where salmon are known to be found lying or resting during their upstream migration. There is no single, simple definition of a salmon lie; however, Joe Bates' classic book *Atlantic Salmon Flies and Fishing* provides extensive descriptions of traditional Atlantic salmon lies.

16. Formed by the Dennys, Two Rivers, and Narraguagus salmon clubs in October 1981; the Pleasant River Fish & Game Association joined in December 1981.

17. Consists of 20-30 Atlantic salmon angling clubs and similar private natural resource conservation organizations.

Atlantic salmon fishing at the Bangor Salmon Pool in early June of 1926. The salmon ranged from 8 to 19 pounds in weight. The anglers are (from left): Walter Crossman, William West, Fred W. Ayer, Horace Chapman, Frank Covan, Charles Bissell, Guy Peavey, Bion Hanson, unknown boy.

poor runs and fisheries observed in recent years. There is no way of estimating how complete rod catch records were before the mid-1940's; however, information from organized salmon clubs and several studies of salmon fishing in the state suggests that reported catches since the early 1950's probably represent about 80% of the actual total for most rivers.

In reviewing the historical rod catches of Atlantic salmon in Maine (Table 11), it is readily apparent that most (95%) of the salmon have been taken in seven rivers. The Penobscot, with records dating back 115 years, accounts for 56.4% of the known historical catch while the five "Downeast" rivers (Dennys, East Machias, Machias, Pleasant, and Narraguagus) account for 36.5%. Of the five Downeast rivers, the Narraguagus with 13% has been the most productive to anglers, followed by the Dennys (11.5%) and Machias rivers (7.2%). The Sheepscot River, which is often called a Downeast river although it is found in central Maine, accounts for another 2.4% of documented statewide catches. Although the Machias historically produced the largest salmon runs of the Downeast rivers, few residents angled for salmon before 1954. Many pools on the Machias River are relatively inaccessible and, unlike the easily accessible bank fishing sites on the Narraguagus and Dennys Rivers, it is more effectively fished from a boat or canoe. Complete, historical rod catches for all of Maine's salmon rivers are recorded in Appendix 2.

Development of Organized Salmon Angling Clubs

The Penobscot Salmon Club was organized in 1884, and by 1887 a 31-foot x 45-foot clubhouse and 100-foot long horse shed had been built (by Thomas F. Allen in association with F. W. Ayer) on the

The Saco River Salmon Club operates a private hatchery that produces Atlantic salmon fry for the Saco River salmon restoration program. Salmon eggs are provided annually by the US Fish and Wildlife Service.

Brewer shore of the Bangor Salmon Pool. The 40 club members (dues were rather pricey at $10.00 per year) included some of the Bangor area's most prominent citizens. One account of early breakfasts at the clubhouse noted that "members gathered each April first, each with a setter dog, a pound of beefsteak and a quart of whiskey, the steak being for the dogs. When properly fortified, the Isaac Waltons gathered their rods and began the day's activities."

When fire destroyed the original buildings a new clubhouse was built, and the Penobscot Salmon Club was incorporated in 1923. Competition among club members to catch the first salmon of the season was always fierce, leading to the tradition, established in 1912, of sending the first salmon of the season to the president of the United States.

The 1930 removal in the town of Dennysville of a dam that had restricted salmon access to the lower Dennys River for many years generated an increased interest in the Atlantic salmon fishing in eastern Maine. This led to the formation of the second oldest salmon fishing club in the state on April 13, 1936—the Dennys River Salmon Club. The Club, in a gesture of visionary foresight, immediately bought out the local gill net and weir fishermen and aided in having the state legislature pass a law in 1937 prohibiting the use of weirs and gill nets in the river. The Dennys River, which was named after an Indian Chief who fished in the area for many years, was soon known as the outstanding salmon river in the nation for fly fishing, and membership in the Dennys River Salmon Club swelled to nearly 750 members (Bartlett and Robinson 1988). In 1947 the club was incorporated under a new name—the Dennys River Sportsman's Club.

The opportunity for most people to participate in leisure time activities such as salmon fishing declined during World War II; however, the end of the war stimulated a renewed interest in the sport. The Maine legislature and federal government initiated programs to restore salmon runs and fisheries, and additional salmon fishing clubs were established. The Narraguagus Salmon Association was formed in the late 1940's, and additional salmon clubs were organized throughout the state as salmon runs and fisheries improved due to restoration efforts by various state and federal agencies. A complete list of Maine Atlantic salmon fishing clubs appears in the panel opposite.

In addition to the salmon fishing clubs listed above, numerous other private conservation groups, including local Fish and Game and Rod and Gun Clubs, Conservation Associations, Trout Unlimited Chapters, and so forth, throughout Maine have members who have fished actively and regularly for Atlantic salmon.

C. Z. Westfall presents a "Presidential Salmon" to President George W. Bush at Walker's Point, Kennebunkport, Maine, on May 25, 1992. This was the last Penobscot River salmon actually presented to the President, ending a tradition that began in 1912.

The Presidential Salmon Tradition

Historically, the first fresh-run salmon caught at the Bangor Salmon Pool became as much of a sign of spring as the melting April snows, and competition arose between two local Bangor hotels to purchase the first salmon to offer fresh salmon to their customers (Hennessey 1987). However, in 1812 angler Karl Anderson decided to send a salmon to William Howard Taft as a gesture designed to contribute "to the city's honor and respect" for the president. Interestingly enough, Mr. Anderson only saw fit to ship the second (not the first) salmon he caught on April 1, 1912, to President Taft. After that, competition among anglers vying for the presidential salmon was keen each April 1st. Beginning in 1914, the first salmon caught at the Pool was either purchased by a local group of businessmen or the Penobscot Salmon Club and shipped via train to Washington. Maine's first salmon graced the White House table annually until 1954 when dams and pollution took their toll on the Penobscot River causing salmon runs and the sport fishery to dwindle. The traditional open-

Maine's Presidential Atlantic Salmon

Date Caught	*Angler*	*Weight of Salmon (lb)*	*President*
April 1, 1912	Karl Anderson	11	William Taft
April 4, 1913	Charles Bissell	16	Woodrow Wilson
April 1, 1914	Michael Flanagan	18	Woodrow Wilson
April 1, 1915	John Thomas	16	Woodrow Wilson
April 6, 1916	Jeanette Sullivan	10	Woodrow Wilson
April 6, 1916	Michael Flanagan	11	Woodrow Wilson
April 6, 1917	John Thomas	15	Woodrow Wilson
May 27, 1918	John Doane	15	Woodrow Wilson
April 2, 1919	Charles Bissell	15 1/2	Woodrow Wilson
April 2, 1920	Michael Flanagan	12	Woodrow Wilson
April 2, 1921	Michael Flanagan	16	Warren Harding
April 2, 1922	J. Edward Canning	20	Warren Harding
April 15, 1923	Adolph Fischer	15	Warren Harding
April 1, 1924	J. Edward Canning	16 1/2	Calvin Coolidge
May 17, 1925	Adolph Fischer	20	Calvin Coolidge
April 11, 1926	Frank S. Rand	7	Calvin Coolidge
April 1, 1927	Walter Crossman	12 3/4	Calvin Coolidge
April 1, 1928	Robert Blair	15	Calvin Coolidge
April 1, 1929	Horace Chapman	14 1/4	Herbert Hoover
May 1, 1930	J. Edward Canning	10	Herbert Hoover
April 7, 1931	Horace Chapman	7 1/2	Herbert Hoover
April 12, 1932	Robert Blair	16	Herbert Hoover
April 1, 1933	Walter Crossman	14	Franklin Roosevelt
April 23, 1934	Lothrop Coldwell	7 1/2	Franklin Roosevelt
April 1, 1935	Walter Higgins	8 1/2	Franklin Roosevelt
April 9, 1936	Charles Bissell	11 1/2	Franklin Roosevelt
April 1, 1937	Walter Crossman	12	Franklin Roosevelt
April 5, 1938	Adolph Fischer	7 1/4	Franklin Roosevelt
April 1, 1939	Horace P. Bond	13 1/4	Franklin Roosevelt
May 20, 1940	Don Phinney	8	Franklin Roosevelt
May 22, 1940	Osgood Nickerson Robert Weston	10 3/4	Franklin Roosevelt
May 24, 1941	Paul Atwood	9	Franklin Roosevelt
May 11, 1942	Horace P. Bond	8	Franklin Roosevelt
April 18, 1943	Adolph Fischer	20	Franklin Roosevelt
May 15, 1944	Guy Carroll	9	Franklin Roosevelt
May 24, 1945	Harold Hatch	9	Harry Truman
May 11, 1946	Robert Weston	8 3/4	Harry Truman
April 1, 1947	Donald Smith	7 3/4	Harry Truman
May 5, 1948	Adolph Fischer	8	Harry Truman
May 18, 1949	Adolph Fischer	10	Harry Truman
April 15, 1950	Guy Carroll	7 1/2	Harry Truman
April 1, 1951	Horace P. Bond	16	Harry Truman
April 1, 1952	Guy Carroll	8	Harry Truman
May 17, 1953	Walter Dickson	5 1/4	Dwight Eisenhower
May 31, 1954	Guy Carroll	10	Dwight Eisenhower
May 9, 1964	Harry C. Davis	14	Lyndon Johnson
May 1, 1981	Ivan Mallett	8	Ronald Reagan
May 2, 1982	Leroy Hutchings	7	Ronald Reagan
May 9, 1983	James Coldwell	9 1/2	Ronald Reagan
May 12, 1984	Doug Blanchard	6	Ronald Reagan
May 1, 1985	Carl Small	7 1/2	Ronald Reagan
May 1, 1986	Tom Hennessey	8 1/2	Ronald Reagan
May 2, 1987	George Fletcher	15	Ronald Reagan
May 1, 1988	Charles Caron	8	Ronald Reagan
May 1, 1989	William Ellison	5 1/2	George Bush
May 1, 1990	Greig Barker	7	George Bush
May 1, 1991	Tom Prue	7 1/2	George Bush
May 1, 1992	Claude Westfall	7 1/2	George Bush
May 2, 1993	Scott Westfall	7	William Clinton[18]

18. This fish was never actually presented or sent to the president.

ing day breakfast at the Penobscot Salmon Club and competition for the presidential salmon also ended.

Many salmon continued to be caught in the Penobscot River throughout the period 1954–1980; however, during this period the first Maine salmon of the year was often caught in the Narraguagus River, and one was actually sent to the White House. On May 9, 1964, the presidential salmon was taken by Harry Davis in the Narraguagus River, and the fish was shipped to President Lyndon Johnson.

By the mid-1970's, the Penobscot salmon run (and the Penobscot Salmon Club) had been revitalized, and the presidential salmon tradition was finally reinstated in 1981. Instead of simply shipping the salmon to the president, however, the fish, the angler who caught it, his wife, the governor, the fish and wildlife commissioner, and one of Maine's senators joined Vice-President George Bush in the Roosevelt Room of the White House to revive the old state custom.

Vice-President George Bush accepts the 1981 "Presidential Salmon" on behalf of President Ronald Reagan. The salmon was presented by Maine Governor Joe Brennan (right) and Inland Fish and Wildlife Commissioner Glenn Manuel (center).

After that the newly reinstated tradition became increasingly muddied by politics, as the governor and other state officials, Maine's congressional delegation (the appropriate Democrats or Republicans—depending upon who was president), and other assorted unnecessary "embellishments" (e.g., occasionally a fishery scientist) now joined the fish and the angler in a whirlwind day trip to Washington. Overall, the publicity was beneficial to the statewide restoration program, but an occasional *faux pas* seemed to occur each year. Examples include the presentation of dripping-wet (or still frozen) salmon, the presence of assorted unknown White House aides accepting the fish for the president, lengthy delays before arrangements could be made, and funding dilemmas for the entourage to travel to Washington.

Unfortunately, the significance of the first salmon eventually became lost in the annual shuffle involving pomp and circumstance, delivery and protocol, quips and photo opportunities. By 1993, in what was to be the final year of the tradition, arrangements to present the fish to Vice-President Gore, who was scheduled to accept the fish on behalf of President Clinton, remained uncertain into the month of September, and no presentation was ever made. Mercifully, increasingly restrictive angling regulations finally ended the presidential salmon tradition in 1994.

When the Penobscot salmon run is again large enough to allow for a recreational harvest of salmon, and the tradition is again revived—as I believe that it should be—perhaps those involved will take the time to refer to boatbuilder Karl Anderson's original idea in 1912 and also keep in mind one of today's oft-used axioms—KISS.[19] The significance of the Penob-scot River presidential salmon tradition was purely symbolic. Local pride in one of this country's unique natural resources brought the realities of everyday life in Maine to the national forefront each spring. Clean waters, hard work, cooperation between government and industry, and a commitment to future generations was what this annual event was supposed to signify!

Presidential Salmon Tidbits. In 1916 the first *two* salmon caught in the Bangor Salmon Pool were sent to the president. Miss Jeannie Sullivan caught the first salmon, and Michael Flannagan also landed one later the same day. A group of prominent Bangor Democrats shipped both fish to President Wilson.

19. Keep it simple, stupid!

In 1924 Miss Sullivan moved to West Virginia to live with her father. She reportedly gave all of her fishing tackle to her 12-year-old niece, Roselle Sullivan, declaring "you ought to get lots of big salmon with this outfit." A year later, on her first trip to the Bangor Salmon Pool, Roselle caught a 27-pound salmon—the largest fish taken at the Pool in 25 years!

On May 2, 1925, Charles Bissell caught the first salmon at the Bangor Salmon Pool, but he sold the fish to a local fish market for the unheard-of price of $2.00 per pound ($18 total)! Thus, Adolph Fischer's 20-pound salmon, which was sent to President Coolidge, was actually the second to be caught that year.

While most written accounts of the presidential salmon tradition list the names Osgood Nickerson and Robert Weston (it took *two* men to land the fish?) as sending a 10 3/4-pound salmon to President Roosevelt on May 22, 1940, Donald Phinney sent the 8-pound salmon that *he* caught from the Dennys River to the president May 20th!

Bangor sausage-maker Adolph Fischer sent a presidential salmon to the White House in 1925, 1932, 1943, 1948, and 1949; two of his five salmon were 20-pounders!

President Franklin Roosevelt had 13 Maine Atlantic salmon grace the White House table (including the two in 1940), while Woodrow Wilson received nine. Presidents Truman and Reagan each "landed" eight salmon while they occupied the Oval Office!

In 1964 the presidential salmon tradition was resumed—for a one-year period. During the winter of 1963, interest in reviving the tradition was expressed by the angling community. Therefore, the Atlantic Sea Run Salmon Commission agreed to negotiate with the angler catching the first salmon and to ship it to the White House; the Maine Department of Economic Development agreed to arrange for presentation to the president and for news coverage of the event. Harry C. Davis of Cherryfield caught a 14-pound 2-ounce salmon in the Narraguagus River on May 9, 1964. The Salmon Commission, with packaging help from H. P. Hood & Sons in Bangor, shipped the fish to President Lyndon B. Johnson via Air Express, and Maine Congressman Clifford G. McIntyre presented it to the president at the White House. A photo of Mr. Davis landing the salmon graced the Atlantic Sea Run Salmon Commission's 1962–1964 Biennial Report. In 1965 it was back to "normal"—with no plans for continuing the presidential salmon tradition.

When the Penobscot River presidential salmon tradition was again revived in 1981, Maine Governor Joseph E. Brennan struggled to hold the wet and dripping fish away from himself and Vice-President Bush. When asked by reporters if he had much experience with such things, he responded "the only fish I've ever met have been in pool rooms." Later in the ceremonies, an ABC television reporter asked the vice-president if the State of Maine would receive anything in return for the fish. "They already get a lot of my dough for my house (in Kennebunk)" George Bush responded.

> *Many of you have wondered why the Stillwater Pool (Narraguagus River) was such a choice angling site. Drainage of the pool during dam construction provided some of the answers. Numerous large boulders provided well-shaded resting places out of the current; and two large springs provided the cool clear water that salmon seek during warm weather.*
>
> Excerpt from the March 1961 Atlantic Sea Run Salmon Commission Newsletter

"Probably meeting Reagan . . . but not by much" was 87-year-old George Fletcher's reply to a reporter's question of what was more exciting, catching that 15-pound salmon on May 1, 1987, or meeting President Ronald Reagan!

Former logger Neil Donnelly caught the first Penobscot salmon in 1988, but he declined to donate the fish to the president, saying "President Reagan just cut my income in half, so I felt he didn't need my salmon too. I've had two good meals off it and I'm going to have another tomorrow."

On May 2, 1993, Scott Westfall caught what was to become the final Penobscot River presidential salmon. By early August, Mr. Westfall had grown tired of waiting for Maine officials and the Clinton White House to accept the fish. He was probably a little "miffed" by the fact that instead of presenting the salmon to President Clinton, he was now slated to present it to Vice-President Al Gore, who had been delegated the task of accepting the fish

Special Section:

Fishing Maps of Maine's Major Salmon Rivers

Atlantic Salmon Fishing Pools of the Dennys River

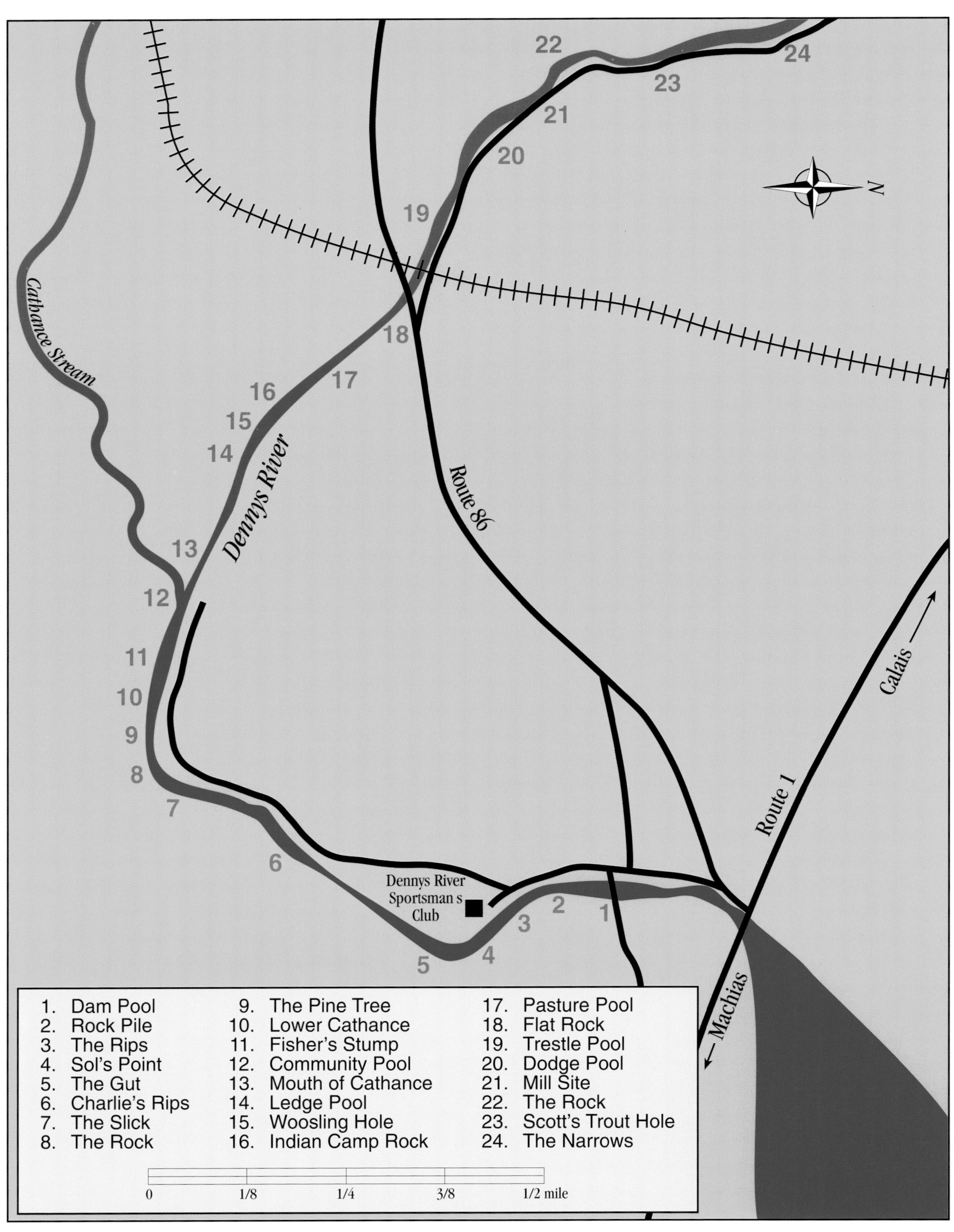

Atlantic Salmon Fishing Pools of the Machias & East Machias Rivers

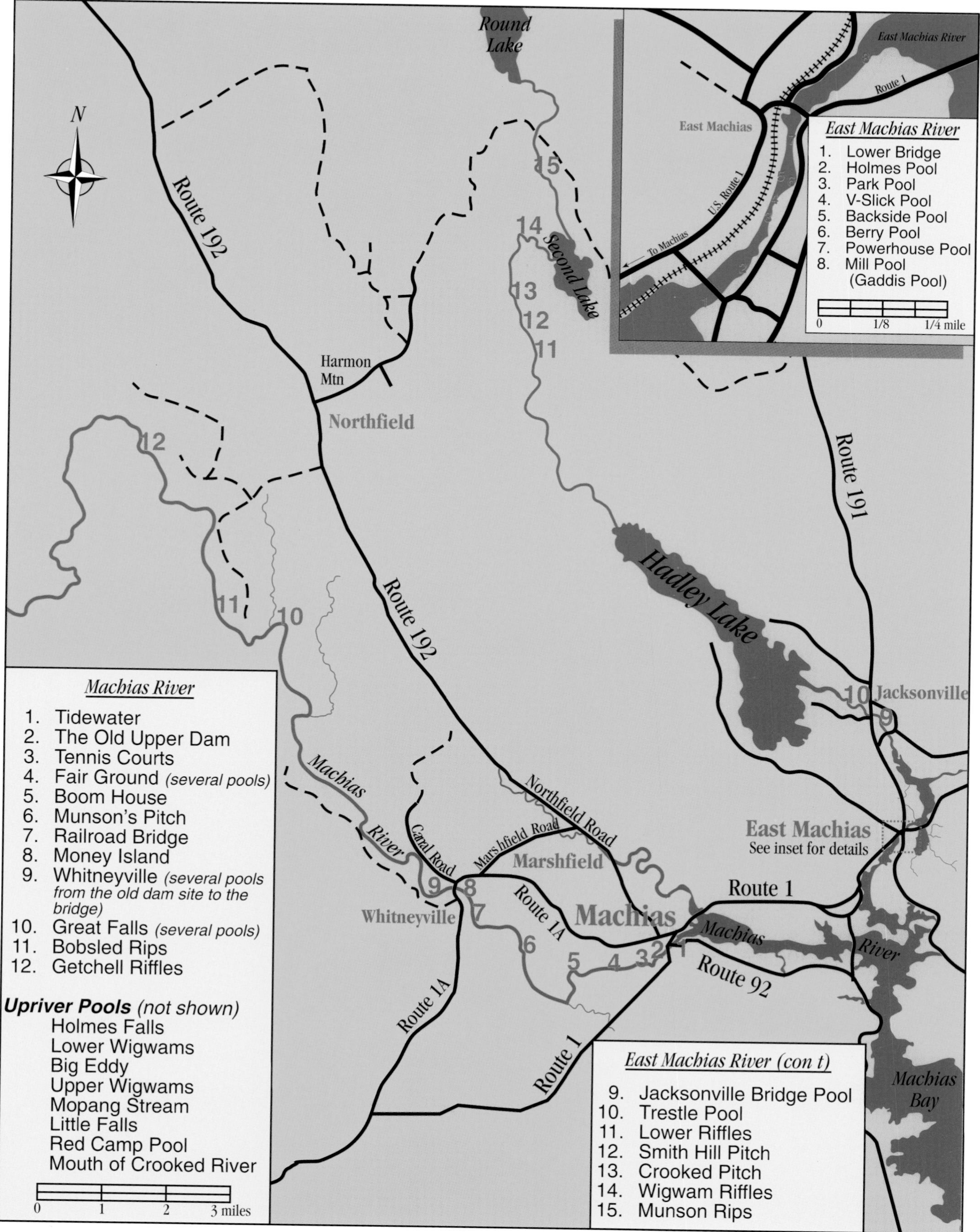
Round Lake
N
Route 192
Second Lake
Harmon Mtn
Northfield
East Machias River
Route 1
East Machias
U.S. Route 1
To Machias
East Machias River
1. Lower Bridge
2. Holmes Pool
3. Park Pool
4. V-Slick Pool
5. Backside Pool
6. Berry Pool
7. Powerhouse Pool
8. Mill Pool (Gaddis Pool)
0 1/8 1/4 mile
Route 191
Hadley Lake
Jacksonville
Machias River
1. Tidewater
2. The Old Upper Dam
3. Tennis Courts
4. Fair Ground (several pools)
5. Boom House
6. Munson's Pitch
7. Railroad Bridge
8. Money Island
9. Whitneyville (several pools from the old dam site to the bridge)
10. Great Falls (several pools)
11. Bobsled Rips
12. Getchell Riffles
Upriver Pools (not shown)
Holmes Falls
Lower Wigwams
Big Eddy
Upper Wigwams
Mopang Stream
Little Falls
Red Camp Pool
Mouth of Crooked River
0 1 2 3 miles
Machias River
Canal Road
Marshfield Road
Northfield Road
Marshfield
East Machias
See inset for details
Route 1
Whitneyville
Route 1A
Machias
Machias River
Route 92
Route 1A
Route 1
Machias Bay
East Machias River (con t)
9. Jacksonville Bridge Pool
10. Trestle Pool
11. Lower Riffles
12. Smith Hill Pitch
13. Crooked Pitch
14. Wigwam Riffles
15. Munson Rips

Atlantic Salmon Fishing Pools of the Pleasant River

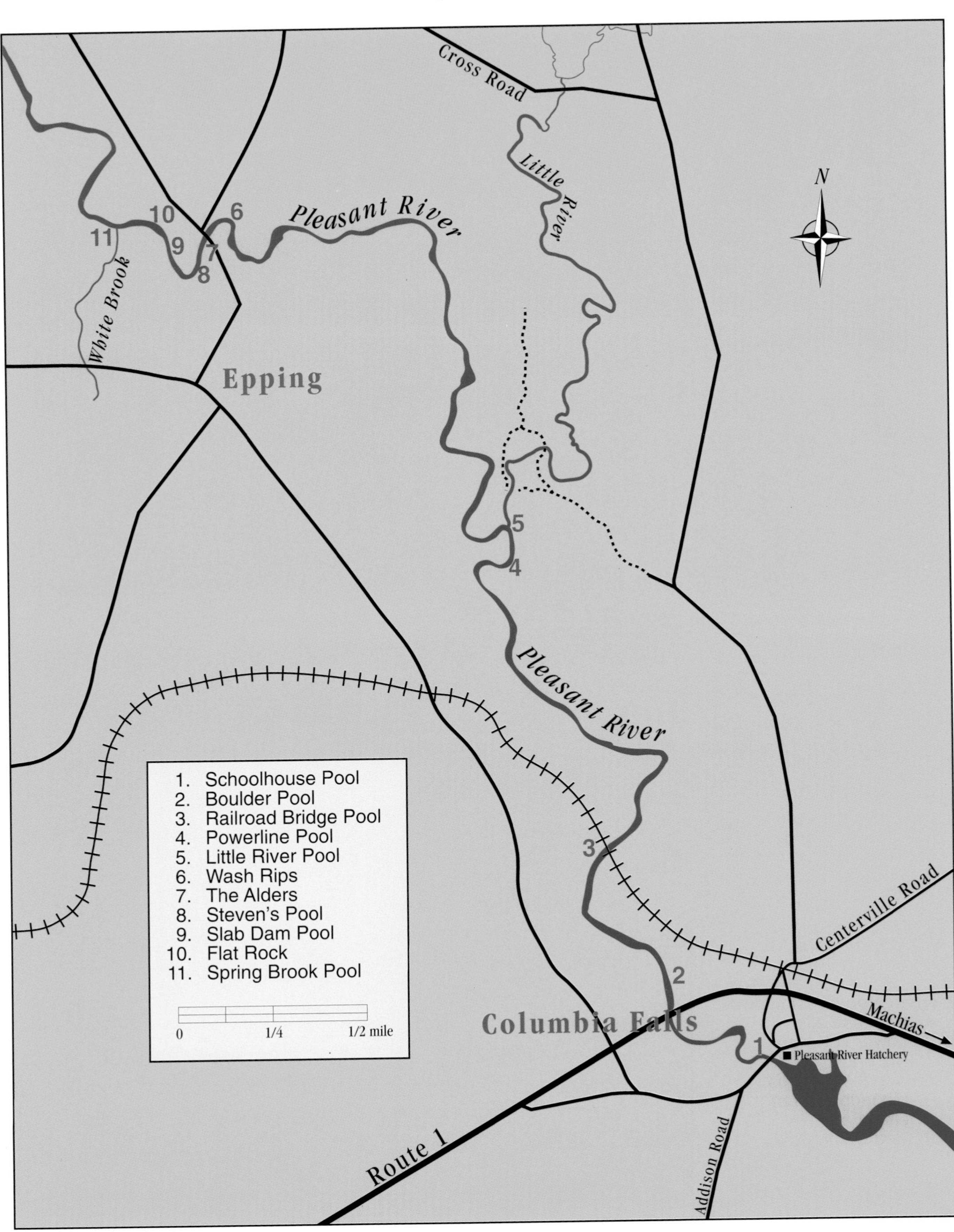

Atlantic Salmon Fishing Pools of the Lower Narraguagas River

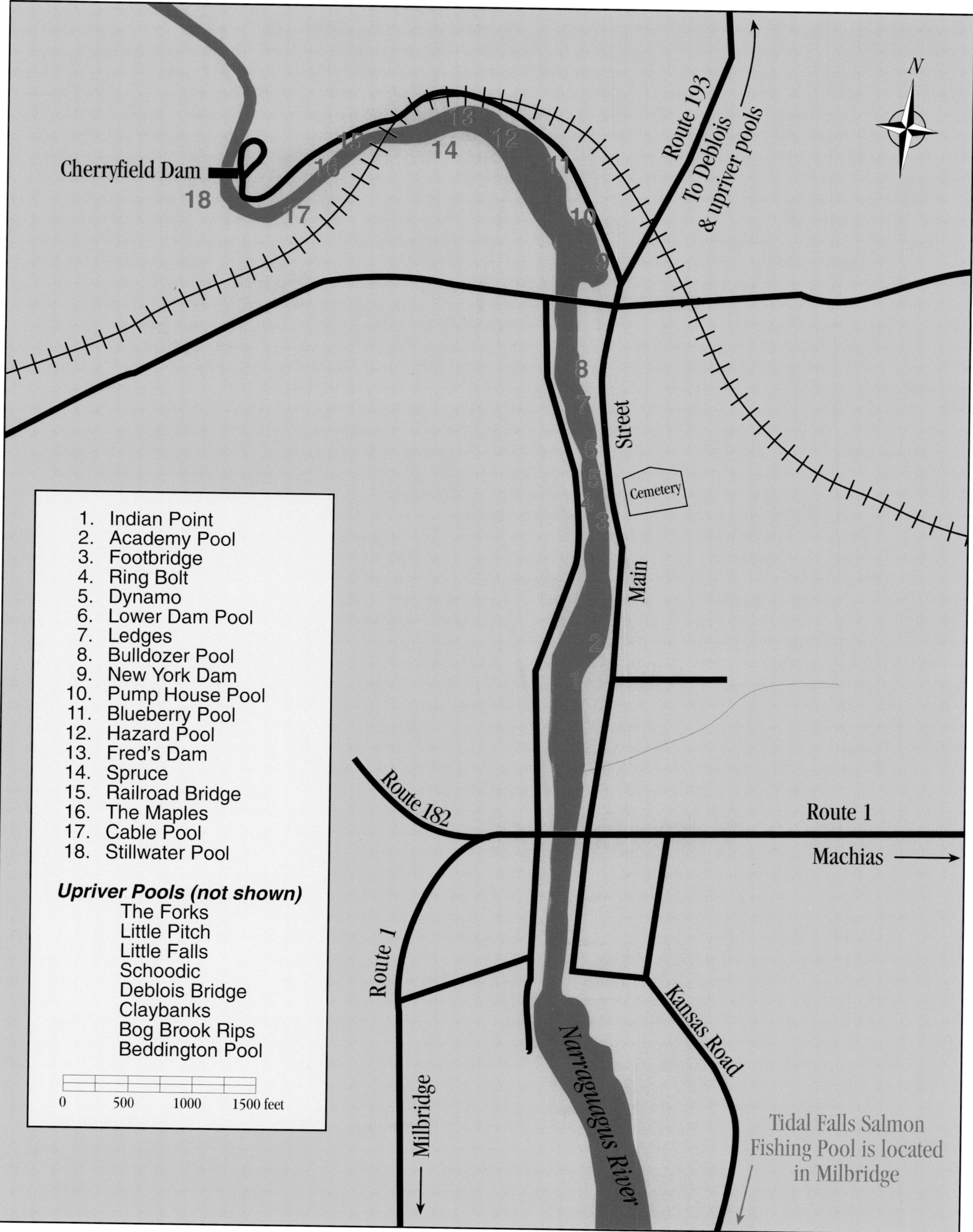
Cherryfield Dam
Route 193
To Deblois & upriver pools
N
Street
Cemetery
Main
Route 182
Route 1
Machias
Route 1
Kansas Road
Milbridge
Narraguagus River
Tidal Falls Salmon Fishing Pool is located in Milbridge
1. Indian Point
2. Academy Pool
3. Footbridge
4. Ring Bolt
5. Dynamo
6. Lower Dam Pool
7. Ledges
8. Bulldozer Pool
9. New York Dam
10. Pump House Pool
11. Blueberry Pool
12. Hazard Pool
13. Fred's Dam
14. Spruce
15. Railroad Bridge
16. The Maples
17. Cable Pool
18. Stillwater Pool
Upriver Pools (not shown)
The Forks
Little Pitch
Little Falls
Schoodic
Deblois Bridge
Claybanks
Bog Brook Rips
Beddington Pool
0 500 1000 1500 feet

Atlantic Salmon Fishing Pools of the Lower Penobscot River

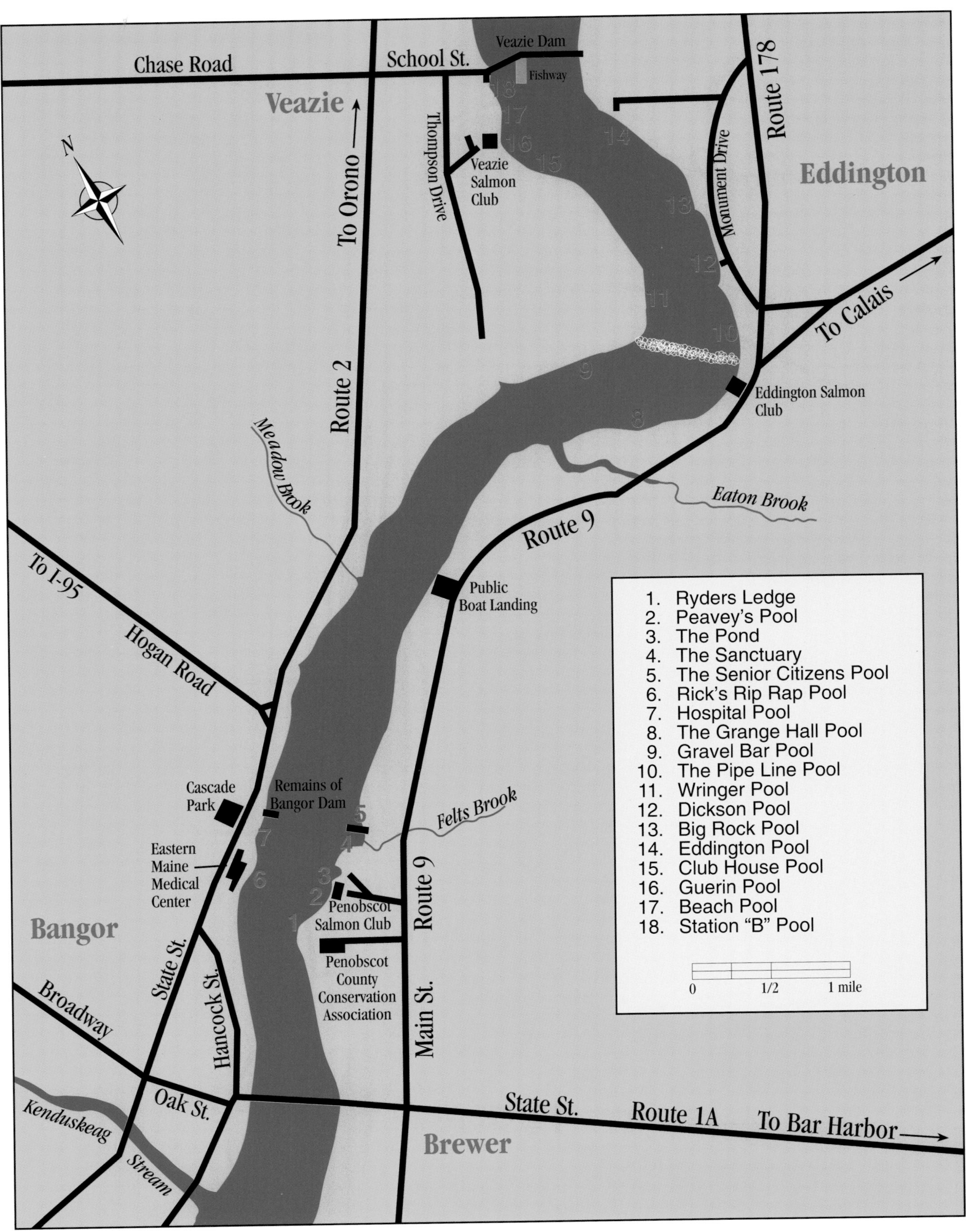

Atlantic Salmon Fishing Pools of the Ducktrap and Passagassawakeag Rivers

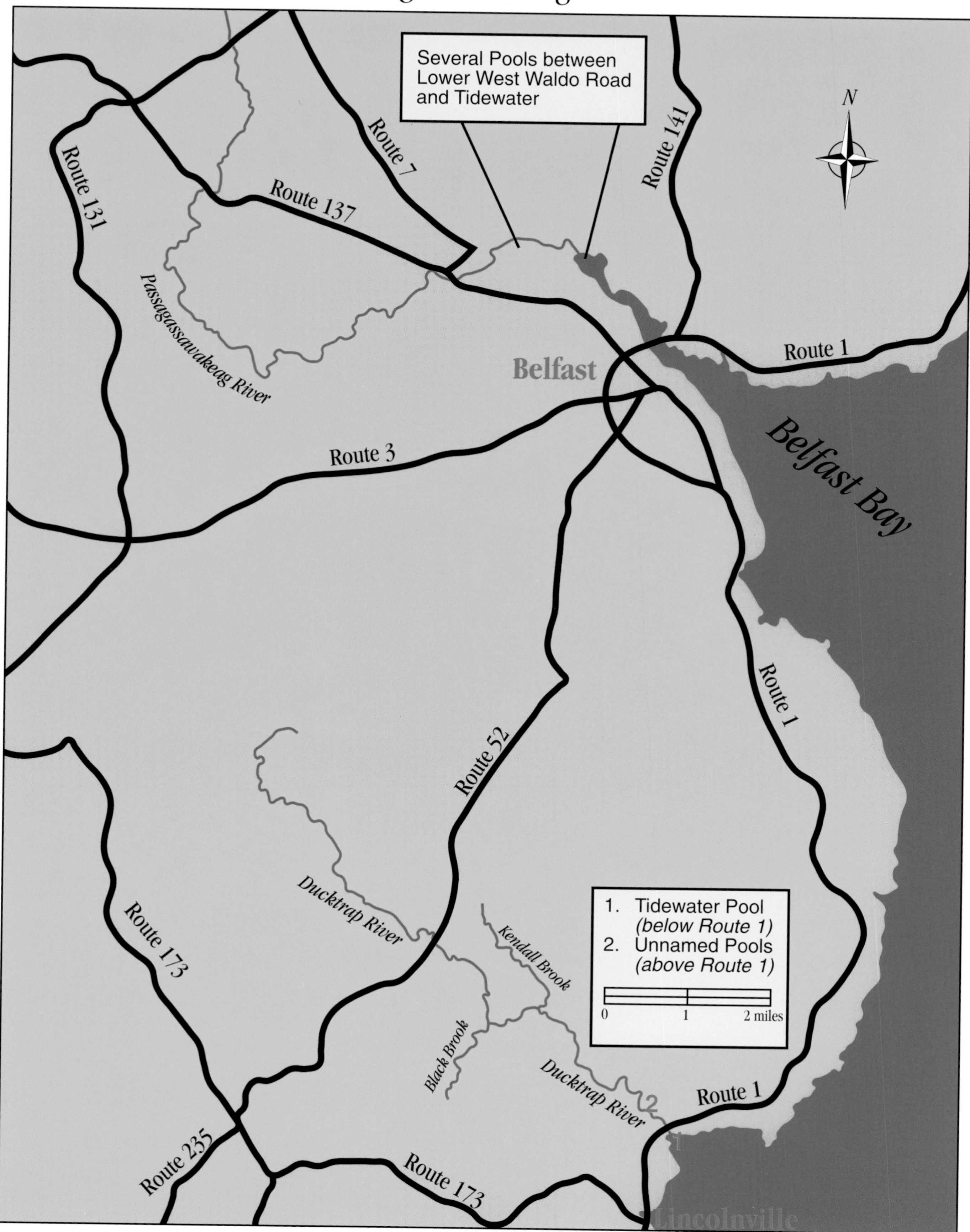

Atlantic Salmon Fishing Pools of the Sheepscot River

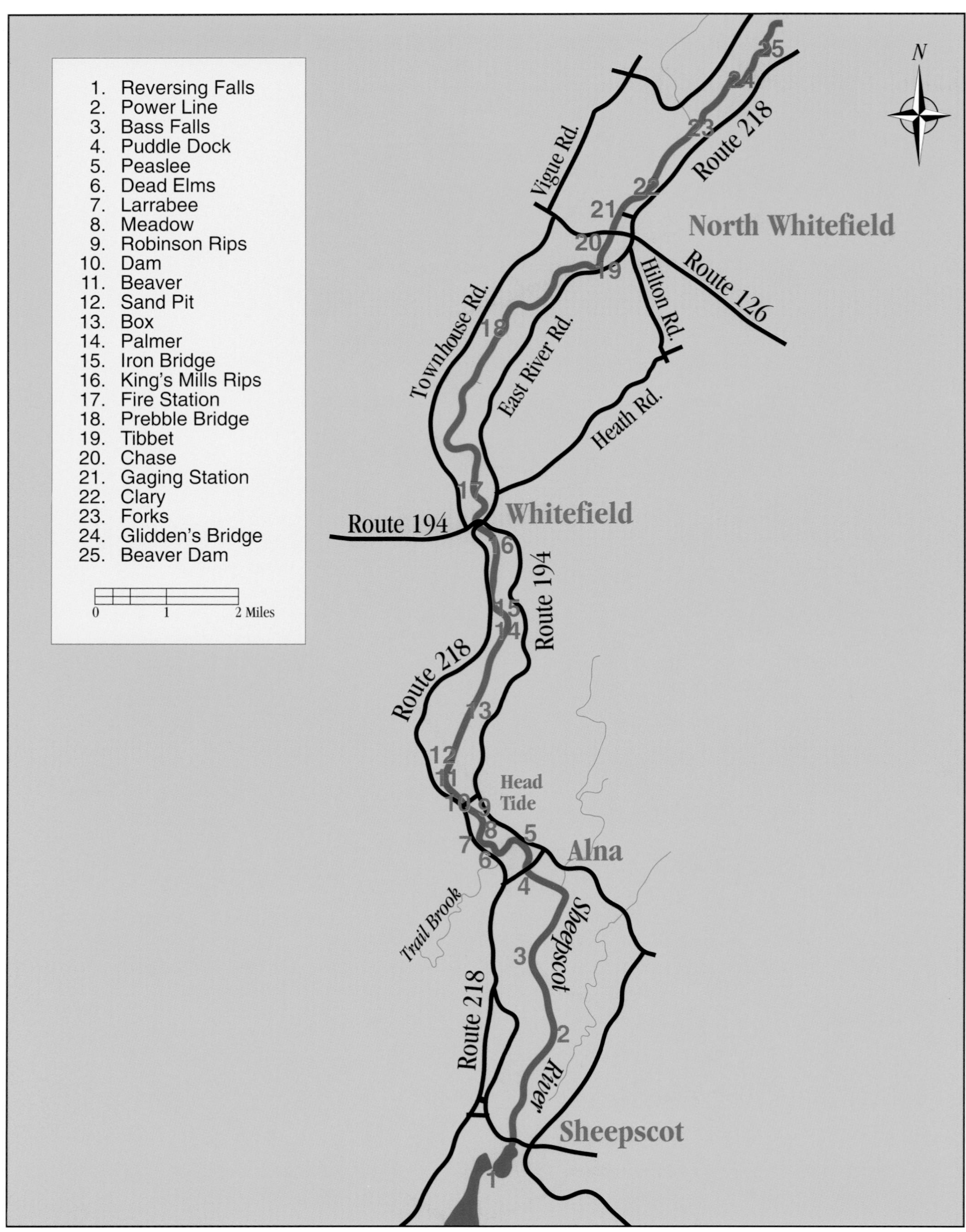
1. Reversing Falls
2. Power Line
3. Bass Falls
4. Puddle Dock
5. Peaslee
6. Dead Elms
7. Larrabee
8. Meadow
9. Robinson Rips
10. Dam
11. Beaver
12. Sand Pit
13. Box
14. Palmer
15. Iron Bridge
16. King's Mills Rips
17. Fire Station
18. Prebble Bridge
19. Tibbet
20. Chase
21. Gaging Station
22. Clary
23. Forks
24. Glidden's Bridge
25. Beaver Dam
0 1 2 Miles
N
Vigue Rd.
Route 218
North Whitefield
Route 126
Hilton Rd.
Townhouse Rd.
East River Rd.
Heath Rd.
Whitefield
Route 194
Route 194
Route 218
Head Tide
Alna
Trail Brook
Sheepscot River
Route 218
Sheepscot

on behalf of the president on September 7. When it became obvious that there there was not going to be a ceremony in the Oval Office that year, Scott Westfall—with the help of his dog Clancy—ate the Presidential salmon of 1993. And so the presidential salmon tradition quietly ended on a rather piquant note.

Two father-son teams sent presidential salmon to the White House—Lothrop Coldwell in 1934, followed by his son, Jim, in 1983. And then there was the back-to-back father-son team consisting of Claude Westfall in 1992 and Scott Westfall in 1993. Make that *one* father-son team . . . .

In 1994, in response to rapidly declining salmon stocks throughout North America, the Maine Atlantic Sea Run Salmon Commission promulgated a grilse-only (i.e., salmon more than 25 inches had to be released) rule that effectively ended the presidential salmon tradition. The first grilse of the year, one of only seven known to have been kept by anglers all year on the Penobscot River, was killed on June 24—long after interest in catching the first salmon had waned. Angling early in the season was actually very good that year, with perhaps 25 salmon that would normally have been "eligible" for the presidential salmon tradition being caught and released on opening day!

Maine's Record Salmon

The modern-day record for a rod-caught Maine Atlantic salmon is 28 pounds, 1 ounce, caught on October 9, 1980, by Howard Clifford of Portland. Although Mr. Clifford refused to disclose which Maine river the 43 1/2 -inch trophy came from, most people think that it was caught at the Tidal Falls Pool on the Sheepscot River. More than half of the largest (20+ pounds) Atlantic salmon taken in Maine in the past 50 years have come from the Narraguagus River, although many salmon greater than 20 pounds in weight have also been taken in the Machias and Dennys. Interestingly, the number of 20-pound salmon recorded by anglers in Maine in the 1970's and 1980's was about the same as for the 1950's and 1960's. Salmon greater than 20 pounds from Maine rivers include the following fish:

Narraguagus River

Lb.	*Oz.*	*Angler*	*Date*
26	2	Harry Smith	1959
24	8	Daniel Brooks	1982
23	12	Fred Wardwell	1947
22		Jim Brooks	1963
22		Warren Schnaars	1982
21	12	John Doane	1949
21	12	Clayton Gay	1985
21	8	Unidentified	1945
21	4	Thomas Bacigaloupo	1972
21	4	William Sheldon	1982
20	8	Harold Loring	1951
20	8	Edward T. Brown	1954
20	8	Dana Bartlett	1991
20	5	Robert Strong	1977
20	1	Leo Gilmore	1957
20	1	James Brooks	1961
20	1	Roy Willey	1980
20		W. O. Kennedy	1948
20		Harold Loring	1951
20		Harry Smith	1954
20		W. W. Cochrane	1954
20		Winthrop Rolfe	1969
20		Barry Joy	1974

Sheepscot River

Lb.	*Oz.*	*Angler*	*Date*
28	1	Howard Clifford[20]	1980
23	8	Joe Dunn	1969
20		Paul Wagstaff	1977

St. Croix River

Lb.	*Oz.*	*Angler*	*Date*
29		unidentified	1898

Dennys River

Lb.	*Oz.*	*Angler*	*Date*
24		Ralph Bagley	1929
23		H. M. Wasson Sr. 1944	
23		Sam Ward	1953
22	12	Fred Callahan	1962
22	8	Don Cushing	1961(?)
22	4	Alton Bell	1957
21	8	J. L. Chute	1937
20	12	H. M. Wasson Sr.	1954
20+		Kip Swedberg	1960
20		Dr. William Sleight	1946

Penobscot River[21]

Lb.	*Oz.*	*Angler*	*Date*
30		W. W. Fogg	1896
30		Ivory Doane	1898
29	8	E. O. Buck	1893
28		J. Henry Peavey	1897

20. Mr. Clifford refused to disclose where this salmon was caught; assigning it to the Sheepscot River is based upon speculation by the author.

21. Penobscot Salmon Club records document large numbers of salmon in excess of 20 pounds during the 1800's. For example, between 1893 and 1899 more than 60 salmon between 20 and 30 pounds were cataloged. Additionally, dozens of salmon recorded at an even 20 pounds caught between 1900 and 1943 are not included in this summary.

Cameron Clark displays the 27-pound salmon that he caught June 19, 1982 on the Machias River.

27		Roselle Sullivan	1925
26	8	E. O. Buck	1896
25	8	Charles Hogdon	1896
25		John Kent	1894
24		Fred W. Ayer	1886
24		Ed Hunt	1887
24		Thomas Allen	1891
24		George Willey	1901
23	4	George Libby	1891
23		Mrs. George Willey	1902
22	12	Mike Flanagan	1912
22	12	Ray Wade	1930
22	7	Dave Hutchinson	1988
22		Robert Taylor	1928
22		Samuel Drinkwater	1901
22		Jennie Sullivan	1902
21	8	Frank Burnell	1984
21		Walter Crossman	1937
20	12	Charles Bissell	1932
20	8	Dr. William Gould	1932
20	8	Clyde Lloyd	1927
20	8	Rick Doll	1984

Machias River

Lb.	*Oz.*	*Angler*	*Date*
27	12	Cameron Clark	1982
27	8	Robert Hinckley	1984
24	8	John Follett	1962
21	10	Henry Dowling	1962
20	8	Ken Van Bramer	1966
20	7	Charles Dowling	1961
20		Ralph Reeves	1961

East Machias River

Lb.	*Oz.*	*Angler*	*Date*
25	7	Ken Beland	1984
19	15	Gene Mallory	1977

Salmon anglers often ask why Maine rivers do not produce "monster" salmon of 30–50 pounds in weight in the way that some Canadian rivers (e.g., Restigouche and Miramichi) do. The answer may be found in two words: *geography* and *genetics*. Compared with many Canadian salmon, Maine salmon must cover much more oceanic "territory" over the same time. To illustrate the point, the author examined several scale samples of 25- to 30-pound Canadian salmon that had spent the same amount of time at sea (three winters) as had Maine salmon weighing one-third less. Maine salmon face a harsh marine environment that requires up to a 6,000 mile "swim" over a two-year period in the Atlantic Ocean; another year (or two) at sea would be required to produce a giant Maine salmon. That is where genetics enters the picture. Producing such a fish would be extremely inefficient for nature—natural selection favors those Maine fish spending three or fewer years at sea. Salmon numbers are also part of the equation. If the Narraguagus or Dennys Rivers experienced a return of 100,000 salmon each year like the Miramichi River, I am sure that there would be occasional 50-pounders in the run too! Also, it should be noted that "southern" Canadian stocks (e.g., Bay of Fundy and eastern N.S. rivers) do not produce these giant salmon, either.

Thoughts on Black Salmon Fishing

Post-spawning Atlantic salmon in freshwater are termed "kelts" by biologists. However, anglers traditionally call them black salmon, racers, slinks, snakes, or other similar contemptuous-sounding names. The reason for these unflattering names is that kelts are normally very thin, having lost 50% or more of their original prespawning body weight. They are also dark in color and rather unattractive to look at—especially the males, which could serve

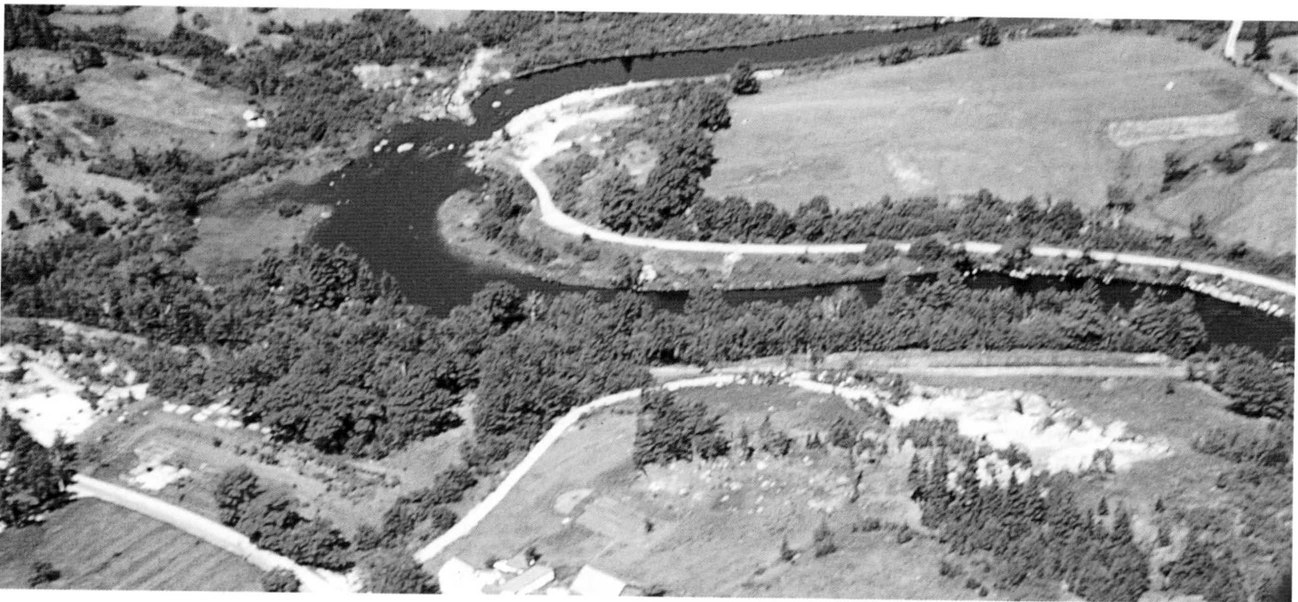

Aerial view of the Stillwater Pool on the Narraguagus River in Cherryfield. This was the most productive Atlantic salmon fishing pool in the river until 1961, when the US Army Corps of Engineers constructed a flood-control dam that destroyed most of the pool.

as models for scary Halloween masks! Salmon angling "purists" consider it unsporting to fish for these fish in their weakened, vulnerable condition.

Various studies suggest that about 10% of Maine kelts descend to the lower freshwater portions of rivers soon after spawning (late October–November), although the majority make the return to sea during April and May of the following year. A few laggards leave in early June, but these fish are the exception to the rule. Generally speaking, kelts and smolts leave Maine rivers at about the same time in the springtime.

Kelt fishing is quite unlike the traditional fishing that takes place for "bright" salmon. Salmon angling in April and early May is usually conducted under high flow and high turbidity conditions resulting from snow melt and spring rains. And, salmon on their way to sea do not frequent the salmon lies they stopped at on their upstream migration the previous year. The most productive kelt fishing areas are in deadwater areas or pools of rivers. As you might expect, a salmon that has not eaten normally for up to a year may be a little hungry. Thus, kelts are rather easy to hook and land for they do not have the energy or stamina of a fish that has just spent 1 to 3 years fattening up on the many delicacies of the sea.

A few kelts were always caught early in the Maine salmon fishing season (April), especially in the Penobscot and Dennys rivers. Few anglers bothered reporting catching them, however, for catching a spent salmon was not considered "sporting," and anglers fishing for kelts were often criticized by anglers who fished seriously for the more "majestic" bright salmon. The first directed fishery for kelts in North America reportedly began in the late 1930's in the Miramichi River in New Brunswick and became popular on the Pleasant and Narraguagus Rivers in Maine during the late 1950's.

It is hard for some people to imagine how the lowly, innocuous salmon kelt could create controversy. However, every decade or so the relative pros and cons of fishing for them are debated in Maine, usually because of a petition to the Salmon Authority or state legislature to prohibit black salmon fishing to "save" these fish so they may return as repeat spawners in future years.

Kelt angling provides a fishery for large salmon early in the season when there is little else to fish for. And, to some anglers, catching a 5- to 10-pound black salmon is as much fun and sporting as catching a brook trout, bass, or pickerel in a Maine river. From a conservation perspective, it can be argued that catching black salmon makes more biological sense than catching bright salmon, for the kelts have already contributed to future generations by spawning the previous year and few (only about 1% in recent years) will survive to return and spawn again.

However, those who would prohibit kelt fishing point to the fact that if those fish are protected to improve their chances of spawning again in future years, then they may return as trophy fish (15–25 pounds in weight) with a much higher reproductive potential (i.e., large salmon produce more eggs).

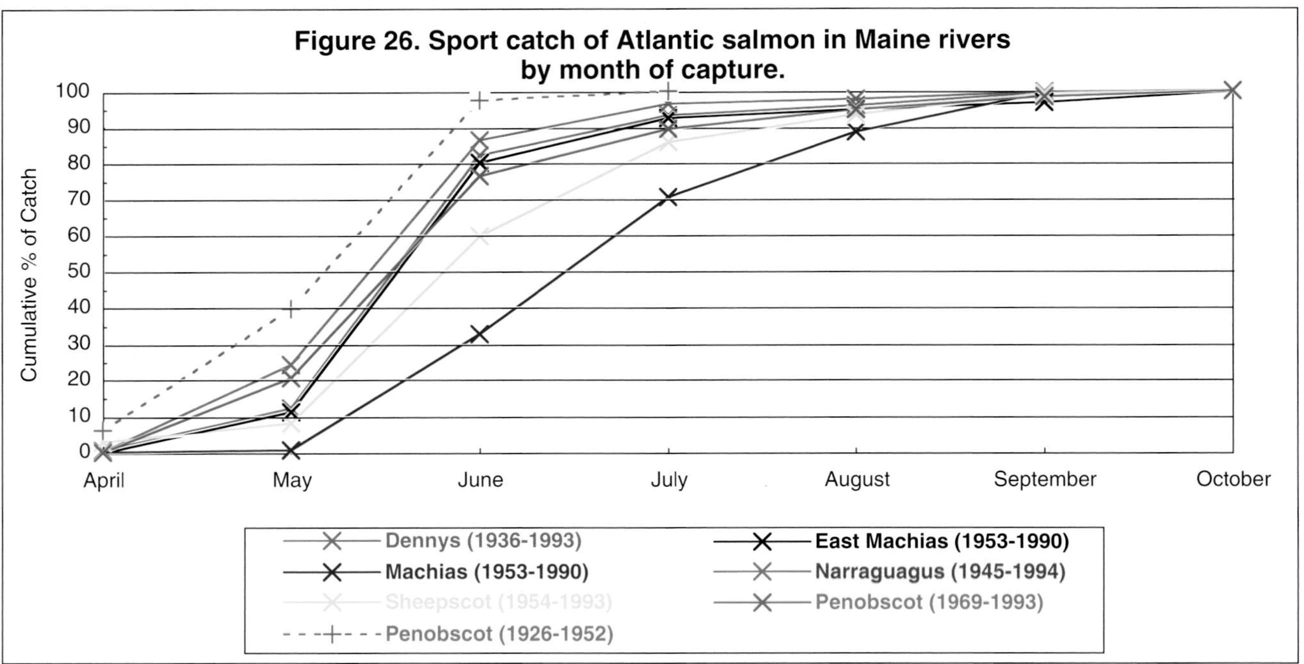

Known catches of kelts in the Pleasant and Narraguagus rivers are reported in Appendix 2. Pleasant River catch records show nearly three times as many black salmon as bright salmon were caught (700 kelts versus 262 bright salmon) during the years 1955–1979, while the Narraguagus River kelt fishery recorded about one half as many black salmon as brights (562 versus 1,147) for the years 1959–1974. Historically, relatively few kelts were caught in all other Maine rivers. In fact, for decades the salmon fishing season on the Dennys River opened on May 1 (versus April 1 on all other rivers) at the request of local anglers in an effort to increase the number of repeat spawning (bright) salmon in subsequent years.

Protecting kelts from a sport fishery should theoretically increase the number of repeat spawners in the salmon run two years later. It is true that repeat spawners are predominantly females, which should increase the proportion of repeat spawners in subsequent generations, since there is evidence that this trait is heritable. However, based on examinations of historical rod-catch records, repeat spawners were no more numerous in Maine rivers without kelt fisheries than in those rivers that had traditional kelt fisheries.

The statewide opening date for Atlantic salmon angling in Maine was advanced from April 1 to May 1 starting with the 1980 fishing season as a reaction to the declining numbers of large (MSW) salmon in Maine rivers. While hindsight is often 20/20, history has shown that fishing for black salmon was not the reason for the decline in the numbers of large salmon returning to Maine rivers. For a more reasonable explanation, the reader is encouraged to review the section of this book that examines commercial fisheries for Maine salmon.

When to Fish for Maine Salmon

The most productive time to fish for Maine Atlantic salmon is easily described: first, fish for them when they are abundant; second, go when the water temperature is lower than 21°C (70°F)! For rivers such as the Dennys, East Machias, Narraguagus, and Penobscot, the months of May and June normally provide the best angling opportunities, with from 80 to 86% of the annual catch occurring by June 30. Later in the season is usually more productive on the Machias, Sheepscot, and Ducktrap rivers, with 40 to 70% of the annual catch occurring *after* June 30 (Figure 26 and Table 12). When salmon are abundant in any given year, angling in September and October is also productive on all Maine rivers.

Exploitation in Maine Rivers: what percent of salmon runs do anglers catch?

Most Atlantic salmon anglers catch only a few salmon each year, which leads them to conclude that their endeavors are not detrimental to the future of the resource. Perhaps it is for this reason that anglers usually recommend limiting the catch of *others* (such as commercial fishermen, seals, cormorants, etc.). However, there is a wealth of information available which reveals that anglers can take 50% (or more) of a salmon run.

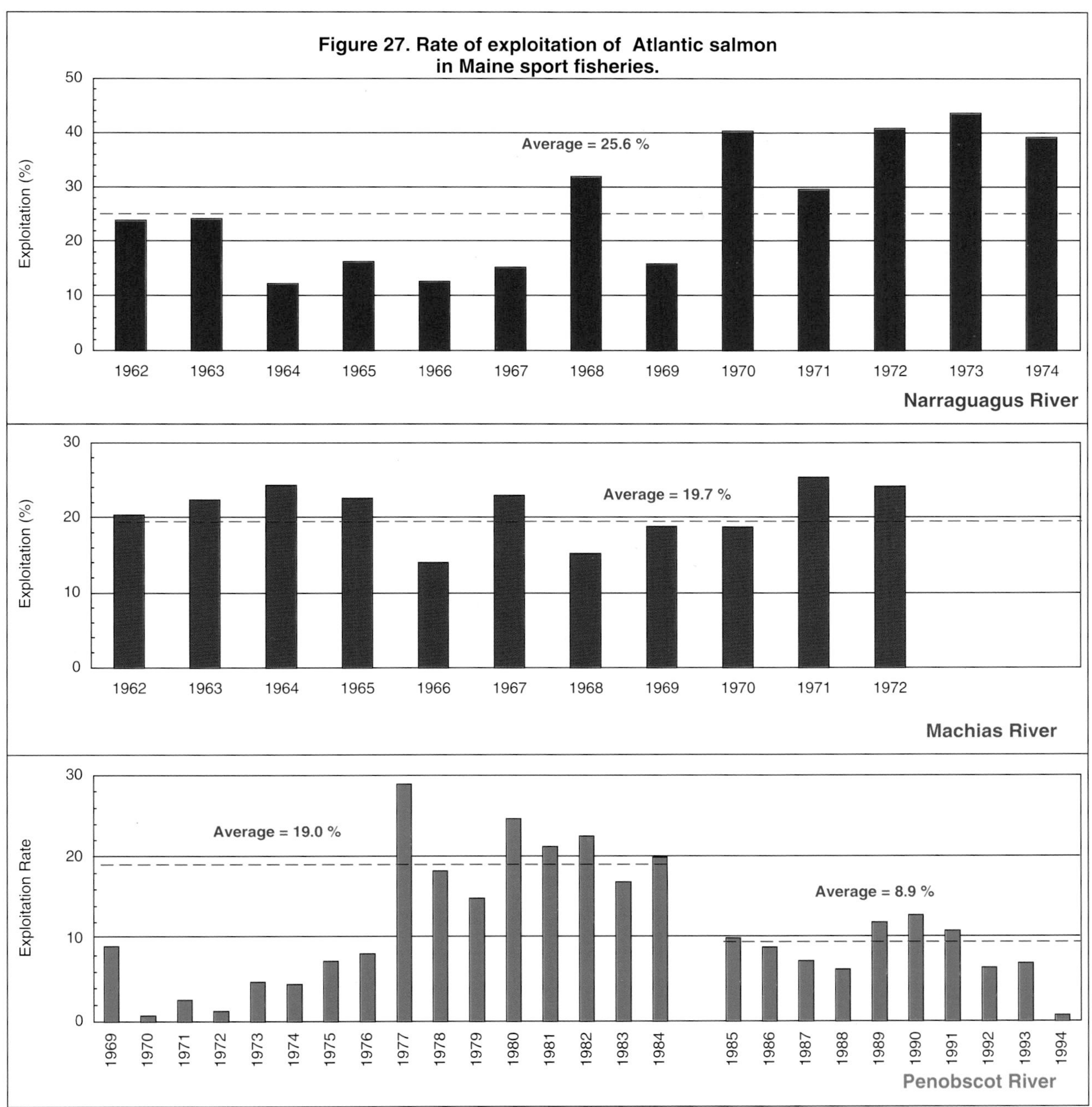

Figure 27. Rate of exploitation of Atlantic salmon in Maine sport fisheries.

Salmon-counting facilities on several rivers and creel census data have provided information on the rate of exploitation of Maine Atlantic salmon in sport fisheries. Overall, anglers are very proficient at catching Maine Atlantic salmon, with up to 43% of the run caught in sport fisheries (Figure 27). An average of more than 25% of the annual Narraguagus River salmon run was taken by anglers during the period 1962–1974, and 20% of Machias River salmon runs were taken from 1962 to 1972. On the Penobscot River, an average of 19% of the annual salmon run was taken before 1985. However, with the institution of highly restrictive sport fishing regulations in 1985, the catch was reduced by more than one-half. It should be noted that these are minimum estimates, since undoubtedly there were salmon caught but not reported to the Atlantic Sea Run Salmon Commission. These figures are comparable to those reported in many Canadian rivers, where, for example, annual exploitation rates of 35% for the Miramichi River are common. Havey and Warner (1985) reported similar exploitation rates (up to 41%) for landlocked salmon in Maine lakes.

All age groups of Maine Atlantic salmon are not exploited equally, however, with significant differences observed for various population age structure segments. Multi sea-winter salmon are often caught at twice the rate of one sea-winter salmon (grilse) because of their earlier entry into Maine rivers. Frequently, wild salmon are exploited to a greater extent than hatchery-origin salmon

Much of the sport fishing for salmon on the Penobscot River takes place from boats. Here, anglers fish above the Pipeline Pool from boats while anglers on shore fish the Wringer Pool. The Veazie Dam may be seen in the background.

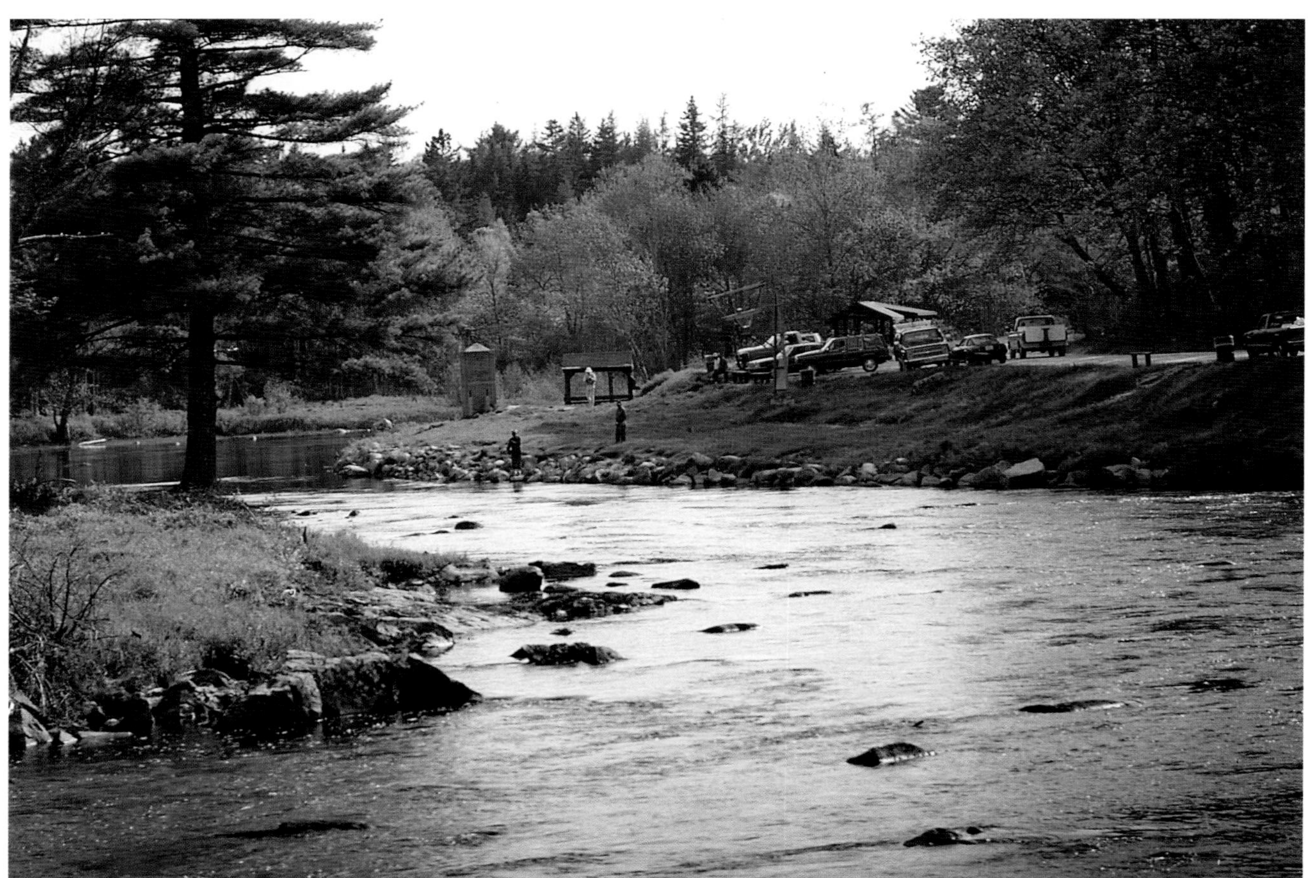

The Cable Pool on the Narraguagus River in Cherryfield is one of the most popular Atlantic salmon fishing sites in Maine.

Ai Ballou with a large salmon that he caught at the Reversing Falls Pool (background) of the Sheepscot River. There is only sufficient room for two anglers to fish this pool; therefore, anglers usually take turns fishing.

Anglers try their luck fishing Charlie's Rips on the Dennys River. The Dennys River Sportsman's Club building may be seen in the background.

The East Machias River is one of the smaller salmon rivers in eastern Maine. The small hydrodam that can be seen in the background was abandoned in the early 1970's.

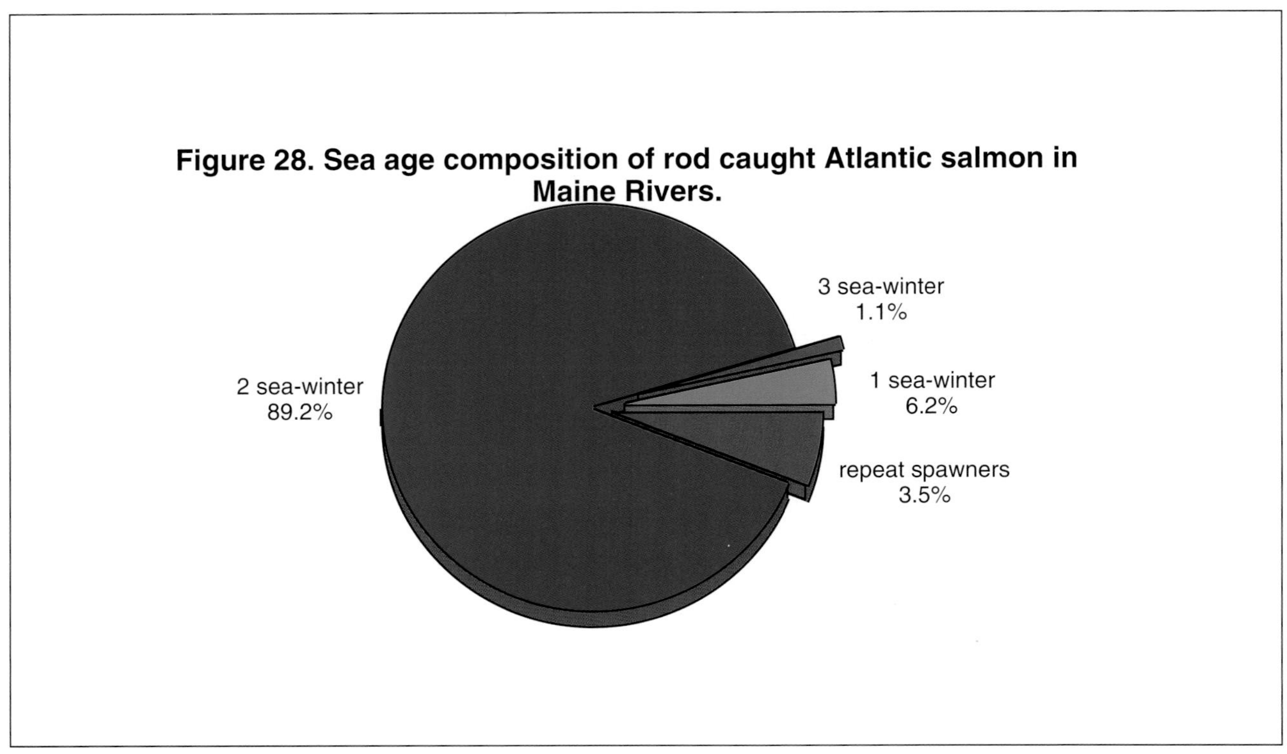

Figure 28. Sea age composition of rod caught Atlantic salmon in Maine Rivers.

(double the rate in Penobscot salmon) because of their earlier run timing which makes them more vulnerable to anglers. Salmon entering Maine rivers later in the season, when lower flows and higher water temperatures are not conducive to angling, are, therefore, less likely to be caught by Maine anglers. Additionally, angling effort for Maine Atlantic salmon typically declines after mid-July in most years, with most fishing activity concentrated in the first half of the season.

Size and Age Structure of Maine Rod-Caught Salmon

The sea-age distribution for Atlantic salmon caught by angling in the seven most productive rivers of Maine are shown in Table 13 (also see Figure 28). While the catch of 2SW salmon is similar for all rivers (86–96%), there are differences in other sea age classes. 1SW salmon (grilse) are more common in the East Machias, Pleasant, Sheepscot, and Penobscot rivers and repeat spawners more abundant in the Machias and Narraguagus rivers. Historically, repeat spawners have been 2 to 4 times more abundant than 3SW salmon in all but the Sheepscot River, where the trend was reversed. These differences are undoubtedly due to many factors, including the following:

Origin of catches: 1SW fish (grilse) are more numerous in hatchery-origin salmon, which have been more abundant in the East Machias, Sheepscot, and Penobscot Rivers in recent years.

Physical differences among rivers: salmon are less likely to survive to return as repeat spawners in a river with many dams (e.g., the Penobscot).

Run timing and angling traditions: there is increased angling effort late in the season in some rivers when 1SW salmon are more abundant.

Periods of record: in some rivers (Dennys, Machias, and Narraguagus), the highest rod catches occurred in the 1950's, 1960's, and 1970's, when 3SW salmon and repeat spawners were more abundant.

Local adaptations: because there is little interbreeding of the salmon stocks in Maine rivers, there may be a genetically based component to these differences.

The average size of Atlantic salmon caught in the sport fishery varies annually; however, detailed length and weight information collected from salmon that were carefully measured at fishway trapping facilities have produced the following approximate average sizes for Maine salmon:

Sea Age	*Length*		*Weight*	
	in.	*cm*	*lb*	*kg*
One sea-winter salmon	22	57	3.7	1.8
Two sea-winter salmon	29	75	9.8	4.5
Three sea-winter salmon	34	86	16.5	7.5
Repeat spawners	35	89	18.0	8.0

Epilogue on Salmon Angling

During my years of service dedicated to the restoration of salmon runs and fisheries in Maine,

The author tends the salmon trap at the Bangor dam fishway on the Penobscot River in this August 1974 photo. The Bangor Salmon Pool and Eastern Maine Medical Center may be seen in the background. In the lower photo (taken inside the trap on October 3, 1969), the author displays an 8-pound female salmon. Note the large, perfectly-shaped fins on the fish - it is undoubtedly a wild salmon!

it has not been uncommon for an ardent salmon angler (usually an "old timer") to chastise me occasionally because I "do not fish for Atlantic salmon." The theory is, how can a **** biologist (adjectives deleted) know anything about Atlantic salmon unless he fishes for them ("like I do," I suppose, is the inference).

In my youthful days, growing up in Western Maine, I fished constantly for anything and everything I could catch. Whether it was 15 brook trout per day from the Swift River, 984 yellow perch caught in one day at a fishing derby on Roxbury Pond, or 84 chain pickerel in one day (my personal best) from Joe Pond, I was a regular Huck Finn. I used everything from a cane pole to catch bullheads at night in Roxbury Pond to sophisticated fly-fishing gear to catch brawny landlocked salmon in the Kennebago River. As a youngster, I guess, I must have fished myself out.

During the 1970's, as a fishery scientist with the Atlantic Sea Run Salmon Commission, my close association with many of Maine's most successful Atlantic salmon anglers throughout the state gave me the "bug" to try fishing for the "King" of gamefish. Consequently, I eventually took up Atlantic salmon fishing with a little help and advice (and some free salmon flies!) from a few people who seemed to know what they were doing at the time. So I fished for Atlantic salmon on the Dennys, Machias, Narraguagus, Union, and Penobscot rivers.

On June 6, 1975, at about 6:30 A.M. I hooked my first salmon while fishing the famous Bangor Salmon Pool. Twenty minutes later I hand-tailed it all by myself—not because it was the macho thing to do, but because another angler (I think it was Charlie Caron) kept missing it with his tailer and I did NOT want to lose that fish! I laid the fish on the bank of the Penobscot River and marveled at its silvery beauty—it was exactly 30 1/2 inches in length and 10 pounds in weight. The only mark on the fish was a tiny, green Carlin tag (number USA-B 64,998) which I had undoubtedly helped to apply to the fish when it was tagged as an 8-inch smolt at the Enfield State Hatchery in November 1972. Three hours later I was tending the Atlantic Salmon Commission trap at the Bangor fishway, collecting biological data from and applying Carlin tags to five live salmon in preparation for taking them to Craig Brook National Fish Hatchery for broodstock purposes.

The contrast between catching and killing the salmon earlier that morning and taking several live ones to the hatchery a few hours later had a profound influence on me. I felt as if I had disgraced my profession—my goal in life was to bring Atlantic salmon back to Maine rivers, not to short-circuit their upstream migration before they had a chance to spawn. It was then that I realized that I could not be an Atlantic salmon fisherman. My association with the species had been too intimate. I fished for salmon a few more times after that, but my heart was just not in it. By the early 1980's I became an advocate of "catch and release" angling for Atlantic salmon—long before it was the popular thing to do—and have remained so ever since.

I have probably handled more than 15,000 live, adult Atlantic salmon during my career—when I handle them to collect biological information I can almost feel their hearts beating in my hands. Irrational? Ridiculous? Anthropomorphism? Perhaps, but every time I come across that little green Carlin tag in the top drawer of my desk at the office, I still feel pangs of guilt.

Mr. S. J. Martin reports to the US Fish Commission that a salmon weighing 21 1/4 pounds was taken in a trapnet at Kettle Island, on the Massachusetts coast, just south of Gloucester, on the 21st of May. The Bangor (Me.) Commercial *says: The king of all the salmon is on exhibition at A. E. Jones' market on Kenduskeag Bridge. The label attached to the fish says it was caught by R. French, Sandy Point. The weight is 46 pounds. Not even the oldest inhabitants can remember of so large a salmon being caught in the Penobscot.*

Forest and Stream, Vol. XXII, June 5, 1884.

Distant Water Commercial Fisheries

In October 1963, a Danish scientist reported the capture of a Narraguagus River salmon about 30 miles north of the Arctic Circle in the commercial fishery off the coast of West Greenland. The salmon had been tagged by Atlantic Sea Run Salmon Commission biologists at the Cherryfield trap on May 7, 1962. After it had spawned in the river that fall, it returned to sea in the spring of 1963 and migrated more than 2,150 miles to the Greenland waters where it was captured. While many fin-clipped Maine-origin salmon had previously been documented in the commercial fisheries off Nova Scotia (dating from 1951), this was the first direct evidence of the major oceanic migrations that Maine Atlantic salmon undertake. Who could have guessed then that 30 years and nearly 2,000 tag returns later Maine salmon would play a major role in the closure of the Greenland salmon fishery in 1993–1994!

Fisheries in Greenland

Although historical records show that commercial fishing for Atlantic salmon in Greenland began in the early 1900's (Kendall 1935; Møller Jensen 1986), it was not until the late 1950's that fishing for the species escalated. From a mere harvest of 13 tons in 1959 the West Greenland fishery rapidly expanded to a high of 2,689 tons in 1971. Before 1965, and after 1975, only Greenlandic vessels were allowed to participate in the fishery. During the 11-year period from 1965 to 1975, vessels from Denmark, Norway, Sweden, and the Faroe Islands also fished for salmon in the West Greenland area. It was at this time that monofilament nylon drift nets were introduced, thereby substantially increasing commercial fishermen's efficiency in taking salmon at sea. However, due to various political pressures, the West Greenland fishery has been managed under a quota system since 1972.

The first Atlantic salmon tagged outside Greenland (it had been tagged in Scotland) was captured in Greenland in 1956. Five years later, in 1961, the capture of a salmon originally tagged in Canada established the presence of salmon from North America. Since then, thousands of tagged Atlantic salmon have been taken in the Greenland fishery. Most (95%) of the North American salmon taken in Greenland originate in Canadian rivers, with the balance originating from United States (primarily Maine) rivers. While ten European countries are known to contribute salmon to the Greenland fishery, it appears that Scotland and Ireland are the main contributors.[22] Analysis of scale samples and other biological data collected from Atlantic salmon in West

22. Fishery scientists refer to the Greenland fishery as a "mixed-stock" fishery because many different salmon stocks are "mixed" together as they feed in the ocean.

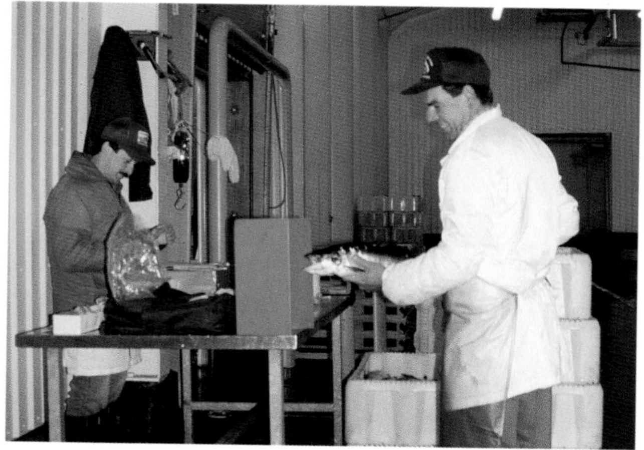

Left: A typical commercial fisherman heads out to set gillnets for Atlantic salmon in Nuuk, West Greenland. Contrary to popular opinion, commercial fishing for salmon at sea is carried out from small boats, not large factory ships. Right: The author scans a commercially-caught salmon for a coded-wire nose tag (CWT) at the fish processing plant in Nuuk, West Greenland, while colleague Peter Downton, from the Canadian Department of Fisheries and Oceans, records data. Between August 19 and September 2, 1989 Ed and Peter scanned 7,591 salmon and recovered 44 CWT's; 5 were from the Republic of Ireland, 1 from Scotland, 4 from England & Wales, 1 from Canada (Miramichi R.) , and 33 from the USA (8 Connecticut R., 8 Merrimack R., and 17 Penobscot R.).

Greenland during the last 20 years indicates that the overall proportion of North American and European salmon is about 50/50, although there is considerable annual variation. For example, the North American component has been as high as 75% in 1990 and as low as 34% in 1971 (data from ICES North Atlantic Salmon Working Group).

Any thorough discussion of the West Greenland fishery for Atlantic salmon would, by necessity, be very complex.[23] In addition to varying annual contributions of adult salmon by at least 12 different countries (not including Greenland itself, which also has one salmon-producing river), the catch at Greenland is also significantly affected by such things as international treaties and environmental conditions. For example, Møller Jensen (1986) attributed the low catches in West Greenland in 1983 and 1984 to cold winters in 1982–83 and 1983–84. Catches in those two years were only about one-third of the quotas established. Conversely, after a warmer-than-normal winter in 1984–85, the catch in 1985 (864 tons) seemed to be limited only by the quota (852 tons) that had been established. The recent low catches of salmon on a worldwide basis, and those in North America in particular, clearly show that the annual marine survival of smolts has a major impact upon the abundance of Atlantic salmon in the West Greenland area.

The distribution of 1,795 Carlin-tagged, Maine-origin Atlantic salmon reported from Greenland[24] is shown in Figure 29. The majority of tags (as many as 400 in one year) have come from the central portions of the coastline (Areas 1C and 1D), primarily because that is where most of the fishing villages and fish processing plants are located. Additionally, in some years adverse environmental conditions in Areas 1A and 1F limit the ability of Greenlanders to fish effectively or even at all. About 95% of the Maine-origin tag returns came from 1SW salmon destined to return to Maine rivers in the year following capture as a typical 8- to 10-pound maiden spawner. The remaining 5% of Maine salmon taken at West Greenland were 2SW salmon (3%) and post-kelts (2%) which would have returned to Maine a year later as 3SW salmon and repeat spawners, respectively. These fish would have returned to Maine as trophy-sized (15- to 25-pound) salmon. Of course, some of these fish would not have survived to return to Maine, since "natural" mortality at sea is currently estimated at 1% per month; therefore, about 88–90% would probably have survived to return to Maine rivers.

The 29 recoveries of tagged, Maine-origin salmon in East Greenland are unique. Unlike West Greenland, where the presence of salmon originating from 12 countries has been documented, salmon originating from only three countries (U.S.A.-Maine, Iceland, and Ireland) have been identified

23. For a thorough history and description of the West Greenland fishery for Atlantic salmon see: Netboy 1968, 1974; Møller Jensen 1986; Reddin and Shearer 1987; Reddin 1988; Buck 1993; Friedland et al. 1993; Friedland and Reddin 1993; Rago et al. 1993.

24. For areas where the exact location of capture could be determined.

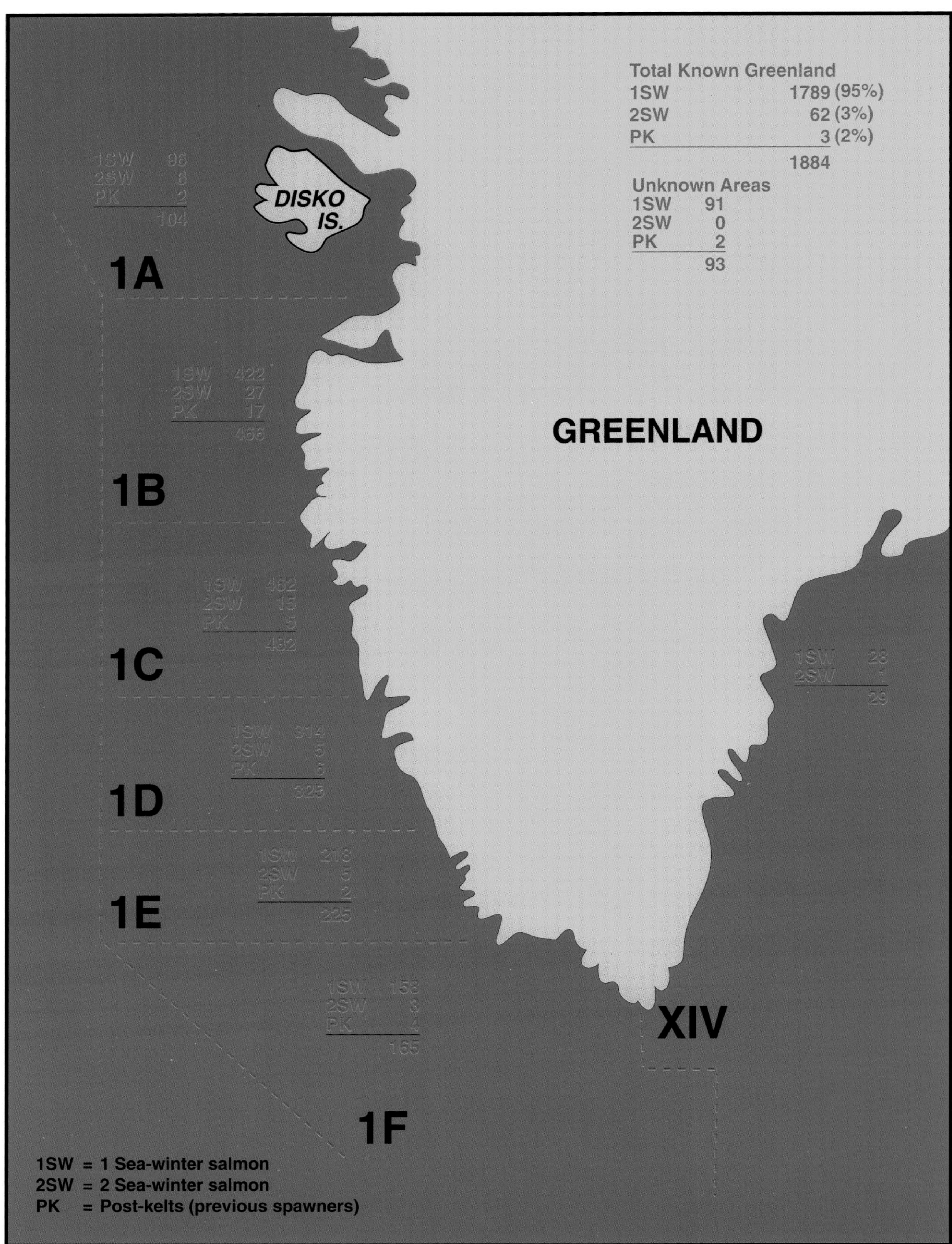

Figure 29. Distribution of Carlin tag returns from Maine-origin Atlantic salmon captured in Greenland, by life stage and NAFO* Division.
***North Atlantic Fisheries Organiation**

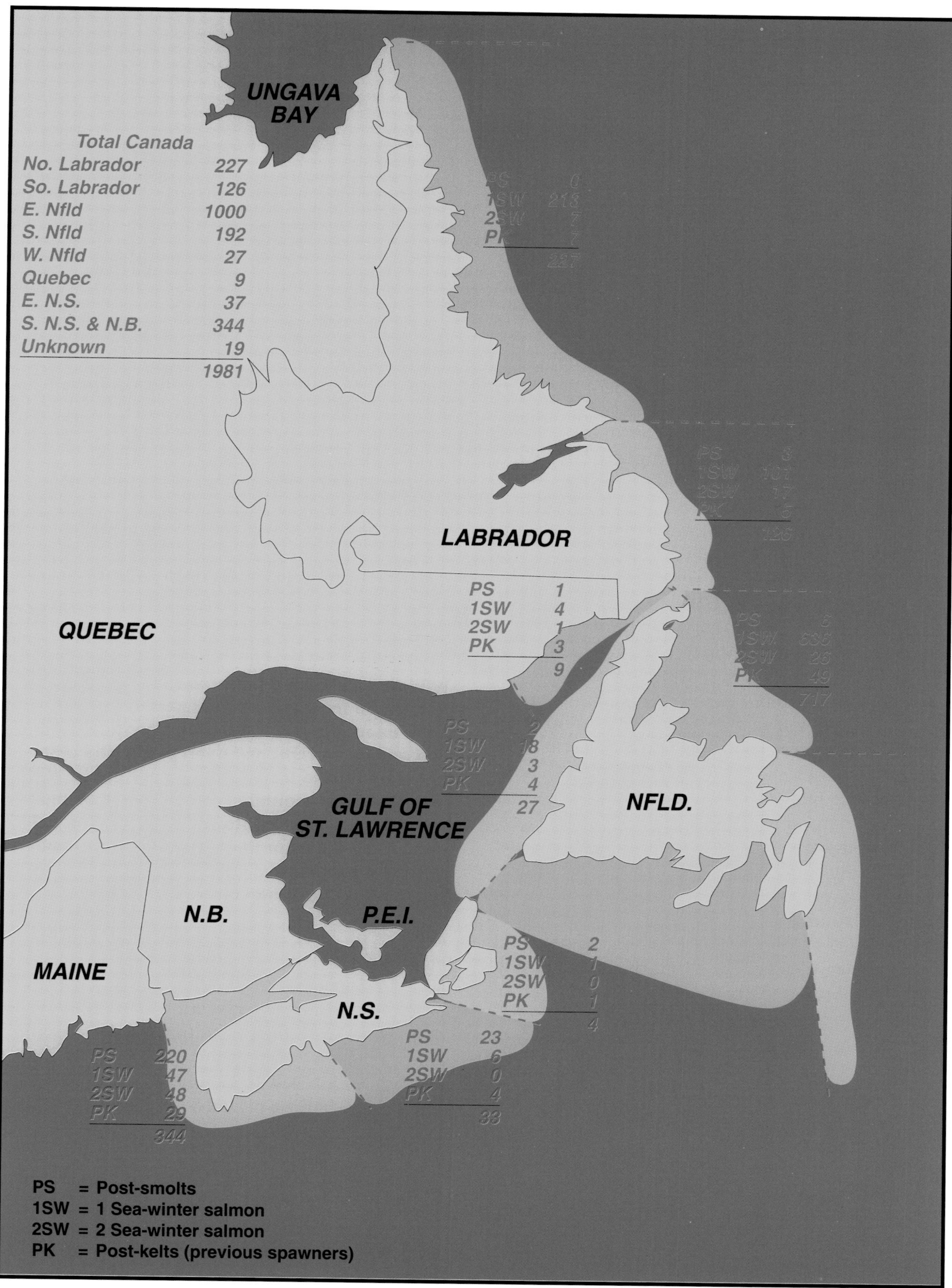

Figure 30. Distribution of Carlin tag returns from Maine-origin Atlantic salmon captured in Canada, by life stage and area.

in East Greenland. The fishery for salmon in East Greenland takes place sporadically, with little or no harvest in some years due to extreme ice conditions. Exploratory (research) fishing for salmon in the mid-1980's did, however, show that salmon are abundant in East Greenland when the salmon's preferred sea temperatures (4-8°C) occur in the area. It is approximately 2,750 miles from Maine to the area in East Greenland where these salmon have been taken!

As evidenced by the cursory tag-return information presented above, Maine salmon are in West Greenland waters from July to November. Although one tagged salmon was captured in June, most have been caught in August and September (49% and 35%, respectively) followed by the months of October (9%), July (5%), and November (2%). The small number of Maine salmon taken in East Greenland waters were captured in August (24%), September (52%) and October (24%).

Fishery scientists who are members of the ICES[25] North Atlantic Salmon Working Group (NASWG) have recently developed a run reconstruction model used to estimate the harvest of Maine-origin salmon at West Greenland. The model, which is based upon the ratio of Carlin-tagged to untagged salmon returning to Maine rivers annually, is used to raise the known tag returns collected in the fishery the previous year to a total estimated harvest in the fishery. The model includes adjustments for tag reporting rates (in commercial fisheries and Maine sport fisheries), non-catch fishing mortality (i.e., fish escaping nets that die later), natural mortality at sea, Carlin tag loss, and fish passage efficiencies at fishways in Maine rivers. Using this model, an average of 1,534 Maine salmon was estimated to have been taken at West Greenland annually, with a range of 216 salmon in 1967 to 3,797 in 1989. The Carlin tagging program in Maine was phased out in 1992 due to increasing costs of applying the tags, decreasing survival of tagged smolts, increasing emphasis upon coded-wire tagging programs, and changing fisheries and sampling programs. However, the Carlin tagging of smolts was reinstated in 1996 and is expected to continue occasionally.

The ICES-NASWG developed an alternative mathematical model to estimate the number of Maine-origin salmon harvested in West Greenland based upon the releases of one-year hatchery-origin salmon in Maine. Termed the proportional harvest method, this model produced an estimated average of 7,524 Maine-origin salmon harvested at West Greenland, ranging from 1,950 in 1992 to 30,492 in 1980. Although this model tended to overestimate the number of salmon taken, it did produce similar trends as the first model described above.

25. ICES is an acronym for the International Council for the Exploration of the Sea, with headquarters in Copenhagen, Denmark.

William and Robert Anderson are commercial fishermen from Makkovik, Labrador. These men have used gillnets to fish for Atlantic salmon, cod and other fish, and even seals (the last being under the ice!). In the upper photo William holds a 10-pound and a 23-pound salmon, while in the lower photo Robert removes a 4-pound salmon from the net. Most of the salmon taken by commercial fishermen in Labrador are produced in Canadian rivers.

The ICES-NASWG developed a third model to estimate the harvest of *all* 1SW U.S. Atlantic salmon (i.e., Maine rivers, Merrimack River and Connecticut River) based upon coded wire tags (CWT's) recovered in the Greenland fishery and the number of CWT's recovered in USA rivers. Since CWT's were not universally used in New England until the mid-1980's, and recovery programs in Greenland were not initiated until 1987, harvest estimates can only be made for the period 1987–1992. Estimates using this method, considered by fishery scientists to be the most accurate, averaged 2,896 Maine salmon annually, ranging from 1,319 in 1992 to 5,571 in 1987.

A complete summary of the estimated harvest of Maine-origin salmon by all three methods is presented in Table 14.

Fisheries in Canada

Recoveries of Maine tagged salmon have occurred through a well-established tag return network in the North Atlantic. Historically, most Canadian commercial fishermen typically returned tags directly to the Maine Atlantic Sea Run Salmon Commission in exchange for a reward of up to $8.00. Additionally, Canadian fishery officers often obtained tags directly from fishermen or employees of fish processing plants, and the tags were returned to Maine via the federal Department of Fisheries and Oceans. The distribution of tag returns from the North Atlantic by sea-age of the fish and by area of capture are shown in Table 15. Most Maine salmon captured in Canada were taken in Eastern Newfoundland and in Labrador, with smaller numbers taken in Nova Scotia and New Brunswick[26] (Figure 30).

Only 215 tagged Maine salmon were recovered in the coastal waters of New Brunswick and Nova Scotia in the Bay of Fundy area, and most (60%) of those were post-smolts. It appears that post-smolts from Maine that enter the Bay of Fundy are probably lost. Indeed, several lots of tagged fish released in Maine that were subsequently captured in this area produced few, if any, subsequent adult returns back to Maine. Most of the Maine salmon recovered in Nova Scotia were taken along the coast from Yarmouth to Halifax, although small numbers of returns were also reported from the Cape Breton Island area.

By far, the greatest number of tagged, Maine-origin salmon have been captured in the commercial fisheries of Newfoundland-Labrador. More than 1,200 tags were recovered from insular Newfoundland, and an additional 361 tags from Labrador. A few Maine salmon apparently migrate through the Straight of Belle Isle as evidenced by the seven tags returned from commercial fisheries in Quebec (fishery area Q9) and southwestern Labrador (Fishery Area 14b, see Figure 29). While Maine salmon have been captured by commercial fishermen throughout the coast of Labrador, the majority (about two of every three) have come from the northern half of the coastline.

The reader should bear in mind that the number of tag returns from any given area does not necessarily reflect the abundance of Maine salmon in those areas. Recoveries of Maine salmon in distant water fisheries depend upon the number of tagged fish at large, the commercial fishing effort, fishing regulations that are in effect, and tag reporting rates. Reporting rates from Canada (and

CARIBOU, MAINE. On Saturday, June 28, editor A. Hall, of the Aroostook Republican of this place caught an eight pound salmon in the pool just below the Caribou Dam, on the Aroostook River. This is the first one caught this season. Took three hours to land him, having only a six-ounce bamboo rod, and using a five cent brown hackle fly."

THE AMERICAN ANGLER, VOL. XVIII, JULY 5, 1890.

A big fish leaped out of the water, striking him and knocking him over backwards. The salmon, which weighed at least 25 pounds, fell into the boat, then jumped out again. In the rumpus, Mr. Peavey broke his fine salmon rod!

ARTICLE IN *MAINE SPORTSMAN*, VOLUME 1, NO. 12, TITLED "A UNIQUE ADVENTURE," ABOUT LEGENDARY PENOBSCOT RIVER SALMON ANGLER, J. HENRY PEAVEY ON MAY 28, 1894.

26. The Canadian government banned commercial fishing for Atlantic salmon in New Brunswick and Nova Scotia in 1984, and significant reductions were made in the salmon fishing season throughout the 1980's in Newfoundland-Labrador. A commercial salmon fishing license buy-out program occurred in the 1980's and 1990's and a complete moratorium on salmon fishing was in effect around the island of Newfoundland from 1992 to 1996.

elsewhere) are extremely variable and are estimated to range from 50 to 90%.

Other Fisheries

Not all Maine Atlantic salmon migrate to either Greenland, Newfoundland, or Labrador. A complete summary of the distribution of more than 7,700 Carlin-tag returns from releases of Maine-origin salmon is presented in Appendix 3. The Maine Atlantic Authority (formerly the Atlantic Sea Run Salmon Commission) has received tag returns from Barregat, New Jersey (one tagged salmon captured on April 18, 1982), to the Faroe Islands (one Carlin and one coded-wire tag recovered in December 1988). The most unusual Carlin-tag returns were submitted to the Atlantic Sea Run Salmon Commission from the State of South Dakota—now *that* was quite a migration for Maine Atlantic salmon![27]

27. "And now, for the rest of the story." Unused Carlin tags from the salmon tagging program in Maine were sent to State of North Dakota biologists who applied them to trout that were released in a trout pond. Anglers catching the trout sent the tags back to Maine for the "reward," as directed by the legend on the tag!

4

Maine Atlantic Salmon Restoration Efforts

4 Maine Atlantic Salmon Restoration Efforts

In The Beginning: The New England Regional Commission, 1865

The Civil War delayed progress in the newly discovered art of fish culture in the United States; however, the return of peace stimulated interest in the subject in the northeastern states. By the mid-1850's Atlantic salmon had been virtually extirpated in many rivers outside Maine, and the demise of many anadromous fish stocks was cause for great concern throughout New England. In 1864, the State of New Hampshire founded the first state fish commission in the U.S., proposed a regional Interstate Commission for restoring and improving anadromous fish runs in New England rivers, and invited neighboring states to participate. In 1865 Massachusetts and Vermont formed their own state fish commissions and joined the Regional Commission, followed in 1866 by Maine, Rhode Island, New York, New Jersey, and, interestingly enough, Michigan.

> *Man's hand is against the salmon, either directly or indirectly. Its extraordinary life cycle makes it uniquely vulnerable to human interference and depredation. The nets of the commercial fisherman and the rod of the angler are but two of the hazards it has to face in its journey up rivers that, throughout the world, have become increasingly polluted, dammed or diverted for human purposes.*
>
> (Netboy 1980)

In 1866 the Regional Commission imported 70,000 salmon eggs from the Miramichi River in New Brunswick, Canada,[28] most of which were planted (as eggs) in the Pemigewasset River and another small, spring-fed tributary to the Merrimack River in Concord, New Hampshire. This small effort was the beginning of a salmon restoration program on the Merrimack River that spanned three decades before it was abandoned because of the lack of adequate fish passage facilities (Stolte 1981).

Dr. Fletcher obtained another 70,000 eggs from the Miramichi River in 1867. These were incubated at two sites in New Hampshire and were destined to be stocked in the Connecticut and Merrimack Rivers. Survival was poor, however, with only 5,000 surviving to hatch—all of which were stocked in the Merrimack drainage.

In 1868, with assistance from the Canadian government, the states of New Hampshire and Massachusetts established a private hatchery 8 miles above Newcastle, New Brunswick, on the Northwest Branch of the Miramichi River with Livingston Stone as superintendent.[29] Although nearly 444,000 eggs were collected that year, only about 32,000 survived to be stocked in the Merrimack River. Hatchery operations were discontinued after 1869 when only 50,000 eggs were sold to the State of Vermont; about 30,000 salmon survived to be stocked in the headwaters of the Connecticut River system. A stable egg supply was desperately needed if the Regional Commission's fledgling salmon restoration efforts were to continue.

There was a strong sentiment throughout the United States for the federal government to halt the decline of fisheries and to coordinate restora-

28. The Commission sent Dr. William Fletcher, a Concord dentist, to Canada to obtain permission from the Province of New Brunswick to collect these eggs.

29. Mr. Stone later went on to become superintendent of federal salmon hatcheries in California and Oregon.

tion efforts among the states. Although most states created their own fish commissions, it was not until 1871 that the federal government became actively involved. On February 9, 1871, the U.S. Congress passed a law that established the United States Commission of Fish and Fisheries. The Commission's first order of business was to "determine whether any and what diminution in the numbers of food-fishes of the coast and the lakes of the United States has taken place" (Wood 1953). After two years of investigations, the Commission, led by Spencer F. Baird, its first commissioner, reported on the extent and causes of the decrease in marine fisheries. In 1872, the U.S. Congress expanded the duties of the Fish Commission to include the propagation of fish. Attempts were made to transfer many Pacific coast species to the East Coast and Atlantic coast species to the West Coast. During this period many European species, including carp and brown trout, were also introduced throughout the country. While there were some successes, most introductions were failures. Shad and striped bass were successfully introduced into California. In the 1880's Pacific salmon fry were stocked into every river south of the Hudson (Wood 1953); however, these latter efforts were unsuccessful in establishing any viable populations. In an attempt to improve the success of subsequent stocking programs the U.S. Fish Commission altered its policy from one of stocking small numbers of fish in many streams to one of stocking large numbers of fish in a few streams. Attempts to introduce Pacific salmonids into many major rivers in the Northeastern United States continued into the mid 1920's. Although adults returned and spawned occasionally (for example, up to 2,000 pink salmon returned to the Dennys River at one time), all of the attempts to introduce Pacific salmon into Maine waters ultimately failed.

Initial Maine Salmon Restoration Efforts: The Atkins Era, 1870–1920

Although Maine's initial entry into the anadromous fish restoration "business" was via the Regional Commission in 1866, the declining fish stocks in the major rivers of the state had been a topic of concern for the first half of the nineteenth century. Historical accounts of attempts to halt the decline of Atlantic salmon runs were usually presented in negative tones. Most accounts typically expounded upon the construction of numerous and often formidable dams, water pollution, and commercial fishing that led to declining salmon runs and fisheries for them. As early as 1818, the citizens of Bangor appointed a committee to advise the state legislature regarding regulating the weirs and commercial fisheries on the Penobscot River (Ford 1882).

The Maine legislature passed a resolution in 1867 authorizing the appointment of two fisheries commissioners whose duties were to examine Maine rivers "for the consideration of the restoration of sea fish, the introduction of new varieties of freshwater fish, and the protection of fish generally in our inland water" (Kendall 1936). As a result, the first fish commission for Maine, one of four in the entire country, was established, and the first two commissioners of fisheries, Charles G. Atkins and Nathan W. Foster, were appointed.

The commissioners' first report (January 16, 1868) stated, "The salmon is suffering from neglect and persecution. So peculiarly is it exposed to the attacks of man, so greedy and relentless has been the pursuit, and so regardless of their necessities has been the management of the waters, that in many rivers, both in Europe and America, it has become utterly extinct, and in very few of the remainder does it yield anything like the number that it was won't." The two men attributed the depletion of fish populations in many of Maine's streams and lakes to impassable dams, overfishing, and pollution (with the first and second as the principal causes). Regarding Atlantic salmon, Commissioner Atkins stated that the "ancient brood of salmon was long ago extinguished by dams that held the salmon in check, while the fishermen caught them out." Atkins' summary of nets and weirs in the Penobscot River characterizes the typical gauntlet faced by returning Atlantic salmon in 1880: 172 weirs, 65 fish traps or pound nets, and 36 gillnets that were either set or drifted in the river. The total reported take of anadromous fish from this gear was 10,106 salmon, 800 shad, 730,000 alewives, and 266,875 pounds of smelt.

In their first report, the commissioners also discussed the protection of freshwater fish and their artificial culture. The report continued with a recommendation that restoration of sea fish to Maine's four large river systems (the Androscoggin, Kennebec, Penobscot, and St. Croix) be undertaken, and it suggested restrictions and limitations to fisheries for salmon, shad, and alewives. Regarding existing fishery laws, the commissioners wrote that "they are founded on no common system and the officers to enforce them are without organization and generally without efficiency." Besides proposing the need for better laws, Commissioners Atkins and Foster noted that the most important work to be accomplished was the construction of fishways.

Commissioner Atkins possessed a great interest in the new field of fish rearing, and, in 1867, made his first attempt at artificial propagation by collecting several thousand landlocked salmon eggs at Sebago Lake in southern Maine. The eggs were successfully collected and transferred to a private hatchery 6 miles from Augusta; unfortunately, only *one* egg hatched! In the fall of 1868, a successful attempt to obtain landlocked salmon eggs occurred at Grand Lake Stream in eastern Maine, when broodfish were collected by angling and from Indians capturing salmon with spears.[30] Earlier that year Commissioner Atkins had also collected 100,000 eggs from commercially caught shad in the Kennebec River at Augusta, hatched them in boxes in the river, and liberated those that survived.

In 1869, the Maine legislature passed an act regulating river and interior fisheries. The act also provided for the appointment of one person to be the commissioner of fisheries. Charles Atkins was appointed to the position, and his first report described attempts to provide for the construction of fishways, introduction of smallmouth bass, and stocking of landlocked salmon with eggs obtained from broodfish collected at Schoodic Lake, which is in the Penobscot River drainage.

In 1870, Atkins purchased 8,000 Atlantic salmon eggs from the Canadian government in Ontario at a cost of $44.80 in gold per 1,000. These eggs were reared at a private hatchery in Alna, Maine, for one year; and about 1,500 fingerlings were stocked into the Sheepscot River in 1871. Finding the cost of imported Atlantic salmon eggs from Canada too high, Atkins decided to establish a hatchery and obtain his own eggs. Atkins initially considered obtaining eggs by collecting adult salmon in the upper waters of the Penobscot drainage; however, he concluded that: (1) how many salmon could be caught on the spawning grounds was questionable, though obtaining a large number of salmon from weir owners was fairly certain; (2) the hatchery should be within easy reach of the railroad and steamboat access, as opposed to the spawning grounds that were "in the wilderness"; and (3) he did not want "the spawn which was taken away to detract from anything from the natural increase of the species in the river, since one should use for parent fish only those that would have otherwise gone to markets, and the accustomed number of adult fish would still be left to deposit their eggs without molestation."

Atkins then conceived and pursued a plan to breed Atlantic salmon captured from the lower Penobscot River. He decided to purchase live fish from Penobscot River weir fishermen in the vicinity of Wetmore (Verona) Island and transport them to a freshwater holding site in Orland using boats with holes in the bottom (locally known as salmon cars). The hatchery that Atkins established in 1871 was in an existing mill on Craig's Pond Brook (now called Craig Brook) and was funded by the states of Maine, Massachusetts, and Connecticut.[31]

From the first 111 salmon purchased in June and July 1871, only 18 survived to provide 70,500 viable eggs. There were many reasons for the high mortality rate. For example, the first group of 12 salmon purchased died in the transportation boat because too few holes had been drilled in it, and the exchange of fresh oxygenated water was inadequate. Many salmon also died in the area where they were being held (in an enclosure in Dead Brook), causing Atkins to transfer nine of them to Craig's Pond[32] because he thought that they, too, might perish.

The first supply of eggs (70,500) was distributed among Maine, Massachusetts, and Connecticut (21,750 each, with 5,250 sent to a "Wm. Clift"). The Maine eggs were sent to a private state hatchery operated by "Messrs. Crockett and Holmes" in Norway, where the resulting fry were stocked into a tributary to the Androscoggin River. Although the cost of obtaining this first group of eggs was relatively high at $18.09 per thousand, Atkins learned how to transport and maintain adult Atlantic salmon broodstock successfully for subsequent operations.

This may have been the first time in history that adult Atlantic salmon were captured in saltwater and successfully transferred directly to freshwater where they were held for up to five months before artificial spawning. Atkins was also the first person to publish (1871 Commissioner's Report to the Governor) in minute detail the "dry" method of spawning Atlantic salmon. He borrowed this technique from "a Russian gentleman named Mr. Vrasski" (published in 1856) and modified it, noting that "the secret of success in fecundation is in keeping water away." This was a very radical idea

30. Since the commissioner of fisheries for Massachusetts shared the expenses involved in this experiment, a portion of the eggs were shipped to Massachusetts in boxes packed with wet sphagnum moss.

31. The other NE states contributed to this effort in exchange for a share of the eggs taken each year.

32. They were observed later that fall to have spawned in the lake within a dozen rods of the outlet on a gravel-bottomed area in 2 to 3 feet of water.

at the time, since "it was supposed that since fishes lay their eggs in water, such an important process in their economy as fecundation could not safely be performed out of water."

Atkins ended his term as Maine fisheries commissioner in 1871 and began his work for the United States Fish Commission in 1872. U.S. Fish Commissioner Spencer Baird, representing the federal government, joined with the states of Maine, Massachusetts, and Connecticut to enlarge Atkins' operations at Craig Brook. The enlarged operation was moved initially to Spofford's Pond[33] in Bucksport. There the salmon purchased for broodstock were transferred from boats and taken overland by horses pulling 90-gallon wooden tanks specifically built for that purpose. This method was also successfully used in the upper Merrimack River in the 1880's. Continuing his salmon experiments at Bucksport in 1872, Atkins purchased 692 salmon from commercial fishermen in the lower Penobscot River, and that fall he collected 1,566,044 eggs. By 1874, when more than 3 million eggs were obtained from 389 female Penobscot River salmon, Atkins had reduced the cost from $44.80 to $2.00 for each 1,000 eggs taken.

Atkins collected more than 9 million Penobscot River Atlantic salmon eggs between 1871 and 1875. Most were shipped to the five other New England states, with the balance going to New York, New Jersey, Pennsylvania, Ohio, Maryland, Michigan, Minnesota, Illinois, Wisconsin, and Iowa. Because some of these states participated in funding the Craig Brook hatchery operations, they were entitled to a share of the eggs obtained each year. In subsequent years, Penobscot River Atlantic salmon eggs were even shipped as far south as Ecuador, and one shipment was made across the Atlantic to England.

> *On the Dennys River we have only to remark that if they would display the same energy in the destruction of the Canadian thistle and Colorado beetle that they have annihilating the salmon, and thus depriving themselves of an important local interest, they would render their town and the state a distinguished service.*
>
> EXCERPT FROM THE *1880 REPORT OF THE COMMISSIONERS OF FISHERIES AND GAME FOR THE STATE OF MAINE.*

The purchase of Atlantic salmon was discontinued in 1876 until the results of the first five years of operations could be evaluated by the U.S. Fish Commission. Although the Bucksport hatchery was closed between 1876 and 1878, Atkins continued his experiments with landlocked salmon and other species of fish throughout the state. He also devoted much of his time to the introduction of black bass to various Maine waters.

In 1877 scattered reports of adult Atlantic salmon returns were noted in the Connecticut and Merrimack rivers. Considerable numbers of salmon were especially noted at the Lowell dam, causing the Massachusetts and New Hampshire commissioners to proclaim support for the Craig Brook Hatchery and to request that hatchery operations be resumed to help rebuild the Merrimack River salmon run.

U.S. Fish Commissioner Spencer Baird reported in 1879 that the introduction of Penobscot salmon into rivers as far south as Pennsylvania and Delaware was a success and that there had also apparently been an increase in salmon abundance in the Penobscot River. Consequently, salmon operations were resumed at Bucksport under the direction of Superintendent Atkins. The previously used salmon holding site in Bucksport (Spofford's Pond) was abandoned in favor of the original Dead Brook site in Orland, because the eggs could be incubated at the nearby Craig Brook Hatchery.

The first year of resumed activity at the hatchery was a disaster for Atkins and his crew; 205 of the 264 salmon purchased died before the fish could be spawned. They achieved satisfactory results later, however, as the methods used to collect, transport, and hold salmon were modified and improved each year. Between 1879 and 1886 more than 3,700 Penobscot River broodstock were purchased from commercial fishermen and 15 million salmon eggs were collected.

Craig Brook Hatchery, with funding from the New England states and the U.S. Fish Commission, was primarily used as an egg collection and distri-

33. In the early years of operation, Atkins experimented with various adult salmon holding facilities including a holding pond in Craig's Brook, an enclosure in Alamoosook Lake at the mouth of Craig's Brook, an enclosure in Dead Brook (part of the Orland River system), and Spofford's Pond in the town of Bucksport.

Collecting Sal

"The method of collection was as follows: The fishermen agreeing to furnish to prevent chafing of the fish; a car was stationed in every neighborhood, and eac brought alongside for the direct receipt of captured fish was provided with a large became low enough to leave the fish stranded on the floor of the box, the salmon a tour of the district, taking in tow the cars containing salmon and leaving empty before high water. A dam and lock at this point making it impossible for the steam miles farther to Dead Brook, where the fish were released in an enclosure of abou having an extreme depth of about 6 feet.

During the season persistent efforts were made to keep the temperature d arranging their interiors so that the water, admitted in a greatly reduced volume, s this method it was necessary to have a separate boat containing a considerable q

on, circa. 1895

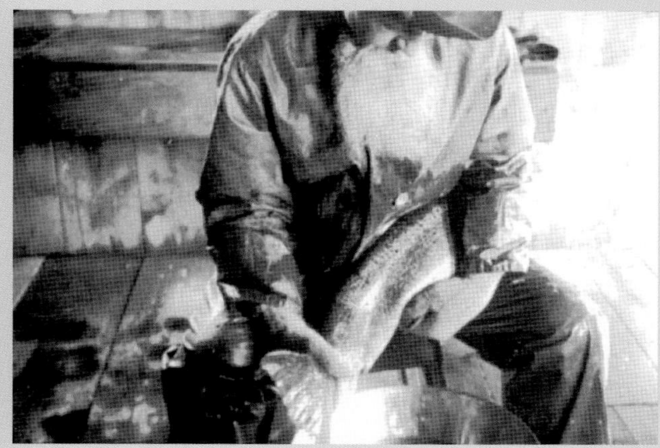

***mon were supplied in advance with large, fine-meshed dip nets, lined with flannel
nan whose weirs were so far from the moorings of the car as to forbid their being
vhich to transport them short distances. As low water approached and before it
efully dipped out and placed in the cars. Once a day the collecting steamer made
neir places. The cars were then towed as far as Orland, arriving there a short time
end farther, the cars were here taken in tow by oarsmen and carried on nearly 2
of a mile up and down a sluggish stream, averaging 3 or 4 yards in width and***

***e cars by means of ice, and positively favorable results were at last attained by
ss through a cooling compartment before reaching the fish. In the application of
f ice to accompany the fleet."***

Excerpts from the 1895 Report of the U.S. Commissioner of Fish and Fisheries.

bution facility. Most often, a large portion of the Atlantic salmon eggs obtained were shipped to private hatcheries and other government facilities throughout the country. For example, Mr. Benjamin Lincoln of Dennysville obtained 20,000 to 40,000 eggs on seven occasions between 1874 and 1890 for fry stocking efforts in the Dennys River. Other private hatchery facilities hatched and stocked salmon fry from locations in Enfield, Dixfield, Rangeley, Machias, Mt. Kineo, Norway, Weld, Caribou, Monson, and Auburn. While some of these facilities stocked salmon fry into Maine rivers that flowed to sea, many of them were used extensively to stock Maine's interior lakes and streams, including Sebago, Moosehead, and the Rangeley lakes.

In 1887 Commissioner Baird assigned Atkins to work for one year at the marine fish hatchery at Woods Hole, Massachusetts. Atkins went there to apply his knowledge of artificial salmon culture to the hatching of cod, flounder, and lobster. During Atkins's absence from the State of Maine, Mr. E. O. Buck was placed in charge of the Craig Brook Hatchery.

During the 1890's and early 1900's, Atkins expanded his fish cultural research to include landlocked salmon, Swiss lake trout, and various strains of European brown trout (Scottish sea trout, Von Behr trout or Loch Leven trout, depending upon where they originated). In addition to being the superintendent at the Craig Brook Hatchery, he was also often placed in charge of several other hatcheries operated jointly by the New England states and the U.S. Fish Commission (for example, the Schoodic and Grand Lake Stream stations). Atkins also experimented with the rearing of all five species of Pacific salmon, as well as steelhead (anadromous rainbow trout), rainbow trout, brook trout, and grayling. During his illustrious career, he also experimented in the rearing and stocking of smelt, shad, white perch, and striped bass in Maine waters. In all, more than 21 species were reared at Craig Brook Hatchery (and other sites) under the direction of Superintendent Charles Atkins.

The United States Fish Commission is making an experiment of planting large numbers of nonindigenous salmon in the Penobscot Basin and other Maine waters with a view to test whether the fishes are adapted to those streams. The species with which trials thus far have been made are the quinnat or chinook salmon (Onchorynchus tschawytscha) *and the steelhead trout* (Salmo gairdneri). *It is intended to plant sufficiently large numbers of yearling fish to fully test the feasibility of the project; and in the event of success two extremely valuable species will have been added to the fishery resources of the Maine streams.*

(Smith 1896)

Operation of the Craig Brook hatchery was funded jointly by the states and the U.S. Fish and Fisheries Commission through 1888. That year Congress changed the name of the U.S. Fish and Fisheries Commission to the U.S. Fish Commission. The federal government also leased, with the option to purchase, the farm enclosing both banks of Craig Brook to establish "a permanent station for the propagation of Salmon-idae, especially the Atlantic salmon" (Kendall 1936). The property (134.68 acres) was purchased on September 4, 1889, for $2,000 from Mr. Thomas Partridge, and by June of the following year several buildings and much needed new hatchery equipment had been installed. Improvements to the roads and grounds at the site were also made during this time. One of the new buildings constructed was a 24- x 50-foot "fly house" which was used to produce large quantities of maggots that served as live food for the small salmon. Tending the maggot house was the job usually given to new hatchery employees or to an employee who was not looked upon favorably by the hatchery manager.

Because of Charles Atkins's first 20 years of pioneering work in the field of fish culture, the first United States federal hatchery for the propagation of Atlantic salmon was officially established on the shore of Alamoosook Lake at the mouth of Craig Brook.

The first rearing tanks for overwintering of salmon were constructed in the cellar of a shed on the property at Craig Brook in 1890, and, by fall nineteen 15- x 50-foot ponds were constructed on the south slope of the property. The release of fingerling salmon was initiated in 1890 in an attempt to increase the survival of those fish stocked. Additionally, less emphasis was placed at this time upon the collection and distribution of eggs and fry to other private and governmental facilities. For the next ten years, Atkins continued to purchase broodstock and collect the eggs each fall and to transport the salmon fry to nearby localities in the Penobscot drainage in the spring. Stocking in the Penobscot River drainage was necessarily limited to those areas that were accessible by train or horse and wagon.

Charles Atkins believed that distributing salmon fry on natural spawning beds in headwater areas might provide better results than simply stocking locally accessible areas. Consequently, in the winter of 1903–1904 he established a small hatchery at Little Spring Brook on the East Branch of the Penobscot River—some 125 miles from Craig Brook Hatchery.[34] For the next twelve years (until 1916) salmon eggs were transferred each winter from Craig Brook Hatchery to the Little Spring Brook Hatchery, and fry were stocked in many headwater areas of the Penobscot drainage that had been inaccessible in prior years when all stocking had originated from the Craig Brook facility.

In 1903 the U.S. Fish Commission was again renamed, this time as the U.S. Bureau of Fisheries, and in 1914 the Bureau appointed Charles Atkins to the position of "fish culturist at large." He served in that position until his retirement six years later. Notably, only fragmentary records of his activities at Craig Brook Hatchery are available after 1914, and it is probably not coincidental that the Little Spring Brook Hatchery ceased operations after the 1915 season.

During the fall of 1921, 445,000 eggs were secured from wild humpback salmon taken from Dennys River, at Dennysville, Me. These were incubated at the Craig Brook (Me.) station, producing approximately 370,000 fry for return to the Dennys River and tributaries. This run of fish resulted from the transfer of humpback salmon eggs from the Afognak (Alaska) station in November, 1917, being the second generation to ascend the river for reproduction. It therefore appears that the humpback salmon has become well established in the waters of the Maine Coast.

Excerpt from the 1922 *Report of the (Maine) Commissioner of Fisheries.*

Quarrels between the Bureau and Penobscot River commercial fishermen over the purchase price of salmon and bonus amounts "for careful handling," led the fishermen to become increasingly uncooperative. This caused the Bureau to choose to import salmon eggs from Quebec and New Brunswick. It was also during this period that the U.S. Bureau of Fisheries undertook the rearing and stocking of large numbers of pink salmon fry in Maine rivers.

The number of salmon broodstock purchased from Penobscot River fishermen declined dramatically. While typical numbers purchased from 1902 to 1918 ranged from 400 to 1,100 annually, numbers decreased to about 200 each year during the period from 1919 to 1921 (Appendix 1). In June 1922, only 51 salmon were purchased from three Penobscot weir fishermen because the federal government had "refused to pay as much of a bonus as formerly for careful handling." Ironically, all 51 salmon escaped from the holding pond. No fish were purchased because of "poor fisherman cooperation" in 1923. After that, the U.S. Bureau of Fisheries evidently concluded that it would be easier to obtain Atlantic salmon eggs from the government of Canada for rearing at Craig Brook and to increase the numbers of other species being reared. For example, 18 million smelt eggs were shipped from Craig Brook Hatchery to the State of Maine hatchery in Oquossoc in 1929.

34. In 1890 Atkins attempted unsuccessfully to capture adult salmon with a weir across the East Branch of the Penobscot, noting that "on account of low water they failed to surmount the dams in the lower Penobscot."

Charles G. Atkins retired on August 21, 1920. He died on September 3, 1921 at the age of 80, leaving behind a spectacular and unparalleled 53-year legacy as a pioneer in Atlantic salmon restoration and research activities in the State of Maine.

Restoration Falters: The Canadian Stocks Era, 1920–1937

From 1920 to 1937 (except 1930[35] and 1934), the U.S. Bureau of Fisheries obtained Atlantic salmon eggs from the Miramichi (New Brunswick) and/or Gaspé (Quebec) hatcheries in Canada (see Appendix 4 for a complete historical summary of sources of salmon eggs used in Maine). These eggs were often obtained in exchange for an equal number of brook trout eggs. The Bureau also imported pink salmon eggs from Alaska, Washington, and Oregon and stocked large numbers of fry throughout Maine during the period 1915–1926. Brook trout egg production reached as high as 7,000,000 annually in the 1920's and 1930's, and landlocked salmon production was greatly expanded at the two other federal fish hatcheries at Green Lake and Grand Lake Stream (originally established by Charles Atkins in 1889 and 1875, respectively).[36] By 1938, for only the second time in 68 years of operation (1934 being the first), the Craig Brook fish hatchery did not hatch any Atlantic salmon eggs.[37]

The shift from native to imported salmon eggs, coupled with an increased emphasis upon rearing other species, left the Maine Atlantic salmon restoration program in a state of suspended animation. Throughout the 1920's and early 1930's, commercial and sport fishermen became increasingly discontented with the continued decline of salmon runs in Maine rivers. Salmon stocking that occurred during this period was undoubtedly very ineffective, with many fry "dumped"[38] into Maine rivers.

Maine Sea and Shore Fisheries Commissioner H. D. Crie (left) and Inland Fish and Game Commissioner George Stobie, who are depicted in this old newspaper photo, visited the Bangor Salmon Pool on June 20, 1932 in order to talk with anglers about improving the condition of the Penobscot River salmon population.

Considering the transportation methods available and the inaccessibility of many rivers, it is doubtful that these releases contributed much, if at all, to future salmon runs.

Late in 1934, two local Bangor sportsmen's clubs (the Penobscot County Fish and Game Association and the Penobscot Salmon Club) established a committee composed of three men from each organization "to make a study of conditions on the Penobscot River with the sole purpose of restoring the salmon run." The committee of six[39] was known as the Penobscot River Salmon Committee; their chief concern was the decline of sport

35. About 4,500 eggs were obtained from one partially spawned female that was captured in Souadabscook Stream, a tributary to the Penobscot River, in Hampden in 1930. This was the first time that eggs were taken directly from a Maine Atlantic salmon in the wild.

36. On October 17, 1933, the U.S. Bureau of Fisheries turned over the operation of the Grand Lake Stream Hatchery to the Maine Department of Fish and Game, and the Department has maintained a landlocked salmon rearing station there for the last 65 years. The Green Lake Hatchery was destroyed by fire in the 1930's; a new, modern hatchery was built at a different site on Green Lake in the 1970's.

37. The U.S. Fish Commission voluntarily closed the hatchery from 1876 to 1878 to evaluate results from the first five years of operation.

38. The author hesitates to use the word "stocked" in this instance; for example, it was not uncommon to release 50,000 –100,000 fry at one site in the lower reaches of a river.

39. Under the chairmanship of Walter S. Higgins of Bangor.

State of Maine • Executive Department • Augusta

August 6, 1939

Honorable Charles E. Jackson
Acting Commissioner, Bureau of Fisheries
Commerce Building, Washington, D.C.

Dear Mr. Jackson:

For a considerable period of time the matter of the decline of Atlantic sea salmon catches in the various rivers of Maine has been most disturbing to me as well as to a large number of the citizens of this State.

As a result of this situation, I requested Commissioner Stobie of our Department of Inland Fisheries and Game and Commissioner Greenleaf of our Department of Sea and Shore Fisheries to jointly undertake a survey and then report to me on the basis of their study.

They have covered the ground very thoroughly and as a result of their investigation, I am respectfully requesting your Department to consider the use of the Federal Hatchery at Orland, Maine, for the exclusive propagation of salmon. It appears that the Hatchery does not raise anything at the present time but trout and while we appreciate this work, we feel that we are in a position to care for the raising of trout in our other hatcheries that have recently been completed, which, in turn, are not adequate nor adapted for the propagation of salmon.

Secondly, I am of the opinion that if this can be arranged we should then present a plan to the next Legislature designed to purchase the fishing rights or weirs in several of our rivers, with the idea of eliminating the weirs which would thereby reasonably compensate many of our citizens.

Thirdly, we propose to give additional attention to the improvement of fishways in various dams that are in our rivers at the present time. For your information, may I now point out that all of the dams in the Penobscot River now contain modern and adequate fishways or fish ladders, so-called. The Dennys River is entirely clear of dams which affords the salmon an opportunity to go to the head waters for spawning purposes without any obstructions. In the Pleasant River and Narraguagus River there appears to be the desirability of improving the fishways in three or four dams. I have requested Commissioner Stobie to proceed with these projects as rapidly as possible and in view of the splendid cooperation that he has always received from the dam owners, I am confident that he will be able to make fine progress. This, it seems to me, will be extremely helpful in aiding us to reach our desired goal.

I do believe, however, that it is vitally necessary for us to have the cooperation of your Department in designating the use of the Orland Hatchery for the exclusive propagation of salmon, which I most urgently request.

Will you kindly advise me whether or not you are willing to assist us along the lines suggested above?

I wish to take this opportunity to thank you for the cooperation that our two Departments have received from you in the past, and in addition, I want to assure you that both Commissioner Stobie and Commissioner Greenleaf are willing to confer with you either in Washington or in Maine at any time you feel that such a conference would be helpful.

Very truly yours,
(signed) Lewis O. Barrows

Stocking Atlantic salmon in the Narraguagus River in the 1930's was an arduous task!

fishing for salmon on the Penobscot River. "In collaboration with the best authority and their own calculations, it was felt that obstructions played the major part in retarding the migration of our fish" wrote the Committee. The Salmon Committee enlisted the aid of the state, through Fish and Game Commissioner George L. Stobie, and the federal government, through the Bureau of Fisheries, for construction of new, up-to-date fishways. In 1936, a second fishway was constructed at the Brewer end of the Bangor Dam (the existing fishway near the center of the dam had been rebuilt in 1923), and new concrete fishways were built at the Veazie and Great Works dams during the winter of 1936–1937. Funding and personnel for the construction of these fishways was provided under the Works Progress Administration (WPA) program. The Committee reported in 1938 that, under the direction of state engineer Carl Crane, the Penobscot had been given the finest set of fishways in the East and that "beyond a question of doubt, their efficiency will enable the brood fish to pass once more to headwaters for reproduction."

Another Attempt: The General Salmon Committee Era, 1939–1946

On August 9, 1939, the Bangor Chamber of Commerce, at the request of the Penobscot Salmon Committee, was host to a day-long conference in Bangor to discuss and formulate a plan for salmon restoration in selected Maine rivers. The conference was conducted by officials of the Federal Bureau of

J. D. Sullivan (left) from New York City had the rare experience of catching an Atlantic salmon at sea. The 16-pound salmon was taken with a clam-baited hook in 50-feet of water near Corea, Maine, in August of 1939. William P. Langdon (right) from Brooklyn, New York, and Robert Dow (who took the photo) from Bangor, Maine, witnessed the event. The salmon was donated to the Atlantic Sea Run Salmon Commission in 1987 and it currently hangs on a wall of the conference room at the Atlantic Salmon Authority's office in Bangor.

Fisheries with representatives of several Maine salmon angling clubs and interested citizens present. The rivers under discussion were the Penobscot, Dennys, Narraguagus, Aroostook, St. Croix, Machias, and East Machias. At the closing session of the Bangor conference, a State of Maine General Salmon Committee was formed to represent the people of the state who were interested in salmon restoration efforts. "The Committee was assisted in every way possible by the State Fish and Game Department and Federal Bureau of Fisheries," wrote General Salmon Committee Chairman Horace P. Bond in 1940. Mr. Bond represented the Penobscot Salmon Club; additional members of the General Salmon Committee attending were Raymond S. Foster (Machias Valley Sportsmen's Club, Inc.), Herbert H. Allen (Dennys River Salmon Club), Raymond Plummer (Narraguagus Fish and Game Association), Stephen E. Beckett (Calais Rod and Gun Club), and Fred L. Urquhart (Aroostook Valley Fish and Game Club).

Much to the surprise of the Penobscot Salmon Committee, a letter was received from Maine Governor Lewis Barrows showing his displeasure with having not been invited to the August 9 conference in Bangor. Because of declining commercial fisheries for Atlantic salmon throughout the state, the governor had also initiated his own disjointed but parallel effort to establish an Atlantic salmon restoration program. Only three days before the Bangor Conference, on August 6, 1939, Governor Barrows had sent the letter reprinted on page 101 to the acting commissioner of the Federal Bureau of Fisheries in Washington, D.C.

The Maine General Salmon Committee was not well organized during the mid-1930's, and there was disagreement among the members as to the possibility and means by which Atlantic salmon runs might be restored. A New England-wide salmon restoration organizational effort was initiated later in 1939. At the request of David Alward, president of the National Wildlife Federation, the U.S. Bureau of Fisheries called a meeting of the conservation commissioners of all of the New England states to discuss the problem of declining salmon runs and sport and commercial fisheries for the species. The commissioners asked for a report on the subject that was subsequently prepared by two scientists from the Federal Bureau of Fisheries (Harrington and Rounsefell 1940). They worked in cooperation with Maine Fish and Game Commissioner George Stobie, the other New England Fish and Game commissioners and Raymond Dow, who represented the Penobscot Salmon Committee. The report—widely recognized as the impetus for a renewed New England salmon restoration program—presented information that was currently available, reported on the possibilities for salmon restoration, and recommended a program suggesting effective methods for carrying out Atlantic salmon restoration work. Recommendations in the report included:

In order that the Atlantic Sea Run Salmon Commission carry out its duties and provide whatever such regulations as may be deemed remedial of any adverse condition proven to exist, a propagation and research program has been established. The research program, designed to furnish scientific information on the environmental requirements of Atlantic salmon during those periods of their life cycle in which they are present in brackish and freshwaters, is provided by the U.S. Fish and Wildlife Service and the Maine Atlantic Sea Run Salmon Commission.

COMMISSIONERS HORACE BOND, ROLAND COBB, AND RAYMOND DOW IN THE FIRST *BIENNIAL REPORT OF THE ATLANTIC SEA RUN SALMON COMMISSION.*

1. A comprehensive survey of New England rivers from mouth to source to show: number and kind of obstructions, extent and degree of pollution, the condition and extent of spawning areas, and the suitability and capacity of the streams for young salmon.

2. On the basis of the above, select the most suitable stream for restoration and management experiments.

3. Obtain state laws prohibiting or severely limiting the capture of salmon anywhere on the river or within a suitable distance from its mouth.

In 1938 Bangor Hydro-electric Co. constructed the "Station B" plant at the Veazie Dam on the Penobscot River, adding two new generators for the production of electricity. A vertical-slot fishway was constructed in the log sluice at the center of the dam (background) in 1970.

4. Provide a means of determining the number of fish that spawn naturally.

5. Obtain a supply of salmon eggs for hatching and planting each year for at least five years to assist in rebuilding the natural stock.

6. Mark wild parr and smolts in different tributaries and hatchery-reared parr and smolts to determine: the value of tributaries for spawning and nursery grounds, the best age to release hatchery stock and the optimum size of spawning run for each tributary.

7. After 10 years, or less, should results be sufficiently successful, open the streams to controlled fishing.

8. Study the possible advantages and disadvantages to be derived from introducing more desirable species of West Coast salmon—a species with value to sport and commercial fishermen and whose early life history would offer a minimum of competition to Atlantic salmon.

A Memorandum of Understanding was signed in September 1939 by the U.S. Bureau of Fisheries and the Maine Departments of Inland Fish and Game and Sea and Shore Fisheries as a result of recommendations from the Harrington and Rounsefell report. The Memorandum established a program of biological research and investigation and called for the collection of Dennys River salmon broodstock in the fall of 1939 and Penobscot River salmon broodstock starting in 1940. Because of this Memorandum, the first stripping of Maine female sea salmon done in 20 years was undertaken in the fall of 1939 under the direction of George Montgomery, superintendent of the federal hatchery at Orland, and Arthur Briggs, superintendent of hatcheries of the State of Maine.

In 1940 the University of Maine also joined in the combined salmon restoration effort by establishing the William Converse Kendall Fellowship. It sponsored graduate student research on Atlantic salmon in the Dennys and Penobscot Rivers from 1940 to 1942.

The original Memorandum of Understanding was amended on October 10, 1941, to establish biologically based principles relating to salmon propagation and stocking procedures, and to establish a Research Committee to coordinate the salmon work of the three agencies noted above. The Research Committee, composed of Dr. George Rounsefell (U.S. Bureau of Fisheries), Dr. Gerald Cooper (Maine Department of Inland Fish and Game), and Warden Lester Stubbs (Maine Department of Sea and Shore Fisheries), prepared two reports in 1943 (March 23 and October 22). These reports showed which Maine rivers were most suitable for immediate restoration, described fieldwork carried out by Kendall Fellowship students at the University of Maine, and provided recent redd count information from the Dennys River. In addition, they provided information relating to salmon fishing at the Bangor Salmon Pool, results of various stocking experiments, and notes on the 1943 salmon runs in the Dennys, East Machias, St. Croix, and Narraguagus rivers. The report also recommended the institution of a long-term research program, and assigned personnel to carry out the work, "for at least 10 years (two generations of Atlantic salmon)." The Research Committee noted the need for the following: (1) an annual count of the number of spawners, (2) the restriction of all fishing in streams under restoration, (3) the collection of accurate statistics of the numbers of salmon taken, and (4) the development of

The first three members of the Atlantic Sea Run Salmon Commission are shown in this 1947 photo (from left: Horace Bond, Richard Reed, George Stobie). The first official meeting of the Commission took place on December 1st of that year.

protocols for the collection of salmon broodstock from fishways.

America's increasing participation in World War II interrupted the new salmon restoration program that had been so carefully laid out in the early 1940's. For example, it was noted that "no men were available for the Kendall Fellowship, and at one time girls were considered for possible use in the field (Bryant 1951)."[40]

During the mid-1940's the Atlantic States Marine Fisheries Commission (ASMFC), representing all of the states along the Atlantic coast except South Carolina, expressed a renewed interest in salmon restoration along the eastern seaboard. The ASMFC recommended that the State of Maine resolve the problems inherent in the overlapping jurisdiction of the two existing state fishery agencies (Inland Fish and Game and Sea and Shore Fisheries) by creating a special commission with sole authority over Atlantic salmon. In 1945, pursuant to a legislative act, Governor Horace Hildreth appointed a special three-person commission (Frank L. Baker, W. Lloyd Byers, and Sam L. Worcester) to study the remaining salmon resource and to report to the next session of the legislature. Their report, submitted on January 1, 1947, listed "impassible dams, deforestation, pollution by industrial development, over fishing with gillnets and traps, destruction of young salmon during their seaward migration by water diversion tubes to power plants or turbines, and drought conditions" as the factors that caused Maine's Atlantic salmon resource to be "brought to a bad condition." Their report also listed the following measures that the group felt were necessary to restore Atlantic salmon to prominence in the state:

1. Creation of a single administrative unit within state government with sole authority over salmon in both fresh and saltwater.
2. Construction of approved fishways and more attention to assure young salmon a safer passage to sea.
3. Uniform regulations.
4. Reduction of water pollution.
5. Construction of water control structures to augment flows.
6. Reduction and control of predator species.
7. Stocking.

State Government Makes a Commitment: The Atlantic Sea Run Salmon Commission Era, 1947–1995.

Because of the report of the Governor's special commission, the 93rd session of the Maine Legislature created the Atlantic Sea Run Salmon Com-

40. Evidently the idea of female researchers wasn't considered too seriously, for, until the war ended, the only ongoing activity in Maine was the rearing and stocking of salmon fry and fingerlings by the few men who worked at the hatcheries. Eventually, even the Research Committee meetings that were normally held to review the program were finally discontinued in 1945.

mission (ASRSC), which came into existence on August 13, 1947. Commission members included the commissioner of inland fisheries and game, the commissioner of sea and shore fisheries, and a public member appointed by the governor. It was only fitting for the governor to appoint Horace P. Bond as the first public member on the ASRSC, since he was instrumental in formation of the Maine General Salmon Committee in 1940. Today, Horace Bond is universally recognized as the founder of the modern-day Atlantic salmon restoration program in Maine. He served as the public member of the Atlantic Sea Run Salmon Commission until November 20, 1967, and was chairman for most of those 20 years (from August 3, 1951).

One initial action of the Atlantic Sea Run Salmon Commission was to amend the October 10, 1941, agreement between the U.S. Fish and Wildlife Service and the Department of Inland Fisheries and Game and Sea and Shore Fisheries to include two additional signatories: the Atlantic Sea Run Salmon Commission and the University of Maine. That agreement, dated April 15, 1948, established a three-person Research Committee to serve as a coordinating agency for all salmon restoration and management work in Maine. The Committee advised all parties concerning the research program and made recommendations to the Salmon Commission concerning salmon rearing and stocking, fishways, dams, fishing regulations, pollution abatement, and other needed measures. The Salmon Commission agreed to base its salmon fishing regulations on recommendations of the Research Committee.

The Fish and Wildlife Service provided a senior biologist to plan and supervise the research program (the ASRSC paid half of his salary), while the University of Maine agreed to provide "office and laboratory space, including usual services and utilities." The Service further agreed to propagate and rear Atlantic salmon at the Craig Brook Hatchery, while the Department of Fisheries and Game agreed to propagate and rear salmon "whenever the program called for a larger output than can be handled at Craig Brook." The Inland and Sea and Shore Fisheries Departments also agreed to help the Atlantic Sea Run Salmon Commission "in the marking and stocking of young salmon, catching and transporting adult spawning salmon, attending weirs and traps, and such field tasks as may be required."

> *Although no rod catch was reported from the Bangor Salmon Pool, large numbers of salmon have been seen below the hydroelectric installation at Veazie and jumping in the vicinity of the fishway in the Veazie Dam.*
>
> Maine Atlantic Sea Run Salmon Commission, Biennial Report for 1956–1958.

Decisions regarding how many spawning salmon were to be taken from any stream were based upon Research Committee recommendations. Additionally, all parties agreed that no fewer than 50% of the salmon hatched from eggs collected in any stream were to be returned to that stream unless the stream was "specifically declared by the Research Committee to be in unsuitable condition to afford a favorable habitat for sea run salmon."

In 1948 the Inland Fisheries and Game Department provided the services of a full-time biologist to the program, and the U.S. Fish and Wildlife Service appointed the senior biologist. The Inland Fish and Game biologist was Lyndon H. Bond,[41] eldest son of the Salmon Commission's Public Member, Horace Bond. The Service's chief biologist of Atlantic Salmon Investigations was George A. Rounsefell. Together, these two men prepared a report (Rounsefell and Bond 1949) that described what was known about the condition and extent of the Atlantic salmon resource in Maine and how the restoration program was to be organized and carried out. It included a review of the suitability of Maine salmon streams for salmon runs and a historical summary of salmon stocking efforts since the restoration program had been resumed in 1939.

The report also described attempts to introduce coho salmon into the Pemaquid and Ducktrap rivers. This program was designed to try to provide a saltwater sport fishery for this species in the estuaries of Maine streams that lacked deep pools where adults could spend the summer (as Atlantic salmon do). Because coho salmon stayed in saltwater until just before spawning in the fall, the Research Committee believed that the state could

41. Lyndon Bond enjoyed a distinguished career with the Inland Fisheries and Game Department over 35 years, most of which were spent as chief of the Fisheries Division.

provide an additional fishery: this program was not designed to replace the Atlantic salmon where the species existed.[42]

Research Report Number 1 of the Atlantic Sea Run Salmon Commission laid out in great detail the needs of the statewide Atlantic salmon restoration and management program and presented a long-term work program to address those needs. The major needs identified then (November 1, 1948) were virtually the same ones identified during the Charles Atkins era and generally acknowledged as highly important today. Do these recommendations sound familiar?

> ***Environmental Needs:*** catalog physical obstructions to salmon migration; experiment with various types of fishways; measure water temperatures; survey extent of spawning rubble, riffles and pools for adults; catalog types and sources of water pollution.
>
> ***Biological Needs:*** determine food requirements of parr in streams; evaluate effects of predators fish and birds; determine effects of beavers, otters and seals.
>
> ***Habitat and Life History Needs:*** collect age and growth of young salmon; do comparison to hatchery stock; determine adult salmon/age of maturity; determine stream carrying capacity for salmon; determine what percent of kelts survive to spawn again; determine if kelts can be held in saltwater and spawn again.
>
> ***Salmon Migrations:*** determine size, age and season of smolt migration; determine the degree to which adult salmon return to their native stream; determine season of adult migration in order to manage fishway operations, fishing season and stream flows.
>
> ***Salmon Spawning:*** determine stream suitabilities; egg survival in redds; effects of eels, lampreys and mammals on eggs in redds.
>
> ***Salmon Numbers:*** count and catch salmon to estimate population sizes and obtain broodstocks; determine numbers taken in sport fisheries; count numbers of young to estimate survival.
>
> ***Salmon Propagation:*** determine effects of diet on growth; survival and cost per fish at each size and/or age; survival (freshwater and marine) of stocked salmon and compare to wild salmon survival; compare landlocked and Atlantic salmon stocked in same stream.
>
> ***Salmon Management:*** reduce losses from all predators; provide adequate summer flows; make barriers possible on all streams; define minimum adequate standards for fishway design.
>
> ***Commercial and Sport Fishing for Salmon:*** close until runs are established; regulate newly stocked streams; educate the public.

Specific work programs were prepared for ten Maine rivers,[43] with experiments involving Atlantic and coho salmon. The Atlantic salmon work program outlined above was divided into jobs and the responsibility for carrying out those jobs was assigned to biologists and wardens of the agencies that signed the 1948 cooperative agreement. The Inland Fisheries and Game Department began rearing salmon at the state hatcheries at Tunk Lake and Deblois, helped in stocking, trapping of salmon at fishways, collecting information on salmon catches in freshwater, and designing and constructing fish protective devices. The Sea and Shore Fisheries Department helped with juvenile salmon marking, experimented with reconditioning kelts in saltwater tanks, compiled data on all salmon caught in tidal waters, operated salmon traps at fishways, and attempted to control mergansers and cormorants. The University of Maine provided a biologist to study salmon food requirements and availability of food in steams. The State Park Commission assigned the Camden Park ranger to watch the weir in the Ducktrap River while the State Sanitary Board assigned chemists to study water quality issues and to recommend pollution abatement programs. The Salmon Commission and U.S. Fish and Wildlife Service personnel operated fish trap-

The Atlantic Salmon Survey Team of the early 1950's. Standing (from left to right) are US Fish and Wildlife Service biologists James Mason and Floyd Bryant. Seated (from left to right) are Atlantic Sea Run Salmon Commission biologists James Fletcher and Richard Cutting.

42. Some of the coho salmon survived to return and spawn. In 1947 Commissioner Stobie estimated that he saw 100–150 coho salmon in the Ducktrap River and Inland Fish and Game personnel captured 41 of them with a beach seine. Seventeen were females that were artificially spawned and 25,000 eggs were sent to the State Hatchery in Raymond, Maine. While coho salmon spawned for a few generations in the Ducktrap River, they did not become permanently established there or in any other Maine rivers where they were introduced.

43. Dennys River, Little Falls (Hobart) Stream, Machias River, Chandler River, Narraguagus River, Tunk Stream, Penobscot River, Marsh Stream, Ducktrap River, Sheepscot River.

A Conservation Lesson in Salmon

An awakened American conscience is making possible restoration of natural resources in directions where hope almost had been lost, and of these last-ditch programs one of the most golden involves the Atlantic salmon. A few years ago it was believed only a matter of time before the Atlantic salmon would become extinct. The Atlantic salmon without doubt is the greatest fresh water game fish. Long before the days of the timber barons with their mighty forests the salmon beat its way up the rivers of the eastern United States to spawn. So plentiful they were, said reports of the day, that their tails and backs came out of the water. Came the sawmills, sawdust, dams, and pollution. Salmon were hit hard. Poor conservation laws helped push them from the picture. They were believed heading out with the buffalo and passenger pigeon. Then the pendulum swung. Sportsmen were the first to rebel. Clubs were formed and a salmon commission was organized. The State of Maine was aroused and the federal government entered the picture. Stream obstructions were removed to give salmon a chance to run up river. Biologists studied conditions. Many of their recommendations were adopted. By 1959 the U.S. Fish and Wildlife Service was rearing slightly more than 200,000 fall-fingerling salmon for supplemental stocking. Salmon are coming back in the Aroostook, Machias, Narraguagus, and Penobscot. Salmon are being caught in the Dennys, East Machias, Pleasant, and Sheepscot rivers, among the others. It has been estimated that a salmon angler spends about $10 a pound for the fish he takes, and in 1959 about $56,000 was spent in Maine by salmon anglers. Maine and federal authorities are confident that salmon are on the way back. There are problems, some financial, to solve. Even now, however, it is possible to fish for salmon on any of these streams without a special license or guide, and most streams are easily accessible. The Maine salmon comeback offers a lesson which should not be lost on future generations.

EDITORIAL APPEARING IN THE
ELIZABETH (N.J.) *DAILY JOURNAL*,
APRIL 13, 1960.

ping facilities, conducted redd counts, surveyed salmon streams, and evaluated the survival of stocked salmon.

In 1948, the Atlantic Sea Run Salmon Commission launched a highly coordinated, cooperative effort to restore Maine's Atlantic salmon runs to their former glory, beginning with "eight salmon rivers with regular salmon runs[44] and stray salmon occasionally reported in 10 streams that do not contain regular runs." There was much work to be done, and little time was lost in carrying out this important mission. The Salmon Commission immediately eliminated the directed commercial fishery, established a sport fishing license ($3.00 for residents, $1.00 for residents under age 21, and $5.00 for nonresidents), and hired its first full-time fishery biologist, James S. Fletcher.[45] In 1950, the Sheepscot (34.2 miles), Ducktrap (9.1 miles), and Narraguagus (104.1 miles) rivers were surveyed, along with Little Falls (13.9 miles) and Tunk Streams (20.7 miles). Some of the more important "problems" identified during these surveys were beaver dams, high water temperatures, and predators. In 1951 the Dennys, Machias, and Aroostook rivers were surveyed by Salmon Commission, Inland Fish and Game, and U.S. Fish and Wildlife Service biologists. Fish passage improvements were made at the gorge on the Machias River in 1949, and the Narraguagus River was cleared of obstructions all the way to Deer Lake in 1951. This included removal of the dam at the outlet of Beddington Lake. The Sheepscot River was the focus of habitat improvement programs (removal of beaver dams and natural obstructions, etc.) in 1952. Fishways and weirs were operated on the Dennys, Narraguagus, and Penobscot rivers to collect broodstock, and rod catches were tabulated in great detail (for example, in 1951 the average weight of salmon caught by anglers in these rivers was 10.0, 11.2, and 10.5 pounds, respectively).

The Cooperative Agreement was amended again in June 1951. Minor additions were made concerning the Salmon Commission's planned procurement of eggs from Canada and research and stocking programs that were to be carried out on the Narraguagus and Machias Rivers and Little Falls Stream. The amendment also assigned Atlantic Salmon Commission personnel to headquarters at the University of Maine in Orono and U.S. Fish and Wildlife Service personnel to headquarters in

Since intensive restoration efforts cannot be initiated simultaneously on all the large rivers in Maine, the Penobscot has been selected as the first large river to receive a concerted effort. Fulfillment of needs on this river will not be easy, but the rewards will be large. Important, too, is the Penobscot River's potential for the development of American shad, alewife, and striped bass fisheries. The Penobscot River Atlantic salmon restoration program will be the base for a model in overcoming the man-made socio-economic problems that affect fisheries and reduce full river utilization throughout the United States. We plan to develop measures which can be used in the restoration of other rivers in Maine, in New England, and indeed throughout our country. Techniques developed and evaluated on the Penobscot model may have wide applications in the restoration of other fisheries facing similar problems of obstructions, pollution, and controlled flows. This model river plan will be up-dated as work progresses and new information is available.

Everhart and Cutting 1967

44. Roughly in order of salmon abundance: Penobscot, Dennys, Narraguagus, Machias, East Machias, Pleasant, and Ducktrap rivers, and Tunk Stream.

45. Jim Fletcher worked out of the Salmon Commission's regional office in Machias until his retirement in 1979. He was instrumental in carrying out Atlantic salmon restoration and management programs in Washington County rivers, especially in the Dennys, East Machias, Machias, and Pleasant rivers.

46. Author's note: Was this decision based upon Beaufort's close proximity to Maine Atlantic salmon rivers?

In 1951 the Atlantic Sea Run Salmon Commission removed the dam at the outlet of Beddington Lake in the Narragugus River drainage. Eight years later, a weir was constructed just upstream of the old dam site in order to count and collect biological data from adult salmon moving upstream and smolts moving downstream. The first photo shows the original dam, the second photo shows the method used to remove the dam, and the third photo reveals free passage for salmon, shad and alewives!

Upstream passage for Atlantic salmon at the "gorge" on the Machias River was improved by the construction of a series of pools (similar to a fishway) during the 1950's. The hydroelectric generating facility, that can be seen on the right side of the photo, was removed in the early 1970's.

Beaufort, North Carolina.[46]

Operation of a two-way fish counting weir on Little Falls Stream and a salmon counting facility in Machias at the head of the gorge provided valuable biological data on Maine salmon smolt and adult runs during the early 1950's. Additionally, releases of marked[47] salmon parr in five rivers contributed to the Salmon Commission's knowledge about the growth and survival of hatchery-reared salmon. For the first time (beginning in 1951), biologists could identify these marked Maine-origin salmon when they were captured in commercial salmon fisheries in the Canadian provinces of Nova Scotia and New Brunswick.

Improvements in fish passage were made by installing fishways in dams on the East Machias, Machias, and Aroostook rivers; sportsmen's groups on the Pleasant and Sheepscot rivers also helped to make those rivers fully accessible to Atlantic salmon.

The U.S. Fish and Wildlife Service's participation in the research phases of the program ended in February 1954; consequently, the Atlantic Salmon Commission added to its staff, first with the employment of Richard E. Cutting in 1955 and then Alfred L. Meister in 1957.[48]

By the mid-1950's, the Atlantic Salmon Commission, with much assistance and support from biologists of the Department of Inland Fisheries and Game, had published ten river management plans, made significant improvements for salmon passage in the Machias drainage, participated in water quality and minimum flow studies, and expanded salmon stocking and survival experiments. In 1954, W. Harry Everhart, chief of Fisheries Research and Management for the Department of Inland Fisheries and Game *and* chief biologist for the Atlantic Sea Run Salmon Commission wrote the following: "the Salmon Commission is enthusiastic over the success of the Atlantic salmon restoration program. A catch of 64 salmon in the Pleasant River shortly after the season opened, nearly as many fish taken in the Narraguagus by Memorial Day as taken in the entire season the year before, over 35% of the Machias fish already above the last obstruction, plans for a fishway to open up the Piscataquis River, and plans to restore the Aroostook River are some of the highlights."

The Atlantic Salmon Commission had completed its inventory of potential Atlantic salmon rivers by the late 1950's and was now armed with the knowledge necessary to formulate restoration plans on a statewide basis. These plans to build up salmon runs were based upon habitat restoration and natural reproduction that would be supplemented with hatchery-reared stocks. A fishway was formed by dynamiting an area in the Pleasant River natural obstruction at Saco Falls, and fish passage improvements were made in Cathance Stream, the major tributary to the Dennys River. Citizen participation in the program was evident with partial funding for the Saco Falls fishway obtained from the town of Columbia Falls and significant funding ($15,000) for the Caribou fishway and trap at the Tinker Dam Falls in New Brunswick by the residents of Aroostook County, Maine.

During the late 1950's, the Atlantic Salmon

47. The Salmon Commission and U.S. Fish and Wildlife Service had a policy of marking all hatchery fish larger than fry.

48. In March 1968, Dick Cutting moved on to a 25+-year career with the Canadian Department of Fisheries and Oceans, while the author filled Mr. Cutting's position on October 28, 1968. Al Meister, chief biologist for the Atlantic Sea Run Salmon Commission for much of his career, was "Mr. Salmon" in Maine until his retirement in 1988.

Commission embarked upon a large-scale research program[49] with the construction of a 400-foot long weir on the Narraguagus River just below Beddington Lake. Operation of the "fish-tight" fence across the river, continuously from April 1960 to December 1966 and seasonally through 1969, provided the agency with a wealth of information about the year-round life history aspects of Maine Atlantic salmon.

Construction of the Beddington weir commenced in August 1958, and by April 1960 operation of the weir had begun. Much of the early knowledge of Maine Atlantic salmon was obtained through the operation of the weir over the next nine years. Salmon smolts were counted during their seaward migration each spring, while adult salmon (and other anadromous fish such as alewives and shad) were counted as they returned from the marine phase of their life cycle. Detailed biological information from each individual fish was obtained, and freshwater and marine survival rates of stocked and wild salmon were estimated from the counts of returning adult fish.

While Salmon Commission biologists were studying Atlantic salmon populations in the Downeast and Penobscot rivers, U.S. Fish and Wildlife Service biologists at the federal laboratory in Boothbay Harbor were conducting similar studies on the Sheepscot River salmon population. A weir was constructed and operated on the Sheepscot from 1956 to 1958 where smolt and adult runs were monitored and various stocking experiments were carried out.

As a result of a flood in 1953 that severely damaged the Craig Brook Hatchery, the U.S. Bureau of Fisheries completely rebuilt the facility during the period 1953–1955 at a cost of more than $350,000. The Bureau also assigned a full-time biologist (Roger P. Dexter) to work on improving the rearing techniques and survival of hatchery-reared salmon and to act as a liaison between the Salmon Commission and the Bureau. Research involving the stocking of hundreds of thousands of hatchery-reared fry and parr during the 1940's and 1950's showed that few returned as adult fish. (Fletcher 1955; ASRSC 1962); therefore, the Commission and the Bureau decided to try to improve returns through the stocking of smolts. An accelerated growing season was instituted by heating the hatchery water, and smolts averaging 6–8 inches in length were produced in about 15 months.

49. During the mid-1950's, a pilot program was conducted by Al Meister on Cove Brook, a tributary to the lower Penobscot River (Meister 1962).

Longtime Atlantic Sea Run Salmon Commission biologist Jim Fletcher releases a bright, 10-pound salmon from the Whitneyville fishway trap on the Machias River. The Whitneyville Dam was removed in the mid-1970's.

These one-year smolts were used in various stocking experiments using Maine-origin and Miramichi-origin[50] salmon stocks from New Brunswick.

In August 1959, the Atlantic Sea Run Salmon Commission appointed an Advisory Council composed of "nine laymen interested in salmon restoration." The nine men selected to be members of the Advisory Council were State Senator James E. Briggs, chairman (Caribou), Reverend Elmer Smith (Portland), Arthur Hutchins (Bath), Walter Dickson (Bangor), Robert Godfrey (Dennysville), Lenwood Royal (Gorham), John Harriman (Portland), Bion Tibbetts (Columbia Falls), and Edward Cates (East Machias). Believing that the Downeast salmon fishing interests were underrepresented on the Advisory Council, representatives of several salmon fishing organizations decided to form their own group to "give support to—not weaken or replace" the Advisory Council. Accordingly, on January 25, 1960 the Maine Atlantic Salmon Federation was formed "to coordinate the efforts of the individual

50. Maine anglers (and government administrators) often cite the immense Atlantic salmon runs and sport fisheries of the Miramichi River as a reason to import Miramichi stocks into Maine. Looking backward in a historical sense, it is obvious that this was the case when large numbers of Miramichi-origin eggs were sometimes imported into Maine. However, in every instance where marked or tagged Maine-origin and Miramichi-origin salmon were released together, Maine-origin stocks demonstrated a much higher rate of survival. Additionally, adult returns from Maine stocks were primarily early-run, 2SW salmon, predominantly females, averaging 8–12 pounds in weight. In contrast, adult returns from Miramichi stocks were primarily late-run, 1SW salmon, predominantly males, averaging 2–4 pounds in weight. Examples like this demonstrate the benefits of genetics and local adaptions to Atlantic salmon restoration and enhancement programs.

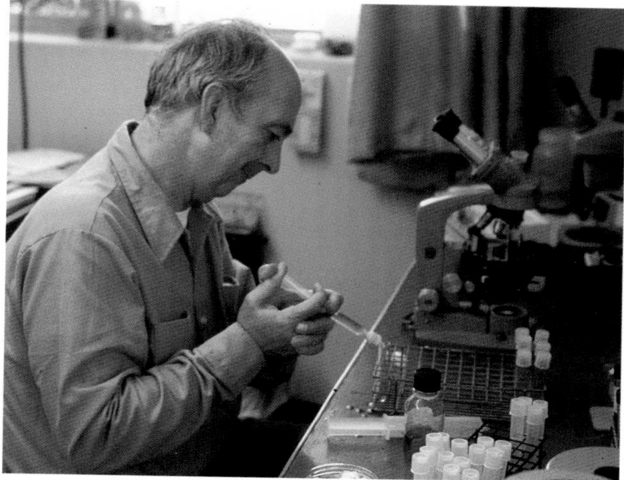

US Fish and Wildlife Service hatchery biologist Roger Dexter checks Maine Atlantic salmon for viral and bacterial diseases at Craig Brook National Fish Hatchery. Good animal husbandry practices, including fish health monitoring, are extremely important in Atlantic salmon stocking programs.

clubs and to foster a spirit of mutual assistance and cooperation between the various member clubs and state and federal agencies. The following six sportsmen's clubs joined the Federation in representing salmon angling organizations throughout the state: Narraguagus Salmon Association, Sheepscot River Atlantic Salmon Association, Dennys River Sportsmen's Club, Lincoln County Sportsmen's Association, Machias Valley Sportsmen's Club, and Pleasant River Fish and Game Association. The organization was formed to promote a "greatly expanded Atlantic salmon restoration program" with the following specific objectives:

- counting weirs on all rivers with established salmon runs
- water control projects on the Narraguagus, Pleasant and Dennys rivers
- studies of predator control
- improved fishways on the Machias River
- an improved stocking program, consistent with research findings
- elimination of transporting adult salmon to the federal hatchery in tank trucks, with resultant high mortality
- an expanded information and education program
- revised and simplified angling regulations such as a uniform May 1 opening, a law requiring registration of all salmon taken, fly fishing only, special licenses for Atlantic salmon fishing, establishment of sanctuaries on every salmon river, and increased salaries for biologists, wardens, technicians, and hatchery and administrative personnel involved in the salmon restoration program.

Beyond an extensive ongoing biological salmon monitoring program, in the early 1960's the Salmon Commission foresaw the need for improved fish passage facilities and regulated water flows in several rivers. A supplemental state appropriation granted to the Salmon Commission by the 100th legislature provided funds for a water control structure and fishways at Cathance Lake and Marion on the Dennys River, improved fish passage at the Machias River gorge, and a water control structure and fishways at Pleasant River Lake and at Saco Falls on the Pleasant River drainage. These programs improved the use of existing salmon habitat and enhanced salmon runs and sport fishing throughout the Downeast (Washington County) area of the state.

In the mid-1960's, fish passage improvements were expanded to other Maine Atlantic salmon rivers. For example, Federal Accelerated Public Works Funds and monies provided by dam owners were used to build fishways at Woodland and Grand Falls on the St. Croix River and at Howland on the Penobscot River. As the statewide salmon restoration program expanded to other rivers, additional hatchery-reared stocks were necessary; therefore, the Department of Inland Fisheries and Game provided holding facilities for 50 adult broodstock (25 each from the Machias and Narraguagus Rivers) at the Deblois State Hatchery and raised 250,000 of these native stocks annually at the Enfield State Hatchery.

Throughout the 1960's, the focus of the Salmon Commission's research program was upon studies being conducted primarily in the Narraguagus and Machias rivers. The number of wild smolts captured at the Beddington weir ranged from 500-2,000 each year, although it was estimated that one-half of the smolts may have been consumed by the pickerel population in Beddington Lake (Barr 1962). The weir also provided data that indicated that a majority (70%) of kelts survived until the following spring. At that time repeat spawners contributed only 5–15% of Maine's salmon runs; therefore, it was felt that many kelts were not able to survive the adjustment required for life in saltwater.[51] It was also during this period in history that the presence of Maine Atlantic salmon was docu-

51. While this may still be an accurate statement, we now know that commercial fisheries in Canada and Greenland were harvesting a large percentage of these fish.

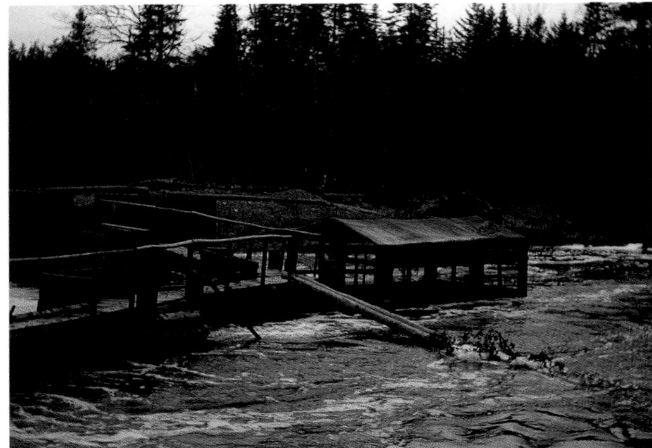

Weirs have been used to count and collect biological data from Maine Atlantic salmon for nearly 50 years. The first photo (clockwise from upper left) illustrates the Little Falls (Hobart) Stream weir, operated in the early 1950's. The next two photos show the Narraguagus River weir at Beddington; this facility was operated year-round from 1960-1966 and seasonally from 1967-1969. The last photo illustrates the Dennys River weir that that was operated seasonally from 1992-1996.

mented in the international salmon arena. Maine salmon originally tagged and released in Maine rivers were now being reported in increasing numbers in the commercial fisheries of the Canadian maritime provinces and in the new salmon fishery at West Greenland. The Greenland fishery brought the world's salmon producing countries together, since tagged salmon originating in many North American and European rivers were now being captured in the same nets.[52]

With passage of the Anadromous Fisheries Act (Public Law 89-304, amended in 1970 to the Anadromous Fish Conservation Act) in 1965, federal

In the mid-1950's the Atlantic Sea Run Salmon Commission constructed a Denil fishway at Saco Falls, a natural impediment to Atlantic salmon migration on the Pleasant River.

52. As a result of concern over the rapidly increasing catch of Atlantic salmon in Greenland, a Salmon Working Group was formed at the June 1965 meeting of the International Commission for the Northwest Atlantic Fisheries (ICNAF) in Halifax, to study the situation. Later that year, at the annual International Council for the Exploration of the Sea (ICES) meeting in Rome, a joint ICNAF/ICES Salmon Working Group was formed to undertake studies and make recommendations regarding international salmon fisheries and management issues. The ICES North Atlantic Salmon Working Group continues to meet annually to assess worldwide Atlantic salmon population trends and to provide scientific advice to the North Atlantic Salmon Conservation Organization (NASCO) which was established in 1984.

funding became available for expanded anadromous fish restoration programs throughout the United States. Consequently, the Atlantic Salmon Commission expanded the Downeast Atlantic salmon restoration program to include the Penobscot and Kennebunk[53] rivers.

In 1967 the Salmon Commission and U.S. Fish and Wildlife Service[54] published a report entitled *The Penobscot River, Atlantic Salmon Restoration: Key to a Model River.* The report noted that "accomplishments on the Machias and Narraguagus rivers prove that successful restoration is both possible and feasible. For salmon even to reach sufficient numbers to support major sport fisheries, the production potential of large rivers must be realized. The Penobscot River represents best the size and type of river to be restored." And so the modern-day Penobscot River Atlantic salmon restoration program began. Anadromous Fish Conservation Act funds were used, with equal funding from dam owners, to construct fishways at the Old Town and Milford dams in 1968, the Bangor dam in 1969, the Veazie and West Enfield dams in 1970, and the Dover-Foxcroft and Guilford dams on the Piscataquis River in 1972 and 1973. Small numbers of hatchery-reared parr and smolts were released throughout the drainage until the new federal Green Lake National Fish Hatchery in Ellsworth Falls became operational.[55]

The author (left) and Chief Biologist Al Meister display a 28-pound male salmon from the Machias River in this November 7, 1969 photo.

Improved fish passage facilities in the Penobscot Drainage coupled with ongoing major improvements in water quality and increased stocking efforts throughout the 1970's and 1980's brought the Penobscot salmon restoration program to the forefront of anadromous fish restoration efforts in the United States. Although similar programs were initiated at the same time elsewhere in New England (e.g., the Merrimack and Connecticut rivers), the success of the Penobscot program was unparalleled. As the salmon run and sport fishery on the Penobscot grew, so did support for the overall program throughout the state; salmon fishing enthusiasts and other conservationists clamored for similar types of programs elsewhere in Maine in "their" rivers.[56]

With the construction of the new Green Lake National Fish Hatchery the need for salmon broodstock in Maine more than doubled. Therefore, to provide an alternative source of broodstock (and to allow more Penobscot River salmon to spawn naturally) a "put-grow-and-take" salmon program

53. The Kennebunk River restoration program was purportedly initiated in an attempt to test the feasibility of providing a salmon fishery in southern Maine. Releases of equal numbers of Atlantic and landlocked salmon smolts were made during the period 1965–1967. A small number of adult salmon returned, and a few were caught by anglers; however, this program was quickly recognized as an ill-fated, politically based attempt to "spread" the available number of hatchery smolts around the state. Stocking of the Kennebunk River was discontinued in 1968.

54. The U.S. Bureau of Fisheries, under the Department of Commerce since 1903, was transferred to the Department of Interior in 1930. In 1956 the U.S. Fish and Wildlife Service Act created the U.S. Fish and Wildlife Service with a Bureau of Sport Fisheries and Wildlife and a Bureau of Commercial Fisheries (originally the U.S. Fish Commission in 1888). In 1976 the Bureau of Commercial Fisheries was transferred to the Department of Commerce, National Oceanic and Atmospheric Administration (NOAA), and renamed the National Marine Fisheries Service (NMFS). In recent years there have been proposals in Congress to eliminate the Department of Commerce and place the NMFS back into the Department of Interior as a branch or bureau of commercial fisheries. Haven't we already been through this scenario?

55. In the late 1960's the U.S. Bureau of Sport Fisheries planned the construction of a major Atlantic salmon hatchery in Maine which would be capable of producing 600,000 smolts annually for the Penobscot River Restoration Program. Construction of the Green Lake National Fish Hatchery in Ellsworth Falls began in 1971 and was completed in 1974.

56. In recent years, as a result of reduced salmon runs and fisheries throughout North American due to reduced salmon survival in the marine environment, some critics have attempted to label the Penobscot program a failure. It should be remembered that the small salmon runs which existed in the lower river during the 1960's have now been expanded to a "core" population of 100–400 wild adult salmon (i.e., those salmon originating from natural reproduction) and up to several thousand hatchery-origin salmon annually. Since 1970, more than 45,000 adult salmon have returned to the Penobscot River, resulting in the most highly utilized sport fishery for Atlantic salmon in the entire United States. The benefits to Maine's economy since its inception have been tremendous.

George Mitchell on the Salmon Restoration Efforts . . . .

Maine's Downeast rivers—the Dennys, East Machias, Machias, Pleasant, Narraguagus, Ducktrap, and Sheepscot—support the last remaining wild Atlantic salmon stocks in the U.S. Atlantic salmon numbers in Maine's Downeast rivers, however, have been declining since the late 1970s. Clearly, Atlantic salmon restoration efforts in Downeast rivers are in trouble and urgently need assistance. Delaying protection and restoration efforts until salmon are listed as endangered will only make these efforts more costly, less flexible and less likely to succeed.

Last year, the Congress approved an amendment that I sponsored to restore federal funding for Maine's Atlantic Sea Run Salmon Commission. Since this independent state agency was established nearly 50 years ago, it has played a critical role in the restoration of Atlantic salmon. This year, the 1993 Interior Department spending bill signed by the President includes $550,000 that Senator Cohen and I secured to help restore native salmon stocks in Downeast rivers.

The funds will be used in part by the U.S. Fish and Wildlife Service and the Maine Atlantic Sea Run Salmon Commission to conduct the necessary studies on native Atlantic salmon stocks in the Downeast rivers to prevent them from becoming endangered and to restore them to sustainable levels.

Maine's native Atlantic salmon are a vital part of our heritage and are an important economic resource. Without the additional support provided this year, the considerable investment that has been made to restore this resource over the past half century will be placed in jeopardy. That must not be allowed to happen. Maine's Atlantic salmon are a priceless gift that once lost, cannot be replaced. Our efforts will help ensure that does not happen.

Excerpts from U.S. Senator George Mitchell's guest column in *The Quoddy Tides*, November 13, 1992.

The new vertical slot type of fishway in the Veazie Dam on the Penobscot River is under construction in this 1969 photo. The cost of the fishway was shared by the US Fish and Wildlife Service and Bangor Hydro-electric Co. The Maine Atlantic Salmon Authority has operated a salmon trap at the exit of the fishway since 1978, where up to 4,200 Atlantic salmon have been counted and sampled annually. About 500-600 salmon are transported to the Craig Brook Hatchery for broodstock purposes, while all others are released to continue their upstream migration.

was initiated in the Union River. Due to the proximity of the lower Union River to the Green Lake Hatchery, and the tourist-rich Bar Harbor summer population, the Salmon Commission and U.S. Fish and Wildlife Service sought to establish another sport fishery for Atlantic salmon in central Maine.[57] Consequently, in 1973 a fish trapping facility was constructed by the Salmon Commission with funding obtained from the state legislature, private local contributions, the owner of the dam in Ellsworth (Bangor Hydro-Electric Co.), and federal funding (50%) through the Anadromous Fish Conservation Act. Originally, an annual stocking of 30,000 smolts below the Ellsworth Dam was envisioned to provide an adult return of 200–300 salmon. With a 20% harvest by anglers (based upon information from other Maine rivers) a rod catch of 40–60 salmon was expected each year, with the balance (160–240 salmon) to be collected for broodstock purposes.

In the early to mid-1980's, the Maine Atlantic salmon restoration program underwent an explosive period of growth. Survival of salmon in the marine environment was high, which produced excellent adult salmon returns (probably 6,000–10,000 total statewide) and sport fisheries[58] (1,000–2,000 salmon harvested annually by anglers) and generated much support for expanding the program to other areas of the state such as the Saco and Aroostook rivers. State and federal government funding was available for expanded and new programs.

The 1980's represented some of the best and worst times for Atlantic salmon management in the State of Maine. In response to public "demand" spurred on by accounts of the good salmon runs and sport fisheries in rivers such as the Penobscot, Narraguagus, and Machias, the Atlantic Sea Run Salmon Commission became actively involved in new or expanded restoration initiatives in the St. Croix, Aroostook, and Saco rivers. At one time, the ASRSC was seriously considering establishing regional offices in northern and southern Maine to handle the expanded work load involved in the newly established statewide salmon restoration program. It was also during this period that the Atlantic Salmon Commission expanded its participation into the international arena by sending staff biologists to distant commercial fisheries in Canada

57. It was thought that fishing for salmon in the Ellsworth area might also take some of the angling "pressure" off of the salmon runs in the Penobscot and Downeast rivers.

58. Except in 1983, when the Atlantic Salmon Commission closed the sport fishery on August 15 because of poor adult returns.

and Greenland to collect biological data that would be used for international salmon management programs.

The Maine aquaculture industry also became fully established in Maine in the 1980's. On two occasions, salmon smolts that were being reared at federal hatcheries for the statewide salmon restoration program, were diverted to the fledgling industry.[59] Salmon angling clubs in Maine and the Atlantic Salmon Federation, upset by the transfer of these publicly reared salmon to private industry, convinced the Maine legislature to increase public representation on the Atlantic Sea Run Salmon Commission from one to three members. Doing so would allow them to outvote the commissioners of Inland Fisheries and Wildlife and Marine Resources in case of future conflicts. Following a second extremely unpopular transfer of smolts to the aquaculture industry in 1985, the Atlantic Sea Run Salmon Commission made a feeble attempt to unite Atlantic salmon conservation efforts on a statewide basis by establishing another Advisory Council. The "new" advisory council, consisting of 12 regional representatives from throughout the state, turned out to be as ineffectual as its predecessors twenty years earlier. The ASRSC finally abolished the Advisory Council in the early 1990's without a single word of protest from the salmon angling interests that were originally so anxious to be represented on it.

Increasing the membership of Atlantic Sea Run Salmon Commission from three to five on June 30, 1987, served to fracture the statewide program into several competing factions. Northern Maine interests competed with those in southern Maine, eastern (Downeast) Maine, and the so-called "Penobscot crowd" (which, was represented by the four Penobscot River Salmon Clubs and, it seemed to some, by the Atlantic Salmon Federation). Unfortunately, this parochialism by various salmon interests persists in some areas of Maine.

In 1983, for the first time since its inception, the Atlantic Sea Run Salmon Commission had adopted a prioritized, biologically based, statewide salmon restoration and management plan. The number one priority of that, and the subsequent 1995 plan, was the maintenance of viable salmon runs and fisheries in the seven Maine rivers with wild Atlantic salmon populations. The plan was historic in that it focused restoration efforts, established priorities, and prevented the ASRSC from going off on tangents (through political arm-twisting) which, in previous years, had diluted available resources and produced unrealistic expectations.

Then the sky literally fell on Maine's Atlantic salmon restoration efforts. First, marine survival for wild and hatchery smolts declined dramatically (by 70–80%) causing salmon runs and sport fisheries to plummet. The catch of wild salmon on the Downeast rivers dropped from several hundred per year to virtually a handful. Adult salmon returns declined statewide from 6,000–10,000 to 1,500–3,000 annually, despite increased stocking efforts, especially in the Downeast rivers of Washington County. The dramatic decline in salmon returns and sport fisheries exacerbated the political infighting. Each of the regional salmon areas in Maine expressed the opinion that too many resources were being "wasted" on the Penobscot River restoration program (the salmon run in the Penobscot did not decline as much as the other rivers in Maine). They also felt that too little effort was being put forth in northern (e.g., Aroostook and other rivers), eastern (e.g., Dennys, Machias, East Machias, and Narraguagus rivers) and southern (e.g., Saco and Kennebec rivers) areas of the state.

The ultimate blow to the Maine salmon restoration program was the "budget crunch" that began in 1989 and resulted in the downsizing of state government agencies and programs throughout the state. The governor and state legislature effectively abandoned the salmon restoration program by eliminating state funding for five of the six existing biological personnel employed by the Atlantic Sea Run Salmon Commission.[60] To make matters worse, declining salmon runs and fisheries resulted in dwindling revenues from the sale of salmon fishing licenses, making it necessary for the Atlantic Salmon Commission to seek other sources of funding to continue to employ two biologists funded by a dedicated revenue account. Fortunately, federal agencies involved in the salmon restoration program were able to provide funds (through contracts with the U.S. Fish and Wildlife Service and National Marine Fisheries Service) for the Atlantic Salmon Commission to continue a reduced restoration program, focusing upon the seven rivers with wild salmon runs.

In the span of a decade Atlantic runs and support for the restoration program had gone from

59. In 1983, 100,000 smolts reared at Craig Brook NFH were provided to Ocean Products, Inc., in order to "jumpstart" the Maine aquaculture industry. In 1985, another 50,000 were provided. OPI repaid the "loan" of these smolts with comparable numbers of fry and parr which were stocked in many Maine rivers in the late 1980's.

60. The salmon restoration program could not "compete" for state funds against various other state programs deemed to be of higher priority (for example, human services, education, state prisons).

their highest of highs to their lowest of lows, and the State of Maine had relinquished its programmatic control, by default, to the federal government agencies. Now abandoned by state government, many new programs started in the 1980's were left to fend for themselves. As such, salmon angling clubs and other conservation associations assumed responsibility for their own piece of the state restoration program while the statewide program was drastically curtailed.

In November 1991, the U.S. Fish and Wildlife Service listed five of Maine's seven rivers with wild salmon runs[61] as Category 2 under the Endangered Species Act. At that time, this classification (which no longer exists) meant that the Service was concerned with the dramatic decline in salmon num-bers; additionally, the Service was seeking all available biological information about those salmon populations before considering upgrading those salmon runs to a higher status (threatened or endangered).

In response to the Category 2 listing, the Fish and Wildlife Service and Atlantic Sea Run Salmon Commission, at the urging of their respective staffs, proposed a radically different approach to Atlantic salmon restoration. Retreating from a statewide program involving 16 rivers to one of trying to restore just a few,[62] the Salmon Commission (and U.S. Fish and Wildlife Service) adopted a river-specific rehabilitation program. This program was based on the well-proven biological principle that the best way to restore a salmon run is to use what occurs there naturally. Because wild salmon survive better than hatchery salmon, the Commission and U.S. Fish and Wildlife Service decided to maximize the production of wild smolts through a program that emphasized the stocking of fry to saturate any vacant or underutilized salmon habitat. If Maine rivers are given the opportunity to produce smolts to the maximum extent possible, there is every reason to expect salmon runs and sport fisheries to return to, or exceed, the levels experienced in the 1970's and 1980's. The pendulum of marine survival must first reverse its swing for this shift to take place, and there is evidence that this may already be happening.

In 1992, the Atlantic Sea Run Salmon Commission and the U.S. Fish and Wildlife Service published a report entitled "Prelisting Recovery Plan for Wild Maine Atlantic Salmon Populations" (Baum et al. 1992). The Prelisting Recovery Plan (PLRP) was based upon the concept that conservation efforts could alleviate the need for listing under the state or federal Endangered Species Act by sufficiently improving the status of the species. If listing proved to be necessary, however, the Prelisting Recovery Plan would help the remaining Atlantic salmon populations to proceed without delay toward full recovery. The two agencies also assumed that these prelisting recovery efforts would help to avert controversy that may have occurred without the plan.

The objectives of the PLRP were to stabilize (or increase) existing salmon populations in the seven Maine rivers with wild salmon runs through

> *The State of Maine continues to object to the listing of salmon on the seven Downeast rivers in the strongest possible terms. It should be clearly understood that this Administration has worked with the Services in good faith to develop the (Conservation) Plan as an alternative to listing. Should listing occur, however, all cooperation with the Services will cease, implementation of the Plan will be suspended, and we will pursue all available avenues, including litigation and legislative solutions to prevent this misapplication of the Act.*
>
> Excerpt from letter to the U.S. Fish and Wildlife Service and National Marine Fisheries Service signed by Maine Governor Angus S. King, October 10, 1996.

61. The Ducktrap and Sheepscot rivers, inadvertently omitted in 1991, were added in 1994.

62. Dennys, East Machias, Machias, Pleasant, Narraguagus, Ducktrap, Sheepscot, and a reduced program on the Penobscot.

Current Atlantic salmon spawning techniques at Craig Brook National Fish Hatchery include the use of compressed air to express the eggs from females (top photo). The males, however, are still done (bottom photo) the way that Charles Atkins did it in 1871!

the following six recovery efforts:

1. Develop river-specific broodstocks to initiate a fry stocking program that could be used to maximize the production of wild smolts.
2. Identify the genetic characteristics of all Atlantic salmon stocks in Maine waters.
3. Install seasonal, permanent weirs to collect biological data on existing salmon runs and collect broodstock, as necessary.
4. Identify threats to salmon populations, and reduce or eliminate those threats if possible.
5. Inventory the quantity and quality of salmon habitat in the seven rivers.
6. Compile all available information on the status of these seven salmon stocks (historically and currently), assess recovery progress, and report results annually.

Maine Senator George Mitchell was instrumental in securing much of the funding for implementation of the Prelisting Recovery Plan by the ASRSC and USFWS. In 1992, the U.S. Fish and Wildlife Service converted Craig Brook National Fish Hatchery from a single broodstock and smolt production facility to a multiple broodstock and fry production facility. Between 1992 and 1996, Atlantic Salmon Commission and USFWS personnel collected more than 5,000 wild-origin Atlantic salmon parr from six of the seven rivers[63] and reared them to maturity at the Craig Brook Hatchery. Between 1992 and 1996, the river-specific stocking program resulted in the release of more than 1.2 million fry into the Dennys, East Machias, Machias, Narraguagus, and Sheepscot rivers. It was also during this period that the Atlantic Sea Run Salmon Commission and National Marine Fisheries Service were conducting an exhaustive five-year study of the Atlantic salmon population and salmon habitat in the Narraguagus River. The purpose of the study was to demonstrate to the North Atlantic Salmon Conservation Organization (NASCO), and others, that U.S. salmon rivers remained productive. The Narraguagus River study, now in its second five-year phase of applied research, indeed proved to the world that Maine's rivers can be excellent producers of wild salmon runs if provided with sufficient spawning escapement.

As a result of the dramatic shift to a river-specific stocking program, all stocking in the seven Downeast rivers using Penobscot-origin salmon ceased in 1991. As expected, adult salmon returns declined to record low levels in the next few years. Fortunately, the Canadian government closed the Newfoundland salmon fishery for a five-year period starting in 1992, and a two-year buyout of the Greenland salmon fishery took place in 1993 and 1994. These measures undoubtedly helped to prevent the extinction of Maine's wild Atlantic salmon runs.

On October 1, 1993, a newly formed environmental organization in Concord, Massachusetts by the name of RESTORE: The North Woods petitioned the U.S. Fish and Wildlife Service to list the Atlantic salmon (throughout its historical range in New England) under the Endangered Species Act

63. There was only space available for five Downeast river-specific stocks at Craig Brook National Fish Hatchery; a sixth stock (from the Pleasant River) is being held at a North Attleboro, Massachusetts, hatchery operated by the USFWS. No Ducktrap River stocks are being held, since state and federal biologists have a "forever wild" policy for that river, which precludes stocking with hatchery-reared fish.

Maine Atlantic salmon fry stocking techniques—then and now. In the 1890's, Atlantic salmon fry were held in milk containers and transported and stocked via horse and buggy. Fry stocking in the 1990's is accomplished with the benefit of canoes and insulated holding tanks. Supplemental oxygen is bubbled through the system in order to keep the fish healthy for the many hours that are required to distribute the fry properly. "One behind every rock" is the biologist's motto!

(ESA). RESTORE was joined in its petition by the Biodiversity Legal Foundation of Boulder, Colorado, and Jeffrey Elliott of Lancaster, New Hampshire. The petitioners requested that the Service list the Atlantic salmon throughout its historical range in the United States under the federal Endangered Species Act (16 U.S.C. Sec. 1531 *et. Seq.* (1973) as Amended).

The petition initiated a ninety-day period during which the U.S. Fish and Wildlife Service had to respond to the "merits" of the petition by either dismissing it or accepting it (all or any portions). A positive finding from the ninety-day review process would then start a one-year "clock" (from when the petition was submitted) on a status review of the species seeking all available biological information with which to decide whether any or all U.S. rivers with Atlantic salmon populations should be proposed for listing. The petition resulted in a "what-to-do" panic in the Department of the Interior, since the Fish and Wildlife Service routinely dealt with land mammal, bird, and plant listings under the ESA but not anadromous fish, and certainly not Atlantic salmon! On the West Coast of the U.S. the National Marine Fisheries Service had been dealing with many petitions to list various Pacific salmonids under the ESA; however, the USFWS had not been involved in those proceedings. As an initial effort to respond to the petition, the USFWS held a meeting at its Leetown, West Virginia, lab on October 26, 1993, and established a Genetics Working Group. This group was charged with preparing a short-term plan that would provide the best possible biological and genetics information with which to decide whether or not any of Maine's seven wild salmon runs qualified for listing under the ESA. The Working Group's mission was to summarize all available historical information and to collect additional tissue samples from Maine salmon stocks during the summer of 1994 to obtain current genetics information. The Working Group was composed primarily of USFWS personnel, but included a few others (e.g., the author). An October 1, 1994, deadline was established for the genetics report.

Fortunately, or unfortunately, depending upon your viewpoint, RESTORE submitted its petition to the National Marine Fisheries Service on November 9, 1993, resulting in an internal turf battle between the USFWS and NMFS over which agency would now have jurisdiction over the petition. The NMFS office in Washington, D.C., quickly ruled (over the objections of its regional office personnel in Gloucester, Massachusetts) that the petition had merit, then hastily reversed itself a few days later and withdrew its findings while the two federal agencies huddled at the Washington level. Ultimately, the two agencies signed a cooperative agreement under which they agreed to process the petition jointly, based upon the fact that the Atlantic salmon spends half its life in the freshwater environment and half in marine environment. On January 20, 1994 "the Services" (as the two agencies refer to themselves) published a joint ninety-day finding (although 112 days had elapsed) in the Federal Register that stated that the federal authorities believed that the petition "presents substantial information indicating that the requested action may be warranted. To assure that the review is comprehensive, the Services are soliciting information and data on this species from any interested party. Comments and materials related to this petition finding may be submitted until April 20, 1994."

Maine's leading business and industry representatives and even a few state agencies fired off dozens of responses to protect their own interests from the perceived horrors of listing the Atlantic salmon under the ESA. Maine's blueberry, forestry, aquaculture, and paper industries sincerely believed that listing the salmon could potentially put them out of business and wreak economic havoc in Maine. In the spring of 1994 the forest products industry organized a committee to fight RESTORE's petition. The forestry committee's acronym was "FIASCO," which stood for the Forest Industry Atlantic Salmon Committee.

By August 1994, Project SHARE (Salmon Habitat and River Enhancement) had been formed by a coalition of private industry, state and federal agency representatives, and various other private interests. The goal of SHARE is "to conserve and enhance Atlantic salmon habitat in the Downeast region of Maine through voluntary and mutual cooperation of area landowners and businesses; local, state, and federal agencies; academia; and conservation organizations." Eventually, more than 30 organizations joined SHARE, although the federal agencies never signed the coalition's agreement. Nonprofit status was obtained, and various committees, including a seven-person Steering Committee and three standing committees focusing upon management, research, and education were formed. SHARE has been active in the removal of natural barriers to salmon migration in the Downeast rivers and the replacement of a water control dam gate at Meddybemps Lake and fishway baffles in the Dennys and Pleasant River drainages. Various other activities were undertaken, such as producing an informational brochure and a video and providing funding for a private hatchery on the Pleasant River.

In a new, joint effort to summarize all available scientific information, the Services formed an Atlantic Salmon Technical Working Group (ASTWG). The Working Group was established on April 23, 1994, at the Sheraton Tara Hotel in Danvers, Massachusetts, during an Atlantic Salmon Symposium sponsored by the New England Salmon Association. The first lengthy brainstorming session of the ASTWG occurred on April 26–27 in Gloucester, at the Northeast regional headquarters of the NMFS. Attendees at the meeting included representatives from all state and federal agencies throughout New England. Additionally, several authorities familiar with or involved in the Endangered Species program for the NMFS (from the Washington, D.C., and Seattle, Washington, areas) participated in the meeting. The group reviewed existing scientific data concerning New England Atlantic salmon populations and evaluated the biological validity of listing the species under the ESA. The meeting ended with attendees agreeing that additional information was needed (for that is typically how biologists end meetings). Since everyone initially agreed that all Atlantic salmon stocks outside Maine had been extirpated for several decades, they requested more specific information about Maine Atlantic salmon populations.

Shortly after the first ASTWG meeting in late April, the Services were internally "reminded" of the Federal Advisory Committee Act (or FACA, 5 U.S.C. App. 2) which essentially says that if federal agencies form a committee like the ASTWG they also need to invite public comment and scrutiny of the process. In this instance, such proceedings would undoubtedly have led to the formation of a cumbersome committee consisting of state and federal agencies, business and industry representatives, private conservation groups, and even the petitioners themselves. The Services promptly abandoned the ASTWG and established a six-member Biological Review Team consisting of three representatives from each of the two federal agencies. The Biological Review Team spent the balance of 1994 gathering and summarizing all available information submitted voluntarily to the agencies and additional information obtained through requests to the state agencies and other organizations represented at the April meeting in Gloucester.[64] In January 1995, the Services' Biological Review Team issued their report: "Draft: Status Review for Anadromous Atlantic Salmon in the United States." On March 10, 1995, the Services issued a press release that said that they had determined that available biological evidence indicated that listing the Atlantic salmon as endangered throughout its historic range was not warranted. However, the Services had "determined that sufficient information was available to support appropriate listing actions for the Distinct Population Segment (DPS) that consists of populations in the Sheepscot, Ducktrap, Narraguagus, Pleasant, Machias, East Machias, and Dennys rivers." While noting that the status of Atlantic salmon populations in the lower Kennebec River, Penobscot River, Tunk Stream, and lower St. Croix River "is uncertain and warrants further study," the Services went on to say that work on a proposed rule to initiate the appropriate listing actions under the Act was underway and "the proposal rule will be published promptly."

On Friday, September 29, 1995—one day before a Congressional moratorium on ESA listing actions went into effect—the Services published a notice in the Federal Register proposing to list Atlantic salmon in seven Maine rivers as threatened under the Endangered Species Act. The Services also announced that the State of Maine would be encouraged to take the lead role in developing a Conservation Plan that could possibly be accepted in lieu of listing or, alternatively, would allow the state to retain the lead for management of the salmon if the federal agencies listed the species.

Ironically, also on September 29, 1995, the State of Maine legislature, in a bill signed by Governor Angus King the previous March, abolished the Atlantic Sea Run Salmon Commission, replacing it with a new agency—the Atlantic Salmon Authority. A complete historical summary of the membership of the Atlantic Sea Run Salmon Commission from its inception in 1947 to its abolition in 1995 is provided in Appendix 5.

Modern Atlantic salmon stocking methods employed in Maine include all means of transportation. In these photos salmon are being distributed by canoe, helicopter, and tractor-trailer. Literally hundreds of thousands of salmon can be distributed daily anywhere within the state.

Starting Over: The Atlantic Salmon Authority Era, 1996

In one of its final actions as a state agency, the Atlantic Sea Run Salmon Commission adopted a new five-year (1995–2000) Statewide Atlantic Salmon Restoration and Management Plan in August 1995. The plan was designed to serve as a basis for river-

64. Team members from the National Marine Fisheries Service were as follows: Douglas Beach, Protected Species Program coordinator, Northeast Region, Gloucester, MA; Mary A. Colligan, fishery biologist, Habitat and Protected Resources Division, Northeast Region, Gloucester, MA; and John F. Kocik, research fishery biologist, Population Dynamics Branch, Northeast Fisheries Science Center, Woods Hole, MA. Team members from the Fish and Wildlife Service were Dan C. Kimball, regional fisheries supervisor, Region 5, Hadley, MA; Joseph F. McKeon, fisheries biologist/project leader, Office of Fishery Assistance, Laconia, NH; and Paul R. Nickerson, chief, Endangered Species Division, Region 5, Hadley, MA.

The first dam at Augusta on the Kennebec River was constructed in 1837. When the dam breached in 1974 (above photo) the State of Maine allowed it to be rebuilt without fish passage facilities. At that time the Department of Inland Fisheries and Game wanted to keep European carp (an undesirable species of fish that is related to a goldfish!) below the dam. Now, 25-years later, the State of Maine is battling to have the dam removed in an effort to restore anadromous fish populations to the 17-miles of free-flowing river above the dam. Carp still exist below the dam but their presence has not been an issue in recent years.

specific Operational Plans for all Maine rivers, and the preparation of those plans was expected to be accomplished in 1996. Earlier, on June 7, 1995, the Salmon Commission had also promulgated a statewide catch-and-release rule for salmon angling. Consequently, for the first time in state history, there was no legal retention of Atlantic salmon allowed in any waters of the state. There was little public opposition to the catch-and-release rule in 1995, although, a decade earlier, the Salmon Commission faced stiff opposition when proposing to reduce the season limit from 10 to 5 salmon to increase spawning escapements.[65]

The legislation that created the Atlantic Salmon Authority (ASA) in September 1995 was the result of a "compromise" between those political factions that wanted to abolish the Atlantic Sea Run Salmon Commission altogether, and those that simply wanted an expanded public membership. These factions were made up primarily of a few of the Downeast salmon fishing clubs and the Downeast Salmon Federation, and other politically active groups such as northern and southern Maine angling groups and the Maine Council of the Atlantic Salmon Federation. These latter groups wanted a more diverse and "balanced" membership in the Atlantic Salmon Commission, believing that this would be more representative of the state as a whole. Also of prime importance to the sponsors of the legislation was the need to create an agency that could conduct the business of Atlantic salmon restoration without undue influence or political interference from the commissioners of Inland

65. During the 1980's, the Atlantic Sea Run Salmon Commission gradually reduced the legal sport harvest of Atlantic salmon from two per day and no season limit to one per day and ten per season (1983). This was followed by a season limit of five, only one of which could be greater than 25 inches long (1985), to one grilse per angler per year (1994). Each successive conservation measure was usually vehemently opposed by some Maine salmon anglers and especially by those that fished the Downeast rivers. Although anglers could see that salmon runs were rapidly declining, it "wasn't their fault" that this was happening.

Fisheries and Wildlife and Marine Resources and the governor's office. On paper, the Atlantic Salmon Authority was given "sole authority" over Atlantic salmon in all waters of the state. An eight-member Atlantic Salmon Board was—by law—to be appointed by the governor no later than October 30, 1995. It would consist of the commissioners of Inland Fisheries and Wildlife and Marine Resources, four public members from various regions of the state, and representatives of the Penobscot Indian Nation and the Passamaquoddy Indian Tribe.

The proposed federal listing of Atlantic salmon under the ESA on September 29, 1995, prompted the governor's office to take *de facto* control of Atlantic salmon management in the seven rivers. Rather than appointing the remaining six members of the Salmon Board (the commissioners of Inland Fisheries and Wildlife and Marine Resources had already been appointed to their cabinet positions in January 1995), and thereby allowing the ASA to deal with the listing process, Governor Angus King delayed action until the 1996 special session of the legislature was near adjournment. A bill was then quietly submitted and quickly passed through the Maine legislature.[66] It delayed until July 1, 1997, the ASA's designated "sole authority" over Atlantic salmon in the seven rivers that the Services had proposed for listing as threatened under the Endangered Species Act.

Instead of appointing the Salmon Board of the Atlantic Salmon Authority in October 1995, Governor Angus King responded to the proposed threatened species listing of the seven rivers by issuing an Executive Order on October 20, 1995, creating the Maine Atlantic Salmon Task Force. Inland Fisheries and Wildlife Commissioner Ray B. Owen was appointed chairman of the Task Force, which was also composed of the following additional representatives: the commissioner of marine resources, the commissioner of agriculture, the state forester, representatives of private recreational fisheries interests and Native American sustenance fishers, and representatives of the agriculture, aquaculture, paper, and forestry sectors, and, notably, the governor's office.

The Task Force was given the following tasks: (1) advising the governor on the appropriate response to the proposed listing of Atlantic salmon in the Dennys, East Machias, Machias, Pleasant, Narraguagus, Ducktrap, and Sheepscot rivers, (2) developing a Conservation Plan to address preservation of salmon and their habitat on these seven rivers, and (3) advising the governor on the appropriate response to the federal request for comments on whether any native, naturally reproducing populations of Atlantic salmon remain in the Penobscot, Kennebec, and St. Croix rivers and Tunk Stream.

Commissioner Owen appointed many representatives (others simply showed up at meetings) to six technical working groups formed to advise the Task Force in its mission. The six technical working groups were Genetics, Forestry, Agriculture, Recreational Fishing, Aquaculture, and Status of the Penobscot, Kennebec, St. Croix, and Tunk Stream salmon stocks. Based upon the reports from the six technical working groups and advice from the Task Force, the governor responded to the two federal agencies in a letter with supporting documentation, dated December 27, 1995. In his response the governor stated that "the State of Maine is strongly opposed to the proposed threatened species listing on the seven rivers on the grounds that the stocks of the seven rivers do not meet the criteria for listing under the Act and that listing would be counter productive to the superior protection afforded the species under the existing Maine regulatory mechanism, as enhanced by a voluntary public/private partnership to conserve and restore salmon runs."

As an alternative to listing, the Governor requested that the USFWS and NMFS enter into a Cooperative Agreement with the State of Maine to implement the Conservation Plan that was being developed by the Maine Atlantic Salmon Task Force that he had appointed. The Task Force produced a draft Conservation Plan in November 1996 and initially submitted it to the USFWS and NMFS for "informal" review. Task Force Chairman Owen received more than 20 pages of "informal" comments from the Services on January 23, 1997, and a revised Conservation Plan was issued from the governor's office on March 4. The Services submitted the Plan to a thirty-day public review and comment period in May and a final rule (or withdrawal of the proposed rule) is expected in the fall of 1997.

Once the Task Force had nearly completed its initial draft of the Conservation Plan, the remain-

66. The bill (L.D. 1832) was introduced into the legislature on March 7, 1996, as a "governor's emergency bill," meaning that if passed by a 2/3 majority vote, it would become effective immediately. It was unanimously passed in the Senate (by vote of 27–0) on March 12 and in the House (by vote of 122–0) on March 13. Signed into law (P.L. 1996, Chapter 535) by Governor King on March 13, the bill had raced through the legislative process in fewer than five working days, with no opportunity for public input and without debate in either the House or Senate. In addition to delaying the ASA's sole authority over the seven rivers, the bill added a ninth member (at-large) to the Atlantic Salmon Board.

ing seven members of the Atlantic Salmon Board were finally appointed by the governor and confirmed by the legislature in August 1996. The nine-member Salmon Board began meeting monthly in its attempt to prepare a required report to the Maine legislature on how it plans to "manage the Atlantic salmon fishery in the state and to notify the legislature of any statutory requirements regarding staffing and budgetary matters." What is more important, the Atlantic Salmon Authority has been unable to define its role in the future of Maine's Atlantic salmon restoration program. Since the governor had usurped the ASA's management authority in the seven rivers with wild Atlantic salmon runs, and the Atlantic Salmon Authority is unlikely to be provided with the resources required to work effectively on the other nine Maine Atlantic salmon rivers with salmon runs, there is little real need for the Atlantic Salmon Board. If the U.S. Fish and Wildlife Service and National Marine Fisheries Service continue to fund the majority of Atlantic salmon restoration activities in Maine there is little incentive for the state to change the status quo.

And so "the jury is still out" on whether the Atlantic Salmon Authority represents a genuine effort at beginning a new chapter in the State of Maine's efforts to restore and manage Atlantic salmon or if this is the final chapter of the book on Maine Atlantic salmon as we have known them.

5

The Future of Maine Atlantic Salmon

5 The Future of Maine Atlantic Salmon

An Endangered Species?

The well-documented decline in wild Atlantic salmon populations in Maine during the past decade and the impending decision by two federal agencies on the 1993 petition to list the species as threatened has generated much discussion about the Endangered Species Act. While most people were aware of the fact that the bald eagle was a listed species, most Maine citizens (including those employed by various natural resource agencies) were completely unaware of the applicability of the Endangered Species Act to Maine Atlantic salmon populations. Despite all of the comments submitted to the U.S. Fish and Wildlife Service and National Marine Fisheries Service since 1993, I believe that most of them were irrelevant and often incorrect because they were not based on the best biological information as required by law under the Endangered Species Act.

> *For most Americans mention of the Endangered Species Act conjures up images of a triumphant Spotted Owl perched atop an enormous Douglas Fir, while below a group of unemployed loggers idly drink beer and pitch stones. The Endangered Species Act, some argue, is impeding American economic growth and prosperity—trashing the economy. Indeed, anecdotes abound of butterflies halting shopping projects, mosses scuttling highway extensions, and fish blocking resort development.*
>
> Meyer 1995

What is a species? What is an endangered or threatened species? What is an Evolutionary Significant Unit (ESU)? What is the definition of "reproductive isolation?" If Maine's wild Atlantic salmon populations are listed under the Endangered Species Act, will the state's economy be severely affected?

The Endangered Species Act defines a species as "any subspecies of fish or wildlife or plants, and any distinct population segment (DPS) of any species of vertebrate fish or wildlife that interbreeds when mature." An endangered species is any species that is in danger of becoming extinct in all or a significant portion of its range. A threatened species is any species that is likely to become an endangered species within the foreseeable future.

Since the definition of a species is ambiguous, the National Marine Fisheries Service adopted the term *evolutionary significant unit* (ESU) to create a working definition for the word *species* as it was being applied to Pacific salmon (Waples 1991). The ESU concept is now accepted by both the National Marine Fisheries Service and the U.S. Fish and Wildlife Service.

An evolutionary significant unit is defined as a population of animals that are "substantially reproductively isolated from other conspecific units (meaning other Atlantic salmon populations) and represent an important component in the evolutionary legacy of the species." The basis for this definition lies in the stock concept. It was for this reason that the stock concept and the importance of Maine Atlantic salmon stocks were presented in the first chapter of this book. Differences between salmon stocks are important because their strong homing instinct helps to maintain populations that are locally adapted to physical and environmental conditions. While the basis for the

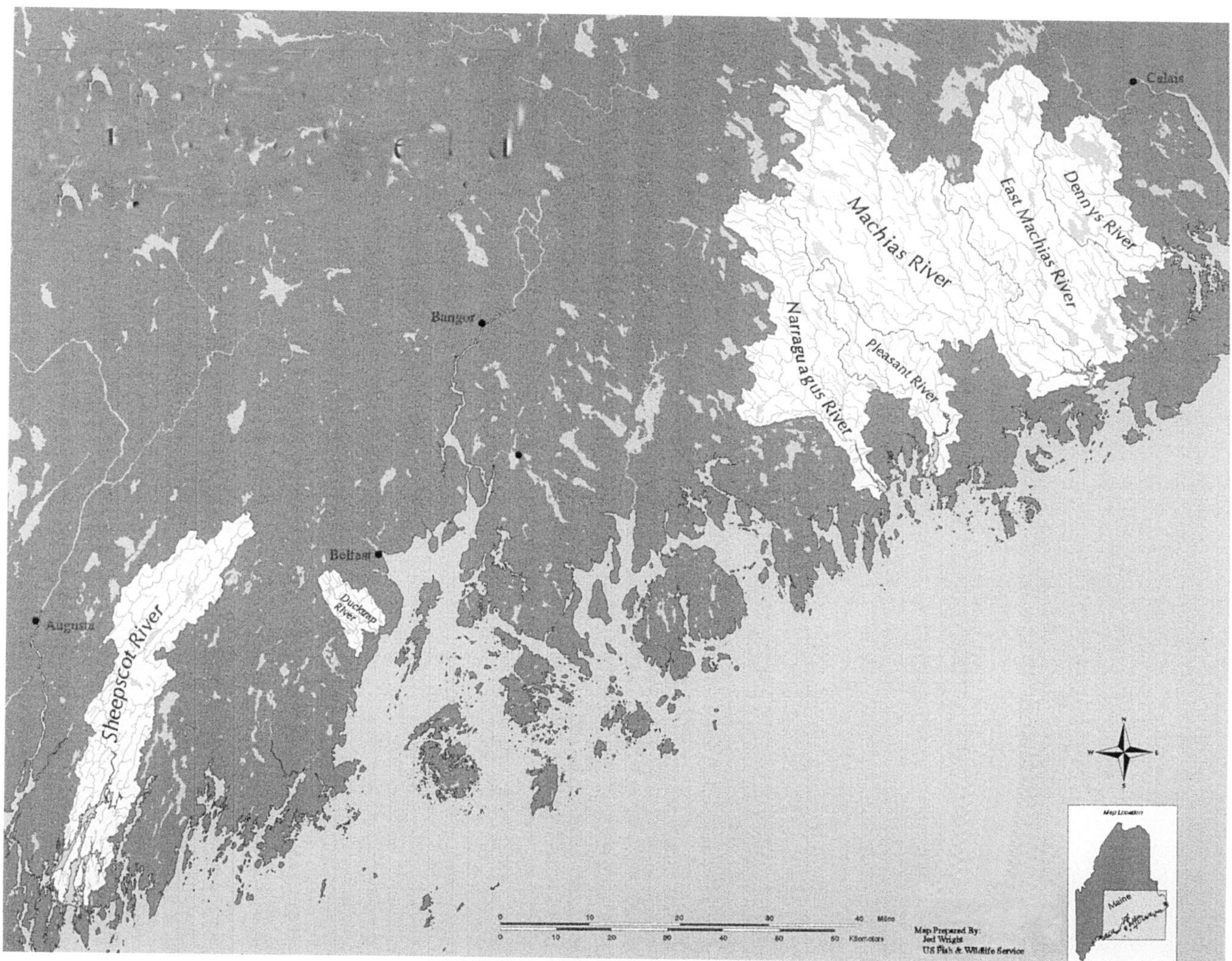

The Atlantic salmon populations in the seven Maine watersheds illustrated in the above photo are being considered for listing as "threatened" under the federal Endangered Species Act. A final ruling by the US Fish and Wildlife Service and National Marine Fisheries Service is expected in the fall of 1997.

definition of an ESU is founded in the stock concept, it is important to realize that the definition allows stocks to be grouped into "units" when information is available to conclude that such groupings are biologically appropriate.

Significantly, the U.S. Fish and Wildlife Service and National Marine Fisheries Service recently adopted (Federal Register Notice, Volume 6, No. 26, dated Wednesday, February 7, 1996) a new interpretation for the term "distinct population segment" (DPS) for the purposes of listing, delisting, and classifying vertebrates under the Endangered Species Act. In making a decision regarding the status of a possible DPS as threatened or endangered, the Services now consider the following three criteria: (1) the *discreteness* of the population segment in relation to the remainder of the species to which it belongs; (2) the *significance* of the population segment to the species to which it belongs; and (3) the population segment's conservation *status* in relation to the Act's standards for listing (i.e., is the population segment, when treated as if it were a species, endangered or threatened?). The terms *discreteness, significance,* and *status* were defined as follows:

> The *discreteness* of a population segment is determined if it satisfies either one of the following conditions: (1) it is markedly separated from other populations as a consequence of physical, physiological, ecological, or behavioral factors; or, (2) it is delimited by international governmental boundaries within which differences in control of exploitation, management of habitat, conservation status, or regulatory mechanisms exist that are significant.
>
> The *significance* of the discrete population segment is determined on the basis of scientific evidence, including—but not limited to—the following: (1) the persistence of the discrete population segment in a setting unusual or unique to the taxon; (2) evidence that loss of the discrete population segment would result in a significant gap in the range of the taxon; (3) evidence that the discrete population segment repre-

> sents the only surviving natural occurrence of a taxon that may be abundant elsewhere as an introduced population outside of its historic range; or, (4) evidence that the discrete population segment differs markedly from other populations of the species in its genetic characters.
>
> The *status* of the discrete population segment will be based on the Endangered Species Act's definitions of those terms and a review of the factors enumerated in section 4(a). It may be appropriate to assign different classifications to different DPS's of the same vertebrate taxon.

Regarding the phrase *substantially reproductively isolated*, the Endangered Species Act does not require that salmon populations be completely isolated, as long as differences are allowed to develop and be maintained. There are many ways that reproductive isolation can occur. Examples include spatial (geography) and temporal (time) isolation, and behavioral and reproductive isolation. While geographical isolation is one way to separate salmon populations, life history (e.g., run timing, spawning) and behavioral (e.g., mate selection, aggressiveness) differences may also bring about the same result. What is more important, the presence of nonindigenous salmon in the stream does not compromise reproductive isolation unless those fish reproduce successfully and their offspring also survive to reproduce in a way that decreases the fitness and survival of the local stocks.

In the pending action upon the 1993 petition to list the Dennys, East Machias, Machias, Pleasant, Narraguagus, Ducktrap, and Sheepscot river Atlantic salmon stocks as threatened, the Services have proposed that these seven rivers represent one ESU (not *seven* as many people think). Arguing against this logic is difficult, since there can be little doubt that: (1) the salmon populations in these rivers are reproductively isolated from other conspecific units (for example, those in Canada), and (2) Maine salmon stocks represent an important evolutionary legacy of the species, in that they are the last remaining populations of naturally spawning Atlantic salmon in the United States.

In building the case for reproductive isolation, there is no indication of interbreeding (successful or otherwise) between Maine and Canadian Atlantic salmon, with the nearest Canadian ESU being the Saint John River salmon population. This is based upon the fact that several hundred thousand Canadian salmon have been uniquely marked or tagged in the last 40 years and only one has been found in a Maine river (a Miramichi River–origin grilse that strayed into the Penobscot River in 1974). Similarly, during the same period nearly two million salmon were tagged and released in Maine rivers and only a few have shown up in the Saint John River. Hatchery-origin salmon are much more likely to stray into other rivers. Thus, these few documented strays illustrate that the straying rate of wild-origin salmon must be extremely low. Additionally, if there was a significant amount of genetic exchange between Maine and Canadian salmon populations, over time they would exhibit similar genotypic (genetic) and phenotypic (life history) similarities; they do not. It is for these reasons that I contend that there is no evidence of interbreeding between Canadian and Maine Atlantic salmon and that there can be little doubt that Maine and Canadian Atlantic salmon populations are reproductively isolated.

With respect to the genetic legacy question, there is evidence to suggest that distinct genetic differences exist between Maine salmon populations and those in Canada and Europe. Maine Atlantic salmon populations are at the southern extent of the range of the species, and it is likely that they are uniquely adapted to survive in our rivers. It has been argued that Maine's wild salmon stocks were eliminated by the dams that prevented access to spawning areas and by the stocking of Canadian salmon stocks in some Maine rivers. In order for these statements to be true, all of Maine's salmon stocks would have had to be eliminated simultaneously for two complete generations (14 years); simply stated, that did not happen.

Interpreting historical records concerning Maine Atlantic salmon populations is problematic because of the difficulty observing and counting salmon accurately. Also, their abundance varies greatly over time due to natural conditions. For example, Rounsefell and Bond (1949) stated that "in 1942 heavy ice jams swept away the dams in the lower Narraguagus River and the salmon run commenced to improve rapidly." If this were an accurate statement, from where did those salmon come? The only artificial stocking to occur in the Narraguagus River was 25,000 parr in 1931 and 85,000 fry in 1936. Most of the few, if any, adult returns from these releases would have occurred in 1935 and 1940, respectively. It is also known that a Mr. Ray Plumber caught a 19-pound salmon in the Narraguagus River on July 26, 1941, which means that this fish was probably a three sea-winter salmon that originated from natural spawning in 1934 or 1935. Similarly, since it is known that there was a good run of salmon in the river in 1943, a substantial amount of natural spawning must have taken place in 1938 (remember from Chapter 2 that Maine salmon typically exhibit a five-year life cycle). Considering the equipment used to transport and stock juvenile salmon at the time (milk cans) and the fact that fish were put into the river in one or two spots, leads me to conclude that: (1) Atlantic salmon were a lot more abundant in the Narraguagus River in the 1930's than it appears from historical records, and (2) the origin of those fish was from natural spawning in the Narraguagus River itself, since the timing of the adult returns did not coincide with the stocking of small numbers of Miramichi River origin stocks that occurred in 1931 and 1936.

Evidently, 1943 was a good year for Atlantic salmon in other Maine rivers thought to be lacking salmon, because alewife dippers in the lower East Machias River reportedly took 50 salmon that year. Clearly, as in the Narraguagus River, there were more wild salmon in the East Machias in the 1940's than portrayed in the Rounsefell and Bond report 1948. Additionally, since very little stocking occurred in the East Machias River (30,000 Penobscot-origin fry in 1917 and 7,000 Dennys-origin parr in 1940) natural spawning must have been taking place in the river for many years. Redd counts in the Dennys River during the period 1940–1943 ranged from 249 (1940) to 471 (1942), indicating that there was a run of 250–500 salmon in the Dennys at that time.

While a few Maine rivers were heavily stocked with salmon fry originating from eggs imported from Canada in the 1920's and 1930's (e.g., the Dennys and Narraguagus), other rivers (e.g., Machias and Sheepscot) received few, if any, such releases of hatchery-reared stocks. I believe that those releases of Canadian-origin salmon would have produced few, if any, adult returns based upon the fact that later experiments with releases of marked fry and parr (in the 1940's and early 1950's) showed that adult returns ranged from "insignificant" to "nil," and the survival of older salmon (regardless of origin) stocked during the period 1962–1970 was also poor (Fletcher 1955; ASRSC 1958; Fletcher et al. 1982; ASRSC unpublished data). Similarly, experiments with Carlin-tagged and fin-clipped hatchery smolts of Miramichi and native origin (Machias and Narraguagus) in the 1960's revealed that survival of the Canadian stocks released into Maine rivers was much lower than that of native stocks. More importantly, most (80–93%) of the Miramichi-origin stocks returned as late-run, one sea-winter salmon (i.e., male grilse), while most (85–95%) of the native stocks returned as early-run, multi sea-winter (i.e., female) salmon (Fletcher et al. 1982; Baum and Jordan 1982; ASRSC unpublished data). Consequently, there is little evidence to support claims that Maine's wild salmon

Although detractors of the Endangered Species Act often describe it as blind to the needs of people and the economy, every government and academic examination of the endangered species process has reached the opposite conclusion: political, economic, and social considerations permeate the listings process. In fact, for every tale about a project, business, or property owner allegedly harmed by efforts to protect some plant or animal species there are over one-thousand stories of virtual 'non-interference.' In reviewing the record of 18,211 endangered species consultations by the Fish and Wildlife Service/National Marine Fisheries covering the period 1987-1991, the General Accounting Office found that only 11% (2,050) resulted in the issuance of formal biological opinions. The other 89% were handled informally—that is to say the projects proceeded on schedule and without interference. Of the 2,050 formal opinions issued a mere 181—less than 10%—concluded that the proposed projects were likely to pose a threat to an endangered plant or animal. And most of these 181 projects were completed, albeit with some modification in design and construction. In short, more than 99% of the projects reviewed under the Endangered Species Act eventually proceeded unhindered or with marginal additional time and economic costs. Given the political and economic screening that occurs in listings cases it is not surprising that no measurable negative economic effects are detectable.

Meyer 1995

stocks are a hybrid of original salmon runs and introduced Canadian stocks.

Conceding that Maine Atlantic salmon are a "species," and that the Maine population (collectively, the distinct population segment encompassing those stocks from the lower Kennebec River to the lower St. Croix River) is biologically different from the Saint John and other Canadian salmon distinct population segments, are they a threatened or endangered species? The answer to that question must be a subjective one. The Services have proposed to list seven Maine salmon stocks as threatened rather than endangered because of the success of ongoing recovery efforts that began two years *before* the petition, and because the Maine DPS is not likely to be in danger of extinction in the near future. This is a logical conclusion, since the total salmon returns to the seven rivers under consideration currently range from about 300 to 500 annually (3,000 to 4,000 if all salmon stocks in the Maine distinct population segment are included), and the river-specific stocking programs and other management measures taken since the late 1980's are expected to increase the numbers of salmon in all Maine rivers during the late 1990's.

If the federal services list the Atlantic salmon in Maine as threatened, will Maine's economy "go down the tubes?" Will timber harvesting be prohibited? Will the blueberry, cranberry, and aquaculture industries in eastern Maine be regulated to the point of bankruptcy? Will local residents be required to obtain a federal permit to till their gardens each spring? The answers to these questions are—of course not! A recent study published by the Massachusetts Institute of Technology (Meyer 1995) concluded that the Endangered Species Act has *not* had a harmful effect on state economies and that protections offered to threatened animals and plants do not impose a measurable economic burden on development activity at the state level. Furthermore, the MIT report stated that the economic effects of endangered species listings are so highly localized, and of such small scale and short duration, that they do not substantially effect state economic performance in the aggregate.

Finally, will the U.S. Fish and Wildlife Service and National Marine Fisheries Service list any Maine Atlantic populations as threatened under the Endangered Species Act? Although the final decision is still several months away, the politics of the situation in Maine clearly will very likely make it difficult for the federal government to list the species, despite the fact that the decision is supposed to be based upon the best available *biological* information. Maine's governor and the entire Maine congressional delegation have made it clear to the Services that they will fight any listing of the Atlantic salmon under the Endangered Species Act. Since the Services will undoubtedly be sued by either the state or the petitioners, they are in a no-win situation. Therefore, it makes sense for the federal agencies to be able to be on the same "team" as the state. Supporting the Governor's Conservation Plan, if it were appropriately revised, would accomplish this. In this way the State of Maine and the federal agencies may be united and could be perceived as supporting the administration's argument that listing is unnecessary while continuing to acknowledge that Maine Atlantic salmon are unique.

During the 16-month period that the Conservation Plan was being drafted, the Services made an extraordinary effort to help the governor's Atlantic Salmon Task Force prepare a document that would (hopefully) avert the *need* for listing. In fact, the National Marine Fisheries Service paid the state $60,000 to hire a person to help put the Plan together. It is doubtful that the Governor's Conservation Plan submitted in March 1997 will fully satisfy the federal agencies' requirements; therefore, changes will probably be necessary. Accepting an appropriately revised Plan will likely be the way that the federal agencies can avert the social and political repercussions that would result from listing, since many people believe that such an action would be counterproductive to the goal of restoring viable salmon runs to Maine rivers. So, the question is not *if* the Services will list the salmon under the Endangered Species Act; rather, what remains to be determined are the words that will be used to justify *not* listing the species.

I believe, without question, that the Maine Atlantic salmon distinct population segment qualifies as an evolutionary significant unit under the Endangered Species Act. However, if the species were to be listed as threatened, the time to do it would have been in the early 1990's when the abundance of wild salmon was at an all-time low. Recent increases in the abundance of Maine's wild salmon runs resulting from the successful application of the 1992 Prelisting Recovery Plan, and the recovery time provided by the four-year period required in responding to the original petition have contributed to averting the need to list at this time. In fairness, the governor's strong response to the perceived "threat" of listing has demonstrated that the state took the petition seriously. At the very least, state government, business, and industry, and various private entities have come to realize that Maine's wild Atlantic salmon populations are a national treasure—even if they cannot proclaim it publicly.

The Challenge of Salmon Restoration in the Twenty-first Century

Given my prediction that Maine Atlantic salmon populations will *not* be listed as threatened under the Endangered Species Act, what is the future of the species in the twenty-first century? In a word—excellent. However, the challenges facing the species are quite different from those at any other time in Maine history. As we revisited each era in Maine salmon restoration history (Chapter 4) such issues as dams, fish passage, predation, overfishing, stocking, and water quality surfaced repeatedly. This is because salmon restoration programs traditionally are designed to mitigate—not remove—the underlying problems that originally caused the need for the restoration program. While many issues of the 1890's remain unresolved in the 1990's, the issues of the twenty-first century will be much more complex.

In some way, shape, or form, the Governor's Conservation Plan for Seven Rivers[67] will likely be accepted and implemented, especially if the federal agencies continue to fund the bulk of the Plan as expected by the state. The mere fact that the Plan exists will help to keep the focus upon protecting salmon habitat and populations until the furor over the proposed Endangered Species Act listing dies down. Once salmon numbers rebound, as I predict they will do (independently of the Conservation Plan), there will be much less adversarial political interest in the species overall. Only then will biological, sociological, political, and economic decisions be made in a rational atmosphere, allowing the restoration program to focus upon the needs of the species as opposed to the perceived threats of listing.

Maine's Atlantic salmon are within the southern part of the range of the species, and this will always pose significant challenges to the restoration of self-sustaining runs in some rivers. Likewise, high water temperatures will continue to be of concern in some rivers, as will competition from nonnative species, low (cyclical) marine survival, and commercial exploitation. Under these less-than-ideal environmental conditions, Maine's small salmon populations are more likely to be adversely affected by natural predation and the effects of the "ultimate predator." Yet, none of these challenges by itself is insurmountable or needs to be mortal to Maine's Atlantic salmon resource.

Throughout my 30 years of Atlantic salmon restoration work in Maine I've been told that all of the problems facing the species are caused by someone else or another entity. Anglers blame predators, inadequate stocking, government bureaucracy, and commercial fishermen. Commercial fishermen also blame predators, along with habitat degradation, and overfishing in rivers by anglers and poachers. Business and industry leaders blame predation, poaching, commercial fishing, global warming, acid precipitation, and inadequate stocking. Scientists blame natural population cycles, "recruitment overfishing," environmental conditions, and political interference.

To some extent, these arguments may be applicable in some specific instances; however, I believe that the following nine issues (not listed in order of priority) will determine the ultimate fate of Maine's Atlantic salmon resources in the twenty-first century:

1. *Water.* The use and management of water in Maine rivers are crucial to the survival of Maine Atlantic salmon populations. Suitable flows are required for juvenile survival and production, adult migration and survival, maintenance of water quality, and angling opportunity. Water is also required for many business and industrial uses and for agricultural purposes. Considering the current government focus upon providing jobs and economic opportunities, the State of Maine will face unprecedented challenges in regulating the use and management of its water resources in rivers with Atlantic salmon populations.

2. *Aquaculture.* The pen-rearing of large numbers of Atlantic salmon in Maine is a reality that must be acknowledged. Considering the huge investment of private capital in the Maine salmon farming industry (presently six freshwater hatcheries, 800 sea cages, an annual salmon harvest valued at $55 million) and the significant number of jobs provided to the locally depressed communities of eastern Maine, the issues associated with interactions of wild-origin and aquaculture-origin salmon are likely to become more complex in the future. The *potential* negative impacts to wild salmon stocks associated with salmon farming operations (genetic and behavioral interactions, introduction or increased incidences of diseases and parasites, etc.) have been well documented in the scientific literature. We are currently limited to such

67. This could be categorized as a business and economic conservation plan, since—in my opinion—Atlantic salmon conservation activities will be allowed to occur as long as they do not adversely affect existing (and future) businesses, industries, and job opportunities in Maine.

actions as reducing the probability of salmon escaping in large numbers and maintaining "good" fish husbandry practices. Also, more studies or research into areas such as the sterilization of farmed salmon or another technological remedy, such as barriers to keep undesirable fish out of Maine rivers, are considered essential. The fact is, domesticated salmon will escape from salmon farms and they will interact with wild salmon. I am not convinced that the current strategy of "minimizing" these interactions is sufficient to protect all of Maine's wild salmon runs in the future.

3. *Hatcheries.* Let me state unequivocally that I believe that hatcheries are a valuable management *tool*, with a valid place in Atlantic salmon restoration and management programs. However, there is an overreliance upon them in Maine and elsewhere at this time. Many people (especially children) now view hatcheries as *the* source of salmon for Maine rivers. It seems as though every salmon fishing club in Maine that does not have a hatchery fervently wants one of its own. If a local hatchery is not an option at this time, many clubs utilize or seek out some other program involving artificial supplementation. Examples of this include the current trend of installing streamside egg incubation boxes or streamside parr rearing units, although there is little, if any, evidence that these programs contribute to future adult salmon returns. While these types of stocking programs are usually justified on social grounds (maintaining public interest, a "hands-on" experience, etc.), there is a danger of promoting false expectations for future salmon runs. Despite the historical lessons outlined in Chapter 4, many people continue to follow the belief that all that is needed to restore Atlantic salmon runs is simply to stock more hatchery-reared salmon and build fishways where they are needed. I believe that weaning the public from the increasing dependence upon hatcheries to supply future salmon runs in Maine rivers will be one of the most difficult challenges facing the State of Maine, especially since rearing adult salmon (in captivity in freshwater and/or sea cages) is now technologically feasible. One has only to be reminded that more than 96 million Atlantic salmon have been stocked in Maine rivers since 1870 (see Appendix 6 for a complete historical summary of the stocking of hatchery-reared salmon in Maine)—yet not one salmon population has been "restored." In my opinion, stocking is not the answer to sustainable and increasing Atlantic salmon runs in Maine rivers.

4. *Unsupervised Private Initiatives.* The recent antigovernment/more local control era has effectively left several Atlantic salmon restoration programs in the hands of volunteers who are well intentioned but inadequately trained in the biological needs of the fish or how to conduct a restoration program. One problem with depending too heavily upon volunteers to carry out many aspects of salmon restoration programs is that they often lack the knowledge about the life history and biological requirements of the species. Unnecessary conflicts regarding such basic matters as salmon stocks, genetics, stocking practices, and evaluation techniques often occur, resulting in dissension between the volunteers and the fishery agencies that they are trying to help. Additionally, volunteer efforts normally begin with a wave of enthusiasm, followed by waning support. The final burden of continuing the effort is left to a few individuals or, more often than not, a few government employees who are left unexpectedly to operate without the necessary support to carry out the initial effort. Atlantic salmon restoration programs involve complex interactions among state and federal government agencies, business and industry representatives, and many private interests. While government can act as the catalyst for the development of partnerships that welcome the use of volunteers, it must always assume a strong leadership role in the planning and execution of long-term, biologically sound Atlantic salmon restoration and management programs in Maine.

5. *Technology.* The use of technology is a double-edged sword for Maine's Atlantic salmon populations. On one hand, many current salmon restoration and management activities depend heavily upon the use of technology. An example is the employment of sophisticated salmon habitat and population monitoring equipment. On the other hand, the history of Atlantic salmon restoration efforts clearly illustrates the failure of technology to solve the human-caused problems that continue to plague salmon restoration programs throughout the world. Reliance upon fishways (both upstream and downstream varieties) to guide salmon past dams and other artificial obstructions is not a substitute for unobstructed passage. Similarly, after more than 125 years of fish culture we know, and continue to show, that the survival rate of hatchery-reared salmon is more variable and lower than that of wild salmon. Yet, humans continue to hope and rely upon technology to "fix" our problems. Recent examples of this misguided dependency upon technology in Maine are plans to install barriers (weirs) on eastern Maine rivers to "exclude" aquaculture escapees and to grow adult salmon in cages to supplement wild stocks. Producing "ge-

netically engineered" salmon that can conquer some of the obstacles that they encounter during their life cycle is also being considered in some areas. Based upon history and current science, I believe that these efforts—if used as long-term solutions—are also doomed to failure. Locally adapted, naturally spawning, wild salmon subjected to natural selection in their native habitats, from mate selection to stream life and ocean migrations, should be the goal; quick fixes for problems created by human activities are not the answers.

6. *Politics.* In number 4 above, I expressed the opinion that government must maintain leadership and supervisory roles over long-term Atlantic salmon restoration and management programs. Here, at the risk of contradicting myself, I must make a plea for government to act in a biologically responsible manner. It is becoming all too easy for various entities, many of which represent small constituencies, and do not represent the majority or what is biologically prudent, to influence Atlantic salmon restoration and management programs unduly. Political agendas and parochialism have no place in these matters. The basic biological needs of the Atlantic salmon have been well documented for more than 100 years, yet it is common for local, state, and national politics (and politicians) to induce changes that can result in profound negative impacts to Maine's Atlantic salmon resources.

7. *Greed.* Atlantic salmon were once abundant in Maine; human greed played a major role in diminishing the resource. Commercial fisheries, sport fisheries, poaching, habitat degradation, dams, stocking practices, and government actions or inactions contributed to the situations that exist today. Once Atlantic salmon runs rebound, as I predict that they will, all aspects of society must guard against a repeat of the history chronicled in Chapter 4. It will be appealing to relax regulations prematurely or to ignore the basic needs of the salmon when they are again more numerous.

8. *Habitat Degradation.* As humans we have outlawed most of the obvious activities that degrade salmon habitat and reduce salmon population levels—for example, building dams, discharging raw pollution, and using DDT. More recently, however, there have been major changes to the salmon's environment (and ours) that have been documented globally. These changes may have long-term consequences for salmon habitat and populations; examples include increased ultraviolet light, acid precipitation, and global warming. Locally, many subtle activities take place annually that may have cumulative effects that ultimately are just as harmful. For example, it is possible that the uses of pesticides and herbicides currently believed to be "safe," water withdrawal operations, or certain types of development projects could subtly influence water quality, reproduction, and development of Atlantic salmon, or other species of animals lower down on the salmon's food chain. Without sounding like an alarmist, I caution that human activities that could alter the biodiversity of the salmon's habitat and its long-term productivity must be monitored constantly. Unfortunately, long-term monitoring programs are often difficult to justify and expensive to carry out, since the activities that are being monitored are perceived to be harmless.

9. *Public Apathy.* In recent years many private conservation organizations, for example the Maine Council of the Atlantic Salmon Federation and many of its affiliates, have worked hard to promote an awareness of and participation in the Maine Atlantic salmon restoration program among their constituents and among young, school-aged children. However, despite their extensive efforts, no organization—public or private—has succeeded in

> *The salmon are a test of a healthy environment, a lesson in environmental needs. Their abundant presence on the spawning beds is a lesson of hope, a reassurance that all is well with water and land, a lesson of deep importance for the future of man. If there ever is a time when the salmon no longer return, man will know that he has failed again and moved one stage nearer to his own final disappearance."*
>
> World-renowned author, angler, and conservationist Roderick Haig-Brown (1974)

arousing *general* public interest in Maine's Atlantic salmon resource on a broad scale. It is for this reason that I believe that public apathy has been, and continues to be, the number one threat to the restoration and management of viable Atlantic salmon populations in Maine rivers. People who do not fish for Atlantic salmon, and those who do, need to be reminded constantly of the intimate connection between Maine citizens, the Atlantic salmon, and our mutually shared habitat.

6

Charles G. Atkins—Maine's Atlantic Salmon Pioneer

6 Charles G. Atkins—Maine's Atlantic Salmon Pioneer

The heroic Atlantic salmon restoration efforts of Charles Atkins, Maine's Atlantic salmon pioneer, were chronicled in Chapter 4. The following few pages represent a humble attempt to expand upon the life of an extraordinary person—someone I unhesitatingly nominate as the Thomas Edison of fish culture in America.

Charles Grandison Atkins, son of Elisha Atkins and Lucy Thaxter Cushing, was born on January 19, 1841, in New Sharon, Maine. After graduating from Augusta High School, he entered Bowdoin college in Brunswick, Maine, in the spring of 1855—at the age of 14.[68] Most of Atkins's classes at Bowdoin were languages—Greek, Latin, English, French, German, Spanish, Hebrew, Italian, and Anglo-Saxon. The balance of his studies involved theology, algebra, trigonometry, calculus, rhetoric, astronomy, chemistry, mental philosophy, analogy, natural history, and "Upham's Treatise on the Will." Given his studies of languages and mathematics at Bowdoin, how and why Charles Atkins eventually became such an outstanding scientist and fish culturist is perplexing.

Atkins was elected permanent president of the class of 1861 three years after graduation. As a student, he was always in good company at Bowdoin, for among the members of his graduating class were students destined to become the founder of Bath Iron Works (Thomas W. Hyde), a president of the University of Maine (Merritt C. Fernald), a president of Norwich University (Charles A. Curtis), and a chief justice of the Maine Supreme Court (Lacilius A. Emory). Other Bowdoin students who graduated with Charles Atkins went on to become doctors (12), lawyers (10), businessmen (9), teachers and clergymen (5 each), one U.S. senator (from North Carolina), and one dentist. Sadly, five of his fellow students were also casualties of the Civil War, and one of those fought for the South!

Charles Grandison Atkins—the State of Maine's Atlantic salmon pioneer. Commissioner of Fisheries for Maine, 1867-1871; fish culturist with the United States Fisheries Service, 1872-1920.

Upon graduating from Bowdoin College in 1861, Charles Atkins traveled to the Midwest where he taught school for six years in Green Bay, Wisconsin. He was drafted into military service in November 1863 while living in Green Bay; however, as was customary during those times, he paid a commutation fee to avoid serving in the military. He returned to Augusta where his father operated a box factory on the Kennebec River, intending to become a doctor of medicine. Instead, in 1867, Charles Atkins was appointed by the Maine legislature as one of the first two commissioners of fisheries for Maine.[69]

At the direction of the Maine legislature of 1866–1867, the duties of the two commissioners were "to examine the rivers of Maine for the consideration of the restoration of sea fish to Maine lakes and tributary streams, the introduction of new varieties of freshwater fish, and the protection of fish generally in inland water." In January 1868, Atkins and fellow Commissioner Foster issued their first report on the condition of Maine rivers and the status of fisheries. They

68. During this time in Maine history, there were three school terms with students attending classes during the spring, summer, and fall. Winter was reserved for work, and it was not uncommon for college students to teach in public school.

69. The other commissioner was Nathan W. Foster.

The fishway at the Bangor dam shown at left (circa 1875) was designed by Charles Atkins.

In this photo from June of 1897 (right), Charles Atkins oversees the collection of Atlantic salmon broodstock at the Bangor dam. Thirty-three salmon were collected and 26 survived to be spawned at the Craig Brook Hatchery in November. An additional 665 live salmon were purchased that year from commercial fishermen for broodstock purposes.

attributed the near extinction of fish populations in many streams to impassable dams, along with overfishing and water pollution (Kendall 1936). The remedial actions proposed by Atkins and Foster and the accomplishments of Charles Atkins are chronicled in greater detail in Chapter 4.

Atkins served as commissioner of fisheries of Maine from 1867 to 1871. During that time his pioneering work in the field of artificial fish culture focused upon trying to collect and rear Sebago (landlocked) salmon; however, he had a keen interest in all of Maine's fishery resources. Atkins collected American shad eggs from adult fish taken in the commercial fishery at Augusta, he studied white perch and determined that they spawned in June and July, and he learned that striped bass were in spawning condition in the Kennebec River each year around the first of July.

Since the commissioners of fisheries felt that the most important work to be done was the construction of fishways, Atkins turned his attention to designing and constructing them in Maine rivers. He is credited with inventing the "fishway," and *the Maine Fisheries Commissioner's Report* of 1877 noted that "the large fishway in the dam at Bangor was designed by Charles G. Atkins, Esq."

Atkins ended his term as fisheries commissioner of Maine in 1871 and, on July 1, 1872, began his work with the United States Fish Commission. He was employed by the Commission and its successor, the U.S. Bureau of Fisheries, until his retirement on August 21, 1920.

Beyond his scholarly works in the area of fish culture, Charles Atkins conducted ground-breaking tagging experiments with Penobscot River salmon from 1872 to 1880. Following spawning operations at Craig Brook Hatchery, Atkins attached aluminum plate tags to a total of more than 1,200 salmon that were ultimately liberated at tidewater in Bucksport in 1872, 1875, and 1880. Atkins noted that the first group of tagged salmon recovered in the spring of 1873 was in poor condition. He observed that the males had faded in color and the hooks on their lower jaws had decreased in size. Additionally, he noted that the female salmon had regained their silvery color, although most were smaller than the previous fall. Atkins also reported that he had found the "germs" of the next litter of eggs in their ovaries. From the 357 tagged salmon released in November of 1875, many kelts were taken in the spring of 1876. More important, three salmon were recovered in the 1877 commercial fishery, "all in good condition and of larger size than when released." In 1880, another 252 tagged salmon were liberated in the Orland River, and this time Charles Atkins offered a small reward to commercial fishermen who returned any salmon bearing tags. Twelve salmon were recovered the following spring (all in poor condition). However, in June 1882, five "prime" salmon were recovered and returned to Charles Atkins. These salmon, ranging from 7 1/2 to 14 1/2 pounds in weight when released in 1880, weighed from 14 3/4 to 21 pounds at capture! Atkins' pioneering tagging experiments led him to conclude that Penobscot salmon were four years old at first maturity, and that they were biennial spawners.[70] He published his work on the biennial spawning of Maine Atlantic salmon in 1885. Additional innovative Atlantic salmon programs that Charles Atkins successfully introduced were the rearing and spawning of captive (domestic) Atlantic salmon broodstock in freshwater in the 1890's, and the reconditioning and spawning of sea run salmon kelts in freshwater during the period 1908–1910. Both of these techniques, which were reintroduced to Atlantic salmon restoration programs throughout New England in the 1970's, continue to be widely utilized in Maine and elsewhere.

It is a pleasure for me to dedicate this book to Charles G. Atkins, Maine's Atlantic salmon pioneer. I will always respect and admire his contributions and accomplishments on behalf of Maine's wild Atlantic salmon, and vow to strive to ensure that his efforts were not in vain.

Atkins published 35 articles in publications of the U.S. Bureau of Fisheries, 12 papers in the *Transactions of the American Fisheries Society*, and he was also the author of the first five reports of the Maine fisheries commissioners. In total, Charles Atkins published more than 100 papers, official reports, essays, and contributions to various popular and scientific journals and magazines of his day (Kendall 1936). Among his published works were portions of the *Manual of Fish Culture* for Atlantic and landlocked salmon published by the U.S. Fish Commission in 1897. In 1908 his article "Foods for Young Salmonid Fishes" won him a $150 prize (in gold) from the Fourth International Fishery Congress.

While he published many of his works, Charles Grandison Atkins's greatest legacy was the many notebooks that he meticulously kept throughout his career. His observations and experiments are often illustrated by his own sketches and drawings, and the neatness and care by which he documented his work are exemplary. Atkins was also an accomplished photographer, who left behind hundreds of carefully cataloged glass plate negatives of his work and local scenes. Much of his work remains hidden in government offices and archives today—probably never published because many of his studies were in various stages of completion. Stop for a moment and consider the wealth of information that Charles Atkins could have left society had he had access to today's personal computer, dictaphone, fax machine and video camera!

Charles Atkins married Nellie Moses of Bucksport on November 24, 1874. They had no children. He died of "renal sclerosis" on September 21, 1921, at the age of 80.

70. Since scale reading was unheard of in those days it was assumed that smolts went to sea at two years of age. Thus, the biennial spawning habit of salmon led Atkins to conclude that the fish would be four years old as maiden spawners.

Epilogue

Epilogue

Chapter 5 outlined many conservation measures that I consider to be crucial to the future of Maine's wild Atlantic salmon populations. As a reminder, those measures *NOT* listed included more hatcheries, added stocking, predator control, more studies, and additional funding. I believe that there are really only two simple measures required to protect and maintain Maine Atlantic salmon:

(1) protect the integrity and diversity of habitats for all life stages of the species, and

(2) protect the integrity and genetic diversity of naturally spawning salmon populations.

> *What we call wildness is a civilization other than our own.*
>
> Henry David Thoreau

As humans, we are biologically, socially, environmentally, morally, and ethically challenged to do the right things in this regard. Aldo Leopold was on the right track (over 50 years ago) when he said that "a thing is right when it tends to preserve the integrity, stability, and beauty of the biotic community."

I view Maine's wild Atlantic salmon as an image of human life. Each year—in fact each day—in the life of the salmon is different. If there is one certainty in the occupation of a fishery scientist, it is the uncertainly of what will occur tomorrow, next month, next year, or five years from now in his or her work with *Salmo salar*. No one knows how many salmon will return to any of Maine's rivers this year or the next. Undoubtedly, there will always be good salmon runs and poor salmon runs, triumphs and disappointments. For me, the conclusion to the end of the salmon run each year sets the stage for anticipation of the mysteries surrounding what is to occur next year; it is but one of those small reasons to look eagerly to the future.

As with humans, each wild salmon is a unique individual. Body lengths and weights vary, as do forms and shapes, spots and colors, marks and scars, and fins and eyes, and even individual temperaments. A salmon can be easily alarmed; likewise, it can also be easily calmed. The Atlantic salmon is sport, and it is food. It is grace and beauty, and awkwardness and ugliness. The mysteries associated with each fish are intriguing to me—where did it come from, what has it experienced during its lifetime, where is it going, what is its fate? The constant uncertainty and the baffling secrets hidden within each salmon's life are also oxymoronic because of the certainty of annual salmon runs and the finality of outcomes. Salmon spawn, parr are produced, smolts leave, adults return to complete the circle of life. In reality, as we humans change and adapt to our environment so, too, do the Atlantic salmon. The fact that we know so much, yet so little, about the salmon is testimony to the stamina, plasticity, and resiliency of the species.

Just when you think you know something about the Atlantic salmon, reality redefines itself and you begin to question what you thought you knew. In working with and appreciating the mysteries of Atlantic salmon, there are few absolutes and no guarantees. None of our cherished beliefs about the species should be permanently engraved in stone. In this book I have attempted to summarize what is currently known about the life history of Maine's wild Atlantic salmon and humanity's attempts to restore and manage the species. Future historians, no doubt benefitting from time and additional information, will be able to expand upon our knowledge of the species and perhaps correct some of our current misunderstandings. Until then, I hope that this book will help to document what occurred in the past and inform and educate a few more people to know and appreciate Maine's wild Atlantic salmon, for I believe that they truly are a national treasure.

References

References

Allan, I. R. H. 1967. Revised terminology list for Atlantic salmon (*Salmo salar* L.). ICES, C.M. 1967/M:19.

Allan, I. R. H., and J. A. Ritter. 1975. Salmonid terminology. J. Cons. Int. Explor. Mer. 37 (3): 293–299.

Anonymous. 1988. Long term management plan for the diadromous fisheries of the St. Croix River. Canadian Manuscript Report of Fisheries and Aquatic Sciences No. 1969. Department of Fisheries and Oceans, Halifax, Nova Scotia. 73p.

Anonymous. 1990. Annual report of the US Atlantic salmon assessment committee. Woods Hole, MA. 29 Jan–Feb. 1990. 37p.

Anonymous. 1993. Report of the North Atlantic Salmon Working Group. Copenhagen, 5–12 March 1993. ICES, Doc. C.M. 1993/Assess: 10. 210p.

Anthony, V. C. 1994. The significance of predation on Atlantic salmon. Proceedings of the NE Atlantic Salmon Conference: A Hard Look at Some Tough Issues. NE Salmon Association, Newburyport, MA. 371p.

Atkins, C. G. 1874. On the salmon of Eastern North America and its artificial culture. Report of the Commissioner for 1872 and 1873, part II. United States Commission of Fish and Fisheries, Washington, DC. 226–337.

Atkins, C. G. 1885. The biennial spawning of Penobscot River Atlantic salmon. Trans. Am. Fish. Soc. XIV, 89–94.

Atkins, C. G. 1887. The river fisheries of Maine. *In* the Fisheries and Fishery Industries of the United States. G. B. Goode and Associates, Section V, Volume 1. 673–728.

Bair, S. H., and G. A. Rounsefell. 1951. An interim report on salmon in the St. Croix, Aroostook, and St. John Rivers. United States Fish and Wildlife Service.

Barr, L. M. 1962. A life history study of the chain pickerel, *Esox niger* Lesueur, in Beddington Lake, Maine. MS Thesis, University of Maine. Orono, ME. 88p.

Bartlett, E., and R. Robinson. 1988. Salmon on the Dennys: 1786–1988. The Ellsworth American. 106p.

Bates, J. D. 1970. Atlantic salmon flies and fishing. Stackpole Books, Harrisburg, PA. 362p.

Baum, E. T. 1981. Evaluation of Penobscot River Atlantic Salmon restoration program. APS-12-R Performance Report (Final). Atlantic Sea Run Salmon Commission, Augusta, ME. 13p + App.

Baum, E. T. 1982. Saint John River Watershed, an Atlantic salmon river management report. Atlantic Sea Run Salmon Commission, Bangor, ME. 60p.

Baum, E. T. 1983. The Penobscot River: an Atlantic salmon river management report. Maine Atlantic Sea Run Commission, Bangor, Maine. 67p.

Baum, E. T., and Atlantic Salmon Board. 1997. Maine Atlantic salmon management plan with recommendations pertaining to staffing and budget matters. Maine Atlantic Salmon Authority, Bangor, ME. 57p.

Baum, E. T. 1995. Maine Atlantic salmon restoration and management plan, 1995–2000. Atlantic Sea Run Salmon Commission, Bangor, ME. 55p.

Baum, E. T., N. R. Dube, and F. M. Trasko. 1988. Penobscot River Atlantic salmon restoration program; progress report 1969–1985. Atlantic Sea Run Salmon Commission, Bangor, ME. 67p.

Baum, E. T., and R. M. Jordan. 1982. The Narraguagus river: an Atlantic salmon river management report. Atlantic Sea Run Salmon Commission, Bangor, ME. 48p.

Baum, E. T., J. Marancik, and P. R. Nickerson. 1992. Prelisting recovery plan for Maine wild Atlantic salmon populations. Atlantic Sea Run Salmon Commission and U.S. Fish and Wildlife Service. 9p.

Baum, E. T., and A. L. Meister. 1971. Fecundity of Atlantic salmon (*Salmo salar*) from two Maine Rivers. J. Fish. Res. Bd. Canada 28: 764–767.

Baum, E. T., E. S. Sawyer., and R. G. Strout. 1982. Survival of hatchery-reared Atlantic salmon smolts vaccinated with a *Vibrio anguillarum* bacterin. No. Am. J. Fish. Mgt. 4: 409–411.

Beland, K. F. 1982. The Tunk river: a report on the watershed potential of Atlantic salmon management. *In* Union and Minor Coastal Drainages East of the Penobscot. Atlantic Sea Run Salmon Commission, Bangor, ME.

Beland, K. F. 1984. Strategic plan for management of Atlantic salmon in the state of Maine. Atlantic Sea Run Salmon Commission, Bangor, ME.

Beland, K. F., N. R. Dube, M. Evers, R. C. Spencer, and E. T. Baum. 1993. Atlantic salmon research addressing issues of concern to the National Marine Fisheries Service and Atlantic Salmon Commission. Annual Report, Grant NA29FLO-131-01. Segment 1. Atlantic Sea Run Salmon Commission, Bangor, ME. 132p.

Beland, K. F., N. R. Dube, M. Evers, G. Vander Hagen, R. C. Spencer, and E. T. Baum. 1994. Atlantic salmon research addressing issues of concern to the National Marine Fisheries Service and Atlantic Salmon Commission. Annual Report, Grant NA29FLO131-01. Segment 2. Atlantic Sea Run Salmon Commission, Bangor, ME. 85 p.

Beland, K. F., N. R. Dube, M. Evers, G. Vander Hagen, R. C. Spencer, and E. T. Baum. 1995. Atlantic salmon research addressing issues of concern to the National Marine Fisheries Service and Atlantic Salmon Commission. Annual Report, Grant NA29FLO131-0, Segment 1, May 1, 1992–April 30, 1995. Atlantic Sea Run Salmon Commission, Bangor, ME. 133 p.

Beland, K. F., J. S. Fletcher, and A. L. Meister. 1982. The Dennys River: an Atlantic salmon river management report. Atlantic Sea Run Salmon Commission, Bangor, ME. 40p.

Beland, K. F., R. M. Jordan, and A. L. Meister. 1982. Water depth and velocity preferences of spawning Atlantic salmon in Maine rivers. No. Am. J. of Fish. Mgt. 2(1): 11–13.

Belding, D. L. 1940. The number of eggs and pyloric appendages as criteria of river varieties of the Atlantic salmon (*Salmo salar*). Trans. Am. Fish. Soc. 69: 285–289.

Benoit, D. 1989. Gray seal predation on Atlantic salmon. SALAR 8(3): 11.

Bentzen, P., and J. M. Wright. 1992. Single-locus DNA fingerprinting of Atlantic salmon from Maine and Newfoundland. Marine Gene Probe Laboratory, Dalhousie University, Halifax, Nova Scotia. 37p. + App.

Blackwell, B. 1996. Ecology of double-crested cormorants using the Penobscot River, Maine. Unpublished Ph.D. Thesis. University of Maine, Dept. of Wildlife Ecology, Orono, ME.

Blackwell, B. F., W. B. Krohn, and R. B. Allen. 1995. Foods of resting double-crested cormorants in Penobscot Bay, Maine, USA: temporal and spatial comparisons. Colonial Waterbirds. 18(2) (Special Publication).

Bley, P. W. 1987. Age, growth, and mortality of juvenile Atlantic salmon in streams: A review. U.S. Fish and Wildlife Service. Biological Report 87(4). 25p.

Bley, P. W., and J. R. Moring. 1988. Freshwater and ocean survival of Atlantic salmon and steelhead: A synopsis. U.S. Fish and Wildlife Service, Biological Report 88(9). 25p.

Booke, H. E. 1981. The conundrum of the stock concept—are nature and nurture definable in fishery science? Can. J. Fish. Aquat. Sci. 38(12): 1479–1480.

Bowen, W. D., and G. D. Harrison. 1996. Comparison of harbour seal diets in two inshore habitats of Atlantic Canada. Can. J. Zool. 74: 125–135.

Boyle, K. J., M. F. Teisl, and S. D. Reiling. 1992. Qualitative and economic evaluations of Atlantic salmon fishing on the Penobscot River. Dept. of Agricultural and Resource Economics. University of Maine, Orono, ME. Staff Paper No. 436. 43p.

Bryant, F. G. 1956. Stream surveys of the Sheepscot and Ducktrap River systems in Maine. U.S. Fish and Wildlife Service, Washington D.C. SSR-Fish. No. 195. 19p.

Bryant, F. G. 1952. A Survey of the Narraguagus River and its tributaries. Maine Atlantic Sea Run Salmon Commission, Augusta, ME. Research Report No. 2. 36p.

Calaprice, J. R. 1969. Production and genetic factors in managed salmonid populations. *In*: T. G. Northcote (Editor), Symposium on Salmon and Trout in Streams. MacMillan Lectures in Fisheries, University of British Columbia, Vancouver, BC. Pp. 377–388.

Coman, D.R. 1966. Pleasant River. Down East Magazine. Camden, ME. 196p.

Cross, T., J. Bailey, G. Friars, and F. O'Flynn. 1993. Maintenance of genetic variability in reared Atlantic salmon (*Salmo salar*) stocks. *In* D. Mills (editor), Salmon in the Sea and New Enhancement Strategies. Fishing New Books, Cambridge, MA. Pp. 356–366.

Cutting, R. E. 1956. Atlantic salmon (*Salmo salar*) habitat in the lower West Branch, Penobscot River, Maine. MS Thesis, University of Maine, Orono, ME. 111p.

Cutting, R. E. 1963. Penobscot River salmon restoration. Maine Atlantic Sea Run Salmon Commission, Orono, ME. 162p.

DeCola, J. N. 1970. Water quality requirements for Atlantic salmon. U.S.D.I. Federal Water Quality Administration. NE Region, Boston, MA. 42p.

DeRoche, S. E. 1967. Fishery management in the Androscoggin River. Maine Department of Inland Fisheries and Game. Augusta, ME. 52p.

Dow, R. 1953. The herring gull-cormorant control program. Maine Department of Sea and Shore Fisheries, General Bulletin No. 1. 26p.

Dube, N. 1983. The Saco River: an Atlantic salmon river management report. Maine Atlantic Sea Run Salmon Commission, Bangor, ME. 29p.

Dube, N. R., and R. M. Jordan. 1982. The East Machias River: an Atlantic salmon river management report. Atlantic Sea Run Salmon Commission, Bangor, ME.

Dube, N. R., and R. M. Jordan. 1982. The Pleasant River: an Atlantic salmon river management report. Atlantic Sea Run Salmon Commission. Bangor, ME. 69p.

Elson, P. F. 1957. Number of salmon needed to maintain stocks. Can. Fish. Cult. 21: 19–23.

Elson, P. F. 1975. Atlantic salmon rivers, smolt production and optimal spawning: an over-view of natural production. *In:* New England Atlantic Salmon Restoration Conference. International Atlantic Salmon Foundation and World Wildlife Fund, Special Pub. Ser. No. 6: 96–119.

Everhart, W. H., and R. E. Cutting. 1967. The Penobscot River, Atlantic salmon restoration: key to a model river. Maine Department of Inland Fisheries and Game and Atlantic Sea Run Salmon Commission, Bangor, ME. 22p.

Everhart, W. H., J. E. Watson, and R. E. Cutting. 1955. Penobscot River salmon restoration. Atlantic Sea Run Salmon Commission and Maine Department of Inland Fisheries and Game, Bangor, ME. 14p.

Fletcher, J. S. 1955. Machias River salmon restoration. Atlantic Sea Run Salmon Commission, Augusta, ME. 25p.

Fletcher, J. S. 1960. Dennys River drainage: fishery management and restoration. Atlantic Sea Run Salmon Commission, Augusta, ME.

Fletcher, J. S. 1960. East Machias River drainage: fish management. Atlantic Sea Run Salmon Commission, Augusta, ME. 21p.

Fletcher, J. S., R. M. Jordan, and K. F. Beland. 1982. The Machias River: an Atlantic salmon river management report. Atlantic Sea Run Salmon Commission, Bangor, ME. 51p.

Fletcher, J. S., and A. L. Meister. 1966. Machias River salmon runs. Biennial Report July 1, 1964–June 30, 1966: Atlantic Sea Run Salmon Commission, Bangor, ME. 21p.

Fletcher, J. S., and A. L. Meister. 1982. The St. Croix River: an Atlantic salmon river management report. Atlantic Sea Run Salmon Commission, Bangor, ME. 42p.

Ford, H. A. 1882. History of Penobscot County, Maine, Williams, Chase and Co., Cleveland, Ohio. 922p.

Foster, N. W., and C. G. Atkins. 1868. First Report of the Commissioners of Fisheries of Maine for 1867.

Foster, N. W., and C. G. Atkins. 1869. Second Report of the Commissioners of Fisheries of Maine for 1868.

Foye, R. E., and C. F. Ritzi, and R. P. AuClair. 1969. Fish management in the Kennebec River. Maine Department of Inland Fisheries and Game, Augusta, ME. 65p.

Fried, S. M., J. D. McCleave, and G. W. Labar. 1978. Seaward migration of hatchery-reared Atlantic salmon, *Salmo salar,* smolts in the Penobscot River estuary, Maine: riverine movements. J. Fish. Res. Bd. Can. 35: 76–87.

Friedland, K. D., and D. G. Reddin. 1993. Marine survival of Atlantic salmon from indices of post smolt growth and sea temperature. *In* D. E. Mills (editor), Salmon in the Sea. Fishing News Books, Blackwell Scientific, Cambridge, MA. Pp. 119–138.

Friedland, K. D., D. G. Reddin, and J. F. Kocik. 1993. Marine survival of North American and European Atlantic salmon: effects of growth and environment. ICES, J. Mar. Sci. 50: 481–492.

Goodwin, H. A. 1942. The Atlantic salmon in the Dennys River. MS Thesis. University of Maine, Orono, ME. 59p.

Gross, A. O. 1944. The present status of the double-crested cormorant on the coast of Maine. AUK 18: 76–103.

Gustafson-Greenwood, K. I., and J. R. Moring. 1990. Territory size and distribution of newly emerged Atlantic salmon *(Salmo salar).* Hydrobiologia 206: 125–131.

Gustafson-Marjanen, K. I., and J. R. Moring. 1984. Construction of artificial redds for evaluating the survival of Atlantic salmon eggs and alevins. No. Am. J. Fish. Mgt. 4: 455–456.

Haines, T. A. 1987. Atlantic salmon resources in the Northeastern United States and the potential effects of acidification from atmospheric deposition. Water, Air, and Soil Pollution 35: 37–48.

Hard, J. J., and R. P. Jones Jr., M. R. Delaney, and R. S. Waples. 1992. Pacific salmon and artificial propagation under the Endangered Species Act. Technical Memorandum NMFS-NWFSC-2. National Marine Fisheries Service, Seattle, Washington. 56p.

Havey, K. A. 1956. Tunk River drainage: fish management and restoration. Maine Department of Inland Fisheries and Game. Augusta, ME.

Havey, K. A. 1961. Union River fish management and restoration. Maine Department of Inland Fisheries and Game. Augusta, ME. 42p.

Havey, K. A. 1963. St. Croix River: fish management and restoration. Maine Department of Inland Fisheries and Game, Machias, ME.

Havey, K. A., and J. S. Fletcher. 1956. The Pleasant River: fish management and restoration. Maine Department of Inland Fisheries and Game and the Atlantic Sea Run Salmon Commission, Augusta, ME.

Havey, K. A., and K. Warner. 1970. The landlocked salmon (*Salmo salar*): its life history and management in Maine. Sport Fishing Inst., Washington, D.C. and Maine Department of Inland Fisheries and Game, Augusta, ME. 129p.

Heggberget, T. G. 1988. Timing of spawning in Norwegian Atlantic salmon (*Salmo salar*). Can. J. Fish. Aquat. Sci. 45: 845–849.

Heggberget, T. G., Lund, R. A., Ryman, N., and Stahl, G. 1986. Growth and genetic variation of Atlantic salmon (*Salmo salar*) from different sections of the River Alta, Norway. Can. J. Fish. Aquat. Sci. 43: 1828–1835.

Hennessey, T. 1987. The Penobscot's Presidential salmon. Bangor Daily News. May 2.

Hennessey, T. 1987. The Presidential salmon. Fins and Feathers, July–August Issue, 76–82.

Hislop, J. R. G., and R. G. J. Shelton. 1993. Marine predators and prey of Atlantic salmon. *In:* D. Mills (editor), Salmon in the Sea and New Enhancement Strategies. Fishing News Books, Oxford, England. Pp. 104–118.

Horton, G. E., M. E. Evers, and E. T. Baum. 1995. 1994 Summary of Atlantic Sea Run Salmon Commission activities on Maine rivers with native salmon runs. Atlantic Sea Run Salmon Commission, Bangor, ME. 6p.

Horton, G. E., M. E. Evers and E. T. Baum. 1996. 1995 Summary of Atlantic Sea Run Salmon Commission activities on Maine rivers with wild salmon runs. Atlantic Salmon Authority, Bangor, ME. 15p.

Hulbert, P. J. 1977. Biological and physical factors bearing on restoration of Atlantic salmon in the Mattawamkeag River, Penobscot River system, Maine. Univ. of Maine. Migratory Fish Res. Institute and Coop. Fish Res. Unit. Part I. 68p.

Jensen, A. J., and Johnsen, B. O. 1986. Different adaptation strategies of Atlantic salmon (*Salmo salar*) populations to extreme climates with special reference to some cold Norwegian rivers. Can. J. Fish. Aquat. Sci. 43: 980–984.

Jordan, R. M., and K. F. Beland. 1981. Atlantic salmon spawning and evaluation of natural spawning success. Final Performance Report AFS-20-R. Maine Atlantic Sea Run Salmon Commission. Augusta, ME. 25p.

Kendall, W. C. 1935. The Fishes of New England. The salmon family. Part 2. The Salmons. Memoirs of the Boston Society of Natural History 9(1). 166p.

Kerswill, C. J. 1971. Relative rates of utilization by commercial and sport fisheries of Atlantic salmon (*Salmo salar*) from the Miramichi River, New Brunswick. J. Fish. Res. Bd. Can. 28: 351–363.

Kincaid, H., J. Mengel, and J. Johnson. 1994. Meristic and morphometric evaluation of parr from Atlantic salmon stocks collected from the Downeast rivers of Maine in 1992 and 1993. Preliminary report submitted to the Federal Atlantic Salmon Technical Working Group. 13p.

King, D. P. F., S. J. Hovey, D. Thompson, and A. Scott. 1993. Mitochondrial DNA variation in Atlantic salmon (*Salmo salar* L.) populations. J. Fish. Bio. 42: 25–33.

King, T. L., and M. R. Smith. 1994. Allozyme analysis and RFLP analysis of PCR amplified regions of mitochondrial DNA from minimally invasive sampling in Atlantic salmon inhabiting the Downeast rivers of Maine. Completion Report Submitted to the Atlantic Salmon Technical Working Group. 12p.

Knight, A. E., and J. C. Greenwood. 1982. Special report—habitat criteria for Atlantic salmon and American shad. *In:* Special report—anadromous fish: water and land resources of the Merrimack River Basin. USFWS, Laconia, NH. Pp. DF1–DF16

Kornfield, I. 1994. Identification of wild, hatchery and cultured Atlantic salmon: discrimination by genetic fingerprinting. Final Report NA26D 0043-01. 34p.

Krohn, W. B., R. B. Allen, J. R. Moring, and A. E. Hutchinson. 1994. Double-crested cormorants in New England: population and management histories. Colonial Waterbirds (18) (Special Publication 1).

Labar, G. W., J. D. McCleave, and S. M. Fried. 1978. Seaward migration of hatchery-reared Atlantic salmon (*Salmo salar*) smolts in the Penobscot River estuary, Maine: open-water movements. J. Cont. Int. Mer. 38(2): 257–269.

Lawson, J. W., G. B. Stenson, and D. G. McKinnon. 1995. Diet of harp seals (*Phoca groenlandica*) in near shore waters in the northwest Atlantic during 1990–93. Can. J. Zool. 73: 1805–1818.

MacKenzie, C., and J. R. Moring. 1988. Estimating survival of Atlantic salmon during the intragravel period. No. Am. J. Fish. Mgt. 8: 45–49.

Maine State Planning Office. 1993. Kennebec River resource management plan: balancing hydropower generation and other uses. Augusta, ME. 196p.

May, B., D. L. Perkins, and R. L. Sawyer. 1994. Genetic analysis of fish genomes and populations: allozyme variation within and among Atlantic salmon (*Salmo salar)* from Downeast rivers of Maine. Completion Report submitted to the U.S. Fish and Wildlife Service under Unit Coop. Agree. #14-16-0009-1553, Work Order #23. 30p.

McCrimmon, H. R., and D. L. Gots. 1979. World distribution of Atlantic salmon, *Salmo salar.* J. Fish. Res. Bd. Can. 35: 422–457.

McDowall, R. M. 1987. The occurrence and distribution of diadromy among fishes. *In*: Common Strategies of Anadromous and Catadromous Fishes. American Fisheries Society Symposium 1: 1–13.

McLaughlin, E. A., and A. E. Knight. 1987. Special report: habitat criteria for Atlantic salmon. U.S. Fish and Wildlife Service, Laconia, NH. 18p.

McLaughlin, E. A., A. V. Sillas, A. E. Knight, V. D. Pierce Jr., N. R. Dube, and L. Flagg. 1987. Saco River strategic plan for fisheries management. U.S. Fish and Wildlife Service, Maine Department of Inland Fisheries and Wildlife, Atlantic Sea Run Salmon Commission, and Maine Department of Marine Resources.

Meerburg, D. J. (editor). 1986. Salmonid age at maturity. Can. Spec. Publ. Fish. Aquat. Sci. No. 89. 118p.

Metcalfe, N. B., and Thorpe, J. E. 1990. Determinants of geographical variation in the age of seaward migration for salmon, *Salmo salar.* J. Anim. Ecol. 59: 135–145.

Meister, A. L. 1958. The Atlantic salmon (*Salmo salar)* of Cove Brook, Winterport, Maine. MS Thesis. University of Maine, Orono, ME. 151p.

Meister, A. L. 1962. Atlantic salmon production in Cove Brook, Maine. Trans. Am. Fish. Soc. 91 (2): 208–212.

Meister, A. L. 1964. Atlantic salmon fishing—a look back. Maine Fish and Game, Spring 1964.

Meister, A. L. 1982. The Sheepscot River: an Atlantic salmon river management report. Atlantic Sea Run Salmon Commission, Bangor, ME. 45p.

Meister, A. L. 1984. The marine migrations of tagged Atlantic salmon (*Salmo salar* L.) of USA origin. ICES C.M. 1984/M: 27.

Meister, A. L., and R. E. Cutting. 1967. A preliminary report of the composition of the spawning runs of Atlantic salmon *(Salmo salar)* in Maine rivers for the period 1962–1966. Int. Com. Northen. Fish. Redbook. 1967. Part III: 53–57.

Meister, A. L., and F. J. Gramlich. 1967. Cormorant predation on tagged Atlantic salmon smolts. Final report of the 1966–67 cormorant-salmon smolt study. Atlantic Sea Run Salmon Commission, Augusta, ME. 36p.

Mendall, H. L. 1936. The home-life and economic status of the double-crested cormorant, *Phalacrocorax auritus auritus* (Lesson). University of Maine Studies, Second Series, No. 38. 159p.

Moller, D. 1970. Transferrin polymorphism in Atlantic salmon *(Salmo salar)*. J. Fish. Res. Bd. Canada. 27: 1617–1625.

Morantz, D. L., R. K. Sweeney, C. S. Shivvell, and D. H. Longard. 1987. Selection of micro habitat in summer by juvenile Atlantic salmon (*Salmo salar*). Can. J. Fish. Aquat. Sci. 44: 120–129.

Myers, R. A., J. A. Hutchings, and R. J. Gibson. 1986. Variation in male parr maturation within and among populations of Atlantic salmon, *Salmo salar*. Can. J. Fish. Aquat. Sci. 43: 1242–1248.

NASCO. 1996. Report of the special session of the Council: The Atlantic salmon as predator and prey. Annual meeting, 13 June. Gothenburg, Sweden. 97p.

National Marine Fisheries Service. 1996. Report of the pinniped task force. National Marine Fisheries Service, Gloucester, Massachusetts.

New England Fishery Management Council. 1987. Fishery management plan for Atlantic salmon. Saugus, MA. 64p. + App.

Nielsen, J. 1961. Contributions to the biology of the Salmonidae in Greenland I-IV Meddelelser om Grønland, Bd. 159, Nr. 8. København. 77p.

North Atlantic Salmon Conservation Organization. 1992. Protocols for the introduction and transfer of salmonids. NASCO, Edinburgh, Scotland. 119p.

Paloheimo, J. E., and P. F. Elson. 1974. Reduction of Atlantic salmon catches in Canada attributed to the Greenland Fishery. J. Fish. Res. Bd. Can. 31: 1467–1480.

Payne, P. M., and L. A. Selzer. 1989. The distribution, abundance and selected prey of the harbor seal, *Phoca vitulina concolor,* in southern New England. Marine Mammal Series 5(2): 115–147.

Peterson, R. H. 1978. Physical characteristics of Atlantic salmon spawning gravel in some New Brunswick streams. Fish. & Mar. Serv. Tech. Rept. 785. St Andrews, NB.

Peterson, A. L., and K. D. Friedland. 1994. River of dreams. Wild Steelhead and Atlantic Salmon 1(2): 41–47.

Pierce, G. J., et al. 1991 Seasonal variation in the diet of common seals *(Phoca vitulina)* in the Moray Firth area of Scotland. Journal Zool. London 223: 641–652.

Power, J. H. 1977. Upstream spawning migration of Atlantic salmon *(Salmo salar)* as observed using radio telemetry. MS Thesis, University of Maine, Orono, ME. 70p.

Power, J. H., and J. D. McCleave. 1979. Riverine movements of hatchery-reared Atlantic salmon *(Salmo salar)* upon return as adults. Migratory Fish. Res. Inst and Dept. of Zoology, University of Maine, Orono, ME. 41p.

Pratt, V. S. 1946. The Atlantic salmon in the Penobscot River. MS Thesis. Dept. of Zoology, University of Maine, Orono, ME. 85p.

Rago, P. J., D. G. Reddin, T. R. Porter, D. J. Meerburg, K. D. Friedland, and E. C. E. Potter. 1993. A continental run reconstruction model for the non-maturing component of the North American Atlantic salmon: analysis of the fisheries in Greenland and Newfoundland-Labrador, 1974–1991. ICES C.M. 1993/M: 25.

Ray, B. B. 1968. The food of seals in Scottish waters. Dept. of Agriculture and Fisheries for Scotland, Doc. No. 2. 23p.

Ray, B. B. 1973. Further observations on the food of seals. Jour. of Zoology 169: 287–297.

Reddin, D. G., and K. D. Friedland. 1993. Marine environmental factors influencing the movement and survival of Atlantic salmon. *In:* D. E. Mills (editor) Salmon in the Sea, Fishing News Books, Blackwell Scientific, Cambridge, MA. Pp. 79–103.

Reddin, D. G., and W. M. Shearer. 1987. Sea-surface temperature and distribution of Atlantic salmon in the Northwest Atlantic Ocean. *In*: Common Strategies of Anadromous and Catadromous Fishes. American Fisheries Society Symposium 1: 262–275.

Reddin, D. G., D. E. Stansbury, and P. B. Short. 1991. Post smolt Atlantic salmon *(Salmo salar* L.) in the Labrador Sea. Can. J. Fish. Aqua. Sci. 48: 2–6.

Reisenbichler, R. R., and J. D. McIntyre. 1977. Genetic differences in growth and survival of juvenile hatchery and wild steelhead trout, *Salmo gairdneri.* J. Fish. Res. Bd. Canada 34: 123–128.

Riddell, B. E., and Leggett, W. C. 1981. Evidence of an adaptive basis for geographic variation in body morphology and time of downstream migration of juvenile Atlantic salmon *(Salmo salar*). Can. J. Fish. Aquat. Sci. 38: 308–320.

Riddell, B. E., W. C. Leggett, and R. L. Saunders. 1981. Evidence of adaptive polygenic variation between two populations of Atlantic salmon *(Salmo salar)* native to tributaries of the SW Miramichi River, N.B. Can. J. Fish. Aqua. Sci. 38: 321–333

Rimmer, D. M., U. Paim, and R. L. Saunders. 1984. Changes in the selection of micro habitat by juvenile Atlantic salmon *(Salmo salar)* at the summer-autumn transition in a small river. Can. J. Fish. Aquat. Sci. 41: 469–475.

Ritter, J. A. 1989. Marine migration and natural mortality of North American Atlantic salmon *(Salmo salar* L.). Department of Fisheries and Oceans, Halifax, Nova Scotia. Canadian Manuscript Report of Fisheries and Aquatic Sciences No. 2041, 136p.

Ritter, J. A., G. J. Farmer., R. K. Mirsa, T. R. Goff, J. K. Bailey, and E. T. Baum. 1986. Parental influences and smolt size and sex ratio: effect on sea age at first maturity of Atlantic salmon. *In:* D. J. Meerburg (editor). Salmonid age at maturity. Canadian Special Publication Fisheries Aquatic Sciences No. 89: 30–38.

Ritter, J. A., and J. R. E. Harger. 1974. Atlantic salmon life stage terminology—a review of existing usage and proposal for improvement. ICES, C.M. 1974/M:23.

Roberts, F. L. 1976. Final report: biochemical genetics of the Atlantic salmon *(Salmo salar).* USFWS Research Contract No. 14-16-0008-829. 26p.

Rounsefell, G. A. 1947. The effect of natural and artificial propagation in maintaining a run of Atlantic salmon in the Penobscot River. Trans. Amer. Fish. Soc. 74: 188–208.

Rounsefell, G. A., and L. H. Bond. 1949. Salmon restoration in Maine. Atlantic Sea Run Salmon Commission, Augusta, Maine. Research Report No. 1. 52p.

Saunders, R. L. 1969. Contributions of salmon from the northwest Miramichi river, New Brunswick, to various fisheries. J. Fish. Res. Bd. Can. 26: 269–278.

Saunders, R. L. 1981. Atlantic salmon *(Salmo salar)* stocks and management implications in the Canadian Atlantic Provinces and New England, USA. Can. J. Fish. Aqua. Sci. 38: 1612-1625.

Saunders, R. L. 1986. The thermal biology of Atlantic salmon; influence of temperature on salmon culture with particular reference to constraints imposed by low temperature. Report of the Institute of Freshwater Research, Drottningholm. 63: 68–81.

Saunders, R. L. 1991. Potential interactions between cultured and wild Atlantic salmon. Aquaculture 98: 51–60.

Saunders, R. L., and K. R. Allen. 1967. Effects of tagging and fin clipping on the survival and growth of Atlantic salmon between the smolt and adult stages. J. Fish. Res. Bd. Can. 24: 2595–2611.

Saunders, R. L., and J. H. Gee. 1964. Movements of young Atlantic salmon in a small stream. J. Fish. Res. Bd. Can. 21: 27–36.

Schill, W. B., and R. L. Walker. 1994. Genetic evaluation of Atlantic salmon populations of the "Downeast" rivers of Maine: RAPD markers. Completion Report submitted to the Atlantic Salmon Technical Working Group. 36p.

Schulze, M. S. 1994. Connecticut River piscivory: estimating the impact of piscivores on the survival and distribution of juvenile anadromous fish in the lower Connecticut River with field surveys and a bioenergetics model. *In:* Mass. Coop. Fish & Wildlife Research Unit Annual Report, October 1993–September 1994.

Siebenmann, M., and K. E. Gibbs. 1994. Macroinvertebrates of the Narraguagus River as long-term indicators of water quality. A preliminary report to the Maine Atlantic Sea Run Salmon Commission. University of Maine, Orono, ME. 25p.

Smith, H. M. 1898. The salmon fishery of Penobscot Bay and River in 1895 and 1896. Extracted from U.S. Fish Commission Bulletin for 1897. Article 4: 113–124.

Soderberg, S. 1975. Feeding habits and commercial damage of seals in the Baltic. Proceedings from the Symposium on seals in the Baltic. Lindingo, Sweden, June 4–6, 1974. National Swedish Environmental Protection Board 591: 66–78

Squires, T. 1985. History of the Augusta dam as it relates to fish passage from 1834 through 1892. Excerpts from reports of the Commissioners of Fisheries of the State of Maine, Augusta, Maine. Biennial Reports 1867–1868 through 1891–1892. Maine Dept. of Marine Resources, Augusta, ME.

Squires, T. S. Jr., and M. Smith, K. E. Beland, J. D. McNeish, and R. A. DeSandre. 1986. Lower Kennebec River anadromous fish restoration plan and inland fisheries management review. Department of Marine Resources. Augusta, ME.

Stasko, A. B., A. M. Sutterlin, S. A. Rommell Jr., and P. F. Eslon. 1973. Migration-orientation of Atlantic salmon *(Salmo salar)*. Int. Atl. Salmon Found. Spec. Publ. Series 4(1): 119–138.

State of Maine and Kennebec Hydro Developers Group. 1987. Agreement between the State of Maine and Kennebec Hydro Developers Group. Augusta, ME. 14 p.

Stenson, G. B. 1994. The status of Pinnipeds in the Newfoundland Region. NAFO Sci. Council. Studies, 21: 115–119.

Stickney, A. P. 1960. Atlantic salmon investigations. *In*: Progress in sport fishing research. USFWS, Circular 81:6–17.

Stilwell, E. M., and E. Smith. 1879. Report of the Commissioners of Fisheries of Maine for 1879.

Stolte, L. W. 1979. A strategic plan for the restoration of Atlantic salmon to the Merrimack River basin. U.S. Fish and Wildlife Service, Laconia, NH. 59p. + App.

Stolte, L. W. 1980. A strategic plan for the restoration of Atlantic salmon to the Connecticut River basin. U.S. Fish & Wildlife Service, Laconia, NH. 94p. + 4 App.

Stolte, L. W. 1981. The forgotten salmon of the Merrimack. U.S. Government Printing Office. Washington DC. 236p.

Symons, P. E. K. 1969. Greater dispersal of wild compared with hatchery-reared juvenile Atlantic salmon released in streams. J. Fish. Res. Bd. Canada 26: 1867–1876.

Symons, P. E. K. 1979. Estimated escapement of Atlantic salmon *(Salmo salar)* for maximum smolt production in rivers of different productivity. J. Fish. Res. Board Can. 36: 132–140.

Symons, P. E. K., and M. Heland. 1978. Stream habitats and behavioral interactions of under-yearling and yearling Atlantic salmon *(Salmo salar)*. J. Fish. Res. Bd. Can. 35:175–183.

Taylor, J. A. 1973. Comparative water quality of Atlantic salmon streams in Maine. MS Thesis. University of Maine, Orono, ME. 80p.

Thorpe, J. E. 1988. Salmon enhancement: stock discreteness and choice of material for stocking. *In*: Atlantic Salmon: Planning for the Future. Proceedings of the 3rd Intl. Atlantic Salmon Symposium, held in Biarritz, France, 21–23 October 1986.

Thorpe, J., and K. Mitchell. 1981. Stocks of Atlantic salmon *(Salmo salar)* in Britain and Ireland: discreetness and current management. Can. J. Fish. Aqua. Sci. 38: 1576–1590.

United States Fish and Wildlife Service. 1989. Atlantic salmon restoration in New England, final environmental impact statement 1989–2021. Newton Corner, MA. 87p + App.

Utter, F. M. 1981. Biological criteria for definition of species and distinct intraspecific populations of anadromous salmonids under the U.S. Endangered Species Act of 1973. Can. J. Fish. Aqua. Sci. 38: 1626–1635.

van den Ende, O. 1993. Predation on Atlantic salmon smolts *(Salmo salar)* by smallmouth bass *(Micropterus dolomieu)* and chain pickerel *(Esox niger)* in the Penobscot River, MS Thesis, University of Maine. Orono, ME. 95p.

Verspoor, E., and W. C. Jordan. 1989. Genetic variation of the *Me-2* locus in the Atlantic salmon within and between rivers: evidence for its selective maintenance. J. Fish. Biol. 35 (Suppl. A): 205–213.

Waples, R. S. 1990. Genetic interactions between hatchery and wild salmonids: lessons from the Pacific Northwest. Can. J. Fish Aqua. Sci.

Waples, R. S. 1991. Definition of "species" under the endangered species act: application to Pacific salmon. U.S. Dept. Commerce, NOAA Tech. Memo. NMFS F/NWC-194.

Waples, R. S., G. A. Winans, F. M. Utter, and C. Mahnken. 1990. Genetic approaches to the management of Pacific salmon. Fisheries 15(5): 19–25.

Warner, K. 1972. Further studies of fish predation on salmon stocked in Maine lakes. Progressive Fish Culturist 344(4): 217–221.

Warner, K., and K. A. Havey. 1985. Life history, ecology and management of Maine landlocked salmon *(Salmo salar)*. Maine Dept. of Inland Fisheries and Wildlife. Augusta, ME. 127p.

Watt, D., and G. H. Penney. 1980. Juvenile salmon survival in the Saint John River system. Can. Tech. Rep. Fish. Aqua. Sci. No. 939, vii+13 p.

Webb, J. H., D. W. Hay, P. D. Cunningham, and A. F. Youngson, 1991. The spawning behavior of escaped farmed and wild Atlantic salmon *(Salmo salar* L.) in a northern Scottish river. Aquaculture. 98: 97–110.

Williamson, W. D. 1832. A history of the state of Maine from its first discovery, AD 1602, to the separation, AD 1820, inclusive. Glazier, Masters Co., Hallowell, Maine. Vol. I, 696p; Vol. II, 729p.

Windsor, M. L., and P. Hutchinson. 1994. International management of Atlantic salmon *Salmo salar* L., by the North Atlantic Salmon Conservation Organization, 1984–1994. Fish. Mgt. and Ecology 1(1): 31–44.

Youngson, A., and D. Hay. 1996. The lives of salmon. An illustrated account of the life-history of the Atlantic salmon. Swan Hill Press. Shrewsbury, UK. 144p.

Tables

TABLE 1. MONTHLY TRAP CATCHES OF ATLANTIC SALMON IN VARIOUS MAINE RIVERS.

Year	Site	May	June	July	August	Sept.	Oct.	Nov.	Total	No. Trucked
					Androscoggin					
1983	Brunswick Dam	0	14	4	0	0	2	0	20	
1984	Brunswick Dam	0	36	18	0	0	36	4	94	
1985	Brunswick Dam	0	9	9	0	0	4	0	22	
1986	Brunswick Dam	0	46	30	1	2	1	0	80	
1987	Brunswick Dam	0	9	2	0	3	12	0	26	
1988	Brunswick Dam	0	9	0	0	3	2	0	14	
1989	Brunswick Dam	0	10	2	1	1	1	5	20	
1990	Brunswick Dam	0	74	24	8	10	68	0	184	
1991	Brunswick Dam	2	6	1	1	7	4	0	21	
1992	Brunswick Dam	0	8	4	0	1	3	0	16	
1993	Brunswick Dam	0	32	6	2	0	6	0	46	
1994	Brunswick Dam	0	7	0	1	8	9	0	25	
1995	Brunswick Dam	0	6	6	0	1	3	0	16	
	Total (1983–1995)	**2**	**266**	**106**	**14**	**36**	**151**	**9**	**584**	
	%	0.3	45.5	18.2	2.4	6.2	25.9	1.5	100.0	
	Cumulative %	0.3	45.9	64.0	66.4	72.6	98.5		100.0	
					Aroostook					
1988	Tinker Dam	0	0	0	5	7	44	0	56	90
1989	Tinker Dam	0	0	0	58	38	8	0	104	113
1990	Tinker Dam	0	0	14	9	25	16	0	64	0
1991	Tinker Dam	0	0	0	0	20	19	0	39	100
1992	Tinker Dam	0	0	10	36	59	18	0	123	315
1993	Tinker Dam	0	0	7	6	26	24	0	63	156
1994	Tinker Dam	0	0	0	0	8	10	2	20	121
1995	Tinker Dam	0	0	0	0	1	17	4	22	140
	Total (1988-1995)	**0**	**0**	**31**	**114**	**184**	**156**	**6**	**491**	
	%	0.0	0.0	6.3	23.2	37.5	31.8	1.2	100.0	
	Cumulative %	0.0	0.0	6.3	29.5	67.0	98.8	100.0		
					Machias					
1946	Machias Dam	X	X	X	100	X	X	X	100	
1947–48	No Trap	X	X	X	X	X	X	X	X	
1949	Machias Dam	0	13	100	186	51	12	0	362	
1950	Machias Dam	0	36	54	54	10	0	0	154	
1951–52	No Trap	X	X	X	X	X	X	X	X	
1953	Machias Dam	0	0	102	145	11	0	0	258	
1954	Machias Dam	0	182	312	39	11	0	0	544	
1955	Machias Dam	6	128	58	96	23	5	0	316	
1956	Machias Dam	0	152	130	85	29	0	0	396	
1957	Machias Dam	13	157	188	72	18	3	0	451	
1958	Machias Dam	2	217	297	92	15	0	0	623	
1959	Machias Dam	1	37	332	339	98	5	0	812	
1960	Machias Dam	7	131	119	31	19	0	0	307	
1961	Machias Dam	1	99	366	108	29	2	0	605	
1962	Machias Dam	14	80	253	22	4	0	0	373	
1963	Machias Dam	6	197	61	67	17	0	0	348	
1964	Machias Dam	14	104	190	60	5	0	0	373	
1965	Machias Dam	0	0	106	135	40	18	0	299	
1966	Whitneyville Dam	7	76	208	112	99	59	0	561	
1967	Whitneyville Dam	0	27	138	48	34	4	0	251	
1968	Whitneyville Dam	0	31	47	80	12	8	0	178	

Machias (conclusion)

Year	Site	May	June	July	August	Sept.	Oct.	Nov.	Total
1969	Whitneyville Dam	0	49	89	36	10	12	0	196
1970	Whitneyville Dam	0	50	125	13	5	1	0	194
1971	Whitneyville Dam	0	18	53	34	23	4	0	132
1972	Whitneyville Dam	0	12	132	45	11	6	0	206
	Total (1949–1972)	**71**	**1,796**	**3,460**	**1,999**	**574**	**139**	**0**	**8,039**
	%	0.9	22.3	43.0	24.9	7.1	1.7	0.0	100
	Cumulative %	0.9	23.2	66.3	91.1	98.3	100.0	100.0	

Narraguagus

Year	Site	May	June	July	August	Sept.	Oct.	Nov.	Total
1962	Cherryfield Dam	2	97	61	13	22	2	0	197
1963	Cherryfield Dam	0	50	38	28	26	5	0	147
1964	Cherryfield Dam	0	46	103	12	58	2	0	221
1965	Cherryfield Dam	2	79	7	2	28	72	7	197
1966	Cherryfield Dam	0	56	22	10	125	46	0	259
1967	Cherryfield Dam	0	110	76	14	79	22	8	309
1968	Cherryfield Dam	2	87	48	7	24	59	5	232
1969	Cherryfield Dam	4	60	29	14	10	5	0	122
1970	Cherryfield Dam	0	53	22	5	3	3	0	86
1971	Cherryfield Dam	0	8	4	13	45	6	0	76
1972	Cherryfield Dam	6	60	107	16	3	7	0	199
1973	Cherryfield Dam	1	45	40	4	6	1	0	97
1974	Cherryfield Dam	4	62	30	2	3	0	0	101
1975–90	No Trap	X	X	X	X	X	X	X	X
1991	Cherryfield Dam	0	24	9	33	3	5	0	74
1992	Cherryfield Dam	0	9	24	11	5	7	0	56
1993	Cherryfield Dam	2	43	16	5	17	4	0	87
1994	Cherryfield Dam	2	21	8	9	7	5	0	52
1995	Cherryfield Dam	3	38	13	0	0	2	0	56
	Total (1962–1995)	**28**	**948**	**657**	**198**	**464**	**253**	**20**	**2,568**
	%	1.1	36.9	25.6	7.7	18.1	9.9	0.8	100
	Cumulative %	1.1	38.0	63.6	71.3	89.4	99.2	100.0	

Penobscot

Year	Site	May	June	July	August	Sept.	Oct.	Nov.	Total
1941	Bangor Dam	0	0	3	3	0	0	0	6
1942	Bangor Dam	1	142	48	X	X	X	X	191
1943	Bangor Dam	0	20	16	6	5	0	0	47
1944	Bangor Dam	0	0	54	8	8	0	0	70
1945	Bangor Dam	0	135	33	0	0	X	X	168
1946	Bangor Dam	0	1	X	X	X	X	X	1
1947	Bangor Dam	X	53	53	X	X	X	X	106
1948–55	No Trap	X	X	X	X	X	X	X	X
1956	Veazie Dam	0	0	0	1	0	1	0	2
1957–68	No Trap	X	X	X	X	X	X	X	X
1969	Bangor Dam	X	X	X	20	17	34	0	71
1970	Bangor Dam	0	52	60	6	13	4	0	135
1971	Bangor Dam	1	22	47	3	21	14	0	108
1972	Bangor Dam	3	133	119	39	32	7	3	336
1973	Bangor Dam	0	166	82	12	9	27	0	296
1974	Bangor Dam	0	226	289	18	13	9	0	555
1975	Bangor Dam	18	420	266	124	67	30	2	927
1976	Bangor Dam	1	222	299	59	21	13	0	615
1977	Bangor Dam	1	165	232	23	39	1	0	461
1978	Veazie Dam	5	754	244	128	205	104	9	1,449
1979	Veazie Dam	4	295	162	166	96	45	0	768
1980	Veazie Dam	30	925	774	224	391	131	2	2,477
1981	Veazie Dam	89	1,013	969	289	314	46	0	2,720
1982	Veazie Dam	64	1,219	1,168	471	270	48	7	3,247
1983	Veazie Dam	5	249	237	103	131	75	0	800

Penobscot (conclusion)

Year	Site	May	June	July	August	Sept.	Oct.	Nov.	Total
1984	Veazie Dam	0	446	661	108	178	61	2	1,456
1985	Veazie Dam	93	1,216	932	275	422	92	1	3,031
1986	Veazie Dam	42	1,518	1,889	348	257	71	0	4,125
1987	Veazie Dam	29	743	1,129	166	172	86	1	2,326
1988	Veazie Dam	43	671	868	838	200	56	0	2,676
1989	Veazie Dam	0	594	1,462	430	179	54	0	2,719
1990	Veazie Dam	0	1,331	924	142	357	168	3	2,925
1991	Veazie Dam	41	641	356	303	99	125	0	1,565
1992	Veazie Dam	27	741	1,053	207	110	76	11	2,225
1993	Veazie Dam	29	617	629	136	121	112	1	1,645
1994	Veazie Dam	13	469	343	163	39	15	0	1,042
1995	Veazie Dam	57	823	282	36	82	62	0	1,342
	Total (1970–1995)	**595**	**15,671**	**15,476**	**4,817**	**3,838**	**1,532**	**42**	**41,971**
	%	1.4	37.3	36.9	11.5	9.1	3.7	0.1	100
	Cumulative %	1.4	38.8	75.6	87.1	96.2	99.9	100.0	

Saco

Year	Site	May	June	July	August	Sept.	Oct.	Nov.	Total
1986	Cataract Dam (West)	0	11	2	4	1	1	0	19
1987	Cataract Dam (West)	0	14	6	0	6	3	0	29
1988	Cataract Dam (West)	0	12	4	1	10	1	0	28
1989	Cataract Dam (West)	0	3	6	2	3	0	0	14
1990	Cataract Dam (West)	0	21	10	0	4	22		57
1991	Cataract Dam (West)	0	0	0	4	0	0	0	4
1992	No Trap	X	X	X	X	X	X	X	X
1993	Cataract Dam (E+W)	0	14	13	1	14	11	0	53
1994	Cataract Dam (E+W)	0	8	1	6	6	0	0	21
1995	Cataract Dam (E+W)	4	18	1	0	8	3	0	34
	Total (1986–1995)	**4**	**101**	**43**	**18**	**52**	**41**	**0**	**259**
	%	1.5	39.0	16.6	6.9	20.1	15.8	0.0	100
	Cumulative %	1.5	40.5	57.1	64.1	84.2	100.0	100.0	

Sheepscot

Year	Site	May	June	July	August	Sept.	Oct.	Nov.	Total
1957	Alna Weir	1	8	7	1	1	19	28	65
1959	Alna Weir	3	30	8	2	15	70		128
	Total (1957–1959)	**4**	**38**	**15**	**3**	**16**	**89**	**28**	**193**
	%	2.1	19.7	7.8	1.6	8.3	46.1	14.5	100.0
	Cumulative %	2.1	21.8	29.5	31.1	39.4	85.5	100.0	

St. Croix

Year	Site	May	June	July	August	Sept.	Oct.	Nov.	Total
1982	Milltown Dam	0	113	106	95	52	50	2	418
1983	Milltown Dam	0	78	42	14	73	35	5	247
1984	Milltown Dam	0	36	31	35	78	58	8	246
1985	Milltown Dam	0	36	52	97	129	24	5	343
1986	Milltown Dam	0	103	106	83	13	13	0	318
1987	Milltown Dam	0	11	69	111	136	34	0	361
1988	Milltown Dam	1	39	61	172	105	18	0	396
1989	Milltown Dam	0	20	91	44	66	13	0	234
1990	Milltown Dam	0	58	18	4	21	9	0	110
1991	Milltown Dam	0	27	28	82	66	3	0	206
1992	No Trap	X	X	X	X	X	X	X	X
1993	Milltown Dam	0	14	20	14	47	9	0	104
1994	Milltown Dam	0	7	0	14	157	3	0	181
1995	Milltown Dam	3	21	16	6	9	5	0	60
	Total (1982–1995)	**3**	**563**	**640**	**771**	**952**	**274**	**20**	**3,224**
	%	0.0	17.5	19.9	23.9	29.5	8.5	0.6	100
	Cumulative %		0.0	17.6	37.4	61.3	90.8	99.3	100.0

Table 1

Year	Site	May	June	July	August	Sept.	Oct.	Nov.	Total
				Union					
1974	Ellsworth Dam	X	X	3	X	7	6	0	16
1975	Ellsworth Dam	0	5	32	15	10	5	0	67
1976	Ellsworth Dam	0	17	138	41	20	3	0	219
1977	Ellsworth Dam	0	0	136	29	27	3	0	195
1978	Ellsworth Dam	0	44	39	41	17	6	0	147
1979	Ellsworth Dam	0	0	16	7	12	1	0	36
1980	Ellsworth Dam	0	0	150	45	10	4	0	209
1981	Ellsworth Dam	0	108	58	52	40	5	0	263
1982	Ellsworth Dam	0	6	107	18	13	2	0	146
1983	Ellsworth Dam	0	27	83	27	5	0	0	142
1984	Ellsworth Dam	0	9	18	11	1	1	0	40
1985	Ellsworth Dam	0	18	39	22	2	0	0	81
1986	Ellsworth Dam	0	7	45	10	0	0	0	62
1987	Ellsworth Dam	0	0	5	37	16	0	0	58
1988	Ellsworth Dam	0	0	4	20	16	5	0	45
1989	Ellsworth Dam	0	4	17	4	1	0	0	26
1990	Ellsworth Dam	0	0	3	15	2	1	0	21
1991	Ellsworth Dam	0	0	0	2	6	0	0	8
1992	Ellsworth Dam	0	0	2	2	0	0	0	4
	Total (1975–1992)	**0**	**245**	**892**	**398**	**198**	**36**	**0**	**1,769**
	%	0.0	13.8	50.4	22.5	11.2	2.0	0.0	100
	Cumulative %	0.0	13.8	64.3	86.8	98.0	100.0	100.0	
	All Rivers	703	19,620	21,369	8,406	6,306	2,594	99	59,098
	%	1.2	33.2	36.2	14.2	10.7	4.4	0.2	100.0
	Cumulative %	1.2	34.4	70.5	84.8	95.4	99.8	100.0	

TABLE 2. MEAN LENGTH AND WEIGHT OF ATLANTIC SALMON FROM THE NARRAGUAGUS AND PENOBSCOT RIVERS.

Class	Number of Fish	Average Length[1]	Range of Lengths	Average Weight[2]	Range of Weights
		Narraguagus, 1962–1966			
1 sea-winter	13	59.7 cm. 23.5 in.	55.1–65.0 21.7–25.6	1.79 kg. 3 lb. 15 oz.	1.2 to 2.4 2–12 to 4–14
2 sea-winter	964	76.1 cm. 30.0 in.	68.6–85.3 27.0–33.6	3.93 kg. 8 lb. 14 oz.	2.8 to 5.8 6–4 to 12–12
3 sea-winter	19	89.1 cm. 35.1 in.	68.6–85.3 33.0–36.0	7.14 kg. 15 lb. 12 oz.	6.6 to 7.7 14–10 to 17–0
Repeat spawner (2nd time)	87	88.8 cm. 35.0 in.	82.6–104.1 32.5–41.0	7.03 kg. 15 lb. 8 oz.	5.6 to 8.7 12–4 to 19–2
Repeat spawner (3rd time)	12	97.7 cm. 38.5 in.	90.7–106.7 35.7–42.0	9.18 kg. 20 lb. 4 oz.	7.8 to 11.0 17–2 to 24–2
		Penobscot, 1987–1988			
1 sea-winter	269	54.5 cm. 21.5 in.	48.0–62.0 18.9–24.4	1.70 kg. 3.70 lb.	1.0 to 2.6 2.2 to 4.3
2 sea-winter	599	72.6 cm. 28.6 in.	61.0–84.0 24.0–33.1	4.32 kg. 9.50 lb.	2.1 to 6.5 4.6 to 14.3
3 sea-winter	29	86.6 cm. 34.1 in.	82.0–95.0 32.2–37.4	7.33 kg. 16.1 lb.	4.1 to 8.8 9.0 to 19.4
Repeat spawner (short absence)	8	81.4 cm. 32.0 in.	71.0–88.0 27.9–34.6	5.69 kg. 12.5 lb.	3.9–8.1 8.6 to 17.8
Repeat spawner (long absence)	89	87.5 cm. 34.4 in.	80.0–108.0 31.4–42.5	7.78 kg. 17.1 lb.	5.6–10.1 12.3 to 22.2

1. Total length used for Narraguagus River salmon, fork length used for Penobscot River salmon.
2. Narraguagus salmon measured in English units, Penobscot salmon measured in metric units.

TABLE 3

NUMBER AND PERCENT OF SEA-AGE DISTRIBUTION OF ATLANTIC SALMON CAUGHT BY ANGLING IN MAINE RIVERS.

		1SW Salmon		2SW Salmon		3SW Salmon		Repeat Spawners		
River	Years	No.	%	No.	%	No.	%	No.	%	Total
Dennys	1947–1994	24	1.1	2,059	95.6	11	0.5	59	2.7	2,153
East Machias	1956–1992	32	5.0	598	92.7	2	0.3	13	2.0	645
Machias	1948–1992	72	4.0	1,593	87.9	28	1.5	120	6.6	1,813
Pleasant	1967–1994	9	6.8	120	90.9	2	1.5	1	0.8	132
Narraguagus	1945–1994	44	1.4	2,799	90.3	59	1.9	196	6.3	3,098
Sheepscot	1967–1994	33	8.5	344	88.2	10	2.6	3	0.8	390
Penobscot	1954–1994	682	11.0	5,377	86.5	48	0.8	109	1.8	6,216
	Total	896	6.2	12,890	89.2	160	1.1	501	3.5	14,447

TABLE 4

NUMBER OF EGGS PER FEMALE ATLANTIC SALMON FROM VARIOUS MAINE RIVERS BY EGG SOURCE, 1871–1995.

			Number of Eggs Per Female by Egg Source			
Year(s)	River	No. of Females	Sea Run	Reconditioned Kelt	Captive Parr Age 3+	Age 4+
1871–1921	Penobscot*	9,737	8,263	–	–	–
1940–1947	Penobscot	320	5,933	–	–	–
1965–1995	Penobscot	5,490	7,420	–	–	–
1939	Dennys	12	9,417	–	–	–
1992–1994	Dennys	10	7,217	–	–	–
1993–1995	Dennys	13	–	5,633	–	–
1994	Dennys	56	–	–	1,969	
1995	Dennys	105		2,098	3,468	
1995	East Machias	65	–	–	2,211	–
1941–1971	Machias	478	6,996	–	–	–
1992–1993	Machias	9	7,326	–	–	–
1994–1995	Machias	6	–	6,577	–	–
1994	Machias	88	–	–	2,222	–
1995	Machias	171	–	–	1,846	3,421
1962–1971	Narraguagus	176	7,404	–	–	–
1994	Narraguagus	59	–	–	2,470	–
1995	Narraguagus	115	–	–	2,206	4,372
1967–1969	Orland	39	6,914	–	–	–
1974–1990	Union	600	7,685	–	–	–
1979	Kennebec	5	10,000	–	–	–
1995	Sheepscot	11	7,136	–	–	–
1995	Sheepscot	22	–	–	2,018	–
1993–1995	St. Croix	36	7,519	–	–	–

*These fish were purchased from commercial fishermen. In later years salmon were captured at the Bangor and Veazie Dams.

TABLE 5

ESTIMATES OF JUVENILE ATLANTIC SALMON DENSITIES FOR VARIOUS MAINE RIVERS
(NUMBER PER $100M^2$ OF HABITAT)

	Density of Age 0+ Parr		Density of Age 1+ and Older Parr	
River	Average	Highest	Average	Highest
St. Croix	–	40	–	11
Dennys	17	24	11	36
East Machias	13	69	4	20
Machias	12	196	14	33
Pleasant	6	19	11	14
Narraguagus	8	18	6	10
Ducktrap	–	42	11	15
Sheepscot	15	31	7	11
Penobscot	–	227	–	102

SOURCE: Atlantic Sea Run Salmon Commission and Atlantic Salmon Authority published and unpublished reports

Table 6

Counts of Atlantic salmon smolts in the Narraguagus and Penobscot rivers.
(Note: daily counts from the Narraguagus River by ASRSC personnel; 3-day counts from the Penobscot River courtesy of Great Northern Paper Co.

	Annual count of smolts in the Narraguagus River at Beddington Weir											Annual count of smolts in the Penobscot River at Weldon Dam							
Date	1960	1961	1962	1963	1964	1965	1966	1967	1968	**Total**	Cum.%	1988	1989	1990	1993	1994	1995	**Total**	Cum.%
April 1	0	0	0	0	0	0	0	0	0	**0**	0.0	0	0	0	0	0	0	**0**	0.0
2	0	0	0	0	0	0	0	0	0	**0**	0.0								
3	0	0	3	0	0	0	0	0	0	**3**	0.0								
4	0	0	0	0	0	0	0	0	0	**0**	0.0	0	0	0	0	0	0	**0**	0.0
5	0	0	0	0	0	0	0	0	0	**0**	0.0								
6	0	0	5	0	0	0	0	0	0	**5**	0.0								
7	0	0	5	0	0	0	0	0	0	**5**	0.2	0	0	0	0	0	0	**0**	0.0
8	0	0	0	0	0	0	0	0	0	**0**	0.2								
9	0	0	6	0	0	0	0	0	0	**6**	0.2								
10	0	0	5	0	0	0	0	1	0	**6**	0.3	0	0	0	0	0	0	**0**	0.0
11	4	0	7	0	0	0	0	0	0	**11**	0.4								
12	0	0	1	0	0	0	0	0	0	**1**	0.4								
13	3	1	3	1	0	0	0	0	0	**8**	0.5	0	0	0	0	0	0	**0**	0.0
14	4	0	1	0	0	0	0	0	0	**5**	0.6								
April 15	0	2	1	0	0	0	0	0	0	**3**	0.6								
16	6	0	0	0	3	0	0	0	0	**9**	0.7	0	0	0	0	0	0	**0**	0.0
17	0	0	0	0	1	1	1	0	1	**4**	0.8								
18	1	5	0	1	0	1	0	0	0	**8**	0.9								
19	2	2	1	0	0	0	0	0	0	**5**	0.9	1	0	0	0	0	0	**1**	0.0
20	1	0	0	0	0	2	0	0	0	**3**	1.0								
21	0	6	0	0	0	0	0	0	0	**6**	1.1								
22	0	0	0	0	1	0	0	0	0	**1**	1.1	0	0	0	0	0	0	**0**	0.0
23	2	0	0	1	0	0	0	0	0	**3**	1.1								
24	0	2	1	0	1	1	0	0	0	**5**	1.2								
25	0	0	1	2	0	2	0	0	0	**5**	1.2	0	0	1	1	0	0	**2**	0.0
26	0	1	1	0	0	0	2	0	1	**5**	1.3								
27	0	0	1	4	0	0	0	0	8	**13**	1.4								

28	0	1	1	1	0	0	2	0	4	**9**	1.6	0	0	1	0	0	1	**2**	0.0
29	1	1	0	2	0	0	0	0	0	**4**	1.6								
30	1	0	0	1	0	2	0	0	8	**12**	1.7								
May 1	1	0	0	0	0	2	0	0	42	**45**	2.3	0	0	2	0	0	3	**5**	0.0
2	1	0	0	0	0	0	0	0	3	**4**	2.3								
3	7	0	0	3	0	1	0	0	1	**12**	2.5								
4	6	0	0	4	0	0	0	0	13	**23**	2.8	0	3	1	13	3	15	**35**	0.3
5	16	0	0	3	3	1	0	0	64	**87**	3.8								
6	31	0	2	5	2	0	0	0	4	**44**	4.3								
7	27	2	1	4	1	0	3	1	25	**64**	5.1	15	9	27	46	1	33	**131**	1.1
8	15	3	1	16	20	5	0	0	24	**84**	6.1								
9	5	0	2	0	5	2	2	1	46	**63**	6.9								
10	19	0	0	0	13	14	2	0	34	**82**	7.9	43	19	27	189	6	130	**414**	3.7
11	30	1	3	45	25	3	0	0	9	**116**	9.2								
12	48	0	0	39	35	4	0	20	13	**159**	11.2								
13	35	3	4	63	78	50	27	23	13	**296**	14.7	214	11	33	133	9	238	**638**	7.6
14	198	2	4	27	20	74	26	28	37	**416**	19.7								
May 15	283	45	2	86	98	4	31	3	0	**552**	26.4								
16	327	17	27	53	294	20	60	1	44	**843**	36.5	113	38	79	179	7	975	**1,391**	16.3
17	305	47	20	61	35	7	11	8	0	**494**	42.4								
18	50	63	18	67	17	2	47	6	24	**294**	46.0								
19	87	10	24	67	32	10	21	2	21	**274**	49.3	152	267	76	290	32	2,123	**2,940**	34.5
20	188	100	20	96	11	88	5	12	0	**520**	55.5								
21	27	92	47	140	46	24	42	28	0	**446**	60.9								
22	32	100	12	43	4	25	43	18	96	**373**	65.4	262	671	40	699	309	298	**2,279**	48.6
23	18	72	14	82	25	29	61	12	32	**345**	69.5								
24	5	31	59	88	25	11	160	8	16	**403**	74.4								
25	9	83	49	80	2	20	53	23	9	**328**	78.3	202	233	25	873	37	264	**1,634**	58.8
26	14	26	57	126	5	8	22	18	3	**279**	81.7								
27	18	12	76	49	4	8	93	54	13	**327**	85.6								
28	11	0	5	33	8	8	10	150	10	**235**	88.4	529	294	33	642	620	211	**2,329**	73.2
29	4	7	58	64	3	9	25	40	11	**221**	91.1								
30	1	8	14	9	5	0	4	22	4	**67**	91.9								
31	3	12	7	8	3	5	3	62	3	**106**	93.2	208	171	14	81	517	172	**1,163**	80.5
June 1	1	7	69	5	36	0	5	15	0	**138**	94.8								
2	0	2	20	4	6	1	4	32	0	**69**	95.6								
3	0	2	24	10	0	5	0	86	0	**127**	97.2	106	357	44	30	673	108	**1,318**	88.6

Date	Annual count of smolts in the Narraguagus River at Beddington Weir											Annual count of smolts in the Penobscot River at Weldon Dam							
	1960	1961	1962	1963	1964	1965	1966	1967	1968	**Total**	Cum.%	1988	1989	1990	1993	1994	1995	**Total**	Cum.%
June 4	0	3	8	5	3	2	0	6	0	**27**	97.5								
5	1	3	106	0	2	2	0	3	0	**117**	98.9								
6	0	1	3	1	17	0	0	5	0	**27**	99.2	16	192	15	38	256	51	**568**	92.2
7	0	1	0	0	0	0	0	1	0	**2**	99.3								
8	0	0	0	0	0	1	0	6	0	**7**	99.3								
9	0	0	12	2	4	0	0	0	0	**18**	99.6	12	109	3	16	126	21	**287**	93.9
10	0	0	0	0	1	0	0	0	0	**1**	99.6								
11	0	0	0	0	1	0	0	0	0	**1**	99.6								
12	1	0	0	0	0	0	0	1	0	**2**	99.6	21	559	4	25	61	16	**686**	98.2
13	0	0	1	0	0	0	1	0	0	**2**	99.6								
14	0	0	0	0	0	0	0	0	0	**0**	99.6								
June 15	0	0	0	0	0	0	0	0	0	**0**	99.6	9	89	7	5	31	15	**156**	99.2
16	0	0	0	0	0	0	0	0	0	**0**	99.6								
17	2	0	0	6	0	1	0	0	0	**9**	99.7								
18	0	0	0	16	0	0	0	0	0	**16**	99.9	0	68	4	3	5	8	**88**	99.7
19	0	0	0	0	0	0	0	0	0	**0**	99.9								
20	0	0	0	0	0	0	1	0	0	**1**	99.9								
21	0	0	0	0	0	1	0	0	0	**1**	100.0	0	33	1	2	0	9	**45**	100.0
22	0	0	0	0	0	0	0	1	0	**1**	100.0								
23	0	0	0	0	0	0	0	0	0	**0**	100.0								
24	0	0	0	0	0	0	0	3	0	**3**	100.0	0	0	0	0	1	0	**1**	100.0
25	0	0	0	0	0	0	0	0	0	**0**	100.0								
26	0	0	0	0	0	0	0	0	0	**0**	100.0								
27	0	0	0	0	0	0	0	0	0	**0**	100.0	0	0	0	0	0	0	**0**	100.0
28	0	0	0	0	0	0	0	0	0	**0**	100.0								
29	0	0	0	0	0	0	0	0	0	**0**	100.0								
June 30	0	0	0	0	0	0	0	0	0	**0**	100.0	0	0	0	1	0		**1**	100.0
Total	1,851	776	812	1,423	895	456	767	700	636	8,316	100.0	1,903	3,123	437	3,265	2.695	4,691	16,114	100.0

Table 7

Geographic distribution of Carlin tag returns from Maine-origin Atlantic salmon in the North Atlantic Ocean, 1963–1995.

Area of Recovery	Number Recovered by Life Stage					
	Post Smolt	1 Sea-Winter	Multi Sea-Winter	Post Kelt	Total Number	% of Total
East Greenland	0	28	1	0	29	0.8
West Greenland	0	1,670	61	35	1,766	46.4
Total Greenland	0	1,698	62	35	1,795	47.1
Faroe Islands	0	1	0	0	1	0.0
Labrador	3	319	26	13	361	9.5
Newfoundland	29	918	59	232	1,238	32.5
Nova Scotia/New Brunswick	245	53	50	34	382	10.0
Total Canada	277	1,290	135	279	1,981	52.0
Total Coastal USA	10	1	18	2	31	0.8
Total Known Areas	287	2,990	215	316	3,808	100.0
Unknown Areas	3	314	15	3	335	
Grand Total	290	3,304	230	319	4,143	

Table 8

Marine migration data for Carlin-tagged Maine Atlantic salmon.

Life Stage at Capture	Maximum Number of Days at Large	Minimum Distance Traveled		Average Rate of Migration		Maximum Rate of Migration	
		Miles	Kilometers	Miles /day	Kilometers /day	Miles /day	Kilometers /day
Post-Smolt	165	1,392	2,240	9–14	15–22	15.7	25.3
1 Sea-Winter	588	2,845	4,579	NM*	NM*	NM*	NM*
Multi Sea-Winter	941	2,689	4,328	NM*	NM*	NM*	NM*
Post Kelt	209	2,689	4,328	10–17	17–28	25.8	41.6

*NM = not meaningful, since these fish spent one or more winters at sea before capture.

TABLE 9

KNOWN DOUBLE-CRESTED CORMORANT PREDATION UPON MACHIAS RIVER HATCHERY-REARED SMOLTS.

Year	Smolt Age	Size No./lb.	Hatchery[1]	Release Date(s)	Number Released	Known Predation[2] Number	%
1966	1	16.8	CBNFH	April 15–18	13,690	796	5.81
	2	9.0	ESH	April 19	19,305	1,388	7.19
	Total 1+2		CBNFH+ESH		32,995	2,184	6.62
1967	1	8.0	CBNFH	April 10–14	14,700	1,326	9.02
	2	7.9	ESH	April 10–14	11,235	1,138	10.13
	Total 1+2		CBNFH+ESH		25,935	2,464	9.50
1968	1	9.1	CBNFH	Feb. 28–29	4,990	121	2.42
	1	8.9	CBNFH	April 8–10	12,870	790	6.14
	1	8.5	CBNFH	May 13–14	4,880	172	3.52
	Total 1		CBNFH		22,740	1,083	4.76
	2	7.2	ESH	April 10	4,845	382	7.88
	2	5.5	ESH	May 8	4,060	224	5.52
	Total 2		ESH		8,905	606	6.81
	Total 1+2		CBNFH+ESH		31,645	1,689	5.34
1969	1	8.0	CBNFH	April 23–24	2,500	336	13.44
	1	4.8	CBNFH	May 21	2,500	28	1.12
	Total 1		CBNFH		5,000	364	7.28
	2	8.3	CBNFH	April 20–23	8,690	1,062	12.22
	2	9.5	CBNFH	May 19	2,295	35	1.53
	2		ESH	May 28	11,360	45	0.40
	Total 2		CBNFH+ESH		22,345	1,142	5.11
	Total 1+2		CBNFH+ESH		27,345	1,506	5.51
1966–1969	1		CBNFH	Feb. 28–29	4,990	121	2.42
	1		CBNFH	April 8–24	43,760	3,248	7.42
	1		CBNFH	May 13–21	7,380	200	2.71
	Total 1		CBNFH		56,130	3,569	6.36
	2		CBNFH+ESH	April 10–23	44,075	3,970	9.01
	2		CBNFH+ESH	May 8–28	17,715	304	1.72
	Total 2		CBNFH+ESH		61,790	4,274	6.92
	Grand Total 1+2		CBNFH+ESH		117,920	7,843	6.65

1. CBNFH = Craig Brook National Fish Hatchery; ESH = Enfield State Hatchery.
2. Includes Carlin tags recovered from cormorant stomachs and Old Man Island, Machias Bay.

TABLE 10

CORMORANT PREDATION UPON MACHIAS RIVER HATCHERY SMOLTS VERSUS TIME OF RELEASE

Time of Release	Number Released	Number of Tags Recovered	% Predation
February 28–29	4,990	121	2.42
April 1–14	43,650	3,636	8.33
April 15–30	44,185	3582	8.11
May 1–14	8,940	396	4.43
May 15–31	16,155	108	0.67

Table 11. Historical sport catch (known number killed and/or released) of Atlantic salmon in Maine rivers (excluding kelts and salmon of aquaculture origin).

Decade	Aroostook	Croix	Saint Dennys	Machias	East Machias	Pleasant	Narraguagus	Union	Penobscot	Ducktrap	Sheepscot	Kennebec	Saco	Misc./ Unk.	Total Catch	% of Total	Average Catch/Yr.
1880's									90						90	0.3	**9**
1890's	4	120							669						793	3.1	**79**
1900's									808						808	3.1	**81**
1910's									903						903	3.5	**90**
1920's			19						1,298						1,317	5.1	**132**
1930's			232						800						1,032	4.0	**103**
1940's			672	8	5	1	386		201		2			1	1,276	4.:	**128**
1950's	2	2	639	140	261	65	654		74	11	80				1,928	7.5	**193**
1960's			403	135	702	144	577		21		172	2		2	2,158	8.4	**216**
1970's			418	184	499	51	865	191	865		184	12	2	84	3,355	13.0	**336**
1980's	11	114	536	355	370	49	688	95	6,052	52	139	69	112	28	8,670	33.7	**867**
1990's	12	15	62	95	31	2	198	0	2,776	3	34	123	32	3	3,386	13.2	**677**
Total	**29**	**251**	**2,981**	**917**	**1,868**	**312**	**3,368**	**286**	**14,557**	**66**	**611**	**206**	**146**	**118**	**25,716**	100.0	
%	0.1	1.0	11.6	3.6	7.3	1.2	13.1	1.1	56.6	0.3	2.4	0.8	0.6	0.5	100.0		
Rank	14	9	3	5	4	7	2	8	1	11	6	10	12	13			
Best Year	1890's	1986	1980	1981	1961	1961	1959	1973	1990	1986	1966	1990	1985	1978	1986		
Kept/Rel	Unk.	5/50	190/20	85	132	45	167	75	431/675	15/10	40	44/60	60/19	28		1,093/528	

Table 12

Rod catches of Maine Atlantic salmon by month and river.

River	Years	April	May	June	July	August	September	October	Total
Dennys	1936 –1993	5	231	1,379	220	53	68	10	1,966
	%	0.3	11.7	70.1	11.2	2.7	3.5	0.5	100.0
	Accum %	0.3	12.0	82.1	93.3	96.0	99.5	100.0	
East Machias	1953–1990	0	63	386	70	12	11	17	559
	%	0.0	11.3	69.1	12.5	2.1	2.0	3.0	100.0
	Accum %	0.0	11.3	80.3	92.8	95.0	97.0	100.0	
Machias	1953–1990	0	5	350	414	197	119	5	1,090
	%	0.0	0.5	32.1	38.0	18.1	10.9	0.5	100.0
	Accum %	0.0	0.5	32.6	70.6	88.6	99.5	100.0	
Narraguagus	1945–1994	1	751	1,943	318	38	57	14	3,122
	%	0.0	24.1	62.2	10.2	1.2	1.8	0.4	100.0
	Accum %	0.0	24.1	86.3	96.5	97.7	99.6	100.0	
Sheepscot	1954–1993	4	8	79	40	10	11	1	153
	%	2.6	5.2	51.6	26.1	6.5	7.2	0.7	100.0
	Accum %	2.6	7.8	59.5	85.6	92.2	99.3	100.0	
Penobscot	1969–1993	1	1,426	3,874	905	368	239	112	6,925
	%	0.0	20.6	55.9	13.1	5.3	3.5	1.6	100.0
	Accum %	0.0	20.6	76.5	89.6	94.9	98.4	100.0	
Total Maine[1]	1945–1994	11	2,484	8,011	1,967	678	505	159	13,815
	%	0.0	18.0	58.0	14.2	4.9	3.7	1.2	100.0
	Accum %	0.0	18.1	76.0	90.3	95.2	98.8	100.0	
Penobscot [2]	1926–1952	118	645	1,109	47				1,919
	%	6.1	33.6	57.8	2.4				100.0
	Accum %	6.1	39.8	97.6	100.0				

1. Pleasant River = limited information available—most catches in June and July. Ducktrap River = limited information available—most catches in September and October.

2. Season closed on July 15 for many years; catch is from the Bangor Salmon Pool only.

TABLE 13

SEA-AGE DISTRIBUTION OF ROD-CAUGHT ATLANTIC SALMON IN MAINE RIVERS.

River	Years	1SW Salmon		2SW Salmon		3SW Salmon		Repeat Spawners		Total
		Number	%	Number	%	Number	%	Number	%	
Dennys	1947–1994	24	1.1	2,059	95.6	11	0.5	59	2.7	2,153
East Machias	1956–1992	32	5.0	598	92.7	2	0.3	13	2.0	645
Machias	1948–1992	72	4.0	1,593	87.9	28	1.5	120	6.6	1,813
Pleasant	1967–1994	9	6.8	120	90.9	2	1.5	1	0.8	132
Narraguagus	1945–1994	44	1.4	2,799	90.3	59	1.9	196	6.3	3,098
Sheepscot	1967–1994	33	8.5	344	88.2	10	2.6	3	0.8	390
Penobscot	1954–1994	682	11.0	5,377	86.5	48	0.8	109	1.8	6,216
	Total	896	6.2	12,890	89.2	160	1.1	501	3.5	14,447

TABLE 14

ESTIMATED HARVEST OF 1SW MAINE-ORIGIN ATLANTIC SALMON IN THE WEST GREENLAND AND NEWFOUNDLAND-LABRADOR COMMERCIAL FISHERIES.

Year of Harvest	Estimated Harvest of 1SW Maine-Origin Salmon					
	Carlin Tag Method		Proportional Method		CWT Method	
	Greenland	Nfld-Lab	Greenland	Nfld-Lab	Greenland	Nfld-Lab
1967	226	242	–	–	–	–
1968 [1]	–	411	–	–	–	–
1969	545	277	–	–	–	–
1970	828	398	–	–	–	–
1971	2,446	295	–	–	–	–
1972	809	105	–	–	–	–
1973	1,212	220	–	–	–	–
1974	2,615	758	–	–	–	–
1975	1,299	1,014	–	–	–	–
1976	1,529	2,230	5,755	–	–	–
1977	886	940	8,797	–	–	–
1978 [2]	1,066	309	7,160	–	–	–
1979	–	–	11,034	–	–	–
1980	2,207	4,631	30,492	–	–	–
1981	1,908	1,147	13,401	–	–	–
1982	1,283	1,603	7,576	–	–	–
1983	488	1,700	2,350	–	–	–
1984	849	1,329	2,640	–	–	–
1985	1,469	2,288	8,370	–	–	–
1986	2,035	552	3,816	–	–	–
1987	2,087	580	6,006	–	5,571	–
1988	2,309	393	5,173	–	3,882	–
1989	3,797	1,722	4,547	–	2,857	–
1990	1,525	780	4,790	–	2,037	–
1991	1,777	1,425	4,048	–	1,707	–
1992 [3]	991	–	1,950	–	1,319	–
Total	36,186	25,349	127,905	–	17,373	–
Average	1,508	1,056	7,524	–	2,896	–

Source: ICES North Atlantic Salmon Working Group

1. No estimate possible for 1968.
2. No Carlin-tagged smolts released in Maine in 1978.
3. Newfoundland fishery closed (moratorium) from 1992 to 1996.
3. Greenland fishery closed in 1993–1994 due to buyout.

TABLE 15

RECOVERIES OF CARLIN-TAGGED MAINE-ORIGIN ATLANTIC SALMON IN THE NORTH ATLANTIC BY SEA AGE AND AREA OF CAPTURE.

Area of Recovery	NAFO Division(s)[1]	Sea Age at Capture				Total	
		Post-smolt	1SW	2SW	Post-kelt	Number	%
West Greenland, north	1A, 1B	0	518	33	19	570	13.8
West Greenland, central	1C, 1D	0	776	20	10	806	19.5
West Greenland, south	1E, 1F	0	376	8	6	390	9.4
East Greenland	XIV	0	28	1	0	29	0.7
Total Greenland		0	1,698	62	35	1,795	43.3
Faroe Islands		0	0	1	0	1	0.0
Labrador, north	2G, 2H	0	216	7	8	231	5.6
Labrador, south	2J	3	103	19	5	130	3.1
Quebec & NW Newfoundland	4S	1	4	1	1	7	0.2
Newfoundland, east coast	3K, 3L	7	850	51	93	1,001	24.2
Newfoundland, south coast	3Ps, 3Pn	19	46	4	134	203	4.9
Newfoundland, west coast	4R	2	18	3	4	27	0.7
Nova Scotia, north and NW coast	4Vn, 4W	25	6	2	5	38	0.9
New Brunswick and SW Nova Scotia	4x, 4T	220	47	48	29	344	8.3
Total Canada		277	1,290	135	279	1,981	47.8
Maine coast	5Y	8	1	16	2	27	0.7
Other USA coastal	6	2	0	2	0	4	0.0
Total USA coast		10	1	18	2	31	0.7
Unknown[2]		3	314	15	3	335	8.1
Grand Total		290	3,303	231	319	4,143	100.0

1. See figures 29 and 30 for illustration of NAFO areas.
2. Tag returns where it was not possible to postively identify the location where the salmon was taken.

Appendices

Appendices

Appendix 1

Historical Maine Atlantic Salmon Broodstock Data, 1871–1995

Year	River	Number collected	Number spawned: Males	Females	Total	Average weight	Number of eggs: Total	Per female	Remarks
1871	Penobscot	111	8	10	18	11.7	72,300	7,230	
1872	Penobscot	692	130	225	355	12.3	1,566,045	6,960	
1873	Penobscot	652	143	271	414	13.3	2,321,935	8,568	
1874	Penobscot	601	178	343	521	14.0	3,056,500	8,911	
1875	Penobscot	511	152	237	389		2,020,000	8,523	
1876	Penobscot	0	0	0	0		0		1
1877	Penobscot	0	0	0	0		0		1
1878	Penobscot	0	0	0	0		0		1
1879	Penobscot	264	40	19	59	12.3	211,690	11,142	2
1880	Penobscot	522	186	227	413	13.0	1,930,560	8,505	
1881	Penobscot	514	126	232	358	16.5	2,693,010	11,608	
1882	Penobscot	586	184	250	434	13.0	2,090,000	8,360	
1883	Penobscot	431	60	207	267	18.3	2,535,000	12,246	3
1884	Penobscot	568	189	240	429	9.9	1,935,185	8,063	4
1885	Penobscot	691	216	285	501		2,422,600	8,500	
1886	Penobscot	205	46	101	147		1,158,775	11,473	
1887	Penobscot	467	102	133	235		1,184,000	8,902	
1888	Penobscot	631	175	250	425		2,253,205	9,013	
1889	Penobscot	410	102	186	288		1,904,000	10,237	
1890	Penobscot	133	25	52	77		533,400	10,258	
1891	Penobscot	268	88	137	225		1,203,285	8,783	5
1892	Penobscot	222	62	108	170		1,108,500	10,264	
1893	Penobscot	242	51	95	146		806,000	8,484	
1894	Penobscot	174	33	38	71		415,350	10,930	
1895	Penobscot	390	68	111	179		1,027,355	9,255	6
1896	Penobscot	684	174	353	527		3,192,125	9,043	
1897	Penobscot	598		350	350		3,506,640	10,019	7
1898	Penobscot	472			365		2,147,675		

NOTES: All broodstock listed are of sea-run origin, unless noted in column 2 as follows:
(K) = reconditioned kelts of sea-run origin
(C) = captive-reared in freshwater from wild-origin parr
(A) = aquaculture origin

1. Hatchery operations suspended to evaluate first 5 years of stocking.
2. Lost most broodstock due to flood.
3. Hard to handle because fish were so large.
4. Fish much smaller this year.
5. Disease killed most of the fry.
6. Lost 109 broodstock en route to Craig Brook.
7. Includes 33 adults trapped at Bangor Dam (26 survived).

Year	River	Number collected	Number spawned: Males	Females	Total	Average weight	Number of eggs: Total	Per female	Remarks
1899	Penobscot	489			408		1,881,610		
1900	Penobscot	213	66	84	150		665,000	7,917	
1901	Penobscot	255			238		832,300		
1902	Penobscot	614			589		2,506,575		
1903	Penobscot	798					3,484,000		
1904	Penobscot	856			230		954,500		
1905	Penobscot	833	234	324	558		2,310,430	7,131	
1906	Penobscot	931	285	393	678		2,804,400	7,136	
1907	Penobscot	784	232	357	589		2,714,500	7,604	
1908	Penobscot	583	151	155	306		1,114,300	7,189	
1909	Penobscot	408	100	174	274		1,456,800	8,372	
1910	Penobscot	797	257	436	693		3,800,200	8,716	
1911	Penobscot	1088	271	305	576		2,149,455	7,047	
1912	Penobscot	1133	385	480	865		3,966,430	8,263	8
1913	Penobscot	927	339	427	766		3,149,655	7,376	
1914	Penobscot	693	201	288	489		2,014,400	6,994	
1915	Penobscot	725	153	279	432		1,953,400	7,001	
1916	Penobscot	1031	396	491	887		3,739,180	7,615	
1917	Penobscot	835	345	414	759		3,024,930	7,307	
1918	Penobscot	870	354	346	700		2,613,400	7,553	
1919	Penobscot	286	116	111	227		797,610	7,186	9
1920	Penobscot	317	154	126	280		911,720	7,236	10
1921	Penobscot	208	111	79	190		572,040	7,241	
1922	Penobscot	51	0	0	0		0		11
1923	Penobscot	0	0	0	0		0		12
1924	Penobscot	0	0	0	0		0		
1925	Penobscot	0	0	0	0		0		
1926	Penobscot	0	0	0	0		0		
1927	Penobscot	0	0	0	0		0		
1928	Penobscot	0	0	0	0		0		
1929	Penobscot	0	0	0	0		0		
1930	Penobscot	0	0	1	1		4,500		13
1931	Penobscot	0	0	0	0		0		
1932	Penobscot	0	0	0	0		0		
1933	Penobscot	0	0	0	0		0		
1934	Penobscot	0	0	0	0		0		

8. 147,789 lbs. of salmon landed in Maine—largest catch in 20 years.
9. Green Lake Hatchery opens again following renovations.
10. 1st fish in new Green Lake Hatchery—landlocked salmon.
11. All broodstock escaped! Big salmon run noted in Dennys River.
12. No broodstock purchased due to poor fisherman cooperation.
13. First time salmon eggs were taken directly from Penobscot River—one partially spent female spawned @ Souadabscook Stream in Hampden.

Year	River	Number collected	Number spawned			Average weight	Number of eggs		Remarks
			Males	Females	Total		Total	Per female	
1935	Penobscot	0	0	0	0		0		
1936	Penobscot	0	0	0	0		0		
1937	Penobscot	0	0	0	0		0		
1938	Penobscot	0	0	0	0		0		
1939	Penobscot	0	0	0	0		0		
1940	Penobscot	104	40	43	83		250,450	5,824	14
1941	Penobscot	7			7	See 1941 Machias			
1942	Penobscot	171	40	118	158		708,945	6,008	15
1943	Penobscot	54	24	23	47		157,240	6,837	16
1944	Penobscot	38	12	24	36		150,000	6,250	17
1945	Penobscot	108	46	52	98		307,400	5,912	18
1946	Penobscot	1			1	See 1946 Machias			19
1947	Penobscot	120	56	60	116		324,475	5,408	
1948	Penobscot	12			12	See 1948 Machias			20
1949	Penobscot	2			2	See 1949 Machias			
1950	Penobscot	29			29	See 1950 Machias			21
1951	Penobscot	0	0	0	0		0		
1952	Penobscot	0	0	0	0		0		
1953	Penobscot	0	0	0	0		0		
1954	Penobscot	0	0	0	0		0		
1955	Penobscot	0	0	0	0		0		
1956	Penobscot	0	0	0	0		0		
1957	Penobscot	0	0	0	0		0		
1958	Penobscot	0	0	0	0		0		
1959	Penobscot	0	0	0	0		0		
1960	Penobscot	0	0	0	0		0		
1961	Penobscot	0	0	0	0		0		
1962	Penobscot	0	0	0	0		0		
1963	Penobscot	0	0	0	0		0		
1964	Penobscot	0	0	0	0		0		
1965	Penobscot	0	0	0	0		0		
1966	Penobscot	0	0	0	0		0		
1967	Penobscot	0	0	0	0		0		
1968	Penobscot	0	0	0	0		0		
1969	Penobscot	70	20	22	42		155,265	7,058	

14. Includes 2 salmon from the Machias River.
15. Used Penobscot Salmon Club tank to transport fish.
16. Heavy losses due to internal and external parasites.
17. Additional 38 released upriver.
18. Additional 60 salmon released upriver.
19. Low water—went to Machias River to obtain broodstock.
20. Sent kelts to Boothbay Harbor lab for reconditioning—all died over winter..
21. Obtained 8 salmon from the Bangor fishway and 21 from the Veazie fishway.

Year	River	Number collected	Number spawned			Average weight	Number of eggs		Remarks
			Males	Females	Total		Total	Per female	
1970	Penobscot	111	17	38	55		269,480	7,092	
1971	Penobscot	73	21	34	55		224,130	6,592	
1972	Penobscot	218	110	114	224		682,745	5,989	
1973	Penobscot	234	34	111	145		831,090	7,487	
1974	Penobscot	305	116	173	289		1,447,785	8,369	
1975	Penobscot	264	109	139	248		972,965	7,000	
1976	Penobscot	307	116	179	295		1,313,995	7,341	
1977	Penobscot	205	69	95	164		710,880	7,483	
1978	Penobscot	313	112	166	278		1,407,930	8,482	
1979	Penobscot	274	103	151	254		1,117,360	7,400	
1980	Penobscot	418	129	214	343		1,506,050	7,038	
1981	Penobscot	469	120	141	261		1,028,000	7,291	
1982	Penobscot	678	162	203	365		1,549,600	7,633	
1983	Penobscot	433	151	211	362		1,557,490	7,381	
1984	Penobscot	521	151	311	462		2,351,800	7,562	
1985	Penobscot	509	218	239	457		1,838,900	7,694	
1986	Penobscot	467	163	295	458		2,376,100	8,055	
1987	Penobscot	471	161	271	432		2,150,165	7,934	
1988	Penobscot	546	233	226	459		1,610,700	7,127	
1989	Penobscot	499	174	316	490		2,427,200	7,681	
1990	Penobscot	538	185	300	485		2,041,700	6,806	
1991	Penobscot	569	191	340	531		2,427,000	7,138	
1992	Penobscot	574	212	351	563		2,448,000	6,974	
1993	Penobscot	486	230	255	485		1,881,870	7,380	
1994	Penobscot	341	200	215	415		1,669,905	7,767	
1995	Penobscot	588	200	380	580		2,735,645	7,199	
1939	Dennys	23	9	12	21		113,000	9,417	[22]
1992	Dennys	6	1	5	6		38,000	7,600	[23]
1993	Dennys	7	0	3	3		19,340	6,447	[23]
1993	Dennys (K)	3	1	2	3		8,590	4,295	[23]
1994	Dennys	4	1	2	3		14,830	7,415	
1994	Dennys (K)		see below	6	6		30,480	5,080	
1994	Dennys (C)		84	56	140		110,240	1,969	
1995	Dennys (K)		see below	5	5		34,155	6,831	
1995	Dennys (C)		197	105	302		303,870	2,894	
1939	E. Machias	2			2		See 1939 Dennys		
1941	E. Machias	2			2		See 1941 Machias		
1995	E. Machias (C)		78	65			143,735		

22. Includes 2 salmon taken from the East Machias River.
23. Also used Dennys River-origin male parr for spawning purposes.

Year	River	Number collected	Number spawned			Average weight	Number of eggs		Remarks
			Males	Females	Total		Total	Per female	
1940	Machias	2			2	See 1940 Penob.			
1941	Machias	63	27	28	55		268,480	9,589	
1946	Machias	100	32	37	69		266,525	7,203	[24]
1948	Machias	23	9	23	32		140,215	6,096	
1949	Machias	186	88	85	173		558,815	6,574	
1950	Machias	79	36	30	66		203,400	6,780	
1957	Machias	77		20			137,535	6,877	
1958	Machias	77		22			138,670	6,303	
1959	Machias	50		19			133,155	7,008	
1960	Machias	17		10			81,910	8,191	
1961	Machias	28		9			71,785	7,976	
1963	Machias	27	7	20	27		150,575	7,529	
1964	Machias	25	5	19	24		139,810	7,358	
1965	Machias	19	4	15	19		127,120	8,475	
1966	Machias	43	6	37	43		287,950	7,782	
1967	Machias	40	11	29	40		131,000	4,517	
1968	Machias	14	4	10	14		76,580	7,658	
1969	Machias	32	8	24	32		190,705	7,946	
1970	Machias	20	4	10	14		70,750	7,075	
1971	Machias	40	7	31	38		169,000	5,452	
1992	Machias	16	9	2	11		15,850	7,925	[25]
1993	Machias	12	4	7	11		50,080	7,154	
1994	Machias (K)	see below		2	2		11,670	5,835	
1994	Machias (C)		83	88	171		195,505	2,222	
1995	Machias (K)	see below		4	4		27,790	6,948	
1995	Machias (C)		238	171	409		484,210	2,832	
1948	Narraguagus	1			1	see 1948 Machias			
1949	Narraguagus	61			61	see 1949 Machias			
1962	Narraguagus	26	16	10	26		72,375	7,238	
1963	Narraguagus	19	5	14	19		131,095	9,364	
1964	Narraguagus	25	4	21	25		162,020	7,715	
1965	Narraguagus	25	4	21	25		139,685	6,652	
1966	Narraguagus	21	4	17	21		142,440	8,379	
1967	Narraguagus	21	4	17	21		146,940	8,644	
1968	Narraguagus	41	10	31	41		182,205	5,878	
1969	Narraguagus	26	4	20	24		160,735	8,037	
1970	Narraguagus	13	3	5	8		46,485	9,297	
1971	Narraguagus	32	9	20	29		119,200	5,960	
1994	Narraguagus (C)		69	59	128		145,710	2,470	
1995	Narraguagus (C)		115	115	230		394,435	3,430	

24. Most broodstock in poor condition—many mortalities noted.
25. Includes 1 spent and 1 partially spent female.

Appendix 1: Historical Broodstock Data

Year	River	Number collected	Number spawned			Average weight	Number of eggs		Remarks
			Males	Females	Total		Total	Per female	
1967	Orland	16	2	5	7		41,110	8,222	
1968	Orland	45	9	31	40		207,940	6,708	
1969	Orland	5	2	3	5		20,595	6,865	
1974	Union	15	8	7	15		54,000	7,714	
1975	Union	57	20	23	43		179,250	7,793	
1976	Union	156	50	61	111		441,830	7,243	
1977	Union	173	68	68	136		490,030	7,206	
1978	Union	147	58	53	111		431,770	8,147	
1979	Union	27	12	12	24		88,670	7,389	
1980	Union	178	39	12	51		90,840	7,570	
1981	Union	249	103	127	230		846,790	6,668	
1982	Union	233	50	50	100		435,410	8,708	
1983	Union	117	56	52	108		450,550	8,664	
1984	Union	39	11	25	36		192,950	7,718	
1985	Union	78	38	37	75		285,740	7,723	
1986	Union	55	24	23	47		211,010	9,174	
1987	Union	39	16	18	34		161,110	8,951	
1988	Union	45	10	10	20		80,710	8,071	
1989	Union	22	12	8	20		67,175	8,397	
1990	Union	21	6	14	20		103,040	7,360	
1979	Kennebec	10	5	5	10		50,000	10,000	
1995	Sheepscot	22	9	11	20		78,495	7,136	
1995	Sheepscot (C)		49	22	71		44,385	2,01	
1993	St. Croix	29	11	15	26		114,000	7,600	
1994	St. Croix	30	11	11	22		80,000	7,273	
1995	St. Croix	16	5	10	15		76,700	7,670	
1995	St. Croix (A)	1	see above	1	1		10,300	10,300	

Appendix 2

Historical sport catches of salmon in Maine Rivers, 1885–1995

(K = number caught and retained; R = number caught and released.)

Year	Androscoggin K	Androscoggin R	Aroostook K	Aroostook R	Dennys K	Dennys R	Ducktrap K	Ducktrap R	E. Machias K	E. Machias R	Kennebec K	Kennebec R	Machias K	Machias R	Narraguagus K	Narraguagus R	Penobscot K	Penobscot R	Pleasant K	Pleasant R	Prestile Str. K	Prestile Str. R	Saco K	Saco R	Sheepscot K	Sheepscot R	St. Croix K	St. Croix R	Union K	Union R	Misc. K	Misc. R	Grand Totals K	Grand Totals R	Grand Totals Total
1936	0	0	0	0	49	0	0	0	0	0	0	0	0	0	0	0	0	0	0	0	0	0	0	0	0	0	0	0	0	0	0	0	49	0	49
1937	0	0	0	0	83	0	0	0	0	0	0	0	0	0	0	0	0	0	0	0	0	0	0	0	0	0	0	0	0	0	0	0	83	0	83
1938	0	0	0	0	68	0	0	0	0	0	0	0	0	0	0	0	0	0	0	0	0	0	0	0	0	0	0	0	0	0	0	0	68	0	68
1939	0	0	0	0	35	0	0	0	0	0	0	0	0	0	0	0	0	0	0	0	0	0	0	0	0	0	0	0	0	0	0	0	35	0	35
1940	0	0	0	0	83	0	0	0	0	0	0	0	0	0	0	0	0	0	0	0	0	0	0	0	0	0	0	0	0	0	0	0	83	0	83
1941	0	0	0	0	12	0	0	0	0	0	0	0	0	0	0	0	0	0	0	0	0	0	0	0	0	0	0	0	0	0	0	0	12	0	12
1942	0	0	0	0	77	0	0	0	0	0	0	0	0	0	0	0	0	0	0	0	0	0	0	0	0	0	0	0	0	0	0	0	77	0	77
1943	0	0	0	0	130	0	0	0	0	0	0	0	0	0	0	0	0	0	0	0	0	0	0	0	0	0	0	0	0	0	0	0	130	0	130
1944	0	0	0	0	62	0	0	0	0	0	0	0	0	0	85	0	0	0	0	0	0	0	0	0	0	0	0	0	0	0	0	0	147	0	147
1945	0	0	0	0	80	0	0	0	0	0	0	0	0	0	11	0	0	0	0	0	0	0	0	0	0	0	0	0	0	0	0	0	91	0	91
1946	0	0	0	0	90	0	0	0	0	0	0	0	0	0	1	0	0	0	0	0	0	0	0	0	0	0	0	0	0	0	0	0	91	0	91
1947	0	0	0	0	58	0	0	0	0	0	0	0	0	0	84	0	0	0	0	0	0	0	0	0	0	0	0	0	0	0	0	0	142	0	142
1948	0	0	0	0	79	0	0	0	8	0	0	0	3	0	111	0	16	0	1	0	0	0	0	0	2	0	0	0	0	0	0	0	220	0	220
1949	0	0	0	0	63	0	0	0	0	0	0	0	2	0	94	0	14	0	0	0	0	0	0	0	0	0	0	0	0	0	0	0	173	0	173
1950	0	0	0	0	41	0	0	0	0	0	0	0	2	0	39	0	9	0	0	0	0	0	0	0	0	0	0	0	0	0	0	0	91	0	91
1951	0	0	0	0	31	0	11	0	0	0	0	0	0	0	53	0	2	0	0	0	0	0	0	0	0	0	0	0	0	0	0	0	97	0	97
1952	0	0	0	0	39	0	0	0	0	0	0	0	0	0	39	0	38	0	0	0	0	0	0	0	0	0	0	0	0	0	0	0	116	0	116
1953	0	0	0	0	39	0	0	0	10	0	0	0	4	0	98	0	16	0	0	0	0	0	0	0	0	0	0	0	0	0	0	0	167	0	167
1954	0	0	0	0	104	0	0	0	15	0	0	0	11	0	60	0	5	0	0	0	0	0	0	0	6	0	0	0	0	0	0	0	201	0	201
1955	0	0	0	0	35	0	0	0	0	0	0	0	27	0	27	0	2	0	0	0	0	0	0	0	32	0	0	0	0	0	0	0	123	0	123
1956	0	0	0	0	89	0	0	0	9	0	0	0	29	0	60	0	0	0	20	0	0	0	0	0	4	0	0	0	0	0	0	0	211	0	211
1957	0	0	0	0	34	0	0	0	2	0	0	0	32	0	27	0	0	0	10	0	0	0	0	0	13	0	0	0	0	0	0	0	118	0	118
1958	0	0	0	0	99	0	0	0	17	0	0	0	105	0	84	0	0	0	13	0	0	0	0	0	16	0	0	0	0	0	2	0	336	0	336
1959	0	0	0	0	133	0	0	0	87	0	0	0	50	1	167	0	2	0	12	0	0	0	0	0	28	0	0	0	0	0	0	0	479	1	480
1960	0	0	0	0	48	0	0	0	14	0	0	0	44	0	21	0	0	0	24	0	0	0	0	0	10	0	0	0	0	0	0	0	161	0	161
1961	0	0	0	0	104	0	0	0	18	0	0	0	132	1	110	0	0	0	45	0	0	0	0	0	13	0	0	0	0	0	2	0	424	1	425
1962	0	0	0	0	54	0	0	0	7	0	0	0	76	0	62	0	0	0	14	0	0	0	0	0	14	0	0	0	0	0	0	0	227	0	227
1963	0	0	0	0	62	0	0	0	2	0	0	0	68	0	47	0	1	0	22	0	0	0	0	0	10	0	0	0	0	0	0	0	212	0	212
1964	0	0	0	0	14	0	0	0	40	0	0	0	78	0	32	0	0	0	2	0	0	0	0	0	20	0	0	0	0	0	0	0	186	0	186
1965	0	0	0	0	22	0	0	0	12	0	2	0	58	0	38	0	0	0	10	0	0	0	0	0	20	0	0	0	0	0	0	0	162	0	162
1966	0	0	0	0	32	0	0	0	14	0	0	0	93	0	76	0	0	0	15	0	0	0	0	0	40	0	0	0	0	0	0	0	270	0	270
1967	0	0	0	0	42	0	0	0	8	0	0	0	75	0	56	0	0	0	10	0	0	0	0	0	30	0	0	0	0	0	0	0	221	0	221
1968	0	0	0	0	3	0	0	0	10	0	0	0	32	0	109	0	13	0	0	0	0	0	0	0	10	0	0	0	0	0	0	0	177	0	177
1969	0	0	0	0	30	0	0	0	10	0	0	0	45	0	22	1	7	0	2	0	0	0	0	0	5	0	0	0	0	0	0	0	121	1	122
1970	0	0	0	0	49	0	0	0	1	0	0	0	45	0	75	0	1	0	1	0	0	0	0	0	6	0	0	0	0	0	0	0	178	0	178
1971	0	0	0	0	19	0	0	0	6	0	0	0	45	0	33	0	3	0	1	0	0	0	0	0	30	0	0	0	0	0	0	0	137	0	137
1972	0	0	0	0	61	0	0	0	4	0	0	0	65	0	139	0	4	0	1	0	0	0	0	0	20	0	0	0	0	0	0	0	294	0	294
1973	0	0	0	0	41	0	0	0	6	0	0	0	35	0	75	0	15	0	2	0	0	0	0	0	20	0	0	0	75	0	3	0	272	0	272
1974	0	0	0	0	49	0	0	0	2	0	4	0	36	0	66	1	26	0	30	0	0	0	0	0	20	0	0	0	4	0	18	0	255	1	256
1975	0	0	0	0	40	0	0	0	30	0	2	0	51	0	111	2	73	0	8	0	0	0	0	0	11	0	0	0	12	0	18	0	356	2	358
1976	0	0	0	0	20	0	0	0	20	0	0	0	25	0	32	3	55	0	1	0	0	0	0	0	10	0	0	0	30	0	5	0	198	3	201
1977	0	0	0	0	26	0	0	0	30	0	0	0	25	0	124	11	186	2	3	0	0	0	2	0	24	0	0	0	50	0	2	0	472	13	485
1978	0	0	0	0	75	0	0	0	59	1	0	0	105	0	133	2	322	38	16	0	0	0	0	0	35	0	0	0	10	0	25	0	780	41	821
1979	0	0	0	0	38	0	0	0	25	0	6	0	66	1	58	0	134	6	8	0	0	0	0	0	8	0	0	0	10	0	13	0	366	7	373
1980	0	0	0	0	190	20	6	0	62	0	4	0	78	1	115	6	810	33	5	0	0	0	0	0	30	0	0	0	20	0	16	0	1,336	60	1,396
1981	0	0	0	0	126	3	0	0	85	0	14	0	53	0	73	6	720	6	23	0	0	0	2	0	15	0	0	0	32	0	0	0	1,143	15	1,158
1982	0	0	0	0	38	3	0	0	37	0	24	0	56	4	79	6	936	3	20	0	0	0	2	0	15	1	1	0	10	0	0	0	1,218	17	1,235
1983	1	2	3	0	28	0	4	0	8	0	18	0	17	1	90	5	162	2	0	0	2	0	1	0	12	3	0	0	6	0	0	0	352	13	365

Year	Androscoggin		Aroostook		Dennys		Ducktrap		E. Machias		Kennebec		Machias		Narraguagus		Penobscot		Pleasant		Prestile Str.		Saco		Sheepscot		St. Croix		Union		Misc.		Grand Totals		
	K	R	K	R	K	R	K	R	K	R	K	R	K	R	K	R	K	R	K	R	K	R	K	R	K	R	K	R	K	R	K	R	K	R	Total
1984	1	0	2	0	68	1	2	0	47	0	1	0	33	8	68	3	360	27	1	0	2	0	2	0	22	0	0	0	0	0	1	0	610	39	649
1985	0	0	0	0	20	0	15	0	30	1	0	0	32	0	57	4	336	356	0	0	0	0	60	19	6	0	8	12	1	0	0	0	565	392	957
1986	1	2	2	0	15	0	15	10	13	2	0	0	46	6	45	1	404	448	[a]	0	0	0	3	1	11	0	5	50	5	8	0	0	565	528	1,093
1987	0	0	2	0	1	1	0	0	14	10	4	0	4	4	37	3	170	111	[a]	0	0	0	13	0	15	3	5	9	5	1	4	0	274	142	416
1988	0	0	2	0	9	0	0	0	14	0	2	0	8	1	35	11	175	125	[a]	0	0	0	3	0	1	0	6	3	2	1	0	0	257	141	398
1989	0	0	0	0	12	1	0	0	31	1	2	0	16	2	39	5	368	500	[a]	0	0	0	3	3	5	0	7	8	4	0	0	0	487	520	1,007
1990	0	0	0	0	33	3	3	0	48	35	46	60	2	0	51	10	431	675	[a]	0	0	0	16	3	9	0	2	4	0	0	1	0	642	790	1,432
1991	0	0	0	0	7	2	0	0	5	0	4	0	2	0	22	6	192	230	[b]	0	0	0	0	0	4	0	2	1	0	0	0	0	238	239	477
1992	1	0	9	0	5	7	0	0	6	3	0	0	3	7	17	45	153	344	[b]	0	0	0	0	0	7	0	1	1	0	0	1	0	203	407	610
1993	0	0	0	0	3	1	0	0	0	3	2	10	0	12	7	20	124	450	[b]	0	0	0	6	6	9	5	1	0	0	0	0	0	152	507	659
1994	0	0	3	0	3	30	0	0	0	12	0	1	0	5	0	20	7	170	[b]	2	0	0	0	1	0	0	0	3	0	0	0	0	13	244	257
1995	[b]	0	[b]	0	[b]	20	[b]	0	[b]	22	[b]	0	[b]	5	[b]	23	[b]	275	[b]	0	[b]	0	[b]	0	[b]	0	[b]	0	[b]	0	[b]	0	[b]	345	345
Total	4	4	23	0	3,000	92	56	10	866	90	135	71	1,814	59	3,194	194	6,292	3,801	320	2	4	0	113	33	618	12	38	91	276	10	111	0	16,864	4,469	21,333

[a] Closed
[b] No kill

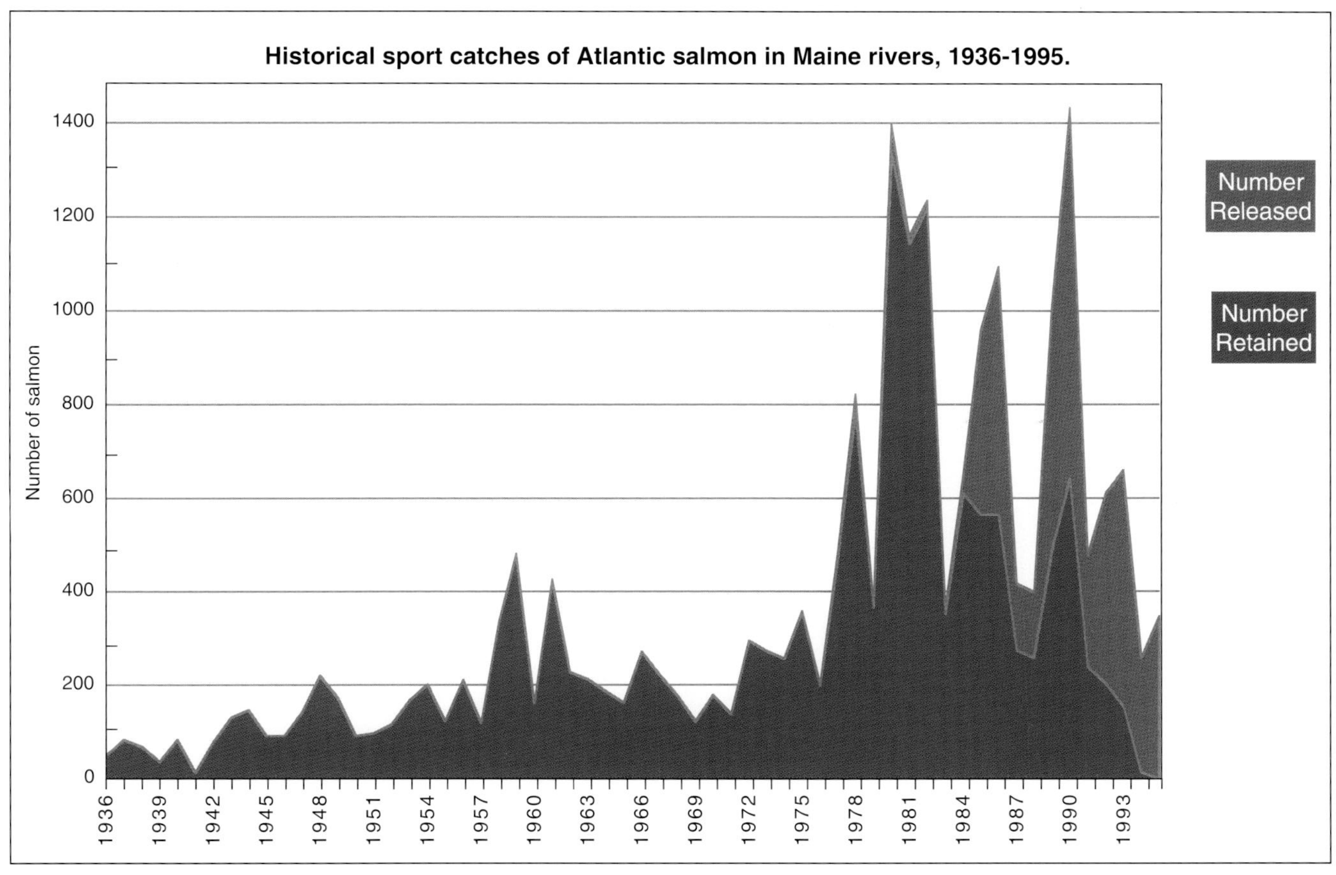
Historical sport catches of Atlantic salmon in Maine rivers, 1936-1995.
Number of salmon
1400
1200
1000
800
600
400
200
0
1936
1939
1942
1945
1948
1951
1954
1957
1960
1963
1966
1969
1972
1975
1978
1981
1984
1987
1990
1993
Number Released
Number Retained

	Androscoggin River				Aroostook River				Ducktrap River		
Year	**Number Killed**	**Number Released**	**Total**	**Year**	**Number Killed**	**Number Released**	**Total**	**Year**	**Number Killed**	**Number Released**	**Total**
1948	0	0	0	1948	0	0	0	1948	0	0	0
1949	0	0	0	1949	0	0	0	1949	0	0	0
1950	0	0	0	1950	0	0	0	1950	0	0	0
1951	0	0	0	1951	0	0	0	1951	11	0	11
1952	0	0	0	1952	0	0	0	1952	0	0	0
1953	0	0	0	1953	0	0	0	1953	0	0	0
1954	0	0	0	1954	0	0	0	1954	0	0	0
1955	0	0	0	1955	0	0	0	1955	0	0	0
1956	0	0	0	1956	0	0	0	1956	0	0	0
1957	0	0	0	1957	0	0	0	1957	0	0	0
1958	0	0	0	1958	0	0	0	1958	0	0	0
1959	0	0	0	1959	0	0	0	1959	0	0	0
1960	0	0	0	1960	0	0	0	1960	0	0	0
1961	0	0	0	1961	0	0	0	1961	0	0	0
1962	0	0	0	1962	0	0	0	1962	0	0	0
1963	0	0	0	1963	0	0	0	1963	0	0	0
1964	0	0	0	1964	0	0	0	1964	0	0	0
1965	0	0	0	1965	0	0	0	1965	0	0	0
1966	0	0	0	1966	0	0	0	1966	0	0	0
1967	0	0	0	1967	0	0	0	1967	0	0	0
1968	0	0	0	1968	0	0	0	1968	0	0	0
1969	0	0	0	1969	0	0	0	1969	0	0	0
1970	0	0	0	1970	0	0	0	1970	0	0	0
1971	0	0	0	1971	0	0	0	1971	0	0	0
1972	0	0	0	1972	0	0	0	1972	0	0	0
1973	0	0	0	1973	0	0	0	1973	0	0	0
1974	0	0	0	1974	0	0	0	1974	0	0	0
1975	0	0	0	1975	0	0	0	1975	0	0	0
1976	0	0	0	1976	0	0	0	1976	0	0	0
1977	0	0	0	1977	0	0	0	1977	0	0	0
1978	0	0	0	1978	0	0	0	1978	0	0	0
1979	0	0	0	1979	0	0	0	1979	0	0	0
1980	0	0	0	1980	0	0	0	1980	6	0	6
1981	0	0	0	1981	0	0	0	1981	0	0	0
1982	0	0	0	1982	0	0	0	1982	0	0	0
1983	1	2	3	1983	3	0	3	1983	4	0	4
1984	1	0	1	1984	2	0	2	1984	2	0	2
1985	0	0	0	1985	0	0	0	1985	15	0	15
1986	1	2	3	1986	2	0	2	1986	15	10	25
1987	0	0	0	1987	2	0	2	1987	0	0	0
1988	0	0	0	1988	2	0	2	1988	0	0	0
1989	0	0	0	1989	0	0	0	1989	0	0	0
1990	0	0	0	1990	0	0	0	1990	3	0	3
1991	0	0	0	1991	0	0	0	1991	0	0	0
1992	1	0	1	1992	9	0	9	1992	0	0	0
1993	0	0	0	1993	0	0	0	1993	0	0	0
1994	0	0	0	1994	3	0	3	1994	0	0	0
1995	0	0	0	1995	0	0	0	1995	0	0	0
Total	4	4	8	Total	23	0	23	Total	56	10	66

Year	East Machias River Number Killed	Number Released	Total
1948	8	0	8
1949	0	0	0
1950	0	0	0
1951	0	0	0
1952	0	0	0
1953	10	0	10
1954	15	0	15
1955	0	0	0
1956	9	0	9
1957	2	0	2
1958	17	0	17
1959	87	0	87
1960	14	0	14
1961	18	0	18
1962	7	0	7
1963	2	0	2
1964	40	0	40
1965	12	0	12
1966	14	0	14
1967	8	0	8
1968	10	0	10
1969	10	0	10
1970	1	0	1
1971	6	0	6
1972	4	0	4
1973	6	0	6
1974	2	0	2
1975	30	0	30
1976	20	0	20
1977	30	0	30
1978	59	1	60
1979	25	0	25
1980	62	0	62
1981	85	0	85
1982	37	0	37
1983	8	0	8
1984	47	0	47
1985	30	1	31
1986	13	2	15
1987	14	10	24
1988	14	0	14
1989	31	1	32
1990	48	35	83
1991	5	0	5
1992	6	3	9
1993	0	3	3
1994	0	12	12
1995	0	22	22
Total	866	90	956

Year	Machias River Number Killed	Number Released	Total
1948	3	0	3
1949	2	0	2
1950	2	0	2
1951	0	0	0
1952	0	0	0
1953	4	0	4
1954	11	0	11
1955	27	0	27
1956	29	0	29
1957	32	0	32
1958	105	0	105
1959	50	1	51
1960	44	0	44
1961	132	1	133
1962	76	0	76
1963	68	0	68
1964	78	0	78
1965	58	0	58
1966	93	0	93
1967	75	0	75
1968	32	0	32
1969	45	0	45
1970	45	0	45
1971	45	0	45
1972	65	0	65
1973	35	0	35
1974	36	0	36
1975	51	0	51
1976	25	0	25
1977	25	0	25
1978	105	0	105
1979	66	1	67
1980	78	1	79
1981	53	0	53
1982	56	4	60
1983	17	1	18
1984	33	8	41
1985	32	0	32
1986	46	6	52
1987	4	4	8
1988	8	1	9
1989	16	2	18
1990	2	0	2
1991	2	0	2
1992	3	7	10
1993	0	12	12
1994	0	5	5
1995	0	5	5
Total	1,814	59	1,873

Year	Kennebec River Number Killed	Number Released	Total
1948	0	0	0
1949	0	0	0
1950	0	0	0
1951	0	0	0
1952	0	0	0
1953	0	0	0
1954	0	0	0
1955	0	0	0
1956	0	0	0
1957	0	0	0
1958	0	0	0
1959	0	0	0
1960	0	0	0
1961	0	0	0
1962	0	0	0
1963	0	0	0
1964	0	0	0
1965	2	0	2
1966	0	0	0
1967	0	0	0
1968	0	0	0
1969	0	0	0
1970	0	0	0
1971	0	0	0
1972	0	0	0
1973	0	0	0
1974	4	0	4
1975	2	0	2
1976	0	0	0
1977	0	0	0
1978	0	0	0
1979	6	0	6
1980	4	0	4
1981	14	0	14
1982	24	0	24
1983	18	0	18
1984	1	0	1
1985	0	0	0
1986	0	0	0
1987	4	0	4
1988	2	0	2
1989	2	0	2
1990	46	60	106
1991	4	0	4
1992	0	0	0
1993	2	10	12
1994	0	1	1
1995	0	0	0
Total	135	71	206

	Dennys River		
Year	Number Killed	Number Released	Total
1936	49	0	49
1937	83	0	83
1938	68	0	68
1939	35	0	35
1940	83	0	83
1941	12	0	12
1942	77	0	77
1943	130	0	130
1944	62	0	62
1945	80	0	80
1946	90	0	90
1947	58	0	58
1948	79	0	79
1949	63	0	63
1950	41	0	41
1951	31	0	31
1952	39	0	39
1953	39	0	39
1954	104	0	104
1955	35	0	35
1956	89	0	89
1957	34	0	34
1958	99	0	99
1959	133	0	133
1960	48	0	48
1961	104	0	104
1962	54	0	54
1963	62	0	62
1964	14	0	14
1965	22	0	22
1966	32	0	32
1967	42	0	42
1968	3	0	3
1969	30	0	30
1970	49	0	49
1971	19	0	19
1972	61	0	61
1973	41	0	41
1974	49	0	49
1975	40	0	40
1976	20	0	20
1977	26	0	26
1978	75	0	75
1979	38	0	38
1980	190	20	210
1981	126	3	129
1982	38	3	41
1983	28	0	28
1984	68	1	69
1985	20	0	20
1986	15	0	15
1987	1	1	2
1988	9	0	9
1989	12	1	13
1990	33	3	36
1991	7	2	9
1992	5	7	12
1993	3	1	4
1994	3	30	33
1995	0	20	20
Total	3,000	92	3,092

	Pleasant River			
Year	Number Killed	Number Released	Total	Number of Kelts
1936				
1937				
1938				
1939				
1940				
1941				
1942				
1943				
1944				
1945				
1946				
1947				
1948	1	0	1	1
1949	0	0	0	0
1950	0	0	0	0
1951	0	0	0	0
1952	0	0	0	0
1953	0	0	0	0
1954	0	0	0	0
1955	0	0	0	4
1956	20	0	20	84
1957	10	0	10	77
1958	13	0	13	78
1959	12	0	12	67
1960	24	0	24	79
1961	45	0	45	99
1962	14	0	14	108
1963	22	0	22	49
1964	2	0	2	20
1965	10	0	10	16
1966	15	0	15	35
1967	10	0	10	0
1968	0	0	0	0
1969	2	0	2	3
1970	1	0	1	0
1971	1	0	1	0
1972	1	0	1	0
1973	2	0	2	0
1974	30	0	30	0
1975	8	0	8	0
1976	1	0	1	0
1977	3	0	3	0
1978	16	0	16	0
1979	8	0	8	0
1980	5	0	5	0
1981	23	0	23	0
1982	20	0	20	0
1983	0	0	0	0
1984	1	0	1	0
1985	0	0	0	0
1986	closed	0	0	0
1987	closed	0	0	0
1988	closed	0	0	0
1989	closed	0	0	0
1990	closed	0	0	0
1991	no kill	0	0	0
1992	no kill	0	0	0
1993	no kill	0	0	0
1994	no kill	2	2	0
1995	no kill	0	0	0
Total	320	2	322	720

	Narraguagus River			
Year	Number Killed	Number Released	Total	Number of Kelts
1936				
1937				
1938				
1939				
1940				
1941				
1942				
1943				
1944	85	0	85	0
1945	11	0	11	0
1946	1	0	1	0
1947	84	0	84	0
1948	111	0	111	0
1949	94	0	94	0
1950	39	0	39	0
1951	53	0	53	0
1952	39	0	39	0
1953	98	0	98	0
1954	60	0	60	0
1955	27	0	27	0
1956	60	0	60	0
1957	27	0	27	0
1958	84	0	84	0
1959	167	0	167	0
1960	21	0	21	28
1961	110	0	110	60
1962	62	0	62	90
1963	47	0	47	78
1964	32	0	32	30
1965	38	0	38	28
1966	76	0	76	30
1967	56	0	56	11
1968	109	0	109	81
1969	22	1	23	21
1970	75	0	75	26
1971	33	0	33	20
1972	139	0	139	12
1973	75	0	75	15
1974	66	1	67	12
1975	111	2	113	25
1976	32	3	35	25-50
1977	124	11	135	25-50
1978	133	2	135	25-50
1979	58	0	58	25-50
1980	115	6	121	25-50
1981	73	6	79	0
1982	79	6	85	0
1983	90	5	95	0
1984	68	3	71	0
1985	57	4	61	0
1986	45	1	46	0
1987	37	3	40	0
1988	35	11	46	0
1989	39	5	44	0
1990	51	10	61	0
1991	22	6	28	0
1992	17	45	62	0
1993	7	20	27	0
1994	0	20	20	0
1995	0	23	23	0
Total	3,194	194	3,388	742

Year	Penobscot River Number Killed	Number Released	Total
1885	40	0	40
1886	50	0	50
1887	60	0	60
1888	70	0	70
1889	35	0	35
1890	25	0	25
1891	20	0	20
1892	21	0	21
1893	87	0	87
1894	51	0	51
1895	61	0	61
1896	112	0	112
1897	125	0	125
1898	51	0	51
1899	53	0	53
1900	67	0	67
1901	112	0	112
1902	120	0	120
1903	39	0	39
1904	51	0	51
1905	115	0	115
1906	111	0	111
1907	117	0	117
1908	39	0	39
1909	37	0	37
1910	103	0	103
1911	64	0	64
1912	153	0	153
1923	90	0	90
1924	111	0	111
1925	72	0	72
1926	354	0	354
1927	112	0	112
1928	170	0	170
1929	119	0	119
1930	111	0	111
1931	248	0	248
1932	82	0	82
1933	36	0	36
1934	41	0	41
1935	57	0	52
1936	203	0	203
1937	110	0	110
1938	20	0	20
1939	8	0	8
1940	23	0	23
1941	5	0	5
1942	23	0	23
1943	5	0	5
1944	12	0	12
1945	42	0	42
Total	4,038	0	4,038

Year	Penobscot River Number Killed	Number Released	Total
1946	13	0	13
1947	48	0	48
1948	16	0	16
1949	15	0	14
1950	9	0	9
1951	2	0	2
1952	38	0	38
1953	16	0	16
1954	5	0	5
1955	2	0	2
1956	0	0	0
1957	0	0	0
1958	0	0	0
1959	4	0	2
1960	0	0	0
1961	0	0	0
1962	0	0	0
1963	1	0	1
1964	0	0	0
1965	0	0	0
1966	0	0	0
1967	0	0	0
1968	13	0	13
1969	7	0	7
1970	1	0	1
1971	3	0	3
1972	4	0	4
1973	15	0	15
1974	26	0	26
1975	73	0	73
1976	55	0	55
1977	186	2	188
1978	322	38	360
1979	134	6	140
1980	810	33	843
1981	720	6	726
1982	936	3	939
1983	162	2	164
1984	360	27	387
1985	336	356	692
1986	404	448	852
1987	170	111	281
1988	175	125	300
1989	368	500	868
1990	431	675	1,106
1991	192	230	422
1992	153	344	497
1993	124	450	574
1994	7	170	177
1995	0	275	275
Total	6,353	3,801	10,154
Grand Total	**10,391**	**3,801**	**14,192**

Year	Misc./Unknown Rivers Number Killed	Number Released	Total
1946			
1947			
1948	0	0	0
1949	0	0	0
1950	0	0	0
1951	0	0	0
1952	0	0	0
1953	0	0	0
1954	0	0	0
1955	0	0	0
1956	0	0	0
1957	0	0	0
1958	2	0	2
1959	0	0	0
1960	0	0	0
1961	2	0	2
1962	0	0	0
1963	0	0	0
1964	0	0	0
1965	0	0	0
1966	0	0	0
1967	0	0	0
1968	0	0	0
1969	0	0	0
1970	0	0	0
1971	0	0	0
1972	0	0	0
1973	3	0	3
1974	18	0	18
1975	18	0	18
1976	5	0	5
1977	2	0	2
1978	25	0	25
1979	13	0	13
1980	16	0	16
1981	0	0	0
1982	0	0	0
1983	0	0	0
1984	1	0	1
1985	0	0	0
1986	0	0	0
1987	4	0	4
1988	0	0	0
1989	0	0	0
1990	1	0	1
1991	0	0	0
1992	1	0	1
1993	0	0	0
1994	0	0	0
1995	1	0	1
Total	112	0	112

Year	Prestile Stream Number Killed	Prestile Stream Number Released	Prestile Stream Total	Year	Saco River Number Killed	Saco River Number Released	Saco River Total	Year	Sheepscot River Number Killed	Sheepscot River Number Released	Sheepscot River Total
1948	0	0	0	1948	0	0	0	1948	2	0	2
1949	0	0	0	1949	0	0	0	1949	0	0	0
1950	0	0	0	1950	0	0	0	1950	0	0	0
1951	0	0	0	1951	0	0	0	1951	0	0	0
1952	0	0	0	1952	0	0	0	1952	0	0	0
1953	0	0	0	1953	0	0	0	1953	0	0	0
1954	0	0	0	1954	0	0	0	1954	6	0	6
1955	0	0	0	1955	0	0	0	1955	32	0	32
1956	0	0	0	1956	0	0	0	1956	4	0	4
1957	0	0	0	1957	0	0	0	1957	13	0	13
1958	0	0	0	1958	0	0	0	1958	16	0	16
1959	0	0	0	1959	0	0	0	1959	28	0	28
1960	0	0	0	1960	0	0	0	1960	10	0	10
1961	0	0	0	1961	0	0	0	1961	13	0	13
1962	0	0	0	1962	0	0	0	1962	14	0	14
1963	0	0	0	1963	0	0	0	1963	10	0	10
1964	0	0	0	1964	0	0	0	1964	20	0	20
1965	0	0	0	1965	0	0	0	1965	20	0	20
1966	0	0	0	1966	0	0	0	1966	40	0	40
1967	0	0	0	1967	0	0	0	1967	30	0	30
1968	0	0	0	1968	0	0	0	1968	10	0	10
1969	0	0	0	1969	0	0	0	1969	5	0	5
1970	0	0	0	1970	0	0	0	1970	6	0	6
1971	0	0	0	1971	0	0	0	1971	30	0	30
1972	0	0	0	1972	0	0	0	1972	20	0	20
1973	0	0	0	1973	0	0	0	1973	20	0	20
1974	0	0	0	1974	0	0	0	1974	20	0	20
1975	0	0	0	1975	0	0	0	1975	11	0	11
1976	0	0	0	1976	0	0	0	1976	10	0	10
1977	0	0	0	1977	2	0	2	1977	24	0	24
1978	0	0	0	1978	0	0	0	1978	35	0	35
1979	0	0	0	1979	0	0	0	1979	8	0	8
1980	0	0	0	1980	0	0	0	1980	30	0	30
1981	0	0	0	1981	2	0	2	1981	15	0	15
1982	0	0	0	1982	2	0	2	1982	15	1	16
1983	2	0	2	1983	1	0	1	1983	12	3	15
1984	2	0	2	1984	2	0	2	1984	22	0	22
1985	0	0	0	1985	60	19	79	1985	6	0	6
1986	0	0	0	1986	3	1	4	1986	11	0	11
1987	0	0	0	1987	13	0	13	1987	15	3	18
1988	0	0	0	1988	3	0	3	1988	1	0	1
1989	0	0	0	1989	3	3	6	1989	5	0	5
1990	0	0	0	1990	16	3	19	1990	9	0	9
1991	0	0	0	1991	0	0	0	1991	4	0	4
1992	0	0	0	1992	0	0	0	1992	7	0	7
1993	0	0	0	1993	6	6	12	1993	9	5	14
1994	0	0	0	1994	0	1	1	1994	0	0	0
1995	0	0	0	1995	0	0	0	1995	0	0	0
Total	4	0	4	Total	113	33	146	Total	618	12	630

	Saint Croix River				Union River				All Maine Rivers*		
Year	Number Killed	Number Released	Total	Year	Number Killed	Number Released	Total	Year	Number Killed	Number Released	Total
1948	0	0	0	1948	0	0	0	1948	220	0	220
1949	0	0	0	1949	0	0	0	1949	173	0	173
1950	0	0	0	1950	0	0	0	1950	91	0	91
1951	0	0	0	1951	0	0	0	1951	86	0	86
1952	0	0	0	1952	0	0	0	1952	116	0	116
1953	0	0	0	1953	0	0	0	1953	167	0	167
1954	0	0	0	1954	0	0	0	1954	201	0	201
1955	0	0	0	1955	0	0	0	1955	123	0	123
1956	0	0	0	1956	0	0	0	1956	211	0	211
1957	0	0	0	1957	0	0	0	1957	118	0	118
1958	0	0	0	1958	0	0	0	1958	336	0	336
1959	0	0	0	1959	0	0	0	1959	479	0	479
1960	0	0	0	1960	0	0	0	1960	169	0	169
1961	0	0	0	1961	0	0	0	1961	424	1	425
1962	0	0	0	1962	0	0	0	1962	227	0	227
1963	0	0	0	1963	0	0	0	1963	212	0	212
1964	0	0	0	1964	0	0	0	1964	186	0	186
1965	0	0	0	1965	0	0	0	1965	160	0	160
1966	0	0	0	1966	0	0	0	1966	272	0	272
1967	0	0	0	1967	0	0	0	1967	221	0	221
1968	0	0	0	1968	0	0	0	1968	177	0	177
1969	0	0	0	1969	0	0	0	1969	121	1	122
1970	0	0	0	1970	0	0	0	1970	178	0	178
1971	0	0	0	1971	0	0	0	1971	137	0	137
1972	0	0	0	1972	0	0	0	1972	294	0	294
1973	0	0	0	1973	75	0	75	1973	272	0	272
1974	0	0	0	1974	4	0	4	1974	255	1	256
1975	0	0	0	1975	12	0	12	1975	356	2	358
1976	0	0	0	1976	30	0	30	1976	198	3	201
1977	0	0	0	1977	50	0	50	1977	472	13	485
1978	0	0	0	1978	10	0	10	1978	780	41	821
1979	0	0	0	1979	10	0	10	1979	366	7	373
1980	0	0	0	1980	20	0	20	1980	1,345	60	1,405
1981	0	0	0	1981	32	0	32	1981	1,143	15	1,158
1982	1	0	1	1982	10	0	10	1982	1,218	16	1,234
1983	0	0	0	1983	6	0	6	1983	350	13	363
1984	0	0	0	1984	0	0	0	1984	609	40	649
1985	8	12	20	1985	1	0	1	1985	565	392	957
1986	5	50	55	1986	5	8	13	1986	1,093	528	1,621
1987	5	9	14	1987	5	1	6	1987	274	142	416
1988	6	3	9	1988	2	1	3	1988	257	141	398
1989	7	8	15	1989	4	0	4	1989	487	520	1,007
1990	2	4	6	1990	0	0	0	1990	642	790	1,432
1991	2	1	3	1991	0	0	0	1991	238	239	477
1992	1	1	2	1992	0	0	0	1992	203	407	610
1993	1	0	1	1993	0	0	0	1993	152	507	659
1994	0	3	3	1994	0	0	0	1994	13	214	227
1995	0	0	0	1995	0	0	0	1995	0	342	342
Total	38	91	129	Total	276	10	286	Total	16,387	4,435	20,822

*Period of record for the AtlanticSea Run Salmon Commission.

Appendix 3

Distribution of tag returns from releases of Carlin-tagged, hatchery-reared smolts in Maine rivers, 1966–1992

		Tag returns from outside of Maine/US				Tag returns from Maine/US				
Year Stocked	Smolts Released	East & West Greenland	Faroe Islands	Canadian Provinces[1]	All Distant Waters[2]	1 Sea-winter Salmon	2 Sea-winter Salmon	3 Sea-winter Salmon	Total Home Waters	Grand Total
1966	82,250	40	0	79	119	26	140	7	173	292
1967	80,715	1	0	11	12	2	6	0	8	20
1968	73,770	6	0	7	13	7	11	1	19	32
1969	76,615	67	0	44	111	2	58	9	69	180
1970	48,210	403	0	63	466	5	270	4	279	745
1971	29,830	95	0	25	120	0	176	20	196	316
1972	52,520	140	0	33	173	3	183	5	191	364
1973	38,030	381	0	119	500	8	383	2	393	893
1974	41,750	129	0	106	235	10	156	0	166	401
1975	28,960	40	0	102	142	12	82	2	96	238
1976	24,980	12	0	19	31	2	81	0	83	114
1977	48,900	9	0	8	17	3	30	1	34	51
1978	0	0	0	0	0	0	0	0	0	0
1979	59,745	81	0	343	424	85	390	1	476	900
1980	49,760	49	0	51	100	24	257	1	282	382
1981	49,950	55	0	93	148	49	113	0	162	310
1982	49,360	9	0	26	35	5	52	1	58	93
1983	49,615	30	0	45	75	7	156	1	164	239
1984	99,340	91	0	102	193	23	262	6	291	484
1985	99,400	81	0	24	105	28	101	0	129	234
1986	100,000	182	0	56	238	47	272	3	322	560
1987	100,000	128	1	24	153	41	163	2	206	359
1988	99,895	111	0	57	168	33	145	0	178	346
1989	52,115	16	0	9	25	2	24	0	26	51
1990	49,870	20	0	16	36	3	24	0	27	63
1991	49,755	6	0	4	10	25	31	0	56	66
1992	50,000	2	0	1	3	2	7	0	9	12
Total	1,585,335	2,184	1	1,467	3,652	454	3,573	66	4,093	7,745
% of Total Returns		28.2	0.0	18.9	47.2	5.9	46.1	0.9	52.8	100

1. Newfoundland-Labrador, Quebec, Nova Scotia, New Brunswick.
2. Does not include post-smolt recoveries.

APPENDIX 4

Number and source of Atlantic salmon eggs utilized in Maine salmon restoration and enhancement programs, 1872–1995

Year	Egg Source	Penobscot	Dennys	E. Machias	Machias	Narraguagus	Orland	Union	Kennebec	Sheepscot	St. Croix	Total Maine	Miramichi New Brunswick	St. John New Brunswick	Saguenay Quebec	Total Canada
1871	SeaRun	72,300										72,300				0
1872	SeaRun	1,566,045										1,566,045				0
1873	SeaRun	2,321,935										2,321,935				0
1874	SeaRun	3,056,500										3,056,500				0
1875	SeaRun	2,020,000										2,020,000				0
1876		0										0				0
1877		0										0				0
1878		0										0				0
1879	SeaRun	211,690										211,690				0
1880	SeaRun	1,930,560										1,930,560				0
1881	SeaRun	2,693,010										2,693,010				0
1882	SeaRun	2,090,000										2,090,000				0
1883	SeaRun	2,535,000										2,535,000				0
1884	SeaRun	1,935,185										1,935,185				0
1885	SeaRun	2,422,600										2,422,600				0
1886	SeaRun	1,158,775										1,158,775				0
1887	SeaRun	1,184,000										1,184,000				0
1888	SeaRun	2,253,205										2,253,205				0
1889	SeaRun	1,904,000										1,904,000				0
1890	SeaRun	553,400										553,400				0
1891	SeaRun	1,203,285										1,203,285				0
1892	SeaRun	1,108,500										1,108,500				0
1893	SeaRun	806,000										806,000				0
1894	SeaRun	415,350										415,350				0
1895	SeaRun	1,027,355										1,027,355				0
1896	SeaRun	3,192,125										3,192,125				0
1897	SeaRun	3,506,640										3,506,640				0
1898	SeaRun	2,147,675										2,147,675				0
1899	SeaRun	1,881,610										1,881,610				0
1900	SeaRun	665,000										665,000				0
1901	SeaRun	832,300										832,300				0
1902	SeaRun	2,506,575										2,506,575				0
1903	SeaRun	3,484,000										3,484,000				0
1904	SeaRun	954,500										954,500				0
1905	SeaRun	2,310,430										2,310,430				0
1906	SeaRun	2,804,400										2,804,400				0
1907	SeaRun	2,714,500										2,714,500				0
1908	SeaRun	1,114,300										1,114,300				0
1909	SeaRun	1,456,800										1,456,800				0
1910	SeaRun	3,800,200										3,800,200				0
1911	SeaRun	2,149,455										2,149,455				0
1912	SeaRun	3,966,430										3,966,430				0

Year	Egg Source	Penobscot	Dennys	E. Machias	Machias	Narraguagus	Orland	Union	Kennebec	Sheepscot	St. Croix	Total Maine	Miramichi New Brunswick	St. John New Brunswick	Saguenay Quebec	Total Canada
1913	SeaRun	3,149,655										3,149,655				0
1914	SeaRun	2,014,400										2,014,400				0
1915	SeaRun	1,953,400										1,953,400				0
1916	SeaRun	3,739,180										3,739,180				0
1917	SeaRun	3,024,930										3,024,930				0
1918	SeaRun	2,613,400										2,613,400				0
1919	SeaRun	797,610										797,610				0
1920	SeaRun	911,720										911,720	1,000,000			1,000,000
1921	SeaRun	572,040										572,040	600,000			600,000
1922	SeaRun	0										0	1,000,000			1,000,000
1923	SeaRun	0										0	500,000			500,000
1924	SeaRun	0										0	550,600			550,600
1925	SeaRun	0										0	1,000,000		500,000	1,500,000
1926	SeaRun	0										0	553,000		546,000	1,099,000
1927	SeaRun	0										0	1,023,200		500,000	1,523,200
1928	SeaRun	0										0	1,026,100		500,000	1,526,100
1929	SeaRun	0										0	1,000,000			1,000,000
1930	SeaRun	4,500										4,500				0
1931	SeaRun	0										0	4,000,000			4,000,000
1932	SeaRun	0										0	1,000,000			1,000,000
1933	SeaRun	0										0	1,000,000			1,000,000
1934	SeaRun	0										0				0
1935	SeaRun	0										0	1,000,000			1,000,000
1936	SeaRun	0										0	1,500,000			1,500,000
1937	SeaRun	0										0	100,000			100,000
1938	SeaRun	0										0				0
1939	SeaRun	0	113,000									113,000				0
1940	SeaRun	250,450										250,450	51,150			51,150
1941	SeaRun				268,480							268,480	50,750			50,750
1942	SeaRun	708,945										708,945				0
1943	SeaRun	157,240										270,240				0
1944	SeaRun	150,000										150,000	50,000			50,000
1945	SeaRun	307,400										307,400				0
1946	SeaRun				266,525							266,525				0
1947	SeaRun	324,475										324,475				0
1948	SeaRun	0			140,215							140,215				0
1949	SeaRun	0			558,815							558,815	305,000			305,000
1950	SeaRun	0			203,400							203,400				0
1951	SeaRun	0										0	200,000			200,000
1952	SeaRun	0										0	415,000			415,000
1953	SeaRun	0										0	300,000			300,000
1954	SeaRun	0										0	302,980			302,980
1955	SeaRun	0										0	503,840			503,840
1956	SeaRun	0										0	496,550			496,550
1957	SeaRun	0			137,535							137,535	509,080			509,080
1958	SeaRun	0			138,670							138,670	464,510			464,510
1959	SeaRun	0			133,155							133,155	700,940			700,940

Year	Egg Source	Penobscot	Dennys	E. Machias	Machias	Narraguagus	Orland	Union	Kennebec	Sheepscot	St. Croix	Total Maine	Miramichi New Brunswick	St. John New Brunswick	Saguenay Quebec	Total Canada
1960	SeaRun	0			81,910							81,910	455,420			455,420
1961	SeaRun	0			71,785							71,785	511,220			511,220
1962	SeaRun	0				72,375						72,375	226,350		296,820	523,170
1963	SeaRun	0			150,575	131,095						281,670	504,000			504,000
1964	SeaRun	0			139,810	162,020						301,830	315,030			315,030
1965	SeaRun	0			127,120	139,685						266,805		303,800		303,800
1966	SeaRun	0			287,950	142,440						430,390		259,000		259,000
1967	SeaRun	0				146,940	41,110					188,050		506,490		506,490
1968	SeaRun	0			76,580	182,205	207,940					466,725				0
1969	SeaRun	155,265			190,705	160,735	20,595					527,300				0
1970	SeaRun	269,480			70,750	46,485						386,715				0
1971	SeaRun	224,130			169,000	119,200						512,330				0
1972	SeaRun	682,745										682,745				0
1973	SeaRun	831,090										831,090				0
1974	SeaRun	1,447,785						54,000				1,501,785				0
1975	SeaRun	972,965						179,250				1,152,215				0
1976	SeaRun	1,313,995						441,830				1,755,825				0
1977	SeaRun	710,880						490,030				1,200,910				0
1978	SeaRun	1,407,930						431,770				1,839,700				0
1979	SeaRun	1,117,360						88,670	50,000			1,256,030				0
1980	SeaRun	1,506,050						90,840				1,596,890				0
1981	SeaRun	1,028,000						846,790				1,874,790				0
1982	SeaRun	1,549,600						435,410				1,985,010				0
1983	SeaRun	1,557,490						450,550				2,008,040				0
1984	SeaRun	2,351,800						192,950				2,544,750				0
1985	SeaRun	1,838,900						285,740				2,124,640				0
1986	SeaRun	2,376,100						211,010				2,587,110			98,500	98,500
1987	SeaRun	2,150,165						161,110				2,311,275			100,000	100,000
1988	SeaRun	1,610,700						80,710				1,691,410				0
1989	SeaRun	2,427,200						67,175				2,494,375				0
1990	SeaRun	2,041,700						103,040				2,144,740				0
1991	SeaRun	2,427,000										2,427,000				0
1992	SeaRun	2,448,000	38,000		15,850							2,501,850				0
1993	SeaRun	1,881,870	19,340		50,080						114,000	2,065,290				0
1993	Kelt		8,590									8,590				0
1993	Total	1,881,870	27,930		50,080						114,000	2,073,880				0
1993	All	1,881,870	27,930		50,080						114,000	2,073,880				0
1994	SeaRun	1,669,905	14,830								80,000	1,764,735				0
1994	Kelt		30,480		11,670							42,150				0
1994	Captive		110,240		195,505	145,710						451,455				0
1994	Total	1,669,905	155,550		207,175	145,710					80,000	2,258,340				0
1995	SeaRun	2,735,645								78,495	87,000	2,901,140				0
1995	Kelt		34,155		27,790							61,945				0
1995	Captive		303,870	143,735	484,210	394,435				44,385		1,370,635				0
1995	Total	2,735,645	338,025	143,735	512,000	394,435				122,880	87,000	4,333,720				0
Grand Total		135,368,730	672,505	143,735	3,998,085	1,843,325	269,645	4,610,875	50,000	122,880	281,000	147,473,780	24,284,010	198,500	2,342,820	26,825,330

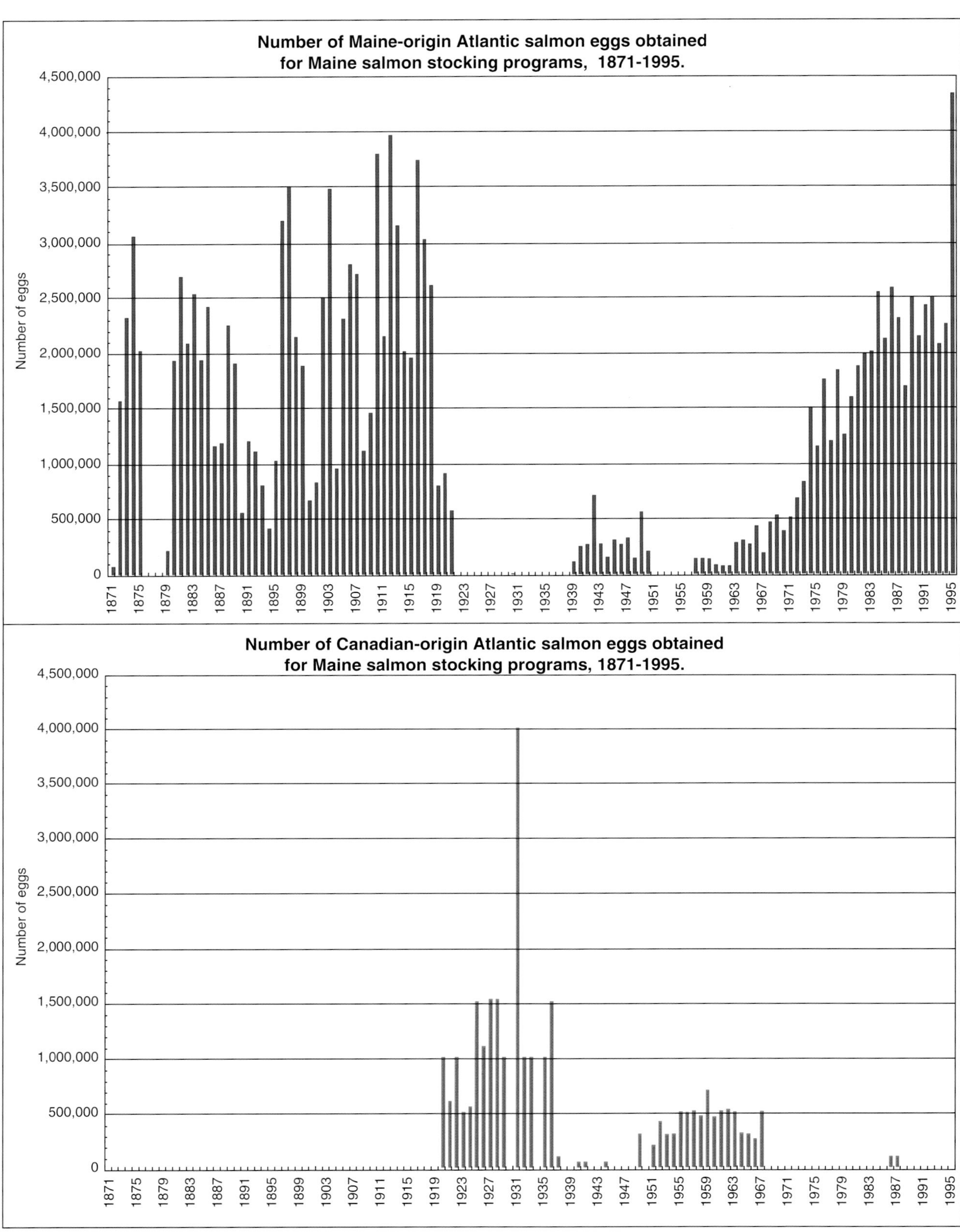
Number of Maine-origin Atlantic salmon eggs obtained
for Maine salmon stocking programs, 1871-1995.
Number of eggs
4,500,000
4,000,000
3,500,000
3,000,000
2,500,000
2,000,000
1,500,000
1,000,000
500,000
0
1871
1875
1879
1883
1887
1891
1895
1899
1903
1907
1911
1915
1919
1923
1927
1931
1935
1939
1943
1947
1951
1955
1959
1963
1967
1971
1975
1979
1983
1987
1991
1995
Number of Canadian-origin Atlantic salmon eggs obtained
for Maine salmon stocking programs, 1871-1995.
Number of eggs
4,500,000
4,000,000
3,500,000
3,000,000
2,500,000
2,000,000
1,500,000
1,000,000
500,000
0
1871
1875
1879
1883
1887
1891
1895
1899
1903
1907
1911
1915
1919
1923
1927
1931
1935
1939
1943
1947
1951
1955
1959
1963
1967
1971
1975
1979
1983
1987
1991
1995

Appendix 5

Members of the Atlantic Sea Run Salmon Commission, 1947–1995.
(Chairman Indicated in bold)

Year	Department of Inland Fish and Game	Department of Sea and Shore Fisheries	Public Members
1947	George J. Stobie	**Richard E. Reed**	Horace P. Bond
1948	George J. Stobie	**Richard E. Reed**	Horace P. Bond
1949	George J. Stobie	**Richard E. Reed**	Horace P. Bond
1950	George J. Stobie	**Richard E. Reed**	Horace P. Bond
1951	George J. Stobie	**Richard E. Reed**	**Horace P. Bond**
1952	Roland H. Cobb	Robert L. Dow	**Horace P. Bond**
1953	Roland H. Cobb	Stanley R. Tupper	**Horace P. Bond**
1954	Roland H. Cobb	Stanley R. Tupper	**Horace P. Bond**
1955	Roland H. Cobb	Stanley R. Tupper	**Horace P. Bond**
1956	Roland H. Cobb	Stanley R. Tupper	**Horace P. Bond**
1957	Roland H. Cobb	Ronald W. Green	**Horace P. Bond**
1958	Roland H. Cobb	Ronald W. Green	**Horace P. Bond**
1959	Roland H. Cobb	Ronald W. Green	**Horace P. Bond**
1960	Roland H. Cobb	Ronald W. Green	**Horace P. Bond**
1961	Roland H. Cobb	Ronald W. Green	**Horace P. Bond**
1962	Roland H. Cobb	Ronald W. Green	**Horace P. Bond**
1963	Ronald T. Speers	Ronald W. Green	**Horace P. Bond**
1964	Ronald T. Speers	Ronald W. Green	**Horace P. Bond**
1965	Ronald T. Speers	Ronald W. Green	**Horace P. Bond**
1966	Ronald T. Speers	Ronald W. Green	**Horace P. Bond**
1967	Ronald T. Speers	Ronald W. Green	**Horace P. Bond**
1968	Ronald T. Speers	**Ronald W. Green**	Hayward W. Higgins
1969	Ronald T. Speers	**Ronald W. Green**	Hayward W. Higgins
1970	Ronald T. Speers	**Ronald W. Green**	Hayward W. Higgins
	George W. Bucknam		
1971	George W. Bucknam	**Ronald W. Green**	Hayward W. Higgins
	Maynard F. Marsh		
1972	Maynard F. Marsh	**Ronald W. Green**	Hayward W. Higgins
1973	Maynard F. Marsh	**Ronald W. Green**	Hayward W. Higgins
1974	**Maynard F. Marsh**	Spencer Apollonio	Hayward W. Higgins
1975	**Maynard F. Marsh**	Spencer Apollonio	Paul C. Fernald
1976	**Maynard F. Marsh**	Spencer Apollonio	Paul C. Fernald

Year	Department of Inland Fisheries and Wildlife	Department of Marine Resources	Public Members
1977	**Maynard F. Marsh**	Vinal O. Look	Paul C. Fernald
1978	**Maynard F. Marsh**	Vinal O. Look	Paul C. Fernald
1979	**Maynard F. Marsh**	Spencer Apollonio	Harlow "Joe" Floyd
	Glenn H. Manuel		
1980	**Glenn H. Manuel**	Spencer Apollonio	Harlow "Joe" Floyd
1981	**Glenn H. Manuel**	Spencer Apollonio	Harlow "Joe" Floyd
1982	**Glenn H. Manuel**	Spencer Apollonio	Harlow "Joe" Floyd
1983	**Glenn H. Manuel**	Spencer Apollonio	Harlow "Joe" Floyd

Year	Department of Inland Fish and Game	Department of Sea and Shore Fisheries	Public Members
1984	**Glenn H. Manuel**	Spencer Apollonio	Harlow "Joe" Floyd
1985	**Glenn H. Manuel**	Spencer Apollonio	Harlow "Joe" Floyd
1986	**Glenn H. Manuel**	Spencer Apollonio	Harlow "Joe" Floyd
1987	**Glenn H. Manuel**	William J. Brennan	Harlow "Joe" Floyd

Year	Department of Inland Fisheries and Wildlife	Department of Marine Resources	1st Congressional District	2nd Congressional District	Member at Large
1987	**William J. Vail**	William J. Brennan	Paul C. Fernald	Peter Wass	Joseph Sewall
1988	**William J. Vail**	William J. Brennan	Paul C. Fernald	Peter Wass	Joseph Sewall
1989	**William J. Vail**	William J. Brennan	Paul C. Fernald	Peter Wass	Joseph Sewall
1990	**William J. Vail**	William J. Brennan	Paul C. Fernald	Peter Wass	Richard J. Warren
1991	**William J. Vail**	William J. Brennan	Paul C. Fernald	Peter Wass	Richard J. Warren
1992	**William J. Vail**	William J. Brennan	Paul C. Fernald	Peter Wass	Richard J. Warren
1993	**William J. Vail**	William J. Brennan	Paul C. Fernald	Peter Wass	Richard J. Warren
	Ray B. Owen	Louise P. Alden			
1994	**Ray B. Owen**	Louise P. Alden	Paul C. Fernald	Peter Wass	Richard J. Warren
1995	**Ray B. Owen**	Louise P. Alden	Paul C. Fernald	Peter Wass	Richard J. Warren
					William H. Nichols Jr.

The initial meeting of the Atlantic Sea Run Salmon Commission was held in Bangor on December 1, 1947.
The final meeting of the Atlantic Sea Run Salmon Commission was held in Whitneyville on August 2, 1995.

Appendix 6.
Historical stocking of juvenile and adult Atlantic salmon in Maine rivers, 1871-1995.

Stocking records for all rivers in the State of Maine are presented in the following order:

6.1	Total: all Maine rivers	6.15	Orland River
6.2	Androscoggin River	6.16	Penobscot River
6.3	Aroostook River	6.17	Pennamaquan (Pembroke) River
6.4	Boyden Stream	6.18	Pleasant River
6.5	Dennys River	6.19	Presumpscot River
6.6	Ducktrap River	6.20	Saco River
6.7	East Machias River	6.21	Sheepscot River
6.8	Kennebec River	6.22	Somesville Stream
6.9	Kennebunk River	6.23	Saint Croix River
6.10	Little Falls (Hobart) Stream	6.24	Saint George River
6.11	Machias River	6.25	Tunk Stream
6.12	Medomak River	6.26	Union River
6.13	Meduxnekeag River	6.27	Upper Saint John River
6.14	Narraguagus River		

The origin of salmon stocked are listed as follows:

D = Dennys River
EM = East Machias River
K = Kennebec River
LLS = Landlocked Atlantic salmon
M = Machias River
N = Narraguagus River
NB = Miramichi River (Miramichi Hatchery), New Brunswick, Canada
O = Orland River
ON = Ontario, Canada (landlocked salmon)
P = Penobscot River
Q = Saguenay River (Tadoussac Hatchery), Quebec, Canada
SC = Saint Croix River
SJ = Saint John River (Mactaquac or Saint John Hatcheries), New Brunswick, Canada
U = Union River

Appendix 6.1

Historical stocking of juvenile and adult Atlantic salmon in Maine rivers, 1871–1995

	Number of juvenile Atlantic salmon								Number of adult salmon		
Year	Fry	0+ Parr	1+ Parr[1]	Total Parr	1-year Smolts	2-year Smolts[2]	Total Smolts	Grand Total	1SW	MSW	Total
1871	0	0	1,500	1,500	0	0	0	1,500	0	0	0
1872	20,000	0	0	0	0	0	0	20,000	0	0	0
1873	245,000	0	0	0	0	0	0	245,000	0	0	0
1874	374,440	0	0	0	0	0	0	374,440	0	0	0
1875	557,070	0	0	0	0	0	0	557,070	0	0	0
1876	0	0	0	0	0	0	0	0	0	0	0
1877	0	0	0	0	0	0	0	0	0	0	0
1878	0	0	0	0	0	0	0	0	0	0	0
1879	0	0	0	0	0	0	0	0	0	0	0
1880	0	0	0	0	0	0	0	0	0	0	0
1881	390,360	0	0	0	0	0	0	390,360	0	0	0
1882	326,800	0	0	0	0	0	0	326,800	0	0	0
1883	232,450	0	0	0	0	0	0	232,450	0	0	0
1884	727,500	0	0	0	0	0	0	727,500	0	0	0
1885	270,000	0	0	0	0	0	0	270,000	0	0	0
1886	0	0	0	0	0	0	0	0	0	0	0
1887	0	0	0	0	0	0	0	0	0	0	0
1888	36,000	0	0	0	0	0	0	36,000	0	0	0
1889	55,000	0	13,960	13,960	0	0	0	68,960	0	0	0
1890	0	0	0	0	0	0	0	0	0	0	0
1891	0	0	207,020	207,020	0	0	0	207,020	0	0	0
1892	0	0	254,200	254,200	0	0	0	254,200	0	0	0
1893	84,000	0	0	0	0	0	0	84,000	0	0	0
1894	0	0	0	0	0	0	0	0	0	0	0
1895	144,740	0	0	0	0	0	0	144,740	0	0	0
1896	0	0	0	0	0	0	0	0	0	0	0
1897	1,642,345	0	19,250	19,250	0	0	0	1,661,595	0	0	0
1898	1,620,000	0	25,160	25,160	0	0	0	1,645,160	0	0	0
1899	445,000	0	150,610	150,610	0	0	0	595,610	0	0	0
1900	908,070	0	0	0	0	0	0	908,070	0	0	0
1901	0	282,400	171,620	454,020	0	0	0	454,020	0	0	0
1902	48,715	0	277,000	277,000	0	0	0	325,715	0	0	0
1903	1,193,000	0	299,120	299,120	0	0	0	1,492,120	0	0	0
1904	2,566,720	0	369,000	369,000	0	0	0	2,935,720	0	0	0
1905	727,460	0	289,100	289,100	0	0	0	1,016,560	0	0	0
1906	1,897,610	0	79,200	79,200	0	0	0	1,976,810	0	0	0
1907	2,156,850	0	39,830	39,830	0	0	0	2,196,680	0	0	0
1908	2,079,510	0	30,000	30,000	0	0	0	2,109,510	0	0	0

1. Includes a small number of age 2+ parr.
2. Includes a small number of 3-year smolts.

Year	Number of juvenile Atlantic salmon								Number of adult salmon		
	Fry	0+ Parr	1+ Parr[1]	Total Parr	1-year Smolts	2-year Smolts[2]	Total Smolts	Grand Total	1SW	MSW	Total
1909	647,790	0	24,430	24,430	0	0	0	672,220	0	0	0
1910	1,217,370	0	232,910	232,910	0	0	0	1,450,280	0	0	0
1911	2,854,080	0	0	0	0	0	0	2,854,080	0	0	0
1912	1,820,350	0	0	0	0	0	0	1,820,350	0	0	0
1913	3,492,460	0	0	0	0	0	0	3,492,460	0	0	0
1914	2,546,290	0	0	0	0	0	0	2,546,290	0	0	0
1915	1,804,310	0	0	0	0	0	0	1,804,310	0	0	0
1916	1,709,810	0	0	0	0	0	0	1,709,810	0	0	0
1917	3,007,850	0	0	0	0	0	0	3,007,850	0	0	0
1918	1,971,000	0	0	0	0	0	0	1,971,000	0	0	0
1919	2,527,000	0	0	0	0	0	0	2,527,000	0	0	0
1920	1,987,500	0	0	0	0	0	0	1,987,500	0	0	0
1921	1,387,000	0	0	0	0	0	0	1,387,000	0	0	0
1922	1,334,000	0	0	0	0	0	0	1,334,000	0	0	0
1923	451,000	0	40,000	40,000	0	0	0	491,000	0	0	0
1924	494,000	0	0	0	0	0	0	494,000	0	0	0
1925	1,410,000	0	0	0	0	0	0	1,410,000	0	0	0
1926	993,640	0	0	0	0	0	0	993,640	0	0	0
1927	1,301,000	0	80,000	80,000	0	0	0	1,381,000	0	0	0
1928	1,073,500	0	80,000	80,000	0	0	0	1,153,500	0	0	0
1929	88,725	0	183,975	183,975	0	0	0	272,700	0	0	0
1930	0	0	88,800	88,800	0	0	0	88,800	0	0	0
1931	679,500	0	340,000	340,000	0	0	0	1,019,500	0	0	0
1932	488,000	0	31,430	31,430	0	0	0	519,430	0	0	0
1933	400,000	4,700	0	4,700	0	0	0	404,700	0	0	0
1934	0	0	0	0	0	0	0	0	0	0	0
1935	0	0	179,000	179,000	0	0	0	179,000	0	0	0
1936	470,000	0	118,000	118,000	0	0	0	588,000	0	0	0
1937	0	0	70,500	70,500	0	0	0	70,500	0	0	0
1938	0	0	0	0	0	0	0	0	0	0	0
1939	0	0	0	0	0	0	0	0	0	0	0
1940	0	22,000	0	22,000	0	0	0	22,000	0	0	0
1941	112,500	40,000	63,500	103,500	0	0	0	216,000	0	0	0
1942	0	75,030	36,350	111,380	0	3,200	3,200	114,580	0	0	0
1943	0	24,500	40,055	64,555	0	6,730	6,730	71,285	0	0	0
1944	0	0	99,810	99,810	0	0	0	99,810	0	0	0
1945	0	0	77,555	77,555	0	16,295	16,295	93,850	0	0	0
1946	0	0	25,355	25,355	0	13,980	13,980	39,335	0	0	0
1947	0	0	144,645	144,645	0	5,640	5,640	150,285	0	0	0
1948	0	80,035	54,825	134,860	0	0	0	134,860	0	0	0
1949	89,365	202,425	50,870	253,295	0	0	0	342,660	0	0	0
1950	184,840	129,350	82,450	211,800	0	0	0	396,640	0	0	0
1951	0	117,500	96,010	213,510	0	2,010	2,010	215,520	0	0	0
1952	6,680	157,145	80,645	237,790	0	0	0	244,470	0	0	0

Appendix 6.1: Historical Stocking in all Maine Rivers

	Number of juvenile Atlantic salmon								Number of adult salmon		
Year	Fry	0+ Parr	1+ Parr[1]	Total Parr	1-year Smolts	2-year Smolts[2]	Total Smolts	Grand Total	1SW	MSW	Total
1953	6,660	99,395	106,790	206,185	0	0	0	212,845	0	0	0
1954	0	227,570	69,470	297,040	0	0	0	297,040	0	0	0
1955	0	258,790	0	258,790	0	0	0	258,790	0	0	0
1956	0	268,400	0	268,400	0	0	0	268,400	0	0	0
1957	0	192,540	0	192,540	0	0	0	192,540	0	0	0
1958	0	206,950	0	206,950	0	0	0	206,950	0	0	0
1959	0	115,555	73,500	189,055	0	0	0	189,055	0	0	0
1960	0	164,810	180,910	345,720	0	0	0	345,720	0	0	0
1961	0	65,705	37,400	103,105	0	0	0	103,105	0	0	0
1962	0	118,520	32,845	151,365	105,640	0	105,640	257,005	0	0	0
1963	0	0	11,280	11,280	101,650	0	101,650	112,930	0	0	0
1964	0	20,075	23,185	43,260	25,205	0	25,205	68,465	0	0	0
1965	0	20,025	53,150	73,175	196,000	0	196,000	269,175	0	0	0
1966	0	30,125	87,685	117,810	205,280	115,735	321,015	438,825	0	0	0
1967	0	8,975	29,555	38,530	164,405	35,985	200,390	238,920	0	0	0
1968	0	0	55,070	55,070	124,195	69,410	193,605	248,675	0	0	0
1969	0	0	0	0	42,370	68,515	110,885	110,885	0	0	0
1970	0	25,000	0	25,000	0	50,990	50,990	75,990	0	0	0
1971	0	0	15,800	15,800	66,830	6,265	73,095	88,895	0	0	0
1972	129,000	0	0	0	8,525	108,595	117,120	246,120	0	0	0
1973	0	0	0	0	12,405	131,150	143,555	143,555	0	0	0
1974	0	0	44,185	44,185	44,245	93,275	137,520	181,705	0	0	0
1975	0	8,200	15,300	23,500	15,760	153,820	169,580	193,080	0	0	0
1976	0	8,250	83,850	92,100	64,710	245,155	309,865	401,965	0	0	0
1977	0	0	0	0	126,785	247,145	373,930	373,930	0	0	0
1978	0	0	126,750	126,750	122,035	173,300	295,335	422,085	0	0	0
1979	28,775	71,150	0	71,150	98,690	266,180	364,870	464,795	0	0	0
1980	0	0	0	0	402,630	279,875	682,505	682,505	118	338	456
1981	201,780	50,500	70,705	121,205	24,690	232,305	256,995	579,980	0	25	25
1982	349,150	118,930	265,155	384,085	148,940	259,740	408,680	1,141,915	0	0	0
1983	20,020	20,320	57,415	77,735	373,925	161,415	535,340	633,095	34	0	34
1984	134,120	34,365	13,800	48,165	658,690	135,595	794,285	976,570	58	29	87
1985	472,210	105,890	62,965	168,855	613,530	108,080	721,610	1,362,675	65	36	101
1986	657,600	53,530	61,385	114,915	709,445	68,990	778,435	1,550,950	50	0	50
1987	746,945	138,885	224,220	363,105	635,750	82,420	718,170	1,828,220	77	9	86
1988	814,390	804,690	51,065	855,755	848,135	87,055	935,190	2,605,335	70	30	100
1989	646,930	202,575	181,125	383,700	522,310	90,485	612,795	1,643,425	86	35	121
1990	962,615	237,765	250,695	488,460	643,065	33,725	676,790	2,127,865	0	0	0
1991	968,275	426,950	134,885	561,835	811,080	29,715	840,795	2,370,905	140	100	240
1992	1,563,955	521,050	138,305	659,355	886,755	8,075	894,830	3,118,140	455	200	655
1993	1,954,040	517,660	9,560	527,220	640,600	0	640,600	3,121,860	194	135	329
1994	1,774,995	254,660	2,430	257,090	648,205	0	648,205	2,680,290	167	33	200
1995	1,136,900	400,760	5,555	406,315	605,100	0	605,100	2,148,315	100	40	140
Sum	67,866,560	6,933,650	7,123,675	14,057,325	10,697,580	3,390,850	14,088,430	96,012,315	1,614	1,010	2,624

Number of Atlantic Salmon Stocked in Maine Rivers, 1871-1995.

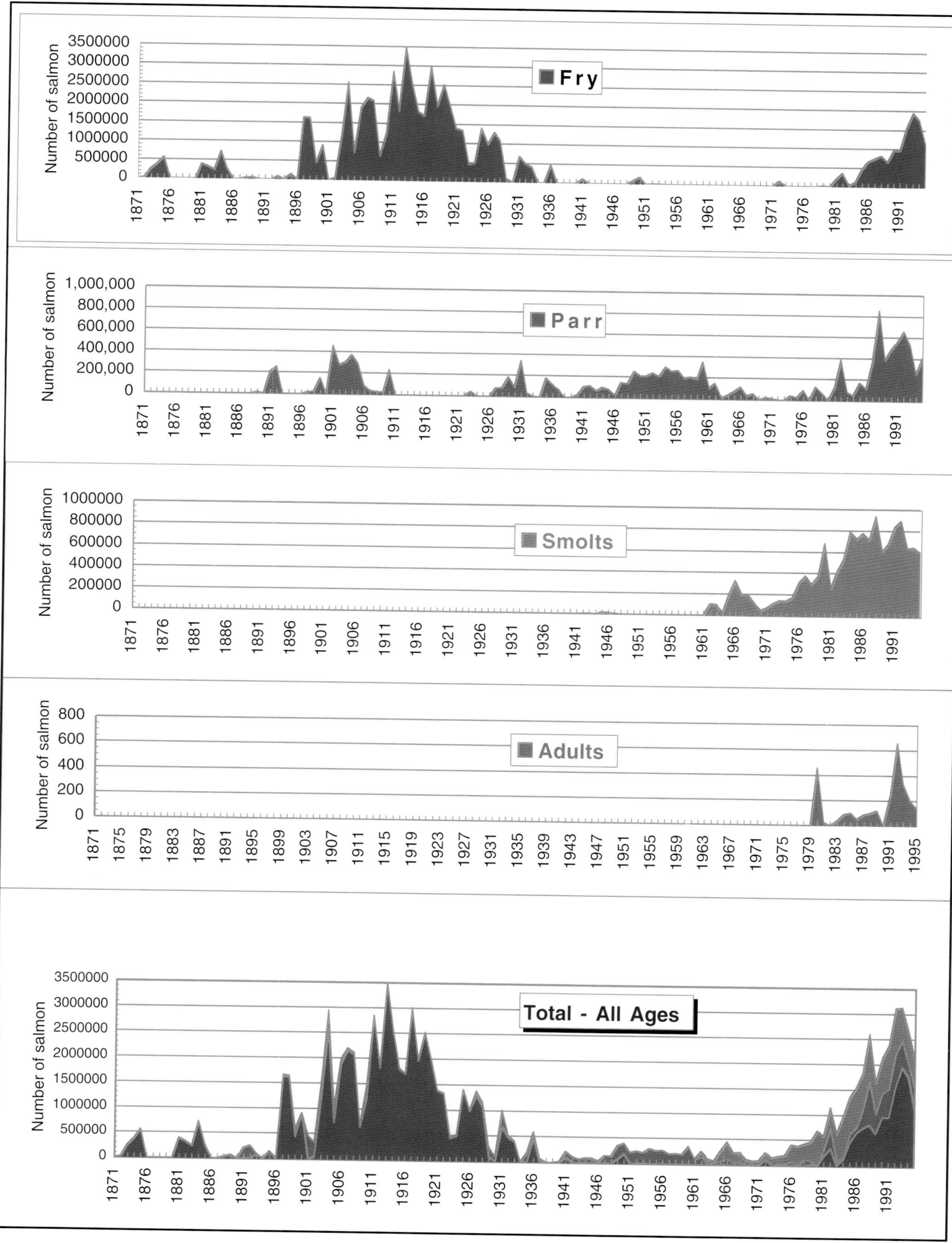

Appendix 6.2
Historical stocking of juvenile and adult Atlantic salmon in the Androscoggin River, 1871-1995.

Year	Fry	Origin	0+ Parr	Origin	1+ Parr	Origin	Total Parr	1-year Smolts	Origin	2-year Smolts	Origin	Total Smolts	Grand Total
1872	20,000	P	0		0		20,000	0		0		0	20,000
1873	130,000	P	0		0		130,000	0		0		0	130,000
1874	95,830	P	0		0		95,830	0		0		0	95,830
1875	50,870	P	0		0		50,870	0		0		0	50,870
1876-1995	0		0		0		0	0		0			None
SUM	296,700		0		0		296,700	0		0		0	296,700

APPENDIX 6.3
Historical stocking of juvenile and adult Atlantic salmon in the Aroostook River, 1871-1995.

Year	Fry	0+ Origin	0+ Parr	1+ Origin	1+ Parr	Origin	Total Parr	1-year Smolts	Origin	2-year Smolts	Origin	Total Smolts	Grand Total	Origin	Adult transfers 1SW	Adult transfers MSW	Adult transfers Total
1872-1894		0		0		0	0		0			0	NONE		0	0	0
1895	144,740	P	0		0		144,740	0		0		0	144,740		0	0	0
1897	146,645	P	0		0		146,645	0		0		0	146,645		0	0	0
1927	0		0		80,000	Q	80,000	0		0		0	80,000		0	0	0
1928	0		0		80,000	Q	80,000	0		0		0	80,000		0	0	0
1929	0		0		40,000	Q	40,000	0		0		0	40,000		0	0	0
1930	0		0		0		0	0		0		0	NONE		0	0	0
1931	0		0		50,000	NB	50,000	0		0		0	50,000		0	0	0
1932	to 1939		0		0		0	0		0		0	NONE		0	0	0
1940	0		10,000	D	0		10,000	0		0		0	10,000		0	0	0
1951	0		20,065	NB	0		20,065	0		0		0	20,065		0	0	0
1952	0		20,100	NB	0		20,100	0		0		0	20,100		0	0	0
1953	0		0		0		0	0		0		0	NONE		0	0	0
1954	0		48,600	NB	0		48,600	0		0		0	48,600		0	0	0
1955	0		70,095	NB	0		70,095	0		0		0	70,095		0	0	0
1956	0		75,130	NB	0		75,130	0		0		0	75,130		0	0	0
1957	0		19,500	NB	0		19,500	0		0		0	19,500		0	0	0
1958	0		69,850	NB	0		69,850	0		0		0	69,850		0	0	0
1959	0		0		73,500	NB	73,500	0		0		0	73,500		0	0	0
1960	0		0		96,450	NB	96,450	0		0		0	96,450		0	0	0
1961	0		0		37,400	NB	37,400	0		0		0	37,400		0	0	0
1962-1977		0		0		0	0		0			0	NONE		0	0	0
1978	0		0		0		0	5,190	U	0		5,190	5,190		0	0	0
1979	0		3,100	P	0		3,100	0		0		0	3,100		0	0	0
1980	0		0		0		0	0		2,595	U	2,595	2,595	P	0	12	12
1981	0		25,150	P	20,450	P	45,600	0		0		0	45,600	U	0	7	7
														P	0	18	18
1982	0		0		0		0	0		0		0	NONE	SJ	0	0	0
1983	0		0		0		0	0		0		0	NONE	SJ	34	0	34
1984	0		0		0		0	0		0		0	NONE	SJ	58	29	87
1985	0		0		1,850	P	1,850	0		0		0	1,850	SJ	65	24	89
1986	84,000	P	0		0		84,000	0		0		0	84,000	SJ	50	0	50
1987	41,400	SJ	0		0		41,400	0		0		0	41,400	SJ	77	9	86
1988	43,300	SJ	0		0		43,300	0		0		0	43,300	SJ	70	30	100
1989	312,600	SJ	14,750	P	0		327,350	0		10,000	SJ	10,000	337,350	SJ	86	35	121
1990	68,600	SJ	0		0		68,600	27,350	SJ	7,570	SJ	34,920	103,520	SJ	0	0	0
1991	74,500	SJ	0		0		74,500	0		9,590	SJ	9,590	84,090	SJ	50	50	100
1992	0		0		16,350	SJ	16,350	0		0		0	16,350	SJ	225	90	315
1993	0		0		0		0	0		0		0	NONE	SJ	85	71	156
1994	0		0		0		0	0		0		0	NONE	SJ	105	16	121
1995	4,300	SJ	0		0		4,300	0		0		0	4,300	SJ	100	40	140
Sum	920,085		376,340		496,000		1,792,425	32,540		29,755		62,295	1,854,720		1,005	431	1,436

Appendix 6.4
Historical stocking of juvenile and adult Atlantic salmon in Boyden Stream, 1871-1995.

Year	Fry	Origin	0+ Parr	Origin	1+ Parr	Origin	Total Parr	1-year Smolts	Origin	2-year Smolts	Origin	Total Smolts	Grand Total
1872-1874			0		0		0	0		0		0	NONE
1875	20,300	P	0		0		20,300	0		0		0	20,300
1876-1972			0		0		0	0		0		0	NONE
1973	0		0		0		0	0		1,000	P	1,000	1,000
1974	0		0		0		0	0		500	P	500	500
1975	0		0		0		0	0		600	P	600	600
1976-1995			0		0		0	0		0		0	NONE
SUM	20,300		0		0		20,300	0		2,100		2,100	22,400

Appendix 6.5
Historical stocking of juvenile and adult Atlantic salmon in the Dennys River, 1871-1995.

Year	Fry	Origin	0+ Parr	Origin	1+ Parr	Origin	Total Parr	1-year Smolts	Origin	2-year Smolts	Origin	Total Smolts	Grand Total
1872-1874			0		0		0	0		0		0	NONE
1875	20,000	P	0		0		20,000	0		0		0	20,000
1876-1880			0		0		0	0		0		0	NONE
1881	3,900	P	0		0		3,900	0		0		0	3,900
1882	0		0		0		0	0		0		0	NONE
1883	20,000	P	0		0		20,000	0		0		0	20,000
1884	39,500	P	0		0		39,500	0		0		0	39,500
1885*	36,000		0		0		36,000	0		0		0	36,000
1886	to 1887		0		0		0	0		0		0	NONE
1888*	36,000	P	0		0		36,000	0		0		0	36,000
1889*	36,000	P	0		0		36,000	0		0		0	36,000
1890	to 1917		0		0		0	0		0		0	NONE
1918	21,000	P	0		0		21,000	0		0		0	21,000
1919	627,000	P	0		0		627,000	0		0		0	627,000
1920	437,500	P	0		0		437,500	0		0		0	437,500
1921	0		0		0		0	0		0		0	NONE
1922	550,000	NB	0		0		550,000	0		0		0	550,000
1923	194,000	NB	0		40,000	NB	234,000	0		0		0	234,000
1924	179,200	NB	0		0		179,200	0		0		0	179,200
1925	112,500	NB	0		0		112,500	0		0		0	112,500
	225,000	Q	0		0		225,000	0		0		0	225,000
1926	5,000	NB	0		0		5,000	0		0		0	5,000
	70,000	Q	0		0		70,000	0		0		0	70,000
1927	100,500	NB	0		0		100,500	0		0		0	100,500
1928	100,500	NB	0		0		100,500	0		0		0	100,500
1929	to 1935		0		0		0	0		0		0	NONE
1936	360,000	NB	0		0		360,000	0		0		0	360,000
1937	0		0		30,000	NB	30,000	0		0		0	30,000
1938-1941			0		0		0	0		0		0	NONE
1942	0		6,000	P	0		6,000	0		3,200	D	3,200	9,200
1943	0		7,000	P	4,150	M	11,150	0		0		0	11,150
1944	0		0		9,000	P	9,000	0		0		0	9,000

Appendix 6.5: Historical Stocking, Dennys River

Year	Fry	Origin	0+ Parr	Origin	1+ Parr	Origin	Total Parr	1-year Smolts	Origin	2-year Smolts	Origin	Total Smolts	Grand Total
1945-1948			0		0		0	0		0		0	NONE
1949	0		5,005	P	0		5,005	0		0		0	5,005
1950	0		9,955	M+N	0		9,955	0		0		0	9,955
1951	0		10,225	NB	0		10,225	0		0		0	10,225
1952	0		20,000	NB	0		20,000	0		0		0	20,000
1953	0		0		0			0		0		0	NONE
1954	0		51,150	NB	19,530	NB	70,680	0		0		0	70,680
1955	0		50,455	NB	0		50,455	0		0		0	50,455
1956	0		45,915	NB	0		45,915	0		0		0	45,915
1957	0		9,900	NB	0		9,900	0		0		0	9,900
1958	0		9,850	NB	0		9,850	0		0		0	9,850
1959	0		0		0			0		0		0	NONE
1960	0		28,000	M	47,500	NB	75,500	0		0		0	75,500
	0		19,900	NB	0		19,900	0		0			19,900
1961	0		20,350	NB	0		20,350	0		0		0	20,350
1962	0		41,450	NB	0		41,450	0		0		0	41,450
1963-1964			0		0		0	0		0		0	NONE
1965	0		0		0			25,570	NB	0		25,570	25,570
1966	0		0		28,015	M	28,015	20,000	NB	0		20,000	48,015
	0		0		15,750	N	15,750	0		0			15,750
1967	0		0		0			0		0		0	NONE
1968	0		0		0			20,510	NB	0		20,510	20,510
1969-1971			0		0					0			NONE
1972	0		0		0		0	0		7,020	N	7,020	7,020
1973	to 1974		0		0			0		0		0	NONE
1975	0		0		3,000	P	3,000	0		4,160	P	4,160	7,160
1976	0		8,250	P	0		8,250	0		8,910	P	8,910	17,160
1977	0		0		0		0	0		0		0	NONE
1978	0		0		0		0	14,820	P	0		14,820	14,820
			0		0			15,395	U	0		15,395	15,395
1979	0		0		0		0	10,230	P	0		10,230	10,230
1980	0		0		0		0	0		15,220	U	15,220	15,220
1981-1982			0		0								NONE
1983	20,020	P	0		0		20,020	5,220	U	0		5,220	25,240
1984	0		0		0		0	3,290	U	0		3,290	3,290
1985	0		0		0		0	4,500	U	0		4,500	4,500
1986	0		8,255	PU	0		8,255	5,440	P	0		5,440	13,695
1987	24,000	P	0		0		24,000	9,040	U	0		9,040	33,040
1988	29,900	P	0		0		29,900	14,290	P	0		14,290	44,190
			0		0			11,445	U	0		11,445	11,445
1989	11,900	P	0		0		11,900	12,130	P	0		12,130	24,030
1990	20,200	P	0		0		20,200	25,810	P	0		25,810	46,010
1991	25,200	P	0		400	P	25,600	11,700	P	0		11,700	37,300
1992			0							0			NONE
1993	32,700	D	0		0		32,700	0		0		0	32,700
1994	20,000	D	0		0		20,000	0		0		0	20,000
1995	84,000	D	0		0		84,000	0		0		0	84,000
Sum	3,441,520		351,660		197,345		3,990,525	209,390		38,510		247,900	4,238,425

* Estimated from 40,000 eggs received.

APPENDIX 6.6

Historical stocking of juvenile and adult Atlantic salmon in the Ducktrap River, 1871-1995.

Year	Fry	0+ Origin	Parr	1+ Origin	Parr	Origin	1-year Smolts	Origin	2-year Smolts	Origin	Total Smolt	Grand Total
1872-1984			0		0		0		0		0	NONE
1985	15,000	P	0		0		0		0		0	15,000
1986	8,000	P	0		0		0		0		0	8,000
1987	15,000	P	0		0		0		0		0	15,000
1988	10,150	P	0		0		0		0		0	10,150
1989	17,040	P	0		0		0		0		0	17,040
1990	17,500	P	0		0		0		0		0	17,500
1991-1995			0		0		0		0		0	NONE
Sum	82,690		0		0		0		0		0	82,690

APPENDIX 6.7

Historical stocking of juvenile and adult Atlantic salmon in the East Machias River, 1871-1995.

Year	Fry	Origin	0+ Parr	Origin	1+ Parr	Origin	Total Parr	1-year Smolts	Origin	2-year Smolts	Origin	Total Smolts	Grand Total
1872-1916			0		0		0	0		0		0	NONE
1917	30,000	P	0		0		30,000	0		0		0	30,000
1918-1939			0		0		0	0		0		0	NONE
1940	0		7,000	D	0		7,000	0		0		0	7,000
1941-1965			0		0		0	0		0		0	NONE
1966	0		0		0		0	10,480	NB	14,405	M	24,885	24,885
1967-1972			0		0		0	0		0		0	NONE
1973	0		0		0		0	0		2,010	P	2,010	2,010
1974	0		0		0		0	0		0		0	NONE
1975	0		0		0		0	0		3,015	P	3,015	3,015
1976	0		0		0		0	0		3,915	P	3,915	3,915
1977	0		0		0		0	0		0		0	NONE
1978	0		0		0		0	8,250	P	0		8,250	8,250
	0		0		0		0	3,920	U	0		3,920	3,920
1979	0		0		0		0	5,150	P	0		5,150	5,150
1980	0		0		0		0	0		15,865	U	15,865	15,865
1981	0		0		0		0	0		0		0	NONE
1982	0		0		8,685	P	8,685	0		5,600	P	5,600	14,285
1983-1984			0		0		0	0		0		0	NONE
1985	12,520	P	0		0		12,520	4,500	U	0		4,500	17,020
1986	7,500	P	0		0		7,500	5,250	U	0		5,250	12,750
1987	10,000	P	0		0		10,000	9,000	U	0		9,000	19,000
1988	10,000	P	0		7,500	P	17,500	20,745	P	0		20,745	38,245
1989	29,900	P	6,545	P	8,000	P	44,445	9,275	P	0		9,275	53,720
	0		0		0		0	6,025	U			6,025	6,025
1990	42,000	P	0		10,055	P	52,055	10,135	P	0		10,135	62,190
1991	26,600	P	0		8,295	P	34,895	15,305	P	0		15,305	50,200
1992	to 1995		0		0		0	0		0		0	NONE
Sum	168,520		13,545		42,535		224,600	108,035		44,810		152,845	377,445

Appendix 6.8

Historical stocking of juvenile and adult Atlantic salmon in the Kennebec River, 1871-1995.

Year	Fry	Origin	0+ Parr	Origin	1+ Parr	Origin	Total Parr	1-year Smolts	Origin	2-year Smolts	Origin	Total Smolts	Grand Total	Adult transfers* Origin	1SW	MSW	Total
1872-1880			0		0		0	0		0		0	NONE	P,U	-	-	0
1881	87,460	P	0		0		87,460	0		0		0	87,460	P,U	-	-	0
1882-1988			0		0		0	0		0		0	NONE	P,U	-	-	0
1989	0		0		0		0	0		0		0	NONE	P,U	-	-	447
1990	0		0		0		0	0		0		0	NONE	P,U	-	-	338
1991	0		0		0		0	0		0		0	NONE	P,U	-	-	114
1992	0		0		0		0	0		0		0	NONE	P,U	-	-	515
1993	0		0		0		0	0		0		0	NONE	P,U	-	-	753
1994-1995			0		0		0	0		0		0	NONE	P,U	-	-	0
SUM	87,460		0		0		87,460	0		0		0	87,460		-	-	2,167

* Captive broodstock (reared entirely in freshwater) from Green Lake National Fish Hatchery; originated from Penobscot and Union River smolts.

APPENDIX 6.9
Historical stocking of juvenile and adult Atlantic salmon in the Kennebunk River, 1871-1995.

Year	Fry	Origin	0+ Parr	Origin	1+ Parr	Origin	Total Parr	1-year Smolts	Origin	2-year Smolts	Origin	Total Smolts	Grand Total
1872-1912			0		0		0	0		0		0	NONE
1913	10,000	P	0		0		10,000	0		0		0	10,000
1914-1964			0		0		0	0		0		0	NONE
1965	0		0		0		0	2,000	NB	0		2,000	2,000
	0		0		0		0	2,000	LLS	0		2,000	2,000
1966	0		0		0		0	5,000	NB	0		5,000	5,000
	0		0		0		0	5,000	LLS	0		5,000	5,000
1967	0		0		0		0	5,000	NB	0		5,000	5,000
	0		0		0		0	5,000	LLS	0		5,000	5,000
1968	0		0		0		0	4,425	NB	0		4,425	4,425
1969-1995			0		0		0	0		0		0	NONE
SUM	10,000		0		0		10,000	28,425		0		28,425	38,425

Note: LLS = landlocked Atlantic salmon that originated from Sebago Lake, Maine.

APPENDIX 6.10
Historical stocking of juvenile and adult Atlantic salmon in Little Falls (Hobart) Stream, 1871-1995.

		0+		1+		Total	1-year		2-year			Total	Grand
Year	Fry	Origin	Parr	Origin	Parr	Origin	Parr	Smolts	Origin	Smolts	Origin	Smolts	Total
1872-1946			0		0		0	0		0		0	NONE
1947	0		0		35,370	P	35,370	0		0		0	35370
1948	0		7,035	P	11,725	M	18,760	0		0		0	18,760
1949	0		6,140	M	2,310	P	8,450	0		0		0	8,450
1950	0		10,770	M+N	6,010	NB	16,780	0		0		0	16,780
1951	0		11,905	NB	0		11,905	0		2,010	NB	2,010	13,915
1952	6,680	NB	13,335	NB	9,980	NB	29,995	0		0		0	29,995
1953	6,660	NB	13,215	NB	7,455	NB	27,330	0		0		0	27,330
1954	0		20,040	NB	11,620	NB	31,660	0		0		0	31,660
1955-1995			0		0		0	0		0		0	NONE
Sum	13,340		82,440		84,470		180,250	0		2,010		2,010	182,260

APPENDIX 6.11
Historical stocking of juvenile and adult Atlantic salmon in the Machias River, 1871-1995.

Year	Fry	Origin	0+ Parr	Origin	1+ Parr	Origin	Total Parr	1-year Smolts	Origin	2-year Smolts	Origin	Total Smolts	Grand Total
1872-1874			0		0		0	0		0		0	NONE
1875	1,000	P	0		0		1,000	0		0		0	1,000
1876-1880			0		0		0	0		0		0	NONE
1881	25,000		0		0		25,000	0		0		0	25,000
1882	29,800	P	0		0		29,800	0		0		0	29,800
1883	17,450	P	0		0		17,450	0		0		0	17,450
1884-1921			0		0		0	0		0		0	NONE
1922	50,000	NB	0		0		50,000	0		0		0	50,000
1923-1940			0		0		0	0		0		0	NONE
1941	0		20,000	P	0		20,000	0		0		0	20,000
1942	0		34,000	P	0		34,000	0		0		0	34,000
1943	0		5,000	P	16,000	M	21,000	0		0		0	21,000
1944-1946			0		0		0	0		0		0	NONE
1947	0		0		38,810	P	38,810	0		0		0	38,810
1948	0		0		43,100	M	43,100	0		0		0	43,100
1949	0		24,835	M	7,320	P	32,155	0		0		0	32,155
	0		25,000	NB	0		25,000	0		0		0	25,000
1950	100,150	M+N	29,500	M+N	17,030	M	146,680	0		0		0	146,680
1951	0		0		45,710	M+P	45,710	0		0		0	45,710
1952	0		0		22,430	NB	22,430	0		0		0	22,430
1953	0		43,930	NB	0		43,930	0		0		0	43,930
1954-1956			0		0		0	0		0		0	NONE
1957	0		19,485	NB	0		19,485	0		0		0	19,485
1958	0		17,525	M	0		17,525	0		0		0	17,525
	0		17,440	NB	0		17,440	0		0		0	17,440
1959	0		30,365	M	0		30,365	0		0		0	30,365
	0		15,565	NB	0		15,565	0		0		0	15,565
1960	0		29,795	M	0		29,795	0		0		0	29,795
	0		27,670	NB	0		27,670	0		0		0	27,670
1961	0		2,035	M	0		2,035	0		0		0	2,035
	0		2,035	NB	0		2,035	0		0		0	2,035
1962	0		30,995	M	0		30,995	35,990	NB	0		35,990	66,985
	0		30,575	NB	0		30,575	0		0		0	30,575
1963	0		0		0		0	30,935	NB	0		30,935	30,935
1964	0		0		7,080		7,080	1,585	NB	0		1,585	8,665
1965	0		0		0		0	38,960	NB	0		38,960	38,960
1966	0		0		0		0	13,690	N	19,305	N	32,995	32,995
1967	0		0		0		0	14,700	NB	11,185	M	25,885	25,885
1968	0		0		0		0	9,040	N	8,910		17,950	17,950
	0		0		0		0	18,390	NB	0		18,390	18,390
1969	0		0		0		0	11,215	M	25,670	M	36,885	36,885
1970	0		0		0		0	0		10,670	M	10,670	10,670
1971	0		0		0		0	5,100	M	3,390	MN	8,490	8,490
1972	0		0		0		0	8,525	P	4,370	PM	12,895	12,895
1973	0		0		0		0	0		6,120	P	6,120	6,120
1974	0		0		0		0	0		6,480	N	6,480	6,480
1975	0		0		0		0	0		0		0	NONE
1976	0		0		0		0	5,250	P	11,090	P	16,340	16,340
1977	0		0		0		0	0		0		0	NONE
1978	0		0		0		0	2,665	P	0		2,665	2,665
	0		0		0		0	7,575	U	0		7,575	7,575
1979	0		0		0		0	6,105	P	0		6,105	6,105
	0		0		0		0	4,095	U	0		4,095	4,095

Year	Fry	Origin	0+ Parr	Origin	1+ Parr	Origin	Total Parr	1-year Smolts	Origin	2-year Smolts	Origin	Total Smolts	Grand Total
1980	to 1981		0		0		0	0		0		0	NONE
1982	0		0		0		0	5,500	P	0		5,500	5,500
1983	0		12,025	P	0		12,025	0		0		0	12,025
	0		505	U	0		505	0		0		0	505
1984	0		0		0		0	15,780	U	0		15,780	15,780
1985	0		0		7,000	P	7,000	5,130	U	0		5,130	12,130
1986	7,500	P	8,000	P	0		15,500	0		0		0	15,500
1987	0		12,510	P	10,235	P	22,745	13,555	U	0		13,555	36,300
	0		0		2,090	U	2,090	0		0		0	2,090
1988	30,200	P	0		30,695	P	60,895	14,285	P	0		14,285	75,180
	0		0		765	U	765	16,615	U	0		16,615	17,380
1989	48,550	P	13,785	P	28,000	P	90,335	23,115	P	0		23,115	113,450
1990	75,000	P	10,130	P	17,630	P	102,760	26,090	P	0		26,090	128,850
1991	13,000	P	30,000	P	21,405	P	64,405	21,080	P	0		21,080	85,485
1992	13,790		0		0		13,790	0		0		0	13,790
1993	0	M	0		0		0	0		0		0	NONE
1994	49,970	M	0		0		49,970	0		0		0	49,970
1995	150,000	M	0		0		150,000	0		0		0	150,000
Sum	611,410		492,705		315,300		1,419,415	354,970		107,190		462,160	1,881,575

APPENDIX 6.12

Historical stocking of juvenile and adult Atlantic salmon in the Medomak River, 1871-1995.

Year	Fry	Origin	0+ Parr	Origin	1+ Parr	Origin	Total Parr	1-year Smolts	Origin	2-year Smolts	Origin	Total Smolts	Grand Total
1872-1873			0		0		0	0		0		0	NONE
1874	38,000	P	0		0		38,000	0		0		0	38,000
1875	5,000	P	0		0		5,000	0		0		0	5,000
1876-1995			0		0		0	0		0		0	NONE
Sum	43,000		0		0		43,000	0		0		0	43,000

APPENDIX 6.13

Historical stocking of juvenile and adult Atlantic salmon in the Meduxnekeag River, 1871-1995.

Year	Fry	Origin	0+ Parr	Origin	1+ Parr	Origin	Total Parr	1-year Smolts	Origin	2-year Smolts	Origin	Total Smolts	Grand Total
1872-1925			0		0		0	0		0		0	NONE
1926	92,000	Q	0		0		92,000	0		0		0	92,000
1927	92,000	Q	0		0		92,000	0		0		0	92,000
1928	0		0		0		0	0		0		0	NONE
1929	0		0		40,000	Q	40,000	0		0		0	40,000
1930	0		0		0		0	0		0		0	NONE
1931	0		0		50,000	NB	50,000	0		0		0	50,000
1932-1978			0		0		0	0		0		0	NONE
1979	0		2,100	P	0		2,100	0		0		0	2,100
1980	0		0		0		0	2,730	U	0		2,730	2,730
1981-1995			0		0		0	0		0		0	NONE
Sum	184,000		2,100		90,000		276,100	2,730		0		2,730	278,830

APPENDIX 6.14
Historical stocking of juvenile and adult Atlantic salmon in the Narraguagus River, 1871-1995.

Year	Fry	Origin	0+ Parr	Origin	1+ Parr	Origin	Total Parr	1-year Smolts	Origin	2-year Smolts	Origin	Total Smolts	Grand Total
1872-1917			0		0		0	0		0		0	NONE
1918	225,000	P	0		0		225,000	0		0		0	225,000
1919	437,500	P	0		0		437,500	0		0		0	437,500
1920-1923			0		0		0	0		0		0	NONE
1924	64,000	NB	0		0		64,000	0		0		0	64,000
1925	60,000	NB	0		0		60,000	0		0		0	60,000
1926	50,000	Q	0		0		50,000	0		0		0	50,000
1927	100,500	NB	0		0		100,500	0		0		0	100,500
1928	10,500	NB	0		0		10,500	0		0		0	10,500
	90,000	Q	0		0		90,000	0		0		0	90,000
1929	88,725	NB	0		0		88,725	0		0		0	88,725
1930	0		0		0		0	0		0		0	NONE
1931	0		0		25,000	NB	25,000	0		0		0	25,000
1932-1935			0		0		0	0		0		0	NONE
1936	85,000	NB	0		0		85,000	0		0		0	85,000
1937-1940			0		0		0	0		0		0	NONE
1941	0		20,000	P	0		20,000	0		0		0	20,000
1942	0		10,000	P	0		10,000	0		0		0	10,000
1943	0		12,500	P	5,000	M	17,500	0		0		0	17,500
1944	0		0		9,000	P	9,000	0		0		0	9,000
1945			0		0		0	0		0		0	NONE
1949	29,280	NB	0		0		29,280	0		0		0	29,280
1950	35,000	M+N	9,855	M+N	0		44,855	0		0		0	44,855
1951	0		14,980	NB	50,300	NB	65,280	0		0		0	65,280
	0		14,990	M+P	0		14,990	0		0		0	14,990
	0		20,335	M+N	0		20,335	0		0		0	20,335
1952	0		78,565	NB	48,235	NB	126,800	0		0		0	126,800
1953	0		42,250	NB	99,335	NB	141,585	0		0		0	141,585
1954	0		0		0		0	0		0		0	NONE
1955	0		39,860	NB	0		39,860	0		0		0	39,860
1956	0		48,725	NB	0		48,725	0		0		0	48,725
1957	0		29,640	NB	0		29,640	0		0		0	29,640
1958	0		19,905	NB	0		19,905	0		0		0	19,905
1959	0		19,030	NB	0		19,030	0		0		0	19,030
1960	0		32,395	NB	0		32,395	0		0		0	32,395
1961	0		17,065	NB	0		17,065	0		0		0	17,065
1962	0		0		0		0	35,620	NB	0		35,620	35,620
1963	0		0		0		0	34,660	NB	0		34,660	34,660
1964	0		20,075	N	5,335	N	25,410	18,105	NB	0		18,105	43,515
1965	0		20,025	M	0		20,025	34,185	NB	0		34,185	54,210
1966	0		30,125	N	0		30,125	24,460	N	24,850	N	49,310	79,435
1967	0		0		0		0	15,830	NB	19,110	M	34,940	34,940
1968	0		0		0		0	11,760	NB	6,855	M	18,615	18,615
	0		0		0		0	0		4,945	N	4,945	4,945
1969	0		0		0		0	9,875	N	15,925	N	25,800	25,800
1970	0		0		0		0	0		1,925	MN	1,925	1,925
	0		0		0		0	0		9,895	N	9,895	9,895
1971	0		0		0		0	0		2,875	MN	2,875	2,875
1972	0		0		0		0	0		15,700	PM	15,700	15,700
1973	0		0		0		0	0		5,560	P	5,560	5,560
1974	0		0		0		0	0		0		0	NONE
1975	0		0		0		0	0		5,000	P	5,000	5,000

Year	Fry	Origin	0+ Parr	Origin	1+ Parr	Origin	Total Parr	1-year Smolts	Origin	2-year Smolts	Origin	Total Smolts	Grand Total
1976	0		0		0		0	0		8,430	P	8,430	8,430
1977	0		0		0		0	0		0		0	NONE
1978	0		0		0		0	0		0		0	NONE
1979	0		0		0		0	4,555	P	0		4,555	4,555
	0		0		0		0	5,575	U	0		5,575	5,575
1980	0		0		0		0	0		20,430	U	20,430	20,430
1981	0		0		0		0	0		4,080	U	4,080	4,080
1982	0		0		0		0	0		5,200	P	5,200	5,200
1983	0		7,790	P	0		7,790	0		0		0	7,790
1984	0		0		0		0	5,200	U	0		5,200	5,200
1985	10,280	P	0		0		10,280	4,500	U	0		4,500	14,780
1986	0		0		0		0	7,510	U	0		7,510	7,510
1987	15,105	P	0		0		15,105	9,020	U	0		9,020	24,125
1988	20,000	P	9,545	P	4,440	P	33,985	10,455	P	0		10,455	44,440
	0		3,490	U	1,115	U	4,605	5,215	U	0		5,215	9,820
1989	29,260	P	9,500	P	7,000	P	45,760	22,110	P	4,900	P	27,010	72,770
1990	0		0		0		0	16,750	P	0		16,750	16,750
1991	0		0		0		0	15,225	P	0		15,225	15,225
1992	to 1994		0		0		0	0		0		0	NONE
1995	105,000	N	0		0		105,000	0		0		0	105,000
Sum	1,350,150		530,645		254,760		2,135,555	290,610		155,680		446,290	2,581,845

APPENDIX 6.15

Historical stocking of juvenile and adult Atlantic salmon in the Orland River, 1871-1995.

Year	Fry	Origin	0+ Parr	Origin	1+ Parr	Origin	Total Parr	1-year Smolts	Origin	2-year Smolts	Origin	Total Smolts	Grand Total
1872-1888			0		0		0	0		0		0	NONE
1889	19,000	P	0		13,960	P	32,960	0		0		0	32,960
1890	0		0		0		0	0		0		0	NONE
1891	0		0		103,510	P	103,510	0		0		0	103,510
1892	0		0		0		0	0		0		0	NONE
1893	84,000	P	0		0		84,000	0		0		0	84,000
1894-1942			0		0		0	0		0		0	NONE
1943	0		0		2,290	NB	2,290	0		0		0	2,290
1944	0		0		0		0	0		0		0	NONE
1945	0		0		600	P	600	0		0		0	600
1946-1948			0		0		0	0		0		0	NONE
1949	10,085	NB	0		0		10,085	0		0		0	10,085
1950	9,895	M+N	0		0		9,895	0		0		0	9,895
1951-1962			0		0		0	0		0		0	NONE
1963	0		0		0		0	36,055	NB	0		36,055	36,055
1964	0		0		0		0	5,515	Q	0		5,515	5,515
1965	0		0		0		0	49,370	NB	0		49,370	49,370
1966	0		0		0		0	40,000	NB	0		40,000	40,000
1967	0		0		7,640	O	7,640	19,890	NB	0		19,890	27,530
1968	0		0		0		0	18,525	O	0		18,525	18,525
1969	0		0		0		0	6,790	OP	0		6,790	6,790
1970-1995			0		0		0	0		0		0	NONE
Sum	122,980		0		128,000		250,980	176,145		0		176,145	427,125

Appendix 6.16
Historical stocking of juvenile and adult Atlantic salmon in the Penobscot River, 1871-1995.

Year	Fry	Origin	0+ Parr	Origin	1+ Parr	Origin	Total Parr	1-year Smolts	Origin	2-year Smolts	Origin	Total Smolts	Grand Total
1872	0		0		0		0	0		0		0	NONE
1873	67,000	P	0		0		67,000	0		0		0	67,000
1874	210,000	P	0		0		210,000	0		0		0	210,000
1875	354,900	P	0		0		354,900	0		0		0	354,900
1876	to 1880		0		0		0	0		0		0	NONE
1881	147,000	P	0		0		147,000	0		0		0	147,000
1882	297,000	P	0		0		297,000	0		0		0	297,000
1883	195,000	P	0		0		195,000	0		0		0	195,000
1884	688,000	P	0		0		688,000	0		0		0	688,000
1885*	234,000	P	0		0		234,000	0		0		0	234,000
1886	to 1890		0		0		0	0		0		0	NONE
1891	0		0		103,510	P	103,510	0		0		0	103,510
1892	0		0		254,200	P	254,200	0		0		0	254,200
1893-1896			0		0		0	0		0		0	NONE
1897	1,345,700	P	0		19,250	P	1,364,950	0		0		0	1,364,950
1898	1,482,500	P	0		25,160	P	1,507,660	0		0		0	1,507,660
1899	445,000	P	0		150,610	P	595,610	0		0		0	595,610
1900	908,070	P	0		0		908,070	0		0		0	908,070
1901	0		282,400	P	171,620	P	454,020	0		0		0	454,020
1902	48,715	P	0		277,000	P	325,715	0		0		0	325,715
1903	1,193,000	P	0		299,120	P	1,492,120	0		0		0	1,492,120
1904	2,566,720	P	0		369,000	P	2,935,720	0		0		0	2,935,720
1905	727,460	P	0		289,100	P	1,016,560	0		0		0	1,016,560
1906	1,897,610	P	0		79,200	P	1,976,810	0		0		0	1,976,810
1907	2,156,850	P	0		39,830	P	2,196,680	0		0		0	2,196,680
1908	2,079,510	P	0		30,000	P	2,109,510	0		0		0	2,109,510
1909	647,790	P	0		24,430	P	672,220	0		0		0	672,220
1910	1,217,370	P	0		232,910	P	1,450,280	0		0		0	1,450,280
1911	2,854,080	P	0		0		2,854,080	0		0		0	2,854,080
1912	1,820,350	P	0		0		1,820,350	0		0		0	1,820,350
1913	3,482,460	P	0		0		3,482,460	0		0		0	3,482,460
1914	2,546,290	P	0		0		2,546,290	0		0		0	2,546,290
1915	1,804,310	P	0		0		1,804,310	0		0		0	1,804,310
1916	1,709,810	P	0		0		1,709,810	0		0		0	1,709,810
1917	2,977,850	P	0		0		2,977,850	0		0		0	2,977,850
1918	1,350,000	P	0		0		1,350,000	0		0		0	1,350,000
1919	1,025,000	P	0		0		1,025,000	0		0		0	1,025,000
1920*	628,530	P	0		0		628,530	0		0		0	628,530
	921,470	NB	0		0		921,470	0		0		0	921,470
1921	821,240	P	0		0		821,240	0		0		0	821,240
	565,760	NB	0		0		565,760	0		0		0	565,760
1922	471,520	P	0		0		471,520	0		0		0	471,520
1922	262,480	NB	0		0		262,480	0		0		0	262,480
1923	257,000	NB	0		0		257,000	0		0		0	257,000
1924	250,800	NB	0		0		250,800	0		0		0	250,800
1925	657,000	NB	0		0		657,000	0		0		0	657,000
	243,000	Q	0		0		243,000	0		0		0	243,000
1926	419,640	NB	0		0		419,640	0		0		0	419,640
	256,000	Q	0		0		256,000	0		0		0	256,000
1927	599,500	NB	0		0		599,500	0		0		0	599,500
	258,500	Q	0		0		258,500	0		0		0	258,500

Year	Fry	Origin	0+ Parr	Origin	1+ Parr	Origin	Total Parr	1-year Smolts	Origin	2-year Smolts	Origin	Total Smolts	Grand Total
1928	772,000	NB	0		0		772,000	0		0		0	772,000
1929	0		0		103,975	NB	103,975	0		0		0	103,975
1930	0		0		88,800	NB	88,800	0		0		0	88,800
1931	679,500	NB	0		215,000	NB	894,500	0		0		0	894,500
1932	488,000	NB	0		27,330	NB	515,330	0		0		0	515,330
1932	0		0		4,100	P	4,100	0		0		0	4,100
1933	400,000	NB	4,700	NB	0		404,700	0		0		0	404,700
1934	0		0		0		0	0		0		0	NONE
1935	0		0		179,000	NB	179,000	0		0		0	179,000
1936	25,000	NB	0		118,000	NB	143,000	0		0		0	143,000
1937	0		0		40,500	NB	40,500	0		0		0	40,500
1938-1940			0		0		0	0		0		0	NONE
1941	112,500	P	0		63,500	D	176,000	0		0		0	176,000
1942	0		25,030	M	15,000	P	40,030	0		0		0	40,030
1943	0		0		9,165	M	9,165	0		0		0	9,165
1944	0		0		50,940	P	50,940	0		0		0	50,940
1945	0		0		51,775	P	51,775	0		16,295	P	16,295	68,070
1946	0		0		25,355	P	25,355	0		13,980	P	13,980	39,335
1947	0		0		70,465	P	70,465	0		5,640	P	5,640	76,105
1948	0		61,000	P	0		61,000	0		0		0	61,000
1949	0		30,245	NB	33,000	P	63,245	0		0		0	63,245
1950	0		29,545	M+N	19,605	M	49,150	0		0		0	49,150
	0		0		19,605	NB	19,605	0		0		0	19,605
1951-1953			0				0	0		0		0	NONE
1954	0		68,315	NB	33,350	NB	101,665	0		0		0	101,665
1955	0		68,490	NB	0		68,490	0		0		0	68,490
1956	0		79,310	NB	0		79,310	0		0		0	79,310
1957	0		90,030	NB	0		90,030	0		0		0	90,030
1958	0		42,385	NB	0		42,385	0		0		0	42,385
1959	0		50,595	NB	0		50,595	0		0		0	50,595
1960-1961			0				0	0		0		0	NONE
1962	0		0				0	34,030	NB	0		34,030	34,030
1963-1964			0				0	0		0		0	NONE
1965	0		0		26,210	MN	26,210	29,705	NB	0		29,705	55,915
1966	0		0		0		0	0		7,005	N	7,005	7,005
1967	0		0		21,915	NB	21,915	38,090	NB	5,690	M	43,780	65,695
1968	0		0		25,000	MN	25,000	0		28,925	M	28,925	53,925
	0		0				0	0		12,690	MN	12,690	12,690
	0		0				0	0		7,085	N	7,085	7,085
1969	0		0		0		0	900	MN	8,545	M	9,445	9,445
	0		0				0	0		18,375	MN	18,375	18,375
1970	0		15,000	MN	0		15,000	0		23,280	M	23,280	38,280
	0		10,000	N			10,000	0		2,585	MN	2,585	12,585
	0		0				0	0		1,555	N	1,555	1,555
	0		0				Note: 3-yr smolt			1,080	MN	1,080	1,080
1971	0		0		15,800	N	15,800	33,915	M	0		33,915	49,715
	0		0				0	18,675	P	0		18,675	18,675
1972	129,000	M	0		0		129,000	0		14,470	M	14,470	143,470
	0		0				0	0		45,330	N	45,330	45,330
	0		0				0	0		3,515	PM	3,515	3,515
	0		0				0	0		10,480	P	10,480	10,480
1973	0		0		0		0	4,235	N	44,285	MN	48,520	48,520
	0		0				0	8,170	P	51,600	P	59,770	59,770

Appendix 6.16: Historical Stocking, Penobscot River

Year	Fry	Origin	0+ Parr	Origin	1+ Parr	Origin	Total Parr	1-year Smolts	Origin	2-year Smolts	Origin	Total Smolts	Grand Total
1974	0		0		35,100	P	35,100	34,320	P	17,510	PN	51,830	86,930
	0		0		9,085	PN	9,085	0		48,340	P	48,340	57,425
1975	0		8,200	P	12,300	P	20,500	15,760	P	94,800	P	110,560	131,060
1976	0		0		83,850	P	83,850	54,655	P	180,030	P	234,685	318,535
1977	0		0		0		0	113,760	P	224,355	P	338,115	338,115
	0		0				Note: 3 yr. smolt			325	P	325	325
1978	0		0		126,750	P	126,750	22,560	P	112,325	P	134,885	261,635
	0		0				0	38,560	U	29,035	U	67,595	67,595
1979	28,775	U	65,950	P	0		94,725	38,465	P	112,670	P	151,135	245,860
	0		0				0	11,580	U	123,585	U	135,165	135,165
1980	0		0		0		0	284,305	P	163,805	P	448,110	448,110
	0		0				0	84,710	U	51,980	U	136,690	136,690
1981	201,780	P	25,350	P	50,255	P	277,385	23,095	P	174,510	P	197,605	474,990
	0		0				0	1,595	U	285	U	1,880	1,880
1982	248,150	P	15,075	P	206,430		469,655	107,370	P	222,325	P	329,695	799,350
	0		35,855	U			35,855	0		0			35,855
1983	0		0		12,580	P	12,580	116,745	P	161,415	P	278,160	290,740
	0		0		19,345	U	19,345	164,800	U	0		164,800	184,145
1984	80,050	P	18,795	P			98,845	473,750	P	135,595	P	609,345	708,190
	0		15,570	U			15,570	7,775	U	0		7,775	23,345
1985	196,840	P	26,400	P	11,375	P	234,615	418,760	P	104,435	P	523,195	757,810
1985	0		33,050	U	6,240	U	39,290	54,325	U	0		54,325	93,615
	0		0				0	3,400	PU	0		3,400	3,400
1986	225,750	P	25,705	P	50,970	P	302,425	518,780	P	68,990	P	587,770	890,195
	0		0		410	U	410	1,435	U	0		1,435	1,845
1987	33,115	P	46,140	P	84,140	P	163,395	445,850	P	82,420	P	528,270	691,665
	0		11,995	U	16,940	U	28,935	10,920	U	0		10,920	39,855
1988	431,040	P	0		0		431,040	561,830	P	87,055	P	648,885	1,079,925
	0		0				0	38,070	U	0		38,070	38,070
1989	76,985	P	82,315	P	68,545	P	227,845	329,345	P	65,325	P	394,670	622,515
	0		21,780	U	11,030	U	32,810	21,950	U	0		21,950	54,760
1990	306,825	P	166,450	P	151,770	P	625,045	392,545	P	15,895	P	408,440	1,033,485
	10,350	UP	0		3,510	U	13,860	20,630	U	0		20,630	34,490
1991	398,450	P	202,600	P	104,140	P	705,190	657,785	P	15,015	P	672,800	1,377,990
1992	925,350	P	278,200	P	106,650	P	1,310,200	816,565	P	8,075	P	824,640	2,134,840
1993	1,320,295	P	202,300	P	9,560	P	1,532,155	580,435	P	0		580,435	2,112,590
1994	948,970	P	0		2,430	P	951,400	567,605	P	0		567,605	1,519,005
1995	501,000	P	325,000	P	5,555		831,555	568,400	P	0		568,400	1,399,955
Sum	53,631,510		2,463,775		4,811,290		60,906,575	7,770,155		2,622,510		10,392,665	71,299,240

* 1885 = Estimated from 260,000 eggs to be 234,000 @ 90% (78,000 @ CB and 187,000 @ private hatchery).

* 1920 = A small number of these fry may have been stocked in other Maine rivers, especially some of those in Washington County.

APPENDIX 6.17

Historical stocking of juvenile and adult Atlantic salmon in the Pennamaquan (Pembroke)River, 1871-1995.

Year	Fry	Origin	0+ Parr	Origin	1+ Parr	Origin	Total Parr	1-year Smolts	Origin	2-year Smolts	Origin	Total Smolts	Grand Total
1872	1873		0		0		0	0		0		0	NONE
1874	8,610	P	0		0		8,610	0		0		0	8,610
1875	45,000	P	0		0		45,000	0		0		0	45,000
1876	to 1917		0		0		0	0		0		0	NONE
1918	375,000	P	0		0		375,000	0		0		0	375,000
1919	to 1995		0		0		0	0		0		0	NONE
Sum	428,610		0		0		428,610	0		0		0	428,610

APPENDIX 6.18

Historical stocking of juvenile and adult Atlantic salmon in the Pleasant River, 1871-1995.

Year	Fry	Origin	0+ Parr	Origin	1+ Parr	Origin	Total Parr	1-year Smolts	Origin	2-year Smolts	Origin	Total Smolts	Grand Total
1872-1918			0		0		0	0		0		0	NONE
1919	437,500	P	0		0		437,500	0		0		0	437,500
1920-1949			0		0		0	0		0		0	NONE
1950	0		10,005	M+N	0		10,005	0		0		0	10,005
1951-1953			0		0		0	0		0		0	NONE
1954	0		10,065	NB	0		10,065	0		0		0	10,065
1955	0		10,000	NB	0		10,000	0		0		0	10,000
1956	0		0		0		0	0		0		0	NONE
1957	0		9,030	NB	0		9,030	0		0		0	9,030
1958	0		9,815	NB	0		9,815	0		0		0	9,815
1959-1962			0		0		0	0		0		0	NONE
1963	0		0		11,280	NB	11,280	0		0		0	11,280
1964	0		0		4,595	MN	4,595	0		0		0	4,595
1965	0		0		26,940	NB	26,940	0		0		0	26,940
1966	0		0		0		0	10,000	NB	0		10,000	10,000
1967	0		0		0		0	0		0		0	NONE
1968	0		0		0		0	13,550	NB	0		13,550	13,550
1969-1974			0		0		0	0		0		0	NONE
1975	0		0		0		0	0		3,000	P	3,000	3,000
1976	0		0		0		0	0		1,020	P	1,020	1,020
1977	0		0		0		0	0		0		0	NONE
1978	0		0		0		0	3,100	U	0		3,100	3,100
1979	0		0		0		0	0		0		0	NONE
1980	0		0		0		0	245	P	9,980	U	10,225	10,225
1981	0		0		0		0	0		4,080	U	4,080	4,080
1982	0		0		0		0	5,000	P	0		5,000	5,000
1983-1984			0		0		0	0		0		0	NONE
1985	33,000	P	0		0		33,000	4,110	U	0		4,110	37,110
1986	25,000	P	0		0		25,000	6,530	U	0		6,530	31,530
1987	25,015	P	0		0		25,015	7,475	U	0		7,475	32,490
1988	25,000	P	0		1,800	P	26,800	10,460	P	0		10,460	37,260
1989	26,195	P	2,500	P	0		28,695	7,300	P	0		7,300	35,995
1990	30,170	P	0		0		30,170	10,505	P	0		10,505	40,675
1991	23,000	P	0		0		23,000	0		0		0	23,000
1992	to 1995		0		0		0	0		0		0	NONE
Sum	624,880		51,415		44,615		720,910	78,275		18,080		96,355	817,265

Appendix 6.19

Historical stocking of juvenile and adult Atlantic salmon in the Presumpscot River, 1871-1995.

Year	Fry	Origin	0+ Parr	Origin	1+ Parr	Origin	Total Parr	1-year Smolts	Origin	2-year Smolts	Origin	Total Smolts	Grand Total
1872-1874			0		0		0	0		0		0	NONE
1875	40,000	P	0		0		40,000	0		0		0	40,000
1876	to 1880		0		0		0	0		0		0	NONE
1881	92,000	P	0		0		92,000	0		0		0	92,000
1882-1995			0		0		0	0		0		0	NONE
Sum	132,000		0		0		132,000	0		0		0	132,000

Appendix 6.20

Historical stocking of juvenile and adult Atlantic salmon in the Saco River, 1871-1995.

Year	Fry	Origin	0+ Parr	Origin	1+ Parr	Origin	Total Parr	1-year Smolts	Origin	2-year Smolts	Origin	Total Smolts	Grand Total
1872-1880			0		0		0	0		0		0	NONE
1881	35,000	P	0		0		35,000	0		0		0	
35,000													
1882-1974			0		0		0	0		0		0	NONE
1975	0		0		0		0	0		9,475	P	9,475	
9,475													
1976-1981			0		0		0	0		0		0	NONE
1982	0		2,355	P	0		2,355	0		0		0	2,355
	0		44,745	U	0		44,745	0		0		0	44,745
1983	0		0		0		0	20,340	U	0		20,340	20,340
1984	0		0		0		0	5,130	P	0		5,130	5,130
1985	0		0		23,600	P	23,600	5,100	P	0		5,100	28,700
1986	0		0		10,005	P	10,005	35,170	P	0		35,170	45,175
1987	0		0		69,825	P	69,825	22,015	P	0		22,015	91,840
1988	47,160	P	0		0		47,160	25,140	P	0		25,140	72,300
1989	0		37,760	P	48,550	P	86,310	9,890	P	0		9,890	96,200
1990	0		30,115	P	47,830	P	77,945	10,625	P	0		10,625	88,570
1991	111,000	P	0		0		111,000	10,320	P	0		10,320	121,320
1992	153,600	P	50,205	P	425	P	204,230	19,850	P	0		19,850	224,080
1993	166,500	P	0		0		166,500	20,055	P	0		20,055	186,555
1994	190,355	P	0		0		190,355	20,000	P	0		20,000	210,355
1995	376,000	P	0		0		376,000	19,700	P	0		19,700	395,700
Sum	1,044,615		165,180		200,235		1,410,030	223,335		9,475		232,810	1,642,840

Appendix 6.21

Historical stocking of juvenile and adult Atlantic salmon in the Androscoggin River, 1871-1995.

Year	Fry	Origin	0+ Parr	Origin	1+ Parr	Origin	Total Parr	1-year Smolts	Origin	2-year Smolts	Origin	Total Smolts	Grand Total
1871	0		0		1,500	ON	1,500						1,500
1872-1947			0		0			0					NONE
1948	0		12,000	P	0		12,000	0		0		0	12,000
1949	0		10,200	NB	8,240	P	18,440	0		0		0	18,440
1950	0		19,800	M+N	20,200	NB	40,000	0		0		0	40,000
1951	0		10,010	NB	0		10,010	0		0		0	10,010
1952	0		20,000	NB	0		20,000	0		0		0	20,000
1953	0		0		0		0	0		0		0	NONE
1954	0		29,400	NB	0		29,400	0		0		0	29,400
1955	0		19,890	NB	0		19,890	0		0		0	19,890
1956	0		19,320	NB	0		19,320	0		0		0	19,320
1957	0		14,955	NB	0		14,955	0		0		0	14,955
1958	0		20,180	NB	0		20,180	0		0		0	20,180
1959	0		0		0		0	0	0	0		0	NONE
1960	0		27,050	NB	36,960	NB	64,010	0		0		0	64,010
1961	0		24,220	NB			24,220	0		0		0	24,220
1962	0		15,500	NB	32,845	NB	48,345	0		0		0	48,345
1963	0		0		0		0	0		0		0	NONE
1964	0		0		6,175	Q	6,175	0		0		0	6,175
1965	0		0		0		0	14,210	NB	0		14,210	14,210
1966	0		0		0		0	25,040	NB	0		25,040	25,040
1967	0		0		0		0	10,515	NB	0		10,515	10,515
1968	0		0		0		0	15,980	NB	0		15,980	15,980
1969	to 1970		0		0		0	0		0		0	NONE
1971	0		0		0		0	1,020	M	0		1,020	1,020
1972	0		0		0		0	0		0		0	NONE
1973	0		0		0		0	0		1,025	P	1,025	1,025
1974	0		0		0		0	0				0	NONE
1975	0		0		0		0	0		2,520	P	2,520	2,520
1976	0		0		0		0	3,000	P	0		3,000	3,000
1977	to 1981		0		0		0	0		0		0	NONE
1982	0		0		0		0	5,310	P	0		5,310	5,310
1983	0		0		0		0	5,175	P	0		5,175	5,175
1984	0		0		0		0	5,005	P	0		5,005	5,005
1985	20,080	P	0		0		20,080	3,860	P	3,645	P	7,505	27,585
1986	100,150	P	5,000	P	0		105,150	7,510		0		7,510	112,660
	0		6,570	U	0		6,570						6,570
1987	15,060	P	8,240	P	0		23,300	9,000	P	0		9,000	32,300
1988	40,040	P	9,740	P	0		49,780	10,245	P			10,245	60,025
	0		2,515	U	0		2,515						2,515
1989	28,500	P	13,640	P	10,000	P	52,140	10,235	P	0		10,235	62,375
1990	27,070	P	10,070	P	10,000	P	47,140	16,500	P	0		16,500	63,640
1991	18,000	P	15,000	P	645	P	33,645	14,375	P	0		14,375	48,020
1992	to 1995		0		0		0	0		0		0	NONE
Sum	248,900		313,300		126,565		0	688,765	156,980		7,190	164,170	852,935

Appendix 6.2 2
Historical stocking of juvenile and adult Atlantic salmon in Somesville Stream, 1871-1995.

Year	Fry	Origin	0+ Parr	Origin	1+ Parr	Origin	Total Parr	1-year Smolts	Origin	2-year Smolts	Origin	Total Smolts	Grand Total
1872-1949			0		0		0	0		0		0	NONE
1950	14,795	M+N	0		0		14,795	0		0		0	14,795
1951	0		4,990	NB	0		4,990	0		0		0	4,990
1952	0		5,145	NB	0		5,145	0		0		0	5,145
1953	0		0		0		0	0		0		0	NONE
1954	0		0		4,970	NB	4,970	0		0		0	4,970
1955-1995			0		0		0	0		0		0	NONE
Sum	14,795		10,135		4,970		29,900	0		0		0	29,900

Appendix 6.23

Historical stocking of juvenile and adult Atlantic salmon in the Saint Croix River, 1871-1995.

Year	Fry	Origin	0+ Parr	Origin	1+ Parr	Origin	Total Parr	1-year Smolts	Origin	2-year Smolts	Origin	Total Smolts	Grand Total	Adult transfers Origin	1SW	MSW	Total
1872	0		0		0		0	0		0		0	NONE				0
1873	10,000	P	0		0		10,000	0		0		0	10,000				0
1874	22,000	P	0		0		22,000	0		0		0	22,000				0
1875	20,000	P	0		0		20,000	0		0		0	20,000				0
1876-1896			0		0		0	0		0		0	NONE				0
1897	150,000	P	0		0		150,000	0		0		0	150,000				0
1898	137,500	P	0		0		137,500	0		0		0	137,500				0
1899-1924			0		0		0	0		0		0	NONE				0
1925	112,500	NB	0		0		112,500	0		0		0	112,500				0
1926	101,000	NB	0		0		101,000	0		0		0	101,000				0
1927	150,000	NB	0		0		150,000	0		0		0	150,000				0
1928	100,500	NB	0		0		100,500	0		0		0	100,500				0
1929-1939			0		0		0	0		0		0	NONE				0
1940	0		5,000	D	0		5,000	0		0		0	5,000				0
1941-1948			0		0		0	0		0		0	NONE				0
1949 1	0		101,000	NB	0		101,000	0		0		0	101,000				0
1950-1965			0		0		0	0		0		0	NONE				0
1966	0		0		43,920	N	43,920	51,610	NB	50,170	M	101,780	145,700				0
1967	0		8,975	NB	0		8,975	55,380	NB	0		55,380	64,355				0
1968	0		0		5,070	NB	5,070	12,015	NB	0		12,015	17,085				0
	0		0		25,000	M	25,000	0		0		0	25,000				0
1969	0		0		0		0	13,590	M	0		13,590	13,590				0
1970-1979			0		0		0	0		0		0	NONE				0
1980 2	0		0		0		0	0		0			NONE	SJ	118	326	444
1981	0		0		0		0	0		13,670	P	13,670	13,670				0
	0		0		0		0	0		6,295	U	6,295	6,295				0
1982	101,000	U	17,150	P	2,605	P	120,755	19,900	P	80	P	19,980	140,735				0
	0		3,750	U	47,435	U	51,185	0		0		0	51,185				0
1983	0		0		14,445	P	14,445	20,040	U	0		20,040	34,485				0
	0		0		11,045	U	11,045	0		0		0	11,045				0

Appendix 6.23: *Historical Stocking, Saint Croix River*

Year	Fry	Origin	0+ Parr	Origin	1+ Parr	Origin	Total Parr	1-year Smolts	Origin	2-year Smolts	Origin	Total Smolts	Grand Total	Adult transfers Origin	1SW	MSW	Total
1984	54,070	P	0		13,800	P	67,870	11,860	P	0		11,860	79,730				0
	0		0		0		0	80,665	U	0		80,665	80,665				0
1985	177,740	P	46,440	P	12,900	U	237,080	29,790	P	0		29,790	266,870				0
	0		0		0		0	29,800	U	0		29,800	29,800				0
1986	193,000	P	0		0		193,000	68,990	P	0		68,990	261,990				0
	0		0		0		0	4,470	U	0		4,470	4,470				0
1987	255,500	P	0		25,975	P	281,475	28,455	P	0		28,455	309,930				0
	0		0		15,015	U	15,015	31,300	U	0		31,300	46,315				0
1988	0		0		0		0	78,745	P	0		78,745	78,745				0
1989	0		0		0		0	50,575	P	0		50,575	50,575				0
1990	254,900	P	0		0		254,900	65,765	P	0		65,765	320,665				0
1991	51,025	P	40,000	P	0		91,025	60,220	P	0		60,220	151,245				0
1992	85,305	PM	56,545	P	14,880	P	156,730	50,340	P	0		50,340	207,070				0
1993	0		100,950	P	0		100,950	40,110	P	0		40,110	141,060				0
1994	0		38,600	SC	0		38,600	60,600	SC	0		60,600	99,200				0
1995	600	SC	20,960	SC	0		21,560	17,000	SC	0		17,000	38,560				0
Sum	1,976,640		439,370		232,090		2,648,100	881,220		70,215		951,435	3,599,535		118	326	444

1 Stocked by the Department of Fisheries and Oceans (DFO), Canada.

2 Stocked by DFO from Mactaquac Hatchery, Frederickton, N.B.

APPENDIX 6.24
Historical stocking of juvenile and adult Atlantic salmon in the Saint George River, 1871-1995.

Year	Fry	Origin	0+ Parr	Origin	1+ Parr	Origin	Total Parr	1-year Smolts	Origin	2-year Smolts	Origin	Total Smolts	Grand Total
1872	0		0		0		0	0		0		0	NONE
1873	38,000	P	0		0		38,000	0		0		0	38,000
1874	to 1941		0		0		0	0		0		0	NONE
1942	0		0		21,350	NB	21,350	0		0		0	21,350
1943	0		0		3,450	NB	3,450	0		6,730	NB	6,730	10,180
1944	0		0		30,870	P	30,870	0		0		0	30,870
1945	0		0		25,180	NB	25,180	0		0		0	25,180
1995			0		0		0	0		0		0	NONE
Sum	38,000		0		80,850		118,850	0		6,730		6,730	125,580

APPENDIX 6.25
Historical stocking of juvenile and adult Atlantic salmon in Tunk Stream, 1871-1995.

Year	Fry	Origin	0+ Parr	Origin	1+ Parr	Origin	Total Parr	1-year Smolts	Origin	2-year Smolts	Origin	Total Smolts	Grand Total
1872-1948			0		0		0	0		0		0	NONE
1949	50,000	NB	0		0		50,000	0		0		0	50,000
1950	25,000	M+N	9,920	M+N	0		34,920	0		0		0	34,920
1951	0		10,000	M+P	0		10,000	0		0		0	10,000
1952-1995			0		0		0	0		0		0	NONE
Sum	75,000		19,920		0		94,920	0		0		0	94,920

Appendix 6.26

Historical stocking of juvenile and adult Atlantic salmon in the Union River, 1871-1995.

Year	Fry	Origin	0+ Parr	Origin	1+ Parr	Origin	Total Parr	1-year Smolts	Origin	2-year Smolts	Origin	Total Smolts	Grand Total	Adult transfers * Origin	1SW	MSW	Total
1872-1970			0		0		0	0		0		0	NONE				0
1971	0		0		0		0	8,120	M	0		8,120	8,120				0
1972	0		0		0		0	0		7,710	M	7,710	7,710				0
1973	0		0		0		0	0		19,550	P	19,550	19,550				0
1974	0		0		0		0	9,925	P	11,800	N	21,725	21,725				0
	0		0		0		0	0		8,645	P	8,645	8,645				0
1975	0		0		0		0	0		31,250	P	31,250	31,250				0
1976	0		0		0		0	1,805	U	31,760	P	33,565	33,565				0
1977	0		0		0		0	13,025	U	22,465	P	35,490	35,490				0
1978	0		0		0		0	0		31,940	U	31,940	31,940				0
1979	0		0		0		0	12,935	U	14,955	P	27,890	27,890				0
	0		0		0		0	0		14,970	U	14,970	14,970				0
1980	0		0		0		0	30,640	U	0		30,640	30,640				0
1981	0		0		0		0	0		29,385	U	29,385	29,385				0
1982	0		0		0		0	5,860	U	5,860	P	11,720	11,720	P,U	-	-	484
	0		0		0		0	0		20,675	U	20,675	20,675				0
1983	0		0		0		0	41,605	U	0		41,605	41,605	P,U	-	-	474
1984	0		0		0		0	1,870	P	0		1,870	1,870	P,U	-	-	229
	0		0		0		0	48,365	U	0		48,365	48,365				0
1985	6,750		0		0		6,750	45,755	U	0		45,755	52,505	P,U	-	-	229
1986	6,700		0		0		6,700	48,360	U	0		48,360	55,060	P,U	-	-	875
1987	6,750		0		0		6,750	32,295	U	0		32,295	39,045				0
	0		0		0		0	7,825	PU	0		7,825	7,825				0
1988	0		0		0		0	15,345	P	0		15,345	15,345				0
	0		0		0		0	15,250	U	0		15,250	15,250				0
1989	0		0		0		0	20,360		0		20,360	20,360				0
1990	0		0		0		0	10,150	P	0		10,150	10,150				0
	0		0		0		0	10,210	U	0		10,210	10,210				0
1991	0		0		0		0	0		0		0	NONE				0
1992	0		0		0		0	0		0		0	NONE				0
1993	60,000		111,650		0		171,650	0		0		0	171,650	P,U	-	-	754
1994	0		0		0		0	0		0		0	NONE				0
1995	0		54,800	P	0		54,800	0		0		0	54,800				0
Sum	80,200		166,450		0		246,650	379,700		250,965		630,665	877,315		-	-	3,045

* Captive broodstock from Green Lake NFH; Penobscot and Union River origin

APPENDIX 6.27
Historical stocking of juvenile and adult Atlantic salmon in the Upper Saint John River, 1871-1995.

Year	Fry	Origin	0+ Parr	Origin	1+ Parr	Total Parr	1-year Smolts	Origin	2-year Smolts	Origin	Total Smolts	Grand Total	Adult transfers Origin	1SW	MSW	Total
1872-1984			0		0	0	0		0		0	NONE				0
1985	0		0		0	0	0		0		0	NONE	SJ	0	12	12
1986	0		0		0	0	0		0		0	NONE				0
1987	306,000	SJ	60,000	SJ	0	366,000	0		0		0	366,000				0
1988	127,600	SJ	779,400	SJ	4,750	911,750	0		0		0	911,750				0
1989	66,000	SJ	0		0	66,000	0		10,260	SJ	10,260	76,260				0
1990	110,000	SJ	21,000	SJ	9,900	140,900	0		10,260	SJ	10,260	151,160				0
1991	227,500	SJ	139,350	SJ	0	366,850	5,070	SJ	5,110	SJ	10,180	377,030	SJ	90	50	140
1992	399,700	SJ	136,100	SJ	0	535,800	0		0		0	535,800	SJ	230	110	340
1993	360,755	SJ	102,760	SJ	0	463,515	0		0		0	463,515	SJ	109	64	173
1994	565,700	SJ	216,060	SJ	0	781,760	0		0		0	781,760	SJ	62	17	79
1995	0		0		0	0	0		0		0	NONE				0
Sum	2,163,255		1,454,670		14,650	3,632,575	5,070		25,630		30,700	3,663,275		491	253	744

Order Form

Telephone orders:	**(207) 848-5590**
Fax orders:	**(207) 848-5590**
Online orders:	**ASUnlimitd@aol.com**
Mail orders:	**Atlantic Salmon Unlimited** **P.O. Box 6185** **Hermon, Maine 04402**

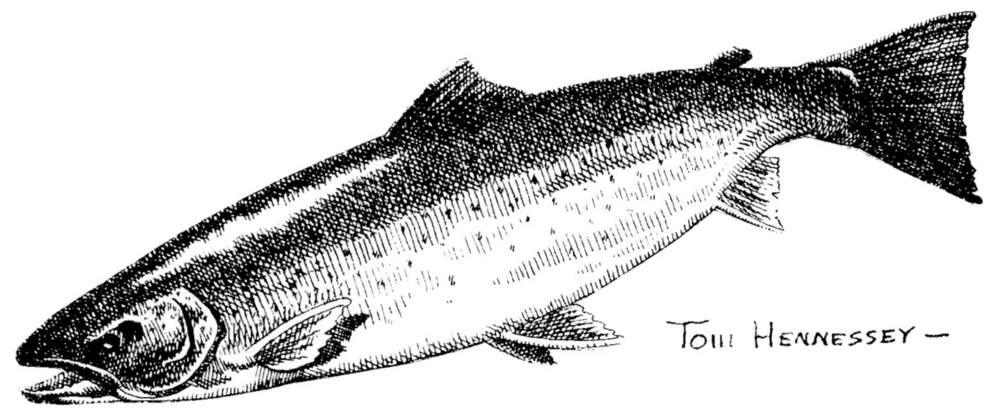

Please send [ ] copies of Maine Atlantic Salmon: A National Treasure **to:**

Name ____

Address ____

City ______________________ **State** _____ **Zip** _______ **Country** _______

Price: $49.95

Sales tax: Please add 6% ($3.00 each) for books shipped to Maine addresses.

Shipping/handling: $4.00 for the first book, $2.00 for each additional book.

(There will be an additional fee for shipments outside of the United States)

Total amount enclosed: ______________________

Method of payment:

☐ Visa ☐ Mastercard ☐ Discover ☐ American Express ☐ Check / money order

Card number: ____

Signature: ______________________________ Exp. Date: __________